ELECTRONIC PUBLISHING '01

Electronic Publishing '01

2001 in the Digital Publishing Odyssey

Proceedings of an ICCC/IFIP Conference
held at the University of Kent at Canterbury,
Kent, United Kingdom
5–7 July, 2001

Edited by

Arved Hübler

Institut für Print- und Medientechnik, Technische Universität Chemnitz, Germany

Peter Linde

Blekinge Institute of Technology, Sweden

John W.T. Smith

The Templeman Library, University of Kent at Canterbury, United Kingdom

IOS Press

Ohmsha

Amsterdam • Berlin • Oxford • Tokyo • Washington, DC

ISBN 1 58603 191 0 (IOS Press)
ISBN 4 274 90454 7 C3055 (Ohmsha)
Library of Congress Catalog Card Number: 2001092112

Publisher
IOS Press
Nieuwe Hemweg 6B
1013 BG Amsterdam
The Netherlands
fax: +31 20 688 33 55
e-mail: order@iospress.nl

Distributor in the UK and Ireland
IOS Press/Lavis Marketing
73 Lime Walk
Headington
Oxford OX3 7AD
England
fax: +44 1865 75 0079

Distributor in the USA and Canada
IOS Press, Inc.
5795-G Burke Centre Parkway
Burke, VA 22015
USA
fax: +1 703 323 3668
e-mail: iosbooks@iospress.com

Distributor in Germany, Austria and Switzerland
IOS Press/LSL.de
Gerichtsweg 28
D-04103 Leipzig
Germany
fax: +49 341 995 4255

Distributor in Japan
Ohmsha, Ltd.
3-1 Kanda Nishiki-cho
Chiyoda-ku, Tokyo 101
Japan
fax: +81 3 3233 2426

PRINTED IN THE NETHERLANDS

Foreword

This book contains the proceedings of the Fifth Conference on Electronic Publishing organised jointly by the International Council for Computer Communication (ICCC) and the International Federation for Information Processing (IFIP).

The Organising Committee of the Conference consisted of:

- John W T Smith, University of Kent at Canterbury, UK - *Chair and Local Organiser*
- Arved Hübler, University Chemnitz, Germany -*Chair of the Programme Committee*
- Dipak Khakhar, Lund University, Sweden - *ICCC and IFIP Liaison*
- Klaus Kreulich, Technical University Chemnitz, Germany - *Assistant Chair of the Programme Committee*
- Peter Linde, Blekinge Institute of Technology, Karlskrona, Sweden - *Advisor to Programme Committee*
- Michael Miller, EntreLevel, UK - *Treasurer*
- Fytton Rowland, Loughborough University, UK - *Exhibition Co-ordinator*

The Programme Committee consisted of:

- Arved Hübler, Technical University Chemnitz, Germany - *Chair*
- Klaus Kreulich, Technical University Chemnitz, Germany - *Assistant Chair*
- Peter Linde, Blekinge, Inst. of Tech., Karlskrona, Sweden - *Advisor to the Committee*
- Ana Alice Baptista, Universidade do Minho, Guimarães, Portugal
- Helene Juhola, VTT Information Technology / Dept. Media, Espoo, Finland
- Elmar Mittler, Nieders. Staats- und Universitätsbibliothek, Göttingen, Germany
- J. Fytton Rowland, Loughborough University, UK
- Harry Rudin, Joint Editor-in-Chief of Computer Networks, Zürich, Switzerland
- John Smith, University of Kent at Canterbury, UK

Earlier volumes in this series

This volume is part of an ongoing series recording the papers presented at the ICCC/IFIP series of conferences on electronic publishing. The previous titles were:

- *Electronic Publishing '97: New Models and Opportunities*
- *Electronic Publishing '98: Towards the Information Rich Society*
- *Electronic Publishing '99: Redefining the Information Chain – New Ways and Voices*
- *Electronic Publishing in the Third Millennium*

All of which are published by and obtainable from: ICCC Press, P.O. Box 9745, Washington, DC 20016, USA. Each volume contains papers from both east and west Europe and the rest of the world giving a snapshot of research and development activity in Electronic Publishing its year of publication. Many of the projects described are still active or have given rise to further work.

Acknowledgements

No event of this kind can take place without a great deal of background administration and technical work. The Editors (on behalf of the Organising Committee) would like to thank Olivia Holmes and Chris Keene for all their efforts.

Arved Hübler, *Peter Linde* and John Smith, May 2001.

Contents

E-Commerce

Sponsoring Institutions

Electronic Publishing '01 –
2001 in the Digital Publishing Odyssey
A. Hübler et al. (Eds.)
IOS Press, 2001

The State and the Content: electronic publishing and policy measures

Giuseppe Vitiello

Programme Advisor, Electronic Publishing, Books and Archives, Conseil de l'Europe

0. Introduction

At the beginning is the author, a brilliant individual or group of people who produce, experiment, innovate. Once the work is there, what happens next?

The relation between the creator and the created thing is quite obvious. In spite of that, experience shows that the created thing has often an independent life and may be associated, grouped and distributed with other related forms of contents and objects. Policies for such dissemination are usually market driven and follow the law of supply and demand and the innovative impulse of individuals and firms. After all, success may be the result of blunt necessity or mere fate.

Experience also shows that governmental action can be applied usefully as a way of regulating, mediating, and balancing the effects of a purely market oriented approach. Policy measures may be direct and affect market mechanisms (in many countries, for instance, printed matters benefit from an advantageous fiscal regime). Sometimes, governmental action can be equally successful when it is indirect and public authorities can act strategically as major owners, providers and users of information.

The aim of the present paper is to analyse governmental policies in the electronic publishing field from a cultural viewpoint. Other areas, such as governmental intervention in the development of information and communication industries or the commercial exploitation of Europe's public sector information, are excluded.[1] Two major foci have been identified. The first concerns content that is stored in public institutions, such as museums, libraries and archives, and form the core part of public heritage. The second is the policy that governments are setting up in relation to the electronic publishing industry.

It can be anticipated that governments feel more at ease in the area of cultural heritage, whereas a lot has still to be done for the private sector, where the need for governmental action is yet to be proven. Latest turbulencies in the sector of the "new economy" as well as the predicament in which electronic publishing industries find themselves may well change this attitude. Cultural electronic publishers are currently in a no-win situation: either they pull back from the field, thus losing their early-mover advantage, or they can go on pouring billions of Euro into a business that is likely to fail altogether. At the end of the day, electronic publishers may drop the belief that free market forces alone would shape the culture-oriented information sector and start to seek for state intervention and favourable regulatory measures. Before governments, too, start to pour billions of Euro into assistance plans, some ideas may well pave the way towards a sound and culture-oriented policy on electronic publishing.

---

[1] Although they have been the object of interesting studies (see European Commission. *Commercial exploitation of Europe's public sector information*, prepared by Pira International LtD, University of East Anglia and knowledgeView Ltd. Luxembourg: Directorate-General for the Information Society (20 September 2000). <www;cordis.lu/econtent>.

1. Policies in the public domain sector

At all levels, public powers have triggered digitalisation plans for the content they store in museums, libraries and archives. Early experiments made evident that such content – as a rule, belonging to the public domain - can and must be made available through websites and, in a more advanced way, through cultural portals. Hence, two major results. On the one hand, museums, libraries, galleries and archive resources are being integrated and their solid co-operation has become a prerequisite. On the other, cultural portals are proliferating with a view to disseminating the information and the content cultural institutions produce or hold. Obviously, it is not merely a question of merging front-end services electronically across them, but rather of setting complex common cultural portals and also a question of reconsidering the traditional ways of communicating and informing about cultural heritage.

In particular, "portal" has become a buzzword for networked cultural information. Portal is described as "something you go through to go somewhere else". In other words, it is a network-specific software that lets users access through a single Web site a range of innumerable data sources on the public Internet, many of them in real time[2]. What differentiates portals from websites and gateways is their ability to incorporate data from multiple sources in multiple formats and to organize it into a single, easy to use menu for a wide range of products and services.

There exists an increasing need to build solid projects and policies concerning the availability of cultural resources through portals. The explanation lying behind this is that there is significant public, political and, to a certain extent, also commercial interest in library, museum and archive heritage. Major investments are being made in information and communication technology to allow virtual access and to extend its benefits across museums, libraries and archives.

Indeed, all these organisations now face issues of digitisation, archiving, preservation, processing, dissemination and new relationships with their users. Use of information and communication technologies appear to have enormous potential for such institutions as they open up opportunities for interoperability and information exchange. Ideally, the user will be able to access, through cultural portals, text, sound and images from a wide variety of sources, often in the context of one-stop-shopping scenarios. This is bound to have considerable impact on the way in which archives, libraries and museums relate to their user communities and become an integral part of the evolving information society.

At the end of the day, it is indeed a question of access and how access is interpreted. At its core, access is about ensuring that as many people as possible have the opportunity to experience for themselves the resources and the collections that the archive, library and museum sector provides. It is obvious that the collection and the services managed on behalf of the public do not exist for they own sake – they exist for a purpose and that purpose has to be primarily defined by the way in which a multiple-faceted public uses and interacts with them.

New technologies have broken down many barriers; however, technology has also introduced many of its own and has shifted the emphasis from barriers regulating the information flow to options concerning policy, legal, financial and technical issues. The policy and financial aspects of cultural portals will be discussed as follows.

---

[2] Pongsathorn Ingpochai *An Introduction to Web Portals*, 1998 <http://www.doc.ic.ac.uk/~pi98/article1>.

1.1 Policy issues

Currently, few countries seem to fully grasp that national information policies represent a key condition for the protection and promotion of cultural diversity, for a wide and equal access to the world's cultural resources and for the progress of the society in general. Though librarian, archival and museum services experience signs of increased public interest, there are still many impediments to a better exploitation and integration of their resources and to enhanced user-friendly techniques.

The main policy issue in the public heritage sector is how to associate, integrate and even merge institutions and departments that have so far worked on a sectoral basis. There are not many examples to be detected in Europe and in the USA. The few may be classified as followed: 1) the "All-in-One" model; 2. the "Primus inter Pares" model; and 3) the "Us and Them" model. Most states are still holding a "Wait-and-see" attitude; this is what could be called the non-model option.

The "All-in-One" model

Resource, the UK Council for Museums, Archives and Libraries is a clear illustration of how the integrated approach may produce significant organisational changes. Resource replaces two separate public bodies working according to the UK characteristic principle of arm's length: the Museums and Galleries Commission and the Library and Information Commission.

The process of merging departments that have not worked in close integration so far is a "revolutionary" act of the Blair government. Libraries and archives have indeed a tradition of co-operation as information institutions. Very often, common professional education for libraries and archives is provided in schools and the UK "information policy" mentions libraries and archives in close association. What is new is the fact that museums are now collaborating with the "information" institutions. This is a promising marriage. All three sectors have heritage missions, but museum professionals have strong communication skills, whereas libraries and archives professionals have a long experience in information management and dissemination.

Problems should not be dismissed. The following is a possible list of hindrances to co-operation among museums, libraries and archives. This list has no precise order of priorities:

a) not all sectors aim at enlarging their public in the same direction;
b) IT skills are unevenly present in the three sectors;
c) collaboration with the private sector is not developed to the same extent;
d) inventory methodologies and searching tools are not the same; their compatibility in the electronic environment is not self-obvious;
e) the attitude of cultural players towards the copyright issue is not the same with museum professionals seemingly being more restrictive than libraries and archives in providing use of their collections;
f) in fact, libraries provide access to a content whose intellectual property belongs to third parties;
g) products/services generated by heritage collections are not the same;
h) in some cases, professional status and remuneration are not the same.

The advanced nature of the UK experience has raised a large debate with inevitable critical voices. Therefore, the information world reproaches that Resource is not aware enough that libraries, museums and archives can become economically important if they learn to team up with non-traditional partners and to think in enterprise terms. The ability of facilitating links and interoperability in the Archive, library and museums community and to foster public/private partnerships is also challenged by Resource's opponents. Resource, however, has already become a model of policy in Europe for the innovative way in which it integrates cultural resources in the light of information and communication technologies.

The "Primus inter Pares" model

In some cases, mainly in Nordic countries, an intersectoral committee has been created and a person has been appointed by the government (usually at ministerial level) to orient and define the points where common work among the three sectors can be undertaken. In Norway, for instance, the National Library is working on, and funding jointly with the Norwegian Council for Cultural Affairs, the preservation plans of the Sound and Image Archive. The members of the working group already established come from different institutions (Norwegian Broadcasting Corporation, the Norwegian Film Institute, the University of Oslo, etc.)[3].

Several countries - such as Sweden, Denmark, Finland and Norway - have created recently national cultural portals, generically called Culture Net, which make available information and resources from museums, libraries and archives.

Although co-operation among these sectors is still at an early stage, some common needs and working streams have been identified:

- standard descriptions (including that of digital images), where there is a lack of skills in the perspective of accessing from a single point resources having different descriptive practices and standards;
- networking different institutions through the elaboration of common metadata;
- codes of use for content belonging to the public domain and delivered to third parties and for content held by public institutions that is produced and distributed by third parties;
- common products and services.

The intersectoral Committee works in an informal way and draws on existing resources in order to set up national digitization plans and establish a common order of priority to ALM projects.

The "Us and Them" model

This model is to be found in particular in the United States where the federal state is absent from the policy landscape and the initiative is left to non-governmental organisations and professional associations. The Clinton Administration has recognised the private sector as the mainstay of IT development in all areas, including the information and cultural sectors. Therefore, cultural organisations are attempting to draw together on their own initiative.

The establishment of the National Initiative for a Networked Cultural Heritage (NINCH) is the reaction of cultural foundations and art and humanities organisations to IT applications in the cultural sector otherwise totally dominated by the private sector controlling electronic superhighways.[4] NINCH's mission is mainly educating their members in nurturing a sense of community among cultural organisations that have seldom co-operated and made advocacy for their interests. The American example is a policy in the cultural field that is situated outside and even opposite the government. The

---

[3] Kulturnett Norge <www.lysator.liu.se/runeberg/admin/foreign.html>.

[4] < http://www.tiesweb.org/digilib/links/org/ninch.html >.

profession ("Us") advocates the need for a common position on matters where the government ("Them") may be suspected to incline exclusively towards meeting the needs and the interests of the private sector.

NINCH advocacy has been successful, for instance, in the case of the vexed area of copyright, where NINCH was instrumental in suspending a proposal for copyright regulations emanated by the US Department of Commerce.

The "Wait-and-See" non-model

This is rather a traditional non-model since it inevitably appears when those in charge of the creation of a policy wait for projects on which the would-be policy could rely. Innovatory projects are therefore initiated by other institutions besides the public authorities and are put "on hold".

Very often, libraries are seen as a public square where information and culture come together for the public, thus bringing together society and public for (digital) information, culture and social interest. Nevertheless, an organized link with other sectors has yet to be established. Most of the projects on common cataloguing and metadata, are therefore awaiting a proper framework policy.

1.2 Who has to pay: the consumer or the taxpayer?

A crucial aspect is whether the costs for a cultural portal should borne entirely by the cultural institution that promotes it or they should be shared with other sponsors and eventually be paid by the consumer. In this respect three patterns of development can be envisaged:

A) the portal is set up by the cultural institution, whether this is public, private or a non-profit organisation, and its costs are totally covered by the institution itself;

B) the portal is set up by the cultural institution that hopes to recover, at least partially, its costs by charging users;

C) the portal is set up by a cultural institution and maintained by a private organisation that uses it as a marketing tool.

In option A, the organisation running the cultural portal creates its own structure and costs are borne by taxpayers. The advantage of such an option is that transparency is ensured and policy choices conform to traditional cultural policies. The disadvantage is that cultural portals become a mere institutional resource and an additional burden put on cultural budgets.

Option B is more a variation of the first than an alternative to it. The philosophy underpinning it is that the portal policy remains in the hands of those agencies - Ministries, independent bodies, non-governmental organisations - that are entitled to carry out national or local cultural policies. Nevertheless, for single products and services, co-operation with the private sector is sought. The advantage is that cultural policy-makers maintain a main stake in policies concerning the development of cultural portals. On the other hand, the commercial potential of resources hosted by the portal is not overlooked. The disadvantage is that the chances for products/services to recover the costs of their production on the Internet are still slim and more linked to expectations than to real life. At the end of the day, it is likely that the bill is sent back again to taxpayers.

In option C, the cultural operator would bear the cost of the digitization plan and the information provider would run the cultural portal, thus relieving the cultural operator from the burden to maintain a steady, although not very expensive, organisation. The advantage is that a private operator would run the portal with a clear commercial vision;

(s)he would link therefore with non-traditional partners in tourism, telecommunications, advertising, car industries, etc. There are several disadvantages. The first is that it is not sure that benefits would be distributed equally within the cultural infrastructure as a whole. The second is the issue of copyright, for which strict requirements should be set in order to keep the property of the content in the public domain. At a world level, there is a risk that the divide between well endowed and less endowed regions in terms of cultural heritage may well increase, with stars in the world of museums, libraries and archives making exclusive alliances with telecom companies and other commercial operators.

It is very likely however that no country will opt for only one of the three options. They will co-exist and be adapted according to the level of wealth, the selected themes and institutions, and to circumstances.

2. Policies in the electronic publishing field

Remember the early 1990's, when the extensive application of Information and Communication Technologies to publishing activities raised justified expectations. Authors were eager to see their works widely distributed and known through networks, producers trusted that their investments would be remunerated by high profits, and distributors forecast cheap information made available to all.[5]

Ten years later, we can see how such forecasts had been overestimated. The commercial benefits of the technological revolution applied to culture-oriented electronic publishing are still more linked to expectations than to factual progress. Cultural and educational publications still follow traditional circuits; in general, their electronic equivalents only add to, and complement, the printed version.

There are several reasons for this. First, electronic publishers usually maintain a "double track" organisational system - the conventional and the digital – for the production and distribution of their materials. Second, contracts between electronic publishers and users (whether individuals or libraries) are confusing and daunting. Third, electronic publishing firms are still fumbling for the win-win business model. Fourth, today's book chain is so rigidly structured that any change has necessarily to result in a change of mentality for their actors. And so on.

Many governments in Europe have allocated a great amount of money for the modernization and the reconversion of cultural industries into the new economy environment. They may be tempted to ask for a review of these projects and to establish their own cultural policy concerning electronic publishing. In fact, they hesitate to do it. The main reason is that no clear model for state support has emerged for the networked dissemination of publications. Except for the copyright issues, where work has been carried out at the European Commission level, it is rare that states have come out with regulatory or overall incentive schemes. Ideas are vague not only on public policies towards electronic publishing but also, and especially, on how public policies towards conventional cultural industries should evolve in the digital environment.

Such policies are indeed different. Until now they have been medium-related. Regulatory measures, support schemes, aids to cultural actors have been different whether they addressed the publishing or the audiovisual sectors. Now that both industries are converging into an overall "convergent industry", with telecommunications partners as allies, a "convergent" policy should be established accordingly. And here comes the problem.

[5] For instance, European Communities. Commission DG XIII/E. *New opportunities for publishers in the information services market. Main report.* Brussels-Luxembourg: ECSC-EEC-EAEC, 1993.

In the publishing sector, democratic requirements imply little regulation for actors entering the market and a wide range of measures within the framework of an incentive-based policy. In this way, the State guarantees the multiplicity and diversity of opinions and expressions, which strict conformity to market laws in the book trade would not be able to maintain. All countries have devised such legal or policy machinery with different policy "mix" and weight of the single actors within the general framework. Such measures can broadly be divided into five categories: legal measures (in particular, the respect of the rights relating to intellectual property); fiscal measures (reduced VAT rate, tax exemption for book import, etc.); mechanisms regulating demand (library lending rights, support to textbooks, fixed book price, massive acquisitions made by libraries, etc.); support for quality content (grants for publishing projects and for translations, etc.); and support for publishing houses and bookselling firms (reduced postal charges, low rate loans, training, etc.).[6]

In the conventional telecommunication sector, the democratic impetus finds its primary expression in the effort to provide universal access to a minimum level of communication services. For telephone providers, for instance, it consisted of an obligation to respect some minimal requirements pertaining to universal service in a particular country, including scarcely populated areas where traffic is low. Deregulation in this field has practically put such burden on the private sector and freed the state from the maintenance of telecommunication companies.

In the broadcasting sector values are reflected in content regulations aimed at assuring that broadcasts provide the diverse information necessary for an informed citizenry. Common values, such as freedom of expression and the right of reply, pluralism, protection for authors and their works, promotion of cultural and linguistic diversity, protection of minors and of human dignity, and consumer protection are among the basic principles that permeate European broadcast policy. The two main regulatory instruments of that policy are the European Convention on Transfrontier Television", established by the Council of Europe on 5 May 1989, and the Television Without Frontiers Directive, established by the European Council on 3 October 1989[7]. In the European film industry, the two policies that support creativity and wider distribution of European films are Media and Eurimages, set up by the European Union and the Council of Europe respectively [8].

As national policies are lacking in the field of electronic publishing (except for the copyright issue), the only possible thing to be done is to define its objectives, scope and related instruments. Any cultural policy should suit the needs of the different actors operating in the cultural electronic publishing chain and keep alive public, social and political concerns in matters such as freedom of expression, the diversity of the content supply and the participation of a well aware and active citizenry. Such policy should aim: "at the greatest freedom, for the greatest number of communication and information suppliers, users, and brokers, and should therefore monitor and correct any situation in

---

[6] The Council of Europe and UNESCO have analysed book policies in several publications. See, for instance, Olivier Baruch, *The book sector and the state: relationships in change*, revised and updated by Jean Richard. In Council of Europe. *Background documents to the Colloquy of Ministers responsible for cultural affairs "A time for choices: towards a democratic policy for books and electronic publishing (Alte Oper, Frankfurt, 16-17 October 2000)*. Strasbourg: Council of Europe, 2000, p. 3-23; Alvaro Garzon. *National book policy. A guide for users in the field.* Paris: UNESCO, 1997.

[7] <http://conventions.coe.int/treaty/EN/cadreprincipal.htm>.

[8] See the web sites of the MEDIA and EURIMAGES programmes, respectively: <http://europa.eu.int/comm/dg10/avpolicy/media/guidelines/ldpromo_en.html> and <http://culture.coe.fr/Eurimages>.

which control of access is subject to market failure and consequently out of balance"[9]. To put it in other words, a communication policy for access should strive for maximum equality in the distribution of communication freedom.

3. Legal issues

As already noted, there has been a clear-cut governmental policy only on the copyright issue. The debate on this matter has enflamed in recent years because of the difficulty of implementing "electronic copyright" and the need of balancing powers between rights-holders and users. In the electronic environment, it is indeed hard to apply copyright when the copy of an electronic document is done at low cost, with no remarkable difference in relation to the original, when transmission is extremely simplified and its dissemination difficult to monitor.

The issue is eminently political and concerns the ownership of intellectual property in the electronic environment and the right of the public to access it. In this respect, the European Union has set a milestone with the draft Directive on the "harmonisation of certain aspects of copyright and related rights in the information society."[10] Another aspect is the legal status of resources belonging to the public domain that are digitalised in and disseminated through heritage institutions (museums, libraries and archives).

3.1 The European Union draft directive

Copyright in the electronic environment is now being defined by the European Parliament and Council draft Directive on the "harmonisation of certain aspects of copyright and related rights in the information society". Authors and publishers have supported this Directive which intends to harmonise measures in order to bring about a coherent and favourable environment for creativity and investment in the framework of the internal market. The practice of freely downloading publications directly from the Internet and of disseminating them world wide is seriously hampered by the draft Directive. It provides for the exclusive right to authorise or prohibit direct or indirect, temporary or permanent reproduction by any means and in any form, in whole or in part the original and copies of copyright protected works. Moreover, the directive provides for exceptions and limitations to the exclusive reproduction right on condition that the rights-holders receive fair compensation. Such limitations are now being established by Member States.

By leaving free member countries to decide whether to assign an exception regime to educational and cultural institutions (like schools, libraries, etc.), the European Parliament did not want to enter into the details of the exemption regime. Therefore, no framework for limitations to the exclusive right has been devised in the recognition that practices in member States are too different to be regulated in a homogeneous way.

---

[9] Van Cuilenberg, Jan and Verhoest, Pascal (1998). "Free and equal access. In search of policy models for converging communication systems". *Telecommunication policy,* vol. 22, n. 3, pp. 171-181. The quotation is at p. 179-180.

[10] *Amended proposal for a European Parliament and Council Directive on the harmonisation of certain aspects of copyright, and related rights in the Information Society (599PC0250)* <http://europa.eu.int/eur-lex/en/com/dat/1999/en_599PC0250.html>.

Licences

A clear pattern of dissemination of electronic publications emerging in the electronic environment is the provision of licenses. Licences are mostly regulated by contract laws but issues such as copyright warranties, perpetual access, choice of law and forum must be taken into consideration especially when one deals with site licences.

Contract law is dominated by the concept of freedom of contract which means that parties to a contract are free to negotiate the terms of use of copyrighted material or indeed waive the rights that the copyright law grants them. Since the Internet/World Wide Web facilitates the establishment of contractual relationships, contract law is becoming the instrument to fill the legal vacuum on the Internet.

User licences are becoming the rule on the Internet[11]. Already, the so-called ‘click-through”, “mouse-click” or “click-wrap” contracts are frequently seen and routinely entered into on the WWW. For the consumer who refuses to accept the conditions of the licence, the information product offered on the web will remain hidden behind a layer of technological protection.

The Guidelines set by the Publishers’ Association[12] suggest several options for use of copyright protected works through licensing and copyright management schemes. For instance, the work can be sold outright so that the user faces no further obligation. Alternatively, the payment of a subscription can be requested for an unlimited number of uses made by individual users. Other options may concern payments made by the user for each time (s)he uses copyright protected works, or else a periodical payment for which the user may be permitted to use a work within a particular locality or site.

Pending issues: the management of electronic rights

An important issue is the management of electronic rights. Although technical problems do not seem to be insurmountable, some issues remain unsolved. Uncertainty concerns, on the one hand, the agencies entitled to deal with the management of electronic rights and, on the other, the nature of copyright limitation. Agencies that could possibly hold negotiations on behalf of publishers are the reproduction rights organisations. In the quasi totality of European countries, they are given the authority to issue blanket agreements that cover the reproduction of copyright protected works beyond normative limits against the payment of a fee. As in some European countries, such as France, reproduction rights organisations are established by law, there is a need to enlarge their mandate and scope of activities and to extend it to the electronic management of rights.

On the other hand, the nature of limitation is expected to be a politically controversial issue for governments. There is a need to work on access practices and on the principle of fair use, i.e. the general practice of lawfully permitted copying or excerpting of copyrighted material in the course of education, scholarship, commentary, or in order to advance learning, and for other societal goals.

The establishment of library and information consortia is definitely instrumental in working towards obtaining perpetual licences. Such consortia should not be prevented from undertaking the necessary steps to archive the content they purchase (to make back-up copies for instance) and from being flexible in the formats and standards chosen for making the content available. Moreover, they should be able to acquire enough autonomy

---

[11] Cf. P. Bernt Hugenholtz, *Code as code, or the end of intellectual property as we know it*, Maastricht Journal of European and Comparative Law <http://www.eblida.org/>.

[12] The Publishers’ Association. *Copyright licensing in an electronic environment*: <http://www.publishers.org.uk >.

from their sponsoring bodies in order to deal with the collective acquisitions of electronic publications.

3.2 Cultural resources belonging to the public domain

Should cultural resources be made available for free or under payment of a fee (moderate though it may be)? Should the digitization plans eventually be paid by taxpayers or users, both commercial and non-commercial? In a nutshell, these are the issues linked to the delivering of cultural resources belonging to the public domain available on the Net that will now be considered. Some states, like France, have already expressed a clear policy statement concerning the condition of their dissemination to the public. This is the statement made by the Comité interministériel pour la société de l'information (CISI) on the development of cultural content on the Internet :

"A programme committee will be created by the Ministry of Culture and Communication in order to develop the following policy: priority to the needs of the great public, digitization of contents of a "general interest" part of the heritage, and free access. A "cultural" portal will be created on the Internet in order to facilitate access to the on-line culture. It will offer free room to the cultural associations which are partners of the public authorities. The multimedia culture network will be extended; in 1998, some one hundred sites of this kind were opened. The Government is decided to reinforce this effort"[13].

Other governments have no definite policy on the conditions of delivery of cultural content, leaving cultural institutions free to decide on their policy or submitting it to the general availability of services in cultural institutions.

4. Other possible policy measures[14]

4.1 Converting direct support to book publishing into schemes on digital printing

Many public authorities, especially in the academic sector, are considering re-orienting their traditional way of supporting the dissemination of the results of research. There may be alternatives indeed to the funding of academic presses or to the contribution to the cost of print dissemination. Research papers and dissertations may be posted on the Web and be made available through print-on-demand systems. Book policies are totally re-designed. Titles being awarded public support are given the chance to reach their direct customers (universities, libraries, and individuals) through networks and not to engage physically cumbersome distribution channels. Instead of providing direct support to the print publication of research and literature, public powers are therefore shifting towards the support of just-in-time marketing and delivery of desired material. This move initiated by public powers is a decisive boost in re-designing a more rational (electronic) publishing chain.

---

[13] Comité Interministériel pour la société de l'information *Développer la culture, les contenus et la présence de la France sur l'Internet.* decisions taken by the on 19th January, 1999. Further details available at: < www.internet.gouv.fr >.

[14] Such measures have been described in detail in Giuseppe Vitiello. "Policy-making: A European Policy for Electronic Publishing". *The Journal of Electronic Publishing*, The University of Michigan Press, March 2001, vol. 6, Issue 3, ISSN 1080-2711 <http://www.press.umich.edu/jep/06-03/vitiello.html>.

Through print-on-demand:

- it is no longer necessary to decide on the size of an edition prior to marketing it;
- the problem of the distribution bottleneck arising from the excessive number of titles offered on the market in relation to the size of the bookshop network which exists to take them is solved;
- all books have an equal chance of being marketed;
- the breakeven point for each book, equivalent simply to the editing and pre-press costs, is much lower;
- on the Internet a book in electronic format is always extant, ready for printing, permanently viewable and always retrievable;
- the current race to consign books to the dustbin, typical of mass-market logic, disappears.

If print-on-demand has such advantages in relation to the printed offer, one may wonder why the technique has not become pervasive in the European publishing context. A few reasons may be mentioned:

- today's book chain is so rigidly structured that any change has necessarily to result in a change of mentality for their actors;
- software dealing with the electronic management of copyright does exist, but is still in an experimental phase;
- formatting texts for print-on-demand has to be adjusted to the software installed on print-on-demand machines;
- techniques of short-run publishing may be more convenient;
- there is a need to establish new contractual agreements with outlet points (in case of electronic distribution, the publisher does not "make" the book);
- major players in the book field use print-on-demand for production; they are starting only now to use it for distribution purposes;
- SME publishing companies have not yet converted their production into the electronic mode; they maintain a "double track system" (print + electronic) and this costs money.

The gradual conversion of public systems supporting published literature and research should facilitate and optimize the changing positions of actors in the publishing business. By setting up well funded programmes, public powers may help re-orienting book professionals towards new tasks and functions, thus guaranteeing creativity and cultural diversity, access to content, and participation by all groups of the population in the information society.

4.2 Reinforcing copyright provisions while implementing "fair use" practices in educational and cultural establishments

In implementing the draft Directive, EU member states will have to confront with the controversial concept of fair use - the general practice of lawfully permitted copying or excerpting of copyrighted material in the course of education, scholarship, or commentary, or in order to advance learning, and for other societal goals.

In the United States, attempts to set up guidelines on the fair use of electronic publications within the CONFU (Conference on Fair Use) framework failed in 1999 for no agreement was reached on two of the thorniest issues concerning electronic publishing:

distance learning and interlibrary loan[15]. In the United Kingdom, the PA/JISC *Guidelines for fair dealing in an electronic environment*[16] identified a series of scenarios where digital copying made either by a librarian or by an individual can be considered as "fair dealing". They do not deal with the inter-library loan of collections of electronic materials made by educational institutions and users – a still unsolved issue.

In European countries, the principle of "fair use" in educational and cultural institutions is far from being generalised. This is the reason why the Council of Europe/EBLIDA Guidelines on library legislation and policy in Europe[17] took a different approach. They suggest that "Governments should establish a legal position for libraries in copyright and neighbouring rights" (art. 9.i) and that "copyright exemptions that apply to printed materials should, as far as possible, also apply to digital materials" (art. 9.ii). There are two important consequences underlined by these two articles. The first is that existing practices in libraries should also be valid in the electronic environment with the principle of public access being safeguarded and not limited by the exclusive right given to authors and producers.

The second is that the application of copyright provisions in libraries (and possibly also in educational and cultural institutions) should be regulated and not left to free negotiations between the public and the private sector. Because libraries in educational and cultural institutions serve the public good, and because they do not benefit by being able to engage in free trade, there is good reason for governments to protect them from free trade. One way to handle this would be for governments to establish collective bargaining bodies in charge of negotiating collective agreements, licensing or other forms of contracts with right holders. This would be a way to preserve the nature of public service ensured by the public information infrastructure.

4.3 Making the case for a reduced VAT rate for electronic publications

In many countries books and some other cultural products enjoy a special fiscal treatment usually consisting of a reduced VAT rate on sales. This principle, which works for categories that correspond to a precise social interest and only benefit the end-consumer, is well acknowledged also by the Council Directive 92/77/EEC of 19 October 1992 supplementing the common system of value added tax amending Directive 77/388/EEC (approximation of VAT rates)[18]. The special VAT rate applied in the book field can be as low as zero - or at least far lower than the standard rate. In Western Europe, only Denmark and Sweden apply the standard VAT rate and tax books up to 25%.[19]

---

[15] Laura N. Gasaway. "Guidelines for distance learning and interlibrary loan: doomed and more doomed"; and Kenneth D. Crews. "Electronic resources and fair use: the outer limits of CONFU"; both in *JASIS. Journal of the American Society for Information Science*, (1999) vol. 50, n. 14, December 1999, respectively p. 1337-1341 and 1342-1345.

[16] PA stands for the Publishers' Association (of the United Kingdom) and JISC for Joint Information System Committee, a strategic advisory committee working on behalf of the funding bodies for higher and further education in England, Scotland, Wales and Northern Ireland. (Guidelines are posted on <http://www.publishers.org.uk>.

17 Council of Europe. Council of Europe – EBLIDA. *Guidelines on library legislation and policy in Europe* (DECS/CULT/POL/book(2000) 1 <http://culture.coe.fr/epba/eng/ecubookR.3.htm>. These Guidelines have no binding nature and do not commit governments to apply them; they are intended to provide guidance for policy-makers, politicians and professionals in drawing-up legal instruments and governmental policies concerning libraries and other information institutions.

[18] Council Directive 92/77/EEC of 19 October 1992 supplementing the common system of value added tax and amending Directive 77/388/EEC (approximation of VAT rates) <http://europa.eu.int/eur-lex/en/lif/dat/1992/en_392L0077.html>.

[19] François Rouet . *VAT and book policy: impacts and issues.* Strasbourg: Council of Europe, 1999.

These measures apply to conventional cultural industries, not the electronic environment. In electronic commerce, the physical means of transport is no longer required, the "goods" are non-corporeal, and the distinction between goods and services is blurring. Moreover, it is practically impossible to determine the content until it is converted from bits and bytes to text.

The European Commission has made an important step forward by issuing the communication on "E-commerce and indirect taxation"[20], designed to simplify the fiscal regime in electronic commerce. The EC proposed that "a supply that results in a product being placed at the disposal of the recipient in digital form via an electronic network is to be treated for VAT purposes, as a supply of services". This proposal is likely to be the regulatory principle underpinning a Community Directive and, as a consequence of the treaties of the European Union, national legislation on indirect taxation. If that happens, there may be a disparity between cultural goods (like newspapers and books, for which a reduced VAT rate is requested), and the same goods delivered in digital form, which would be taxed at the full VAT rate. By making electronic transactions a service, the European Commission would be violating the European Union's principle of neutrality, under which taxation should be neutral and equitable between forms of electronic commerce and between conventional and electronic forms of commerce.

I think that using the culture-oriented electronic publishing chain would be useful in establishing whether a special fiscal regime should be applied to content available on the Internet. Book publishing and electronic publishing organisations should urge the European Union to issue a directive that would standardize indirect taxation on e-commerce according to the principle of neutrality.

4.4 Linking legal deposit of electronic publications to copyright provisions

The principal way governments build national collections of their country's written heritages is by requiring that publications be deposited in central repositories – usually national libraries or specialized archives.

Norway was the first country to require legal deposit of digital publications. In Norway, since 1989, documents of all types on any media have had to be deposited. That law was groundbreaking, as it was passed in a time when electronic publications seemed to be marginal. Denmark followed the Norwegian example and adopted a new Legal deposit act in 1998[21].

Technical problems proved not to difficult to solve; the issue with deposit is access. Publishers hesitate to deposit their electronic products in repository libraries because they are concerned that free access to, and electronic distribution of, those publications would seriously compromise their ability to collect fees. Many web sites provide valuable information, but move or delete information (or parts of it) when it is no longer current. Even now, many articles reference electronic publications that do not exist anymore. The deposit of electronic publications ensures the availability of electronic communication.

If national libraries do not work out appropriate arrangements with publishers to ensure that the public be allowed to access electronic material, there is a risk of creating national "dead collections", deposited for storage purposes and not open to access. The objectives of access, under certain conditions and in compliance with existing laws on copyright, should therefore be explicitly mentioned by legal deposit regulations.

---

[20] European Commission. *E-Commerce and indirect taxation. Communication by the Commission to the Council of Ministers, the European Parliament and to the Economic and Social Committee (374/1998 of 17 June 1998)* < http://www.ispo.cec.be/ecommerce/legal/taxation.html>.

[21] Ingrid Mauritzen – Svein Arne Solbakk *(2000). A study on copyright and legal deposit of online documents.* Helsinki: NORDINFO-rapport nr 1/2000.

Whether legal deposit may become an instrument for a policy on public access at a national level depends very much on the role that national repositories play within national library systems and, even further, on the role libraries play within national information policy and planning. There is no doubt that national libraries could easily lead a consortium of libraries and negotiate for better conditions to access electronic publications on behalf of the other libraries of the country.

In my opinion, if countries were to adhere to a principle of compensation for rights owners, it would have a tremendous impact on the nature of legal deposit and on national libraries themselves, especially those in small or less wealthy countries. The most significant change, however, would concern national libraries themselves. In order to fulfil this objective, national libraries should radically re-think their role in three ways. First, they should create vast repositories of national content in electronic form where copyright issues have been cleared with the rights owners. Second, they should be able to disseminate such content through a network of library consortia and other institutions on a simplified fee-based tariff system. Third, when and where needed, they should establish contacts with a network of sale points where publications available online may be printed locally through print-on-demand techniques and at the payment of an additional fee for value-added services. It is a radical change that is of relevance not only to national libraries but to the entire library and information profession.

5. Conclusions

Today there is a wide recognition that no cultural and societal objective can be pursued without the involvement of public powers in a catalysing, mediatory or facilitating function. Gunter Pauli, an advocate of the sustainability argument, has maintained that: "the first step in developing technologies that are technologically sustainable must be to transform the very nature of technology from a totalitarian 'megatechnology' to a tool, the use of which is restricted by cultural norms" (Pauli, p. 146). The struggle on copyright has certainly drawn the attention of the cultural world around the importance of intellectual property right in the electronic environment. Access to information is the new frontier now open to legislators and policy-makers willing to develop a culture-oriented information society. It took no less than five hundred years for enlightened politicians to notice the impact of the book medium on human development and to define book policies accordingly. It is to be hoped that it will take much less time to set up a model of electronic publishing that is at the service of personal development, freedom of expression and our cultural diversity.

Electronic Publishing '01 –
2001 in the Digital Publishing Odyssey
A. Hübler et al. (Eds.)
IOS Press, 2001

An Evaluation of the Information Needs and Practices of Part-Time, Distance Learning and Mature Students in Higher Education

Fytton Rowland
Iris Rubbert

J.F.Rowland@lboro.ac.uk
I.M.Rubbert@lboro.ac.uk
Department of Information Science, Loughborough University
Loughborough LE11 3TU, UK

Abstract:
This paper evaluates the information needs and practices of part-time, distance learning and mature students in Higher Education (HE) outside the Open University (OU). In recent years, the government has pointed out the importance of individuals engaging in lifelong learning, to remain competitive in a globalised economy, which draws increasingly on successful knowledge creation. In response, the HE sector in the UK offers a growing number of its programmes on a part-time and distance-learning basis for students to remain in full- or part-time employment while studying for further qualifications. We question whether the information-gathering practices of part-time and distance learning students best reflect the pedagogical concept of lifelong learning. Our results show that the majority of universities do not cater for the specialised needs of part-time and distance learners well, which leads to an increasing use of the Internet and employer resources as a substitute for traditional information channels. Students have major problems coping with the complexity of the WWW and they made recommendations on how to improve existing information services in HE.

0. Background: The historical development of part-time and distance learning programmes in the UK

Until the middle of the 19th century much of the HE climate in the UK was determined by the church and cultural elite attending the traditional full-time programmes in the Oxford and Cambridge tradition [1]. Following early Scottish developments, the University of London opened its doors in 1826 to the general public by operating as an external examining body for those students that attended classes in local colleges. In the latter half of the nineteenth century, other universities joined the extension movement, and advances in the print industry together with an improvement in postal services led to the implementation of the first correspondence courses. Fieldhouse points out that these programmes focused on arts and humanities education, concentrating on the middle rather than the working class [2]. At the turn of the century, the British education system was transformed through a standardisation of the university degree structure and tighter control on expenditure for HE, which led to decreasing numbers of short-courses available for mature students in the universities. After World War I, entrance requirements for university attendance were established with the young, full-time student in mind, which transferred the responsibility for post-secondary education to technical colleges and trade unions.

The post-World War II period focused on the restructuring of secondary education, which left the need of enhancement of adult education marginalised [3]. The 1963 Robbins Report recognised the importance of a university expansion programme, but officially excluded any recommendations on the provision for part-time, distance learning or mature students. The implementation of the binary policy, dividing HE from technical colleges and polytechnics, restricted the successful working of democratisation processes, advised just a few years earlier by Robbins. Lowe argues that these developments together with an decrease of adult education through the Workers Educational Association (WEA) led to a demand of a University of the Air, which was to become the Open University who recruited its first students in 1971 [4].

The 1992 Higher and Further Education Act resulted in the abolition of the binary line, and the polytechnics did not consider extra-mural activities or adult education to be a separate entity. Part-time provision for adult students went in line with mainstream undergraduate and postgraduate programmes, and increasingly the pre-1992 universities were forced to adopt the same pattern for their mature students. As most courses were transformed into a modular credit structure, more students formerly studying in a leisurely manner under the 'open' system, had to consider going down the degree route instead. An even more fundamental change was under way as a result of the 1997 Dearing Report, which introduced the term "lifelong learning" as a new pedagogical concept for the new millennium. From the beginning, the report established an educational policy that is anchored in a much broader cultural context involving recognition of the individual's development beyond secondary and higher education:

'The purpose of education is life-enhancing: it contributes to the whole quality of life. This recognition of the purpose of higher education in the development of our people, our society, and our economy is central to our vision. In the next century, the economically successful nations will be those which become learning societies: where all are committed, through effective education and training, to lifelong learning.' [5]

The Dearing Report compared the perception of part- and full-time students about their institutions and programmes of study [6]. Part-time students were particularly restricted in terms of institutional choice because of family and work commitment (over 90% were in full-time employment). As a result, part-time students were also less flexible regarding their choice of programme, academic reputation, teaching record and research status. Full- and part-time students were well informed about the specific content of a programme but lacked awareness on non-academic skills covered in the course. A majority of part-time students (58%) were encouraged by their employers to engage in educational activities and of those who enrolled for a particular programme, 79% received financial support from their company. Part-time students reported an improvement in all three areas under that of their full-time colleagues with the exception of writing skills and self-motivation. On the other hand, it was striking that 6% of all part-time students reported a deterioration of their self-motivation. Interestingly, the Dearing Report excluded the perception of part-time students on library resources, computing and laboratory facilities and other specialised equipment needed for their study programme.

It therefore appeared that the time was right for a study of the information practices of part-time and distance-learning students. In addition, the emergence of the World Wide Web as a medium for the delivery of publications in electronic form has altered the practical possibilities dramatically over the past five years.

1. Our Research

1.1 Introduction: selection of sample

The aim of the research project was to ascertain current practices and future prospects in the use of professional-level information services by students who are located remotely from their institutions of higher education or who study on a part-time basis, which restricts their access to institutional information services. We emphasised the contribution to this provision that may be made by electronic information resources available via the Internet, and evaluated the students' perception of possible cost implications for such a service. In addition, we assessed the student perception of future developments in information services in the HE sector. We specifically excluded students at the Open University from our survey, since their information needs are provided for in a very specific and structured way by the Open University's system which other universities would not be able to emulate.

As the project anticipated a general exploration of the lifelong learning environment, an equal distribution of respondents across the mode of study, subject area and the level of qualification had to be achieved. The starting point for the sampling procedure was information taken from the Internet, which allowed the identification of distance learning, part-time and short-course programmes. In addition to contacting programme tutors directly, students were also approached through the use of e-mail discussion lists. In the end, 77 students volunteered to participate in the study and another 160 addresses of students were received from a number of course administrators, which were used for the distribution of the questionnaire only.

For this study, 30 semi-structured telephone and personal interviews and two focus groups were conducted. In addition, 220 students from 17 universities and 31 different departments were approached to complete a questionnaire, which was available in printed form and on the WWW. A higher than average response rate was expected as the researchers established e-mail contact with nearly half of all respondents prior to the distribution of the questionnaire.

1.2 Telephone and Face-to-Face Interviews

Three face-to-face and 27 telephone interviews were carried out to help in the design and supplement the results of the questionnaire. The interviewees were chosen from different part-time and distance learning programmes in the UK. The respondents split into 16 postgraduate taught, seven research postgraduate, five undergraduate and one short course student. One student classified herself as a lifelong learner after she has completed all of her HE as a mature student. It was interesting to see that none of the 16 students studying on a distance learning basis pursued their course of study full-time. Four of the distance-learning students were based outside the UK and six respondents were non-native English speakers. The telephone interviews were based on an open topic guide and monitored four pre-defined subject areas: information sources that are currently used by the students, problems related to obtaining subject-related information, the future of information service provision and the mapping of an 'ideal world of information scenario'.

1.3 Focus Groups

The two focus groups consisting of seven participants each, were conducted after the completion of half of the telephone interviews. As a result, the research team had a clear indication of problems associated with the provision of information services, which helped in the design of a topic guide for the focus group meetings. Altogether, five of the participants had been interviewed prior to the focus group meetings. It was anticipated that this would not bias the group behaviour as the general perception of respondents on the provision of information sources was not likely to change on the basis of the telephone interviews. In contrast, a positive discrimination could be achieved as these respondents could probe the other participants because they were more familiar with the topic. Fewer interactions were needed by the moderator, which led to a considerable improvement of group dynamics.

The first focus group was conducted at Birmingham University and consisted of students who were studying for either an Executive MBA (part-time evening) or a MSc in Economic Development (part-time day-release). The second focus group was held at Loughborough University with seven participants, studying in five different disciplines. All but one participant (MBA, University of Birmingham) studied at Loughborough University in either evening or day release mode. One of the participants was a full-time, distance learning student based in Glasgow. All other participants were in full-time employment and lived within daily commuting distance from their university.

1.4 Questionnaire Survey

The questionnaire was returned by 106 students, which represents a response rate of 48 per cent. The respondents studied for a diverse range of subject areas (Business, Education, Social Science & Humanities, and Science & Engineering) on undergraduate (11%), taught postgraduate (55%), and research postgraduate (17%) level. In addition, 17% of the students were participants in short courses. As the over-representation of taught postgraduate programmes reflects well the availability of part-time and distance-learning programmes outside the OU, we decided not trying to achieve an equal distribution among courses. During the interviews a number of respondents pointed out that they do not have all the formal qualifications necessary for following a postgraduate degree, but it seemed that a majority of departments were more flexible with the admission of mature students because their work experience was often taken as a substitute for formal academic qualifications.

2. Data Analysis and Results

2.1 The information flow from traditional resources

The biggest barriers to using university libraries [7] for all the students were time and geographical constraints. Over one-third of the respondents never entered their or any other university library during their course of study. More than three-quarters of the part-time students found that the opening hours of the university library are not tailored to their needs and another 34% of the respondents visit a university library only between one and three times per month. The interviews and focus groups revealed the following main problem areas in information provision by university libraries:

- restricted opening hours during vacation periods that hit part-time students in full-time employment most
- short-loan collections which could not be used due to a 24-hour return policy
- inter-library loan services of some institutions operate with a long delay
- strong competition for material because part- and full-time students use the same reading lists

Students recognised that in most institutions library staff would try to adapt to the special needs of part-time and distance learning students. Some of the universities operated special distance learning units, which would provide mail deliveries and an extended electronic information network. A majority of the respondents had to purchase core reading material with an average expenditure of £40-60 per module.

Even though public libraries are recognised by students as a possible source of information, they generally do not cater for the specialised information needs of students in higher education. Nevertheless, the interviews revealed that students found staff in public libraries friendlier and more helpful compared with the university librarians. In addition, the inter-library loan service of public libraries compared favourably with that of universities.

Even though the respondents were critical about libraries, books and journals still emerged clearly as the most frequently used information source by our students. Even though the Internet makes life a lot easier as it saves valuable time, there was a general agreement between respondents that nothing compares to the traditionally published information material because of its mobility, flexibility, easy scanning, more comfortable reading position with less constraint on the eyes, and the option of storing texts for a long period of time. The Internet is frequently used to order books through online bookshops, but students generally prefer to read study material on paper than on the screen. Newspapers and magazines represent a valuable information channel particularly for social science and business students.

Anyone deciding to study for a degree or postgraduate qualification would probably expect to receive an introduction on the availability of information sources in one form or the other. Only 46% of the respondents received such an introduction, which included information on library and Internet resources. Our study has shown that such an introduction was only common among social science and humanities students (77%) and least likely to be offered in business schools (65%) and education departments (54%). It was expected that part-time and distance learning students would receive a special introduction on the availability of information services, as their access to the university libraries is considerably restricted. But interestingly, our results revealed that the introduction to information services had no impact on the quality rating of library and Internet resources with 7% of the students considering the quality of both as unsatisfactory.

2.2 The information flow from electronic resources

Our survey suggests that distance learning and part-time students make increasingly use of electronic information sources. Only 12% of the respondents did not have an Internet access at home, and a lot of time is spent searching the WWW for information. Nearly half of all students spend more than 10 hours a month on-line and only 3% of the students make no use of the Internet at all. Considering the access difficulties to university libraries, it was a surprise to find that a majority of students (52%) do not spend more than 6-10 hours per month on the Internet. A majority of students who spent long hours on the Internet (>10 hours per month) were also regular library visitors (Fig. 1).

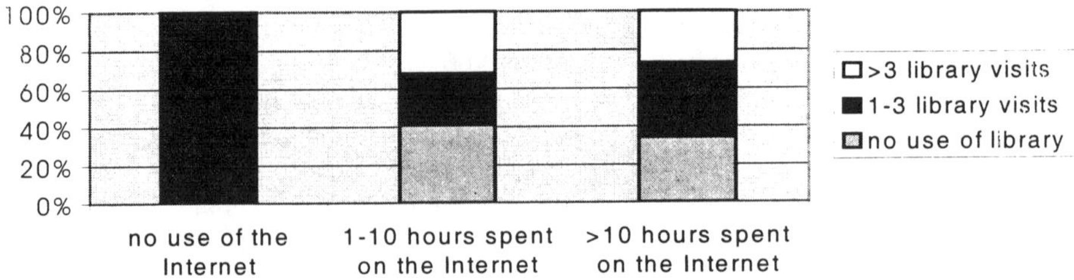

Fig. 1 Library visits in relation to hours spent on the Internet

Even though the Internet is very popular with students, it is not a medium without conflict. The Internet did not emerge as an alternative information channel for those students who were unsatisfied with their university library as a majority (67%) would also give the Internet a rating of a just pass or unsatisfactory.

Students still enjoy studying more than searching for study materials (64%), which might be mainly due to the difficulties associated with accessing the library rather than searching for books *per se*. In addition, students appeared to be very impatient with search engines and information systems, particularly science and engineering and business students (Fig. 2). Almost half of all students (49%) do not invest more than ten minutes in finding out how an information system or search engine works. Overall, an information service provider would have lost nearly three-quarters of its customers if they could still not understand the information system after 15 minutes.

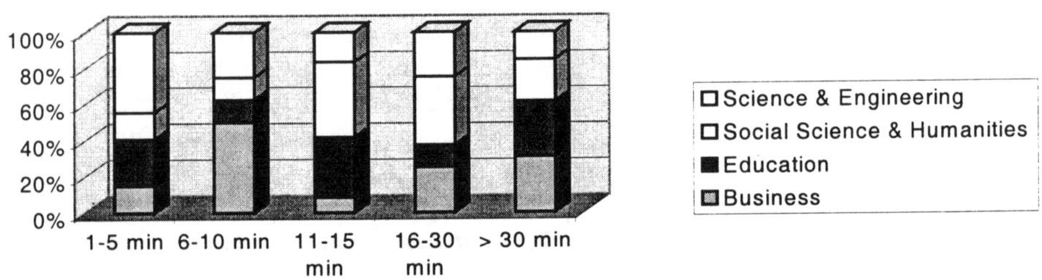

Fig. 2 Maximum timeframe for working out how an information system or search engine works

Generally students seem to be familiar with search engines, as three-quarters of the respondents had no difficulties searching for relevant information sources. Nevertheless, the majority believe that a lot of the search engines are too general and they would appreciate a service that would be more specific for their academic and professional development. There was an indication that the most and least frequent users of the Internet were less likely to spend a long time with a new information system or search engine (Fig. 3).

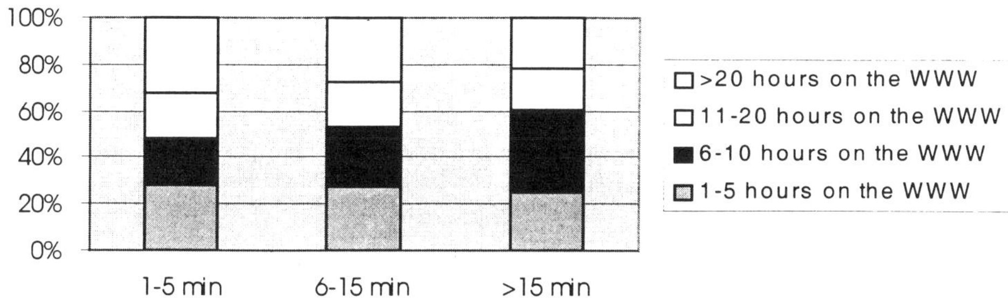

Fig. 3 Usage of the Internet in relation to the time students are prepared to spent with a new information system or search engine

Our results indicate that there is a split between Internet users on the topic of being able to filter relevant information. Half of the students often feel overwhelmed by the amount of information that is provided on the Internet and question its quality. In fact, the focus group discussions revealed that students would welcome the implementation of subject-related gateway services, which would operate as an electronic library with the additional feature of a quality assurance system of commercial websites and e-mail discussion groups.

Nearly half of the respondents (48%) found that there is high competition for books in university libraries, and part-time or distance learning students are normally the ones who get the last pick. As a result, over three quarters (77%) wished that there was an electronic library that would send students material on request via e-mail. Students did not agree on how much such a service should cost (Fig. 4). There seemed to be a general perception that such a service should be offered free of charge, as the information service provider would be able to recover its cost through advertising campaigns. On average, social science and humanities students are willing to pay a higher price per electronic document delivery compared with all other students. Business and science and engineering students are most reluctant to using a service on a pay per view basis, mainly because they feel that the Internet already provides enough information for them free of charge.

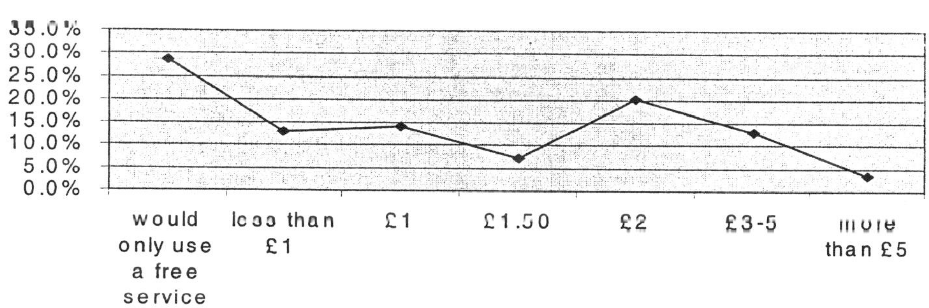

Fig. 4 Maximum price a student would be willing to pay for an electronic document delivery

The two least used information sources are TV/radio and e-mail discussion groups. The former may be subject to increasing commercialisation, which may effect the quality of TV and radio programmes. Only one-third of the respondents is subscribed to e-mail forums. The interviews and focus groups revealed that discussion forums are often considered as lacking quality and providing information that is not really relevant to the course of study. Generally, the more time students spent on the Internet, the more likely they were to subscribe to e-mail discussion forums.

2.3 The Impact of the Work Environment on Part-time and Distance Learners

For mature students the work environment represents an important access channel to information resources. When asked for the character of their current employment contract, the majority of respondents answered that they were working on either a full-time (76%) or a part-time (15%) basis. Science and engineering students, in particular, tend to work more flexibly, with over a quarter them in part-time or casual work. Their flexible work patterns give these students a greater opportunity to visit their university library (43% at least once week). This compares favourably with the business students, of which over half (58%) have never seen their university library at all. This group is perhaps more likely to take their information from the Internet, considering that all business students had access to the WWW from work and 85% from home.

We were surprised to find that only one of our students claimed to be unemployed considering the governmental efforts for better access to HE among those without a job [8]. Vocational training schemes, supported by Training and Enterprise Councils or Local Enterprise Councils, seem to receive a higher backing than formal academic qualifications. Governmental support is minimal and does not cover the full tuition fees, referring the unemployed who aim for a postgraduate degree to university access funds and family support [9]. As a result, it was no surprise to find that 44% of our students received full and 15% part-funding from their employers. The remaining 41% of students were self-funding and, indeed, during the interviews we heard many times that the reason for pursuing their programme on a part-time basis was the fact that they had to finance themselves.

We were not able to establish a correlation between those employers funding the studies of their employees and the provision of information services by the same company. The provision of electronic information resources by the employer had no effect on the number of library visits or the hours students spent on the Internet. The interviews and focus groups revealed that there was a greater level of satisfaction among those students who had access to a company library. Especially, international corporations offered extensive library resources, which often included a physical library that offered an international inter-library loan service, portal services and e-mail discussion forums. Respondents working in smaller companies often found a substitute in library and information resources offered by professional associations.

Internet access at work was granted to 87% of all students. In addition, the employer provided general electronic information resources for 43% of the students, which was welcomed by the respondents with one-third of the students being moderate to frequent users of this information service. On the other hand, internal company information was of little use to the respondents and could not be really integrated in the course of study.

A majority of mature students are members of professional associations (62%), whose information services are valued highly as another important work-related information channel. Only five respondents were not satisfied with the information that was provided by this body, which appears negligible considering that over half of the members of professional associations judged their information service to be very good or good.

3. Discussion and Conclusions

Most of the HE institutions did not provide sufficient support for part-time and distance learning students to pursue their courses successfully. A particular concern was the recognition by students that they would be able to achieve better results if they had better access to information resources.

As a result, it was not surprise to see employers emerging as a blessing for a lot of students working for multi-national corporations, as they normally provide well-maintained company libraries and access to electronic information services. But not all students have the luck to work for these corporations, and especially employees of smaller, national companies, who want to enhance their careers prospects in a changing economic climate of the global community, are the ones to suffer most from restricted access to information resources.

Even though it is realised that an upgrade of existing facilities need to be evaluated on the basis of cost-benefit considerations, simple operational changes could be achieved without high capital investment. Mulvaney and Lewis report on the implementation of a new distance learning initiative for the education library at Birmingham University that was mainly based on operational changes but implemented nearly all the recommendations given by distance learning students [10]. Surprisingly, more than two years later, hardly any of these changes had been introduced to the central library service. The changes made at the education library covered nearly all the recommendations that were given during the focus group meeting but unfortunately, these respondents are unlikely to be the beneficiary and will remain standing in front of closed library doors.

A number of suggestions come from the students themselves:

- special library opening hours for part-time students (two 'long' evenings per week, also operated during vacation periods)
- an electronic reservation service, which would allow students to book material in advance
- closer liaison between subject librarians and departmental staff to check on the availability of reading material
- special introductory sessions which are subject-related and focus on the information needs of part-time students
- alternative reading lists to those of full-time students, which would take pressure off existing resources
- evaluation of websites by lecturers on the quality of information
- postal loans for distance learning students
- increased information networking between students, departmental and library staff

An emerging question, which will need to be addressed by lecturers teaching part-time and distance learning students, is the integration of electronic information resources into the curriculum. Even though publishers are increasingly investing in ICT as a substitute for the existing distribution models, some issues remain unresolved. Adequate pricing mechanisms are not sufficiently developed yet and copyright regulations will need to be adapted [11]. As long as solutions are not found to these problems, publishers will be reluctant to make further high capital investments in ICT channels. Subject-specific information pools that target mainly part-time and distance learning students are likely to be driven furthest down the agenda.

Until these issues are resolved, the best possible solution would be the implementation of subject-related gateway services through commercial information service providers. This would allow students to experience a slow adjustment from the traditional university library to the electronic information network. Our research has shown that mature students work under particular financial constraints, as they often do not receive financial support from their employer and have family commitments. As a result, the success of such a new service will ultimately depend on the utilisation of a suitable pricing mechanism. Students are only prepared to make a minimal contribution, which raises the question of how to recover the remaining costs. The students in this study showed a high level of appreciation for advertising in electronic information services, which might need to be considered as one possible contribution in a gateway service. In addition, electronic bookshops are highly used among part-time and distance learning students, which might need to be regarded as an important augmented product to the subject gateway.

The study has shown that the information needs and practices of part-time, distance learning and mature students in a lifelong learning environment have been rapidly transformed by the use of ICT in the higher education sector. Even though electronic facilities make the information-gathering exercises of part-time and distance learning students easier, there is still a long way to go until the institutional information layer will be optimised in HE sector. Adjustments will need to be made by information services departments to guarantee the future success of undergraduate and postgraduate programmes. The distinct information needs of part-time and distance learners are often not recognised by universities, and only few programmes offer a specialised information service provision for these students.

Clearly, the major problems associated with part-time and distance learning studies are the emerging time constraints, as nearly all students studying in this mode also hold demanding full-time jobs. As a result, key demands on the implementation of better information practices centre around the optimisation of time management. Ultimately, according to Freeman, this would mean recognising the student as a consumer of higher education information services [12]. In a country where students pay tuition fees higher than in any other European country, it must be questioned whether British learners have the right to request unique support. Key demands made by students relating to information services are listed above.

With an increase in distance learning courses, more universities provide specialised distance learning units, which have been welcomed by our respondents. Compared to the part-time students, whose needs go often unaccounted among full-time students, more specialised services are offered for distance learners. Not surprisingly, a lot of part-time students feel like the fifth wheel of the higher education community, dragged along but with no special support. Considering that part-time study opportunities foster the integration of local communities with their local HE institution, there might be a need to increasingly create part-time in addition to the existing distance-learning units.

The study has shown that the emerging conflicts between traditional and electronic information resources is embedded in a much wider transformation of our cultural practices, of which education is just one. The recognition of the book as the primary educational resource is still apparent, especially among mature students. On the other hand, the introduction of the Internet in a lot of work environments has led to an increased use of these facilities. Due to the time constraints, students are often forced to use electronic resources even though they would prefer to use a traditional university library. Critics have argued that the increased use of ICT among students leads to an information overload, leaving the student stranded on piles of information, robbed of the ability to transform this information into knowledge. Ultimately, it must be assessed to what extent library and information services take responsibility for this development and are liable to create and optimise the learning environment for distance learning and part-time students.

The study has shown that most of the student needs could be satisfied with the implementation of a subject-related gateway. Students had particularly difficulties identifying the quality of information that is provided on the Internet. If an information service provider would guarantee the academic relevance and quality of material through either expert abstracts and/or a grading system of material, a better assurance could be given to students that they are going into the right direction with their literature reviews. Ideally, the gateway service should provide the following facilities in order of their importance:

- a good subject-related search engine
- access to an abstract and indexing service, including international references
- access to newspaper and magazine archives
- access to websites of relevant governmental departments, NGOs or professional associations
- e-mail discussion forums and electronic bulletin boards

Some of the demands students made will be easier to implement than others. Where a new service needs to be provided, cost-benefit calculations must decide on the usefulness of specific facilities.. Existing library services often only need to make small operational changes to meet the needs of part-time and distance learning students better. In some institutions, awareness should be raised of the fact that individual members of library staff have the potential to transform the learning experience of part-time and distance learning students from pain to pleasure. Part-time and distance learning students put a lot of time, effort and money into their educational development – all stakeholders in the education community should recognise that, and help to make their experience enjoyable in order to create a truly learning society.

4. Acknowledgement

We thank the ingenta Institute for funding this research.

5. References

1. Tight, M. **Higher Education: A Part-time Perspective**. Buckingham: SRHE and Open University Press, 1991
2. Fieldhouse, R. **A History of Modern British Adult Education**. Leicester: NIACE, 1996
3. Simon, B. **Education and the Social Order**. London: Lawrence & Wishart, 1991
4. Lowe, R. **Education in the Post-War Years: A Social History**. London: Routledge, 1988
5. The National Committee of Inquiry into Higher Education **Higher Education in the Learning Society. Report of the National Committee**. Norwich: HMSO, 1997, pp. 7-8
6. The National Committee of Inquiry into Higher Education Higher **Education in the Learning Society. Report 2, 3 and 4**. Norwich: HMSO, 1997
7. Unwin, L. *et al*. **The Role of the Library in Distance Learning**. London: Bowker Saur, 1998
8. Employment Action Plan (1999), http://www.dfee.gov.uk/eap/index.htm
9. http://www.dfee.gov.uk/secondchances/chaper13_2_ba.html and http://www.dfee.gov.uk/secondchances/chapter25_7_ba.html
10. Mulvaney, T.K. and Lewis, E. Analysis of Library Services for distance learning students at the University of Birmingham. **Education Libraries Journal**, Vol. 41, No. 1, 1998, pp. 29-34
11. Bide, M. *et al.* Some proposals regarding copyright clearance and digitisation in higher education. **Journal of Information Science**, Vol. 23, No. 6, 1997, pp. 393-406
12. Freeman, M. Consuming Interest: a personal view of the student as a consumer of higher education library services. **Education Libraries Journal**, Vol. 40, No. 1, 1997, pp. 25-28

Electronic Publishing '01 –
2001 in the Digital Publishing Odyssey
A. Hübler et al. (Eds.)
IOS Press, 2001

Interaction with electronic documents using the library metaphor

Guadalupe Muñoz-Martín, Ignacio Aedo, Paloma Díaz

Computer Science Department (University Carlos III of Madrid)
Avda de la Universidad, 30 28911-Leganés, Madrid, Spain
+34 91 624 9499 - lupe@inf.uc3m.es

The information available in the Internet could be more useful if in addition to its accessibility, it would be organized as users require. Internet users can feel lost if they can not find information management and retrieval services like those provided by traditional libraries. In the belief that the use of the traditional library metaphor for documents over the Internet will improve their management, we have developed a model for digital libraries called the VILMA model, and a prototype that implements it. VILMA's user interface utilizes a spatial metaphor where the typical elements (such as books, shelves, etc.) are presented in a three-dimensional world. Moreover, VILMA is composed of the three main elements of a traditional library: information entities, metadata, and processes. In VILMA, the information entities that form the library's collection, are documents in the Internet, and the metadata are those required by the Dublin Core Metadata Set. There are two types of processes in VILMA: public, which are all those related to the user, and technical, that have to do with traditional librarian's tasks. Public processes are subscription, identification, searching (analytical, expert, accidental) and customising, while technical processes are selection of documents, acquisition, classification and cataloguing, indexing, maintenance and notification. In this paper, we will present the VILMA model, and its prototype.

0. INTRODUCTION

One of the main concerns of human beings along their whole history has been the preservation and dissemination of the information to keep trace of their culture and to share knowledge. Some of the people in charge of the storage and management of information are the librarians. Librarians have years of experience organizing large quantities of diverse information. They have examined the problem of information retrieval and created regulated rules and standards to organize information, like the Dewey Decimal System [DDC, 96], the Universal Decimal Classification (UDC) scheme [McIlwaine, 95], or the classification scheme devised by the Library of Congress (LCC) [Chan, 86].

The entity in which librarians perform such activities is the library. Although libraries exist since long time ago, they have suffered an evolution mainly due to the change of the material that it organizes, and the advance in the tools that librarians use to perform their tasks. Librarians have achieved their goals making use of the means that were available at every moment in such a manner that the evolution of these means has driven the evolution of the library itself. This evolution has produced three different types of library, each one based on the previous. Before we could talk about digital libraries we had the so-called automated libraries, that were similar to traditional libraries in many ways, but with some use of technology for their management. Traditional libraries have been managing information stored in physical means such as paper or videotapes, and now, there is a new kind of medium, the electronic one. Current traditional libraries (automated libraries) are combinations of old libraries and the use of new technologies. As the technology advances, libraries are evolving into digital libraries. They utilize the new electronic medium in a bigger percentage than the automated ones. A digital library has been described as a federated structure that provides humans both intellectual and physical access to the huge and growing world-wide networks of information encoded in multimedia digital formats [Birmingham et al., 94]. A digital library must provide all of the services found currently in traditional libraries, based on principles of selection, acquisition, access, management and preservation, related to a specific client community, as well as new services made possible by the digital media and computer networks [Gladney et al., 94].

Nowadays, the availability of information has experienced an explosion mainly due to the advance of the technology and the growth of the Internet. But this explosion is tied down by chaos: there is no order or consistency among all the information available. Besides, it gets worse when whoever might produce whatever. Although some people talk about the Internet as if it was a digital library, the reality is that Internet is like a big repository of chaotic information, but not a library [Lynch, 97]. The information available in the Internet is unorganized because there is no single entity indexing it in the way a library catalog does. Moreover, the anarchic Internet does not contain standards for information management, and therefore, search mechanisms are forced to look for keywords in unstructured data. For these reasons, according to [Ferguson and Durfee, 98], users of the Internet feel lost when they can not find information management and retrieval services like those provided by traditional libraries where you make use of the librarians' knowledge, the cataloging and classification mechanisms, the notification support, or the personalized search tool among others.

In this paper, we present the model for digital libraries called VILMA (VIrtual Libraries with a Multi-layer Architecture) based on the traditional library metaphor for the management of information available in the Internet by means of a multi-layer architecture. Digital libraries using this metaphor will be able to manage information as traditional libraries do, but they will also take advantage of the new electronic medium. Also, to take the metaphor further, we propose the use of a user interface based on virtual reality in the belief that it will improve the usability of the digital library.

1. THE ELEMENTS OF THE LIBRARY AND THEIR EVOLUTION

As pointed out by [Nürnberg et al., 95], there are three main elements in a traditional library: information entities, metadata, and processes. Information entities are every item in the library (single or multiple as long as the whole set is a unit of information) that provides complete information about something. Metadata are information about the information entities in the library and how it is accessed and they should identify unequivocally every document. Processes are all the actions taken over the information entities or the metadata in the library. These elements have been changing as an adaptation to the needs of the library evolution. This section presents these changes.

1.1 Information entities

They are physical documents such as books, journals, videotapes or CD-ROM's in traditional and in automated libraries, but in digital libraries we have both physical and digital documents. Digital documents are files stored in computers and could be just digitized copies of physical documents, or proper digital documents such as a collection of electronic hyperdocuments. The whole set of information entities in a library, traditional or digital, is called a collection.

1.2 Metadata

Most of the metadata necessary to identify the information entities does not depend on the medium in which these entities are stored, but some do. Some medium-independent are title, author or subject, and others medium–dependent are the size or the number of pages when the medium is paper, or the number of bytes when the medium is electronic. Another important issue related to metadata is how to access it, because they are also information entities that have to be stored somehow. Another important element related to metadata in a library is a thesaurus, that is a list of subject headings or descriptors usually with a cross-reference system for use in the organization of a collection of documents for reference and retrieval. The whole set of metadata information, the thesaurus and the indexes necessary to access it is called a catalog. As information entities do not vary from traditional to automated libraries, metadata is almost the same for both of them.

There have been several rules, called cataloguing rules to specify the metadata, like the ISBD (International Standard Bibliographic Description) since 1974. But traditional and automated libraries differ in how they store the metadata. Traditional libraries do it in paper cards that can be accessed browsing them in ordered catalogues, but automated ones store the metadata in electronic records that conform to standards such as MARC (MAchine Readable Catalog). User's interface to this metadata are OPAC's (Online Public Access Catalog). However, as digital libraries contain both physical and digital entities, which metadata are necessary for these entities change when we think of electronic documents. Electronic documents have other attributes related to the electronic medium that need to be stored such as locations, document versions or date of last modification [Heery, 96]. Metadata in this case could be stored as electronic records or could be included in the electronic document to facilitate its extraction. Currently there are several efforts to achieve a standard for digital document metadata. Some kinds of available metadata sets are: HTML META-tags, IAFA (Internet Anonymous FTP Archive) templates, Dublin Core metadata sets or the USMARC bibliographic records.

1.3 Processes

These are different when we talk about traditional, automated or digital libraries. For the first and the second one, these activities are the same, and only differ in that automated libraries use automation systems to perform some of them. These processes have been divided by [Arms, 90] in two groups: Public, such as circulation, reference, and assistance; and Technical, such as acquisition, cataloging, or shelves ordering. For digital libraries it has been described different processes such as Collection Administration, Acquisition, Cataloguing and Indexing, Borrowing, and Readers Services [Landoni and Catenazzi, 93]. A more detailed division based on the previous one distinguishes two levels of services for digital libraries [Muñoz et al., 98]: Reader-oriented, such as subscribing, walking through the library to access other services, browsing through the library shelves and through a hierarchical structure, searching through the library catalogues, consulting or asking for advice from the librarian, customizing or creating a personal user library; and Librarian-oriented, such as information acquisition, storage and maintenance of the information, cataloguing, and indexing.

Although some of the processes could sound similar among the three types of libraries, the use of digital technology to perform them incorporates substantial differences between namesake ones. For traditional and automated libraries public services that could be analogous to the reader-oriented in digital ones force readers to go physically to the library to be able to access them while digital libraries allow remote access. Remote access involves several issues such as that the library could be distributed to make a better use of the resources, readers might use different languages, several users could use concurrently the same services, and the access could be at any time, among others. Also, technical/librarian-oriented services have to be performed manually by the librarian in traditional and automated libraries but they could also be carried out automatically in digital ones. This fact implies that human expertise that is crucial for these tasks has to be simulated by computer programs. Also, resource sharing could be done using the advantage of remote networked access.

2. VILMA model

VILMA (VIrtual Library with a Multi-layer Architecture) is a model of digital library developed in order to assess the traditional library metaphor including the new features derived from the electronic media. This model provides a personalized acquisition and cataloguing system, and a virtual reality user interface that may allow a more simple access to the system. On this basis, after a first schema for the architecture, the research has evolved into the implementation of a prototype. The objective of the development of such prototype is not just the achievement of a final product, but also to verify its applicability, that is, the capability of being implemented as a real and efficient product. The next subsections present both the model and the prototype.

2.1 VILMA model

The model being developed tries to handle the three elements that a digital library should be composed of (data, metadata and processes) without loosing modularity, flexibility and scalability. Figure 1 shows a general view of this model, which is explained briefly next. This model has three main layers, called "Public Processes" (PP), composed of those processes that interact with the user, such as subscribing, identification, browsing, searching, customizing, consulting and walking processes, "Technical Processes" (TP), composed of those processes that manage the collection, such as the selection of documents, acquisition, classification, indexing and maintenance processes, and "Repository Processes" (RP), in charge of the communication between the PP layer and the catalog. These layers communicate among them to provide the library functionality as follows.

In this model, the data collection, that is, the information entities, is obtained from the web, and it remains located in the web. The TP layer will select documents from the web based on the classification of the library and on the user preferences (arrow F) and it will acquire them to include them in the library (arrow H). When a document is acquired, it is classified to obtain its metadata, and it is indexed in the library catalog through the RP layer (arrows G and J). This layer is also in charge of the catalog maintenance, that is, to keep updated metadata of the data collection (arrows G and J), and of notifying new acquisitions to the users (arrow C). The PP layer handles all the processes related to the user. It will get, through the interface (arrows A and B), all data about every user to keep their profiles and to allow them to customize their own view of the library and it will show this personal view getting every user's information through arrows D, B and A. It will also get the users search queries and will pass them (arrow E) to the RP layer to find the required information from the catalog (arrow J). Through arrow I, the RP layer will be able to get a complete document when a user request it.

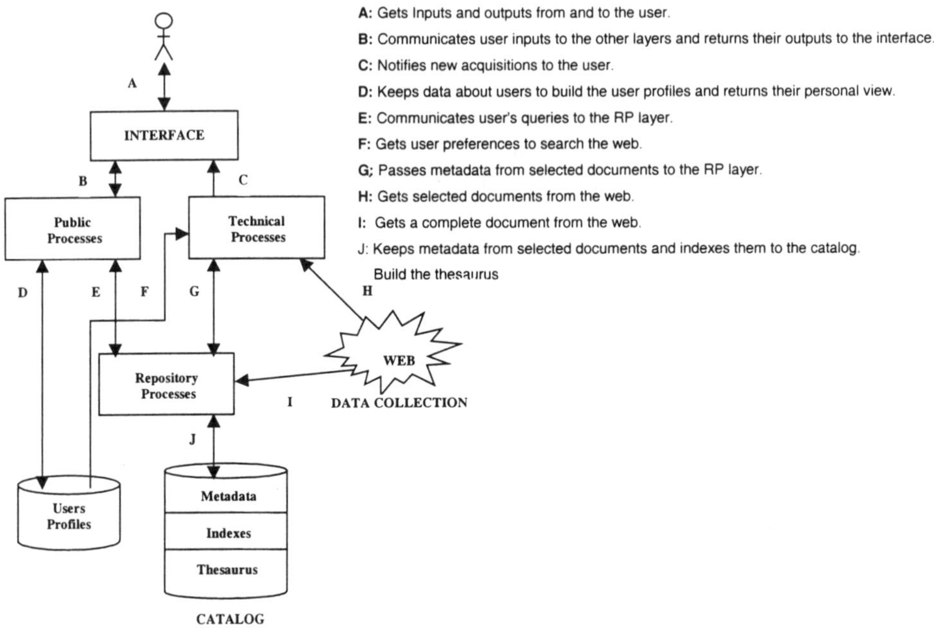

Figure 1. VILMA model

2.1.1 Public Processes Layer

This layer is in charge of all the communications with the user, and therefore will consists of a user interface that handles this communication. For the design of the user interface of an interactive system as a digital library is, we need to specify several points. According to [Shneiderman, 98], and his Object-Action Interface (OAI) model, we need: to identify which objects will be placed in the interface, to perform a task analysis, and to define the interaction styles. Task analysis refers to discovering what actions will be taken by users related to every particular object of the interface, and interaction styles implies to decide how users will accomplish the tasks and how the objects will be represented. The objects as well as their representation proposed by this model are based on the traditional library metaphor, which are rooms, books, shelves, catalogues, and OPAC. The representation of the objects of the system will imitate the real ones. The interaction styles that this model suggests are supported by the virtual reality, as the means for users to accomplish the tasks. The task analysis has been led by the knowledge about the public processes found in a library. The movement of a user in a library is directed to achieve the realization of any of the public services provided by the library. Thus, when a user comes to a library she will subscribe giving personal information and personal preferences. Once a user is in the library records, she will be able to enter the library after identifying herself. After that, she can browse the documents, read them, search the library catalogues, consult the librarian to get help, or customize her personal view of the library.

The proposal of virtual reality as the interaction style, as well as the use of the traditional library metaphor for the representation of the objects in the interface, is the conclusion of a careful examination of the final purpose of the user interface. Interfaces using virtual reality achieve a closer correspondence between the user's mental model of the computer and the image on the screen because three-dimensional images make a better use of the human visual perception and simulate the same actions taken in real life.

2.1.2 Technical Processes Layer

This layer will handle all the technical processes. These are primarily: Selection of documents, Acquisition, Classification, Indexing, Maintenance and Notification. Documents that belong to a library are chosen among the entire available documents. The modules in charge of this task decide which of those should be acquired in accordance with the library's classification and the users' preferences. This means that when a suitable document is found, a simple analysis of its content must be accomplished to decide whether the document can be chosen or not. Once the document's suitability is clear, this is acquired to be included in the library. The acquisition of a document in this model is not a "real" acquisition in the sense of getting a copy of it. To take advantage of the electronic medium and the web accessibility, the document remains on its original location, and what it is "acquired" is a pointer to that location, and a temporary copy of the document to get its metadata. Before this document can be part of the library, it must suffer a classification and cataloguing process that will extract the necessary metadata in order to identify the document. When this process is completed the document can be indexed to the library. After they are included in the library, as documents are "alive entities" that might change along the time, they require a maintenance procedure to keep them updated. Also, when a document is included in the library, those users who were interested in that type of document receive a notification.

2.1.3 Repository Processes Layer

This layer will manage the users inputs provided by the PP layer to search the catalog, and the outputs that answer those queries. It will serve as the access mechanism to the data collection. This layer as well as the TP one might be distributed and it may implement different approaches; for example, the repositories could use inverted files, relational database management, or others. The choice of one of them does not affect the model and it just depends on the implementation restrictions.

2.2 Implementation

After a first design of the model, a prototype that implements it has been built. This prototype is called VILMA, and this section will show details about the implementation of every layer of the model.

2.2.1 Public Processes Layer

In VILMA's interface, every library's room is graphically represented as a VR-model to have a closer approach to the actual physical library. The whole library is represented as a building and the inner side is divided in three floors and all of them in two rooms, one of them is a hall, and the other is the main room. Every floor is conceptually associated to a concrete public process. Thus, the ground floor provides the subscription, identification and the consulting processes.

First floor is dedicated to search and browsing processes: the user will be able to search the library catalog, and browse the documents in the shelves represented as books. Third floor gives the personal view of the user, that is, it provides the customizing process. Floors are communicated through a lift. The virtual reality allows the user to move from one point to another in this interface to access any of the services. Figure 2 shows several snapshots of this interface. This interface has been modeled using the VRML97 International Standard ISO/IEC 14772-1:1997, and the External Authoring Interface (EAI) to add external behaviour produced by Java programs.

Figure 2. VILMA user interface

2.2.2 Technical Processes Layer

Selection and Acquisition: All documents belonging to the VILMA prototype must fulfill three requirements based on the nature of this digital library. 1) The "market" of the VILMA prototype is the World Wide Web, so they have to be found in the web. 2) The Dublin Core is employed as the Metadata Scheme because it is the most widely used metadata scheme from all those available for web documents, due to its ease of use and interpretability [Miller, 96], thus, they must contain this kind of information. 3) The VILMA prototype will keep computing documents, and the 1998 ACM Classification System has been chosen as the library classification (permission of use given by ACM). Documents must belong to any of the library classification subjects.

Therefore, all documents suffer a pre-classification process. That is why a web crawler written in Java to make it reusable and platform-independent, has been developed to search the web to find suitable documents for it.

Cataloguing and Classification: a "Documents Classification Module" has been written as a Java package. This module uses a simple version of the Extended Boolean Model for the Information Retrieval. In the vector space model of information retrieval [Salton, 71], documents are modeled as vectors in a high-dimensional space of many thousands of terms. The terms are derived from words and phrases in the document and are weighted by their importance within the document and within the corpus of documents. Each document's vector seeks to represent the document in a "vector space", allowing comparison with vectors derived from other sources, for example, queries or other documents. In VILMA we use a set of "Training Documents" which are documents manually classified and then presented to the system as examples of documents that belong to each classification. The system then builds class representatives each of which consists of common terms occurring in the documents known to belong to a particular classification group. When the system subsequently encounters new documents it measures the similarity between the document and the class representatives. Each time a new document is classified it is used to modify the class representative to include its most commonly occurring keywords. This model has been used as the basis of successful algorithms for document ranking, document filtering, document clustering, and relevance feedback [Jones and Willet, 97], [Baeza-Yates et al., 99]. After a document is classified, a "Metadata Extraction module" gets all the metadata elements from the document that are needed to follow the Dublin Core Element Set, version 1.0, which are: Title, Author, Subject, Description, Publisher, Contributor, Date, Resource Type, Format, Resource Identifier, Source, Language, Relation, Coverage and Rights Management, and catalog it.

Indexing: after the classification and extraction of metadata from a document, a program written in Java will index the metadata extracted from the document to the repositories in order to create the library's thesaurus and to facilitate the access to the metadata under a user's search query.

Notification: When a document is included in the library, a notification Java program is in charge of checking those users interested in documents that belongs to the same classification than that document, and send them a warning about the acquisition.

Maintenance of the information: As the documents for VILMA are obtained from the web, a robot will check first that documents still exists, and that all the metadata about every document keeps the same. It will change those metadata that differ from the original. Given that life of web documents is not fixed, a study about the timeline of web documents using Dublin Core is being carried out to provide the robot with the appropriate period for the checking out of metadata.

2.2.3 Repository Processes Layer

This layer consists of the repositories for the library catalog, which stores all the metadata elements for every document that has been indexed to the library. It also consists of the access mechanisms that allow searching this catalog under a user query.. This catalog is a PostgreSQL database running under Linux Debian accessed by the previous modules using JDBC connectivity.

3. RELATED WORKS

In order to verify the novelty and contributions of this work, some of the current digital libraries available via web have been reviewed and compared to the prototype VILMA. The contributions of this research are two: the use of the traditional library metaphor adapted to the electronic and users needs, and the use of the virtual reality for the interface for digital libraries. Thus, firstly we will talk about those that do not use any of them, and secondly we will see those that use any or both of them.

Most of the current digital libraries available via web work as enhanced search engines that use hypermedia to interact with the user. This means that they do not take advantage of the services provided by the traditional library metaphor to manage documents. Also, they keep on using hypermedia based interfaces which, according to [Callaghan and Hand, 96] are limited in function and sophistication. The study carried out by [Theng et al., 00] on the ACM Digital Library, ACMDL (http://www.acm.org), the Networked Computer Science Technical Reference Library, NCSTRL (http://www.ncstrl.org), and the New Zealand Digital Library, NZDL (http://www.nzdl.org) to investigate the purpose and usability of digital libraries throws two main conclusions. First of them is that users prefer traditional library services, and second one is that users feel lost if the digital library do not utilize an appropriate model.

Other reviewed libraries like the previous are: The Library of Congress[1], those from the Digital Libraries Initiative, phase I: University of California Berkeley[2], University of Illinois, University of Michigan[3], University of California Santa Barbara[4], Carnegie Mellon University[5], and Stanford[6], and the German Digital Library Project[7].

However there are some digital libraries that share some of the characteristics of VILMA. For example, the Networked Digital Library of Theses and Dissertations has tried a desktop VR interface as well as an inmersive one [Phanouriou et al., 99].

4. CONCLUSIONS

We have presented a model for digital libraries, and its prototype, that uses the traditional library metaphor in two ways: it implements the services provided by traditional libraries adapting them to the electronic medium in the belief of the generality of these services, and it uses the spatial metaphor for the objects in its interface. This model also provides a virtual reality interface to allow a more realistic interaction with this spatial metaphor. VILMA also provides new services that take advantage of the electronic medium. These features are supposed to improve the management of electronic documents in a network in two different aspects. Firstly it provides all the services needed for documents management. And secondly, because taking advantage of the new electronic medium, it eases the access to the documents in several senses. It makes the reader able to customize her preferences and her library view. It approaches the mental model of the reader to the conceptual model of the system by using metaphors and virtual reality,

The hypothetic value of this model for digital libraries will be checked when the development of the prototype VILMA is finished at the end of March. Then, an evaluation with experts (librarians, CHI experts, etc.) and another with real and potential users will be carried out. The results of these two types of evaluation will be analyzed and will confirm or refute the hypothesis of this research.

5. REFERENCES

[Arms, 90] Arms, C. "Campus Strategies for libraries and electronic information" Ed. Digital Equipment Corporation, 1990

[Baeza-Yates et al., 99] Baeza-Yates, R. and Ribeiro-Neto, B. "Modern Information Retrieval". Addison-Wesley/ACM Press, 1999.

---

[1] http://www.loc.gov/, [2] http://elib.cs.berkeley.edu/, [3] http://dli.grainger.uiuc.edu/, [4] http://www.si.umich.edu/UMDL/,

[5] http://alexandria.sdc.ucsb.edu/, [6] http://www.informedia.cs.cmu.edu/, [7] http://diglib.stanford.edu/, [8] http://medoc.informatik.tu-muenchen.de/

[Birmingham et al., 94] Birmingham, W., Drabenstott, K., Frost, C., Warner, A. and Wills, K., "The University of Michigan Digital Library: This is Not Your Father's Library". In Proceedings of the Digital Library 94 Conference (DL'94). Schnase, J. L., Leggett, J. J., Furuta, R. K., Metcalfe, T. (eds.), 19-21, June 1994, College Station, Texas, U.S.A., pp. 53-59.

[Callaghan and Hand, 96] Callaghan, M. and Hand, C. "Presentation and Representation of Implicit Knowledge in the World Wide Web. Workshop on Knowledge Media for Improving Organizational Expertise - Impacts of new methods and enabling technologies", at International Conference on Practical Aspects of Knowledge Management, Basel, Switzerland, 30-31 October 1996.

[Chan, 86] Chan, L.M., "Library of Congress Classification as an online retrieval tool: potentials and limitations". Information Technology and Libraries, 5 (3), pp. 181-192.

[DDC, 96] Dewey Decimal Classification and Relative Index. Edition 21, 1996. Forest Press, division of OCLC Online Computer Library Center, Inc.

[Ferguson and Durfee, 98] Ferguson, I.A.; Durfee, E.H. "Artificial intelligence in digital libraries :moving from chaos to (more) order". International Journal on Digital Libraries; Vol. 2, N. 1 October 1998.

[Gladney et al., 94] Gladney, H., Fox, E., Ahmed, Z., Ashany, R., Belkin, N., and Zemankova, M. "Digital Libraries: Gross Structure & Requirements". In Proceedings of the Digital Library 94 Conference (DL'94). Schnase, J. L., Leggett, J. J., Furuta, R. K., Metcalfe, T. (eds.), 19-21, June 1994, College Station, Texas, U.S.A.

[Heery, 96] Heery, R. "Review of Metadata Formats", Program, Vol. 30, No. 4, October 1996, pp. 345-373.

[Jones and Willet, 97] Jones, K. S.and Willet, P. eds. Readings in Information Retrieval. Morgan Kaufmann, 1997.

[Landoni and Catenazzi, 93] Landoni, M. y Catenazzi, N. "Hyper-books and visual-books in an electronic library" The Electronic Library, Vol. 11, n 3, june 1993

[Lynch, 97] Lynch, C.A., "Searching the Internet". Scientific American, March, 1997, pp. 52-56. Also available at: URL: http://www.sciam.com/0397issue/0397lynch.html]

[McIlwaine, 95] McIlwaine, I.C., "Preparing traditional classification for the future: Universal Decimal Classification". In: New roles for classification in libraries and information networks: reports from the Thirty-sixth Allerton Institute. Cataloging and Classification Quarterly, 21 (2), pp. 49-58.

[Miller, 96] Miller, M., "Metadata for the masses" , Ariadne, the web version Issue 5, September 1996. Also available at: URL:
http://www.ariadne.ac.uk/issue5/metadata-masses/

[Muñoz et al., 98] Muñoz, G., Aedo, I., Díaz, P. Virtual reality and agents in a digital library. In Proceedings of Second European Conference on research and advanced technology for Digital Libraries (Crete, Greece, September 1998) LNCS 1513 Springer, pp. 681-682.

[Nürnberg, et al., 95] Nürnberg, P. J., Furuta, R., Leggett, J. J., Marshall, C. C., Shipman III, F. M. "Digital libraries: issues and architectures" In Proceedings of the second annual conference on the theory and practice of digital libraries, Digital Libraries' 95. June 11-13, 1995 - Austin, Texas, USA.

[Salton, 71] Salton, G. The SMART retrieval system - experiments in automatic document processing, Prentice-Hall, Englewood Cliffs N.J. 1971.

[Shneiderman, 98] Shneiderman, B. Designing the user interface. Addison Wesley Longman. Chapter 2, pp. 61-67.

*Electronic Publishing '01 –
2001 in the Digital Publishing Odyssey
A. Hübler et al. (Eds.)
IOS Press, 2001*

Only Connect: A study of the problems caused by platform specificity and researcher isolation in Humanities Computing Projects

Claire Warwick and Celine Carty

*University of Sheffield
Department of Information Studies
Regent Court
211 Portobello Street
Sheffield S1 4DP, UK
0114 222 2632
Fax. 0114-2780300
c.warwick@sheffield.ac.uk*

Abstract

The paper presents work performed in a collaboration between the department of Information Studies and the Humanities Research Institute at the University of Sheffield. In it we investigate problems caused by the use of platform specific software by humanities computing projects. The methodology for the project was that of case studies focusing on projects in the history of Natural history and science: The Hartlib Project (University of Sheffield) The Darwin Correspondence Project, (University of Cambridge) The Robert Boyle project (Birkbeck College, London), The Mueller Correspondence Project and The Newton Project (Imperial College, London).

All projects had encountered problems with the use of platform specific formats, and had decided to use SGML as a way of providing a platform independent format that would also help to preserve the material independent of hardware platforms. This was influenced either by advice from other scholars, contact with humanities computing centres, or with national advisory bodies. In particular, projects considered adopting the DTD developed by the Text Encoding Initiative. Despite this enthusiasm a number of problems were encountered with the type of material to be encoded. All but one project therefore chose not to adopt it in its original form.

The paper argues that problems were caused by researchers working in isolation from each other. This can cause the replication of problems that others have already worked on, and expertise not being shared with different projects. Documentation was often not kept up to date because those working on projects have no time to do this. The paper contends that there is a role for outside reportage in the collection and presentation of documentation and its dissemination throughout the humanities computing community.

0. Introduction

The history of humanities computing projects is a relatively short one in comparison to many disciplines in the humanities. Even the oldest initiatives date from the early 1970s. Until recently these projects were also few in number, and not overseen by any national bodies or advisory standards. As a result therefore projects often developed in isolation and found solutions to problems that they met as these occurred. In this paper we will discuss the development of a small group of such projects. We will aim to illustrate some of the problems caused by researcher isolation as the domain grew and developed. This will be done by taking as an example the technical problems posed by platform specificity and attempts to solve this using the international standard of SGML markup.

1. Methodology

The methodology for the project was that of case studies of projects in the history of Natural history and science. Because we wanted to gain rich , qualitative data, representatives form each project were interviewed using a semi-structured approach. (Patton, 1990). (Taylor & Bogdan, 1984). The Hartlib Project (University of Sheffield) formed the original stimulus for the study. It faced particular problems coveting legacy data in platform specific formats, as discussed below. We therefore sought to find out whether any similar problems had afflicted other cognate projects. We chose to investigate The Darwin Correspondence Project, (University of Cambridge) The Robert Boyle project (Birkbeck College, London) and The Mueller Correspondence Project. These projects were chosen not only because of their subject matter, but also because they involved the conversion of legacy data rather than the creation of new information.

The interviewees were:
Hartlib Papers Project: Michael Pidd
Darwin Correspondence Project: Dr Alison Pearn
Boyle Project: Professor Michael Hunter and Dr Charles Littleton
Mueller Correspondence Project Harold Short

2. Descriptions of the projects

2.1 The Hartlib Papers project

The Hartlib papers project. (HPP) was established by the Humanities Research Institute, University of Sheffield in 1988, to create a complete electronic edition including full-text transcriptions and facsimile images of the collected papers of Samuel Hartlib (c.1600 1662). Hartlib's contemporaries considered him to be 'the great intelligencer of Europe' He was half-Prussian and half-English, settled in London and exploited his numerous European contacts to create a vast network for the dissemination of knowledge for the education of all mankind (Paterson, 1991). Letters, manuscripts, requests for information, digests of the latest inventions were summarised, copied and sent out again from Hartlib's office on the most diverse range of subjects (Greengrass, 1994: 80) The Hartlib Papers, made up of over 25,000 folios of manuscripts, have been seen as 'a consciously developed database designed to gather, contain and disseminate information on all subjects' The sheer volume of material in the Hartlib Papers made print publication impossible (Leslie, 1990). Hartlib's and his correspondents' views on the interconnectedness of knowledge were another reason for ensuring that the archive be published in a fully searchable way.

The first edition of the Hartlib Papers was published on two CD-ROMs in 1995. However, platform specific software and formats were used. The transcriptions of the original papers were done in Microsoft Word. The choice of TOPIC, made by Verity Inc., as the search engine was intended to allow for highly sophisticated searching, including the building up of complex subject trees in the final product (Greengrass, 1994). Thus the images also had to be in a compatible format to this, the Verity Image Format (VIF).

However, by the late 1990s problem inherent in such choices were apparent. The project consisted of a large amount of data, 125 megabytes (Mb) in over 5,000 separate files, that was in danger of becoming inaccessible. The CD-ROMs were designed to run on MS-DOS and were therefore not compatible with the Windows-based software that was becoming increasingly widespread by that time. They proved difficult to network and were not millennium compatible. This posed long-term preservation problems for the data and the HRI was aware that they must convert the files to formats that had some longevity and were not platform specific. Hartlib made decisions that they subsequently regretted, but had felt to be the best options at the time the project began, given the advice then available to them. Our research aimed to find out whether other projects in the area had faced such problems, and how they might have coped with and recovered from them.

2.2 The Robert Boyle Project

The Robert Boyle Project is based at Birkbeck College, University of London. The Project is working primarily on the preparation of new print editions of Boyle's complete Works and Correspondence. In October 1997 work, funded by the Wellcome trust, began on the electronic edition of Boyle's work-diaries. These are paperbooks comprising approximately 350,000 words, which Boyle filled throughout his life with a wide range of material related to his various interests in literary, scientific and medical topics. (Littleton & Hunter, 1998).

An electronic edition of Boyle's work-diaries could be seen as a continuation of his work, since Boyle himself had begun to sort them by keywords. Each diary entry will be transcribed, including all emendations undergone by the text during its original writing, arranged in chronological order. There will also be hyperlinks to the apparatus of notes and commentary on the background of people, places or processes, as well as links based on keywords and other indexing methods.

2.3 The Darwin Correspondence Project

The Darwin Correspondence Project is the longest-lived project examined in this study. It was established by Frederick Burkhardt and Sydney Smith in 1974, with the aim of publishing the definitive printed edition of all the known correspondence to and from the naturalist Charles Darwin (1809-1882). Although the Project also has staff in the US, the majority of staff are based at Cambridge University Library (CUL) where the largest single collection of Darwin's letters is held. More than 15,000 letters have been located and the bulk of transcription was completed by the mid-1980s (Pearn, 1999b).

Although the publication of printed books remains the Project's primary purpose, the use of computers throughout its history makes it a particularly interesting case study since the Project's life 'spanned almost the whole history of computing in the humanities' (Pearn, 1999b). Although there are plans to convert all the letters into SGML for electronic publication the pilot project will be the conversion of the calendar, which is a list of the letters. This was chosen because it was already highly structured into fields, was complete in itself and was small enough to be completed in a reasonable period of time. It was also considered less likely to be the source of copyright problems, and could be expected to increase interest in the published volume. New letters are being discovered at a rate of about sixty a year (http://www.lib.cam.ac.uk/Departments/Darwin/intro.html) so it requires frequent updating and is therefore well suited to online publication.

2.4 The Mueller Correspondence Project

This project was established in 1988 with the aim of publishing a scientific biography and selected correspondence of Baron Ferdinand von Mueller (1840-1896). Mueller, a German who moved to Australia in 1847, served as chief Government Botanist for many years, was director of Melbourne's Botanic Gardens and has been called the father of Australian botany. The first of three print volumes of selected correspondence was published recently (Home, 1998). After the publication of the print volumes all 12,000 letters will be made available electronically. (Lucas & Short, 1999). The transcriptions of the letters are in Microsoft Word and include extensive critical apparatus. The electronic edition will also include a chronological list of letters, a thematic index and a name register of all the people referred to in the correspondence. It is likely that there will be both a CD-ROM and an online publication.

3. Results

3.1 Hartlib papers

3.1.1 Platform Specificity

In the early stages of text conversion projects researchers often did not realise the problems that the use of proprietary formats might cause. HPP chose Microsoft Word as a positive step. Sheffield University had just adopted Word institution-wide so it was familiar and easy to use (Paterson, 1991). Word was thought to make future conversion easy, particularly by using rich text format (RTF) (Robinson, 1994). They did not realise that this might render data inaccessible in the future until much later in the project.

In the early 1990s no national bodies existed to advise projects about such choices. However, in 1997 a national body, the Arts and Humanities Data service was set up, and began to advise projects that proprietary practices should only be used as a last resort. (Beagrie and Greenstein, 1998). The alternative to proprietary formats and software is to use standard formats. The standard that The AHDS began actively to promote was SGML, since it allows complex capture and representation of data, but limits users as little as possible. (Haynes et al, 1997:37). The Oxford Text Archive , which became one of the service providers for the AHDS had been using SGML for many years. However, with a tiny staff and budget and no brief to publicise the standard, knowledge about its usefulness had been slow to spread. How then did the projects in our sample make decisions about proprietary formats, and whether to adopt standards?

3.1.2 The choice of SGML

The HRI, to which HPP belongs now uses SGML for all its projects. This is partly because of a commitment to what Michael Pidd, the technical manager, called the 'intellectual truth' of SGML. Other reasons were that a standard such as SGML aided preservation, made it possible to publish to multiple media for a variety of different audiences from the same master and to perform sophisticated searching. Another advantage was that the ability to parse documents using the DTD means that 'the emphasis can shift from the technical side onto the editing side'.

3.1.3 The question of DTDs

SGML is a platform-independent, flexible and 'permissive' standard (Haynes et al, 1997). Robinson, 1994, argues that SGML is therefore particularly suited to scholarly text encoding projects. SGML files could also be considered 'a permanent, or even an archival, medium' However, SGML has a number of drawbacks: the mark-up itself is very verbose and SGML itself is complex. Furthermore, writing and testing a DTD can be a long process.

These disadvantages led some member of the scholarly community to feel a need to create guidelines on how to apply SGML to text encoding projects. The Text Encoding Initiative was formed as a result. (Burnard, 1995). SGML was adopted as the chosen syntax of the TEI because it had recently been made an ISO standard and offered the possibility of platform-independent interchange (Hockey, 1996). The TEI aimed to provide a framework which prevented each new text encoding project from having to develop its own SGML tags and DTD from scratch (Robinson, 1994). The first version of the TEI Guidelines was published in 1994, and the most recent version (TEI P3) was released in 1999 (Sperberg-McQueen & Burnard, 1999).

The HRI, however, had not adopted it for the second edition of the Hartlib Papers. Although the HRI follows the TEI Guidelines when writing DTDs, Michael Pidd felt the TEI DTD often made things more complicated for a humanities computing project. One reason was that, because the DTD was designed to be very wide-ranging, it did include sufficient detail, 'since we happen to focus on very specific archives and very specific documents requiring very specific treatments, the TEI DTD just doesn't cover it'.

The sheer size of the TEI DTD made it 'off-putting' to novices, since it includes a large number of files and can seem unwieldy. One of the TEI editors has even admitted that 'the TEI's desire to exclude no-one has led to a multiplication of distinctions at first sight rather bewildering' (Burnard, 1995). Michael Pidd prefers to use TEI-Lite, the slimmed down version of the dtd, and often advises people to look at the TEI-Lite DTD when they are trying to write their own project DTD.

Although it is usually implied that the adoption of SGML must begin with writing a DTD, Michael Pidd 'fundamentally disagrees' with this approach. He usually advises that people begin by deciding what the document structure and tags are going to be without writing a formal DTD. This avoids the need to constantly revise a DTD as new features come to light in the documents. Once the tags and document structure are in place, writing a DTD will take very little time for an experienced person.

3.2 The Robert Boyle Project

3.2.1 The Choice of SGML

Advice from both Jeremy Black at the Sumerian Text Corpus[1] and Michael Pidd at the HRI helped convince the Robert Boyle Project to choose SGML for the electronic work-diaries. Littleton and Hunter (1998) liked its durability and the potential for sophisticated manipulation of the tagged elements. Its platform independence and the advantages of working with a recognised standard, tried and tested on other projects were also important.

[1] The Electronic Text Corpus of Sumerian Literature is based at the University of Oxford (http://www-etcsl.orient.ox.ac.uk). It is preparing a complete electronic corpus of over 400 literary works composed in the Sumerian language in ancient Mesopotamia, accompanied by an English prose translation and bibliographical information. All of the texts are being encoded in SGML and made available on the website.

Although this is a relatively young project, what is essentially 'legacy data' must now be converted into SGML, since the initial transcription of the diaries had begun in Word 97 for Windows. This would have allowed easy transfer to Idealist for the initially planned CD-ROM publication (On The Boyle 1997). The project now plans, however, to web publish the material after possible conversion to XML by the HRI.

Like Robinson, Michael Hunter also saw one of the great advantages of SGML to be its roots in the scholarly approach. Charles Littleton said that 'every day that I continue to work on these files in Word is a day wasted [...]. It makes no sense to tag in Word'. However, they were concerned that the use of proprietary software to tag the SGML might in itself cause problems in case the files become contaminated with any proprietary coding or became hard to extract from the package as a result.

3.2.2 SGML in practice

The decision to use SGML raised a number of other questions, in particular that of the DTD. This highlights some difficulties associated with manuscript encoding projects in particular, and with many digitisation projects in general.

3.2.3 The question of a DTD

Initially Charles Littleton considered developing a DTD for the work-diaries, from scratch. However, he soon realised that this would be difficult and time-consuming since he was working alone and did not have a background in SGML. The Project staff had initially felt that the TEI DTD was unwieldy and were aware of the difficulties that the Sumerian Text Corpus had experienced with it. They also felt that the TEI DTD was not well suited to manuscript projects in general as marginalia can be problematic within the TEI DTD and the overall structure of the TEI DTD is designed primarily to deal with the structural requirements of printed materials.

The OTA, who had advised the project to adopt the TEI DTD offered to help the Project staff overcome any problems they encountered. So they decided to use the TEI DTD. They saw this as an opportunity to 'test TEI and see how it works'. The advantage was that the Project staff would not have to attempt this task alone but can benefit from the expertise of the OTA. However, they recognise that they will need to modify the TEI DTD to deal with the problems identified. Even then, it was felt that the solutions offered by the OTA to the problem of marginalia, for example, 'seem to be stretching TEI a bit'.

The time taken to choose the DTD meant that transcription began before a DTD was in place. Charles Littleton, like Michael Pidd, felt that, although people are generally advised not to do so, he 'wouldn't have got to the know the material as I did if I hadn't worked in this way'.

Charles Littleton pointed out how labour-intensive editing for electronic projects can be: it involves a great deal of rather mechanical work which has to be done by someone with a detailed knowledge of the material and of the subject matter. Although the amount of material in the work-diaries is small compared to some digitisation projects, it has still taken longer than anticipated and involved a steep learning curve for the editor, as much in the techniques needed to mark up the documents as in the theory behind SGML. As is often the case, the editor had no previous experience of working with SGML and is completely self-taught. His task is made more difficult by working alone, which he commented could be 'quite isolating'.

This last point demonstrates another advantage of working with the OTA and the HRI, as it allows the editor to collaborate with other people and helps 'reduce the diversity' of mark-up. Electronic text projects can often develop independently of each other, with staff on each of them working from scratch to develop a DTD or a mark-up scheme. Although Hunter points out that a single standard is not necessarily universally appropriate, lack of discussion about editorial practices and their underlying rationale 'has left each new editor approaching his or her task to reinvent the wheel' (Hunter, 1995: 298).

3.3 The Darwin Correspondence Project

3.3.1 Platform Specificity

The initial decision to use computers on the Project in the late 1970s was purely to sort the 13,000 paper slips which held the calendar entries. Once the calendar entries had been entered on the museum cataloguing package MUSCAT, it became apparent that the computerised records could be used as a way to publish both the calendar and the letters (Pearn, 1999b). Over the next twenty years, however, technological changes have meant that the files have had to be migrated over five mainframe computers and several text-handling programs. Two typesetting languages and three plain-text editors have been employed.

3.3.2 The Choice of SGML

There were several reasons for considering SGML. The CUL was proposing to replace their computer system: the Project's master files were stored on the CUL's mainframe, a VMS ALPHA cluster, but it was unlikely that a proprietary library system would allow them to continue in this way. The Project had also begun to experience problems with their current typesetting package, which, for example, did not allow the incorporation of scanned images. They needed to move to a new 'integrated solution' which would address these difficulties.

Furthermore, in July 1997 the then HRB wrote to all the projects it was funding stating that any computer data generated as a result of their funding should be offered for deposit to the AHDS. The accompanying letter from the AHDS explained the benefits of such deposit, including long-term preservation. This coincided with a growing awareness in the Project of the potential of the electronic database as a resource in its own right (Pearn, 1999b). In response to the letter two members of the Project staff attended an information day at the OTA, where they were introduced to the potential benefits of SGML. (Pearn, 1999a, b).

The Darwin Project is unusual in that it has used platform-independent formats from the outset. The Project was split between the US and the UK, with each site using different platforms and operating systems and hardware. Different software was also used for various stages of data entry, manipulation and typesetting, 'so a device-independent format was essential' and ASCII was chosen . Staff working on the Project have always come from a humanities rather than a computing background, and so have tended to favour standard formats because they did not have the technical expertise to exploit the latest technological developments and they needed to use formats that offered 'disinterested, intelligible and long-term technical advice and help' (Pearn, 1999b). Dr Pearn called this 'one of the best decisions ever made' and it has influenced the Project's attitude to standard formats ever since. This attitude therefore influenced their enthusiasm for SGML.

Although the master files are in ASCII, the Project uses some proprietary software during the editing process. The ASCII files are transferred into Microsoft Word as 'MS-DOS text only with line breaks' for footnoting because Word is more readable and offers the facility to cut and paste text. However, the editorial staff have noticed some problems with such limited use of propriety software:

> *When we were going from Word 6 to Word 97 we are getting contamination in our files, even though we're saving files as text only with line breaks. We are having some problem with contamination.*

This was another factor that influenced the decision to use SGML.

3.3.3 SGML in practice

The use of SGML offered a flexible route to both hard copy and electronic publication It would permit the Project to update their typesetting package and it also allows for better verification of file structure (Pearn, 1999b). This in turn means that the mark-up can be more sophisticated, so that searching of the master files can also be improved. SGML does not 'close down any other options' as it is easy to convert to other formats and it can be refined over time (Pearn, 1999a). In this way, SGML can be seen as offering the solution to all of the technical problems faced by the Project. It also addresses the issue of future-proofing and this was mentioned in the interview as an important reason for choosing SGML.

The fact that SGML is non-proprietary, well-tested, standard and device-independent makes its adoption 'entirely consistent with the lessons learned from twenty-five years of experience' Not only is it non-proprietary itself, SGML also allows the Project to 'reduce present dependence on non-supported software' (Pearn, 1999b). It is even felt that using a standard that is growing in currency will make it easier to hire staff with some existing experience, avoiding the need to train people in Project-specific mark-up.

3.3.4 The question of a DTD

An initial discussion paper stated that 'it would be desirable for our implementation to conform to the Guidelines of the TEI, to ensure the greatest degree of platform-independence' (Pearn, 1999a). This paper also recognised the need for outside help in writing the DTD and establishing the tags to be used. However, in the interview Dr Pearn explained that although the OTA had offered help, the Project had not yet received any real support and so: 'I spent quite a bit of time trying to see how we could use TEI for what we wanted and I couldn't do it, I couldn't make it fit.' She added that she had initially been 'really surprised' that she could not make TEI work but that she had since come into contact with other projects who had encountered the same difficulties with TEI and had also decided against using it. The Project has therefore begun work on writing its own DTD. However, Dr Pearn raised an interesting point about the difference between projects creating SGML files from scratch to those, like Darwin and Hartlib, that are converting existing files.

> *I think that if you're creating new files then it is important to have a good DTD to begin with and really think about what you're trying to do. But if you've already got files, [...] then perhaps the best thing to do is map what you've already got into SGML, so all accents and stuff like that and basic mark-up and basic fields that will map very easily, and not worry too much about having a DTD.*

3.4 The Mueller Correspondence Project

3.4.1 The Choice of SGML

From the outset the project wanted to use SGML, which would be converted to HTML for web publication. The 'fundamental reason' for this was future-proofing: Harold Short pointed out that this was the underlying principle of the TEI. However, another benefit of XML in particular was that it allowed 'maximum accessibility' in electronic databases. The Mueller project were 'not happy working in a proprietary format'. (Harold Short)

3.4.2 SGML in practice

Like the Hartlib Papers Project, the original transcriptions were done in Microsoft Word. However, they aim to convert all the Word files so that the XML files can become the master files for the Project. Most of the conversion work is done on the RTF, since like Hartlib, they were found to be easier to work with. The difficulty of converting legacy data such as Word files was recognised by Harold Short:

> *Where we are now depends quite a lot on the way things were when they started and when people started they did things entirely in the light of the existing technology or in the light of what they then understood about what they wanted to do.*

This statement sums up the experience of all the projects in this study and describes the main difficulty faced by many humanities computing projects.

3.4.3 The question of a DTD

A special DTD was written for this Project. However, Harold Short emphasised that this was only because the TEI DTD for correspondence was not yet fully developed and that they used TEI as far as they could. Apart from his personal commitment to TEI, he also had an organisational commitment as Chair of the ALLC, 'so almost as a matter of principle I would want to use TEI'. The input of the TEI into the development of XML was given as another factor underlining its importance to the future of humanities computing.

However, Harold Short readily accepts that SGML and TEI can often seem daunting, especially to busy academics with no previous knowledge or experience of humanities computing, who are simply looking for a way to future-proof their work

> *SGML is complex because the whole thing of thinking about documents in that kind of way is complex and I think, if people are starting from scratch, it takes a while to understand the implications of what's going on and then when you consider, in addition to the complexities of understanding that aspect of it, there is also the technical barrier.*

He added that the editors of the TEI often encounter this difficulty when they go to speak to people about using TEI and SGML. However, despite having 'a sort of missionary role', he stressed that 'they don't intend to say or even give you the impression that you can't do good humanities research without using the TEI'.

4. Documentation

The previous section has shown, therefore, that many editing practices emerged over time as a matter of trial and error. For example, Darwin's decisions to avoid proprietary formats were directly opposed to Hartlib's adoption of Word. Decisions to adopt SGML were often a result of informal contact between friends, and more latterly influenced by newly formed national bodies. Would it therefore, have been helpful if more formal documentation had been available, or more structured fora for the sharing of expertise?

Documentation is described as vital to a data resource's viability. (AHDS, 1998). Flanders (2000) argues that 'documentation is arguably the most important part of a humanities computing project's long-term existence 'because it allows a project to maintain consistency and continuity internally as well as communicating externally to the larger community'. She emphasises that this contributes to an institutional memory, which would otherwise be lost when project members leave. The AHDS advises that detailed documentation is especially important in the case of projects where non- standard or proprietary formats are used. (Beagrie and Greenstein, 1998). These arguments are undoubtedly sensible, but their dates show that this knowledge had been hard won over a period of time, and may not have been realised by many projects early in their life cycle. Indeed new projects may still not see this as an important part of their remit. For example, although the CCH strongly encourages projects to keep documentation, the Mueller Correspondence Project only keeps informal records of meetings and emails, since it is not a funded project.

Only the Darwin project in the present study kept substantial documentation stating the reasons and decision-making processes underlying their choices. (Pearn, 1999a, b). Transcription guidelines relating to layout and mark-up have probably existed since the beginning of the project and computerisation began by sorting out the calendar, so structure has always been crucial. Though ironically Dr Pearn observed that it was hard to be certain about this, when working in such a long-lived project. These guidelines have not remained static, however, and they 'still come across some files that have got out-of-date coding.'

In 1995, Hunter's (of the Boyle project) article had discussed the importance of documenting editorial practices and decisions in that way that a print editor would consider usual. (1995: 278). Both Hunter and Littleton, when interviewed, agreed that more detailed documentation on the whole process of a digitisation project is needed. Hunter regretted that the Boyle Project does not even posses a complete 'oral history', much less a written one. Similarly, there is currently no policy to create and maintain documentation on the electronic work-diaries.

While project staff may be too busy to create and maintain project documentation, Michael Hunter felt that there was a 'role for reportage' by an outside body so that some written record is preserved. This could document decisions and processes involved in various projects, in order to provide an overview or guide to 'current best practice'. They saw this as a crucial means of avoiding the 'reinvention of the wheel' and a way of keeping those working on digitisation projects in touch with each other.

Alison Pearn from the Darwin project recognised that documentation is 'such a difficult thing and yet it's something that would be so useful'. When writing the conference paper on the history of computing in the Project, she found that it was hard to gather all the information she needed:

> *There were things where I thought "I don't really know how that happened, I hope nobody asks me". It's ironic that a project that deals with history and the preservation of history hasn't preserved its own history at all.*

One of the founders of the Project, Frederick Burkhardt had considered writing a history of the Project, though this would focus on the paper publication. However, the Project staff are more concerned about technical issues as documentation will be required as part of the deposit of archives with the OTA.

Communication may be improved where projects are related to larger Humanities Computing Centres. Two projects in this study operated within larger units, the CCH and the HRI. Staff in both centres agreed that they can help to overcome the isolation, which leads to people who set out to use SGML or TEI abandoning it because it is too difficult or time-consuming. Staff at the centres are also able to provide technical advice and to keep up to date with new developments in humanities computing, when specialist subject academics have no time to do so.

5. Conclusion

It is apparent that the specific characteristics of a humanities computing project depends very much on the material being dealt with but much depends on decisions made early on. All of the projects reported experiencing problems of some kind with proprietary formats or software, and all were keen to guard against such difficulties by adopting standard formats.

The primary reason given for the adoption of a platform-independent format such as SGML was the need for 'future-proofing'. One of the motivating factors behind the move to SGML seems to be the work of funding bodies and academic data services in encouraging the deposit of electronic archives. However, a variety of other reasons for the use of SGML were also given, including its flexibility, the ability to produce both hard copy and electronic publication from one master and the fact that SGML is a recognised international standard.

Despite the positive attitude of all the projects towards SGML, they reported a number of difficulties with its implementation, especially on terms of writing or choosing a DTD. Although all the projects wanted to follow the TEI Guidelines, it is telling that only one has chosen to adopt the TEI DTD. This was also influenced by Harold Short's personal commitment to TEI and the ALLC. The limitations of the TEI DTD with relation to manuscript encoding in particular were cited as the reason in most cases. It could perhaps be concluded from this that TEI has not yet achieved its aim of providing a simple, accessible standard for all scholarly encoding projects. This is partly due to the inevitable complexity of SGML but also the difficulty posed by trying to be 'all things to all men'. The specificity of the needs of projects working on manuscripts letters and papers often seemed to require more than the TEI DTD offers. There is however a palpable desire within the humanities computing community to embrace such standards.

Perhaps the most unexpected result of the interviews was the issue of documentation. All projects reported the difficulty of creating and maintaining project documentation. However, all commented on how useful such documentation would be, particularly for the older projects, as it would provide an essential link with the past. Those projects based in institutions that have no centralised humanities computing centre pointed out how isolating working in this field can sometimes be.

It seems that often the most useful information and advice comes from other people working in humanities computing but that contact of this kind can be limited. Conferences go some way towards solving this problem. However, there is a clear need for improved communication between different. It was telling for example that many projects were under the impression that the difficulties they experienced with DTDs were unique to themselves, and were unaware that such difficulties were relatively common. The existence of centres such as the HRI and the CCH go some way towards achieving this, but there is room for much improvement, particularly in for projects which have access to little or no institutional support or expertise. Often interviewees were not aware of the existence of some of the other projects discussed in this report.

It was suggested more than once that the present study would be an extremely useful way to improve the documentation of and communication between similar projects. This was something that had not been foreseen when the study was being planned but has turned out to be one of the most interesting aspects of the research, and one which we hope to be able to continue in future.

6. References

All URLs last visited on 17.04.01

AHDS (1998). *Creating a Viable Scholarly Data Resource.* August 1998. http://www.ahds.ac.uk/deposit/viable.html

Beagrie, N. & Greenstein, D. (1998). *A strategic policy framework for creating and preserving digital collections.* Arts and Humanities Data Service. http://www.ahds.ac.uk/manage/framework.html

Burnard, L. (1995). 'Text Encoding for Information Interchange: an introduction to the Text Encoding Initiative. July 1995'. http://www.hcu.ox.ac.uk/TEI/Papers/J31

Flanders, J. (2000). 'Writing about it: documentation and humanities computing'. *Paper given at ALLC Conference, Glasgow, July 2000.* http://www2.arts.gla.ac.uk/allcach2k/Programme/session1.html#111

Greengrass, M. (1994). 'The Hartlib Papers Project: an electronic edition of the past for the future'. In: Armstrong, C.J. & Hartley, R.J. (eds.), *Changing patterns of online information: UKOLUG State-of-the-Art Conference 1994*, pp.73-87. Oxford: Learned Information Ltd.

Haynes, D., Streatfield, D., Jowett, T. & Blake, M. (1997). *Responsibility for Digital Archiving and Long Term Access to Digital Data: A JISC/NPO study within the Electronic Libraries (eLib) Programme on the Preservation of Electronic Materials.* London: David Haynes Associates.

Hockey, S. (1996). 'The ACH/ACL/ALLC Text Encoding Initiative: an overview.' (TEI J16). http://quirk.oucs.ox.ac.uk/TEI/History/CS/teij16.txt

Home, R.W. et al. (eds.) (1998). *Regardfully yours: selected correspondence of Ferdinand von Mueller. Vol 1: 1840-1859.* Bern: Peter Lang.

Hunter, M. (1995). 'How to edit a seventeenth-century manuscript: principles and practice'. *The Seventeenth Century*, 10(2), pp.277-310.

Leslie, M. (1990). 'The Hartlib Papers Project: text retrieval with large datasets'. *Literary and Linguistic Computing*, 5(1), pp.58-69.

Littleton, C. & Hunter, M. (1998). 'Boyle on the Web'. *On The Boyle: a newsletter of work in progress on Robert Boyle* (1627-91), 2, pp.8-10.

Lucas, A.M. & Short, H. (1999). 'Anticipating Technical Advance in Recreating a Scattered Correspondence: the Mueller Correspondence Project'. *Paper given at DRH Conference, September 12-15th 1999, King's College, London.* http://www.kcl.ac.uk/humanities/cch/drhahc/drh/abst152.htm

Paterson, A. (1991). 'Windowing the past: a seventeenth century technological archive and its electronic exploitation'. In: Lucker, J.K. (ed.), *IATUL Proceedings: Proceedings of the 14th Biennial Conference of IATUL, Cambridge, Mass. USA, July 8-12 1991: New Technologies and Information Services - Evolution or Revolution?*, pp.164-168.

Patton, M.Q. (1990). *Qualitative evaluation and research methods.* 2nd ed. London: Sage.

Pearn, A. (1999a). 'Electronic development in the Darwin Correspondence Project: discussion paper'. [Unpublished].

Pearn, A. (1999b). 'The Darwin Correspondence Project: evolution of an electronic resource'. *Paper given at DRH Conference, September 12-15th 1999, King's College, London.* http://www.kcl.ac.uk/humanities/cch/drhahc/drh/abst13.htm

Robinson, P. (1994). *The transcription of primary textual sources using SGML.* Oxford: Office for Humanities Communication.

Sperburg-McQueen, C. & Burnard, L. (eds.) (1999). *Guidelines for Electronic Text Encoding and Interchange.* (Rev.ed., May 1999).http://www.hcu.ox.ac.uk/TEI/Guidelines/

Taylor, S.J. & Bogdan, R. (1984). *Introduction to Qualitative Research Methods: the search for meanings.* 2nd ed. New York: John Wiley.

*Electronic Publishing '01 –
2001 in the Digital Publishing Odyssey
A. Hübler et al. (Eds.)
IOS Press, 2001*

Personalized Information Services – an Electronic Information Commodity and its Production

Dipl.-Inform. Thomas Ritz
*Fraunhofer IAO
Nobelstr. 12
70 569 Stuttgart, Germany
Thomas.Ritz@iao.fhg.de*

Abstract

Personalization has become a buzzword in the last months when talking about the internet and the World Wide Web. Nowadays, a lot of sites promise personalization features, but the services provided differ a lot.

Most of the recent publications utilize personalization as a marketing tool, which helps to address customers in a one-to-one marketing manner. Apart from this, personalization and more personalized information services can be seen as unique information commodities supplied by content providers. In order to maximize benefits, the production tools have to be perfectly integrated into the production process applied for the production of recent mass publications. In this paper, we present a definition and characterization of personalization and resulting information goods and sketch an integrated production framework applicable mainly for publishers to provide personalized information services as a unique product in their portfolio. Finally, the paper discusses usability aspects of personalized information services.

0. Introduction

The broad availability of myriad of information and information sources for consumers and the industry, such as the web, has raised the expectations towards services from information suppliers to new heights. To compete against free online services, value added services need to be developed, for which customers are willing to pay a premium fee. The media industry as the classical content owners have to be considered as key players in this development. This has two main reasons:

1. The already existing customer binding and customer's trust in quality
2. The interest of publisher in raising revenues by reuse of contents

Today users are looking for high quality information which they expect from publishers (NN, 1999). Accordingly, the users trust in the skills of editors, likely known, e.g. from the daily news, to filter information regarding customer's needs (c.f. (Ryan, 1999)). This is fostered by Hess (Hess, 1999), stating that in 1998 10% of all Internet users refer to contents provided by media companies.

Already in 1997, Middelhoff (Middelhoff, 1997) predicted the raising importance of contents as key success factor for the media industry. Due to the fact that the elaboration of contents (editorial work) is very expensive, many others stretch the importance to reuse contents (i.e. (NN, 1999)). Thus, the economies of scale holds true also in the publishing industry (c.f. (Shapiro/Varian, 1998) or (Ryan, 1999)).

But how to create new products out of the existing contents? Berghel (Berghel, 1999) argues that it is a misunderstanding to see quantity and variety as success factors for electronic publishing. Moreover, Sander (Sander/Kröger, 1998) postulates an enlargement of the magic triangle, known from project management, towards a "magic rectangular" comprising Cost, Time, Quality and, and what's new, Quantity as major success factors. Facing these success factors, Palmer (Palmer/Eriksen, 1999) gives first hints on activities creating real added value and which kind of publisher will benefit:

table 1: value added publishing

Activity	Type of Publisher Benefited	Technical Requirements
Customized Product	All	Agents, "push" technology
Subscription	All	Micro-payment system
Market intermediary	Publishers specialized on topic or region	Customizable use profiles
Enhanced distribution	Regional specialization	Subscriber database, "push" technology
Archive	Depends on content, role in marketplace as authoritative sources	Search capability, micro-payment scheme

Accordingly, Berghel (Berghel, 1999) postulates following activities to come to an "Value-Added-Publishing", using the Internet far beyond a new distribution channel:

- content enhancement
- encouragement of synergy between and among information providers, consumers, and the resources they share
- addition of interactivity and feedback loops to traditional delivery systems
- reorientation of both the information provider and information consumer toward, "process" of publishing rather than a focus on individual products and services
- meta-level analyses and intelligent restructuring of document collections
- Ad hoc document quality ranking and recommending systems

Most of these activities may be addressed by providing personalized information services.

1. Personalised Information services

1.1 Definition

As stated before, lots of services are labelled personalised service. A definition based on common characteristics will result in a generic definition like "Personalization is a service provided based on a user profile". Which individual services generated using these profiles is still uncertain.

Allen as well as Nielsen (sees (Allen, C. 2000) and (Nielsen, J. 2000)) attempt to distinguish personalization and customisation, while looking at the level of control granted to the customer of the service. Nielsen (Nielsen, J. 2000) defines customisation to be "under direct user control" whereas personalization is "driven by the computer" and based "on some form of model of that user's needs". I.e. Bell (c.f. (Bell/Moffat, 1996)) presents such a formal approach, defining vectors that describe the user profile, the document collections and mappings between these measures.

Another definition is given by IBM (IBM Developer Works 2000): "*Personalization* is a *process* of *gathering* and *storing* information about visitors, *analysing* the information, and, based on the analysis, *delivering* the right information to each visitor at the right time". This definition reveals already the process character behind personalization. This makes personalization an information service, matching classical definitions of a service (c.f. i.e. (Hermes)), what we will call in the following *Personalised Information Service*. But there is still the open question of what might be the right information.

To tackle this problem, Bender ((Bender, 1996)) defines *"Newsworthiness"* as that which is important for the individual and the community (the relation between individual and community interest will be investigated in detail later on). In addition to this, a new dimension appears nowadays. Relying on the paradigm of media independent publishing, it became possible to serve several media from one information source (see i.e. (Matzer, 2000) or (Glotz, P. 2000)). Thus, new information and communication demands are stimulated, making the appropriate media important for profiling users' interests. Sakagami (Sakagami et al., 1998) intends to state more precisely the user interest, focusing on "information freshness". Therefore, he proposes that the "freshness" of information is not only reflecting on the dispatch of information. Furthermore, it has to contain whether the consumer already reads it (for formal models see (Sakagami et al., 1998)).

The definition as follows tries to integrate the dimensions found in definitions cited before:

- process
- user interest (textual)
- demand in schedule
- demand in media

Def. 1: A *Personalised Information Service* is a service towards a customer comprising

1. *filtering* of information out of former *gathered* and *qualified* information regarding users textual *interest*
2. *presentation* of this information using a user defined *time schedule* and *media* appropriate with recent user environment.

As seen before the term interest can be used quite differently. First of all it can focus on the content of the information. But it can also reflect on a time context as shown by the information freshness approach (c.f. (Sakagami et al., 1998)). In real life these preferences are complex structures formed by weighted interest resulting in a profile or preference structure. This shows the similarity to classical economical approaches towards preferences and use (c.f. (Varian, 1991)), leading to an abstract model of interest.

The *media* focuses on the communication channel, which is used to disseminate and present the information for the consumer. Certainly every media creates constraints towards the presentation of the former filtered information (i.e. audio, video capabilities). But also the users' environment can determine the appropriateness. But in the end it is a user preference or a result of user preference and thus part of the user profile.

1.2 Typologies

It was shown that personalized information services are hard to define and a variety of recent existing services match the former given definition. To discuss personalization in more particulars, a categorization of personalization services is needed.

Especially if an IT system learns the user profile from the user behavior, the personalization is not a one step process. In contrary, this process is continued. The gradual process of personalization is sometimes called "creeping personalization" (see (Graham, J. 2000)). Kania (Kania, D. 2000) refers to different models of personalization:

- *Personalized web experience* -- The user's experience itself can be personalized on the fly based on the user profile and their real-time click stream. Basically, these web pages, or parts of pages, are highly dynamic and change during the user's experience.
- *Personalized Information* – Each one of your customers can create their own special and unique version of your web site. Or you can provide personalized recommendations based on a user's unique profile. (This has been the most common form of personalization.)
- *Personalized Service* -- At an additional level of sophistication, you can connect users with personalized customer service for both sales and supporting the customer. These systems can be totally automated or can be a hybrid system that also involves human beings. Dell Computer's order tracking system is an example of an automated personalized service system. An example of a hybrid system is connecting the buyer with an expert customer representative who can make highly personalized recommendations, which are facilitated by the web and/or e-mail.
- *Personalized Community* -- Targeted online communities or discussion forums based on particular interests or needs. These can be built for both business-to-consumer and business-to-business markets. For example, if you are a clothing retailer, you can have several targeted discussion forums within the women's clothing section based on several categories including work formal, work casual, casual, formal/party, accessories, shoes, etc.
- *Personalized Cross-Selling/Up-selling* -- Presenting unique recommendations as users are adding items to their shopping cart, or in an "after-marketing" fashion when a bill is presented or in future e-mail or direct mail communications.
- *Personalized Auctions* -- It is an optimum personalization service where customers get the right product at the right price.

table 2: personalization technologies

Personalization Technologies			
Push by Agent		Pull by User	
Site Control	User Control	Site Control	User Control
Rule Based Matching	Matching Agents	Attribute Search	Menu Select
Feedback & Learning	Community Rating	Full Text Search	Playback
	Collaborative Filtering		

Also Luedi (Luedi, 1997) gives a categorisation of personalization. First he distinguishes push respective pull delivery. Using push *delivery,* the contents are sent actively to the users. In contrast, the users have to take the active part if *pull delivery is* applied. Distinguishing for both methods whether the user defines the filtering methodologies or the site brings Luedi to the following categories of personalization:

- *rule-based-matching:* according predefined rules (i.e. customer clusters) the end user is provided with information
- *matching agents:* an agent searches for information on behalf of the user
- *feedback and learning:* the information system learns from user behaviour and provides information regarding these user profiles
- *attribute search:* the user can search by category (i.e. by industry)

- *full-text-search:* in contrast to search by attributes, the user can search for keywords in the full text (instead of searching for semantic entities like author etc.)
- *community rating:* the quality of information is ranked by the users and others present the information to users regarding the rankings made.
- *collaborative filtering:* as extension to feedback and learning, the learning mechanisms make use of the behaviour of other users (likely with similar profiles), too.
- *menu select:* the users navigate through the information system based on a predefined structure menu.
- *playback:* in order to raise customer binding to a information service, all information regarding the user is used to contact him (i.e. he is welcomed by name when entering a web site).

1.3 Samples

Already in 1996, Bender (Bender et al., 1996) describes sample services performed at the MIT, meeting the former elaborated definition of personalised information services. In the meantime, numerous services emerged. Within the framework of the former mentioned PEACH project a best practice analysis was covering more than 600 web services. All services were evaluated whether the user can tailor one or more of the following items:

- *Topics:* The user can define areas of interest. The information is filtered accordingly to the defined areas. The investigation revealed that there are lots of ways to define the interest profile and to present the information regarding the profile (see results).
- *Layout:* The user selects the media for delivery. This comprises in most cases Web, email, SMS, WAP, PDA or FaxOnDemand services.
- *Sources:* The end user can define the information sources (i.e. newspapers) which should be searched for information. This is important especially for meta search or meta filter engines.
- *Bookmarking:* The end user can use a bookmarking service. This can either mean that the user can bookmark certain areas within one web site or that the end user can manage several web information sources.
- *Quantity:* The end user can define the quantity of information, which should be delivered to him.
- *Times of delivery:* The end user can define a time schedule for the delivery

The study revealed that most services allow the tailoring of the layout and the areas of interest. Surprisingly, the number of services offered for mobile devices as mobile phones or hand held devices was relatively small. The study came up with huge differences regarding the usability of the services provided. For our development we will rely on the best practices found. Concerning the business model applied for the provision of the personalised information service most publishers seemed to be conservative. In most service banner ads are placed and very few services applied business models as pay-per-view.

Another interesting aspect was brought up when analysing methods for the acquisition of user profiles. The study resulted in a categorisation of these methods:

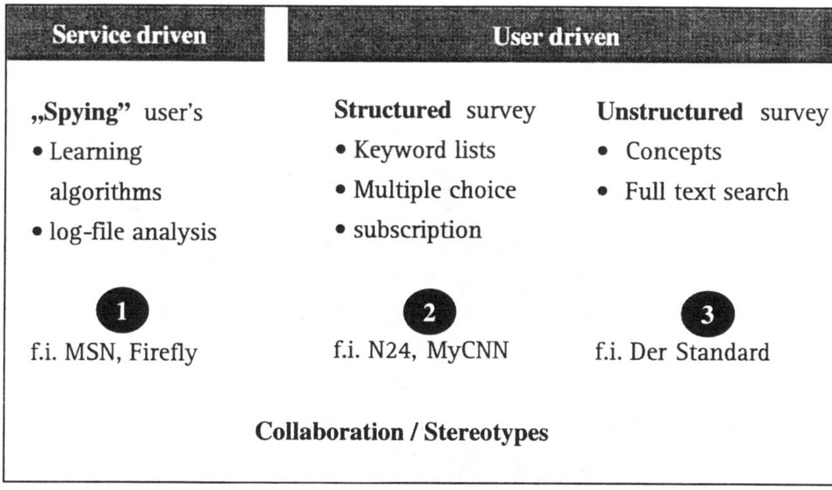

figure 1: three ways to acquire a user profile

2. The production of personalised information services

We assume a generic value chain for the production of personalised information services comprising content acquisition, content processing, content composition, and delivery to

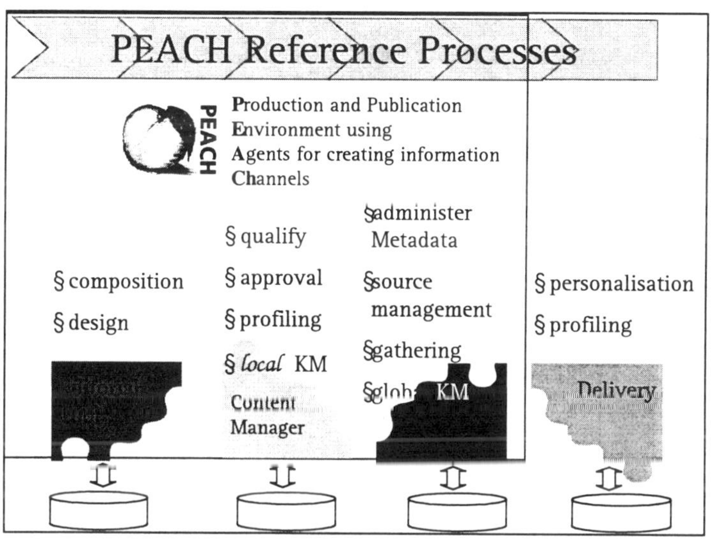

figure 2: Covering the complete value chain for production and provision of personalised information services

the end user. To produce and provide a personalised information service, manifold applications are used today. But from our perspective, there is no tool available covering the complete value chain. Thus, an integration is needed (c.f. (Neuhold, 1998)). As mentioned before, there are certain key-technologies available today covering parts of the value chain:

To support the content acquisition, we see functionality provided by content management systems. This functionality can be improved by services granted by tools used for information retrieval. The use of (collaborative) agents might help to make the information process more effective. Standards and means used for Digital Libraries and Bibliographic Databases might also deal with fruitful inputs. Editorial tools are well

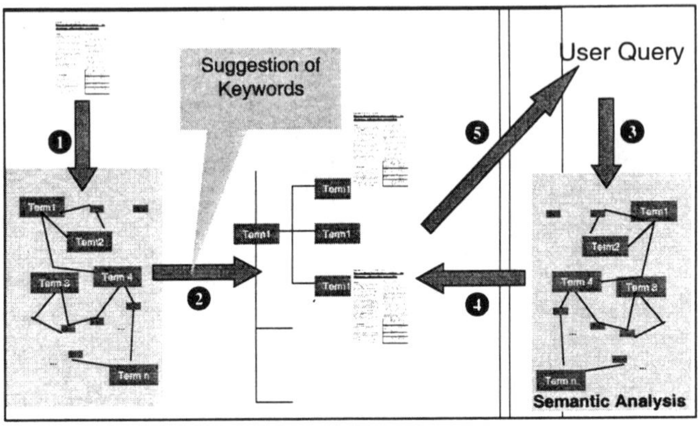

figure 3: Content Qualification and generating user profiles based on semantic nets

developed and perfectly integrated in the production processes of publishers. Therefore, a tool can rely on these services in order to support Content Processing and Composition. Functionality known from Internet portals can be used to transfer the personalised information towards the end user. Therefore, the portal has to be integrated with the content management solution in place.

Further impacts may arise by employing an appropriate business model for placing personalised information services. A survey amongst publishers revealed that this is one of the major concerns of the publishers. Further investigations showed that the publishers would prefer mostly business models close to the business model employed for the recent print products. Thus, ads are mentioned as an important business model and recent researches focus on improving these business models while sticking to the processes used since decades inside the publishing companies.

Within the European funded project PEACH (http://www.vis.iao.fhg.de/peach) we try to attempt this integration and to test the resulting application in a professional test bed. Therefore the PEACH system combines already available systems, defines the integration methods and specifies functionality, which have to be developed from the scratch. We see semantic classification and semantic know how as glue between the different applications involved. In order to deal with personalized information services a user model is crucial for the PEACH delivery system. The same time the semantic know how could be used to define the user profile. The users enter only a vague description of his interests. The semantic know how maps this to the classification scheme (keywords) already applied for classifying the documents. Thus the process could be summarized as shown in *figure 3*.

1. Qualification of contents during editorial process making use of semantically analysis
2. As a result of this qualification, the contents are assigned to a keyword tree

Presentation - Layer	• templates
	  • html pages
	  • wap pages
	  • email services
	  • ...
	• Snippets (Predefined /Predesigned pices interacting with business objects)

Busines - Logic- Layer	• business objects
	  • user model
	  • content filtering
	  • content conversion tools (xml based)

Data - Layer	• relation databases
	  • user model
	  • content metadata
	  • clusterinformation
	• xml files
	• rich media files
	  • pictures
	  • streaming video
	  • audio files

figure 4: The 3-Tier-Architecture

3. User formulates his research interest in his own words. With the help of semantic classification the user query is mapped to the same keyword tree the contents are assigned to these contents are presented to the user, matching his articulated areas of interest (5).

The PEACH delivery system is structured following a 3-Tier approach (c.f. *figure 4*). This approach ensures that the business logic components could be reused for several media, by handling the particular presentation in the presentation layer. The data layer comprises the atomic information. Mostly relational databases will be employed to handle well-structured information as the user model, metadata information etc. Additionally to this, some either unstructured or dynamic changing structured information has to be handled. For text based information (as the text and the structure of articles) we rely on XML structures based on NewsML (c.f. http://www.iptc.org/NewsML). This XML structures could be shown to the

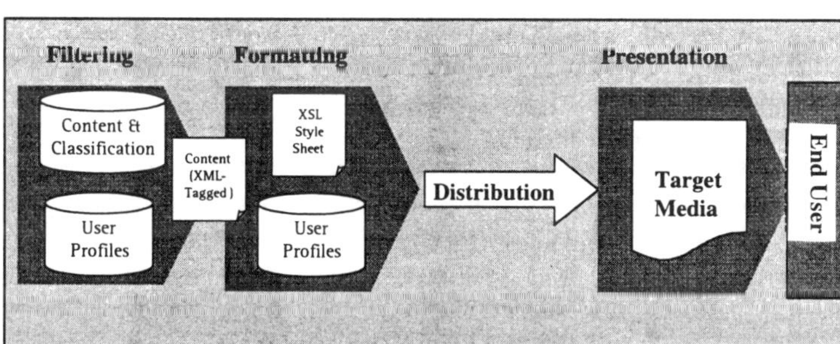

figure 5: The overall process of selecting and formatting contents could be shown as follows

end user by emptying XSL Stylesheets, which filter the information needed and arrange them as defined by the publisher. Furthermore the XML contents may include external entities pointing to flat files as streaming media, pictures and audio files. Again the meta data describing these files are handled employing a relational database system.

The business objects are designed to deal with basic functionality which can be easily embedded in the presentation layer and which encapsulates the data layer from direct access. This is extremely important for critical functions (i.e. dealing with the user profile), cause business rules i.e. for handling privacy issues have to be defined and validated once.

The presentation layer has to deal with interfaces for the different targeted media for information distribution. This layer have to be defined in a way granting a great level of flexibility to the designer of personalized information services. Therefore we came over to design templates for the different distribution media, defining the structure and the look and feel of the service. For designing templates i.e. Macromedias Dreamweaver could be used. To deal with a more modular structure the PEACH system will be shipped with a set of predefined snippets covering the most needed functions and which could be tailored (i.e. designed) regarding the publisher particular needs and requirements.

3. How to Master Interface Design for Personalised Information Services

3.1 Personalization is not the actual goal task users want to perform

The intention of personalised information services is to provide users with individually tailored news and information. It is to optimally support them retrieving information within their scope of interest in the desired coverage, access time, and media. Personalization is also about making online information easier to access, more efficient in use, and providing an individual, personal online experience for the users. Thereby personalization can be considered twofold: as a feature that supports the information supply of a particular information provider, or as an autonomous concept which is to grab and filter information and contents from several information sources and individually present it to the users. In either case the superordinated goal is to help the users getting the information they want in an efficient and pleasing way. Yet the hurdle with achieving this goal is that the information system must first know the users' interests, needs, and preferences. Many of the existing personalization services put the strain of gathering this information on the users. Users are confronted with incomprehensive registration forms, prompting the users to explain their life story in data. Next they have to bother with seemingly endless personalization and customisation features, having to choose from dozens of check boxes or enter cryptic search and keyword strings. The result is that many users either give up before having finished the personalization process or they end up being frustrated because the effective results often stay behind the expectations of the users. Such systems seem to ignore that personalization is not the actual goal task of the users but rather just getting the information they are interested in.

Therefore, personalization services must be easy to set up and use in order to find widespread acceptance with the users. The central unit that is to focus on is the user interface, the visual part of the application with which the users have deal. No matter how complex technical processes are behind an application the user interface is to hide this complexity from the users and to 'translate' pure technical cohesion into a 'language' users can understand. Users don't want to operate an application – they just want to use it. The keyword here is Usability which is determined by the degree of effectiveness, efficiency, and personal satisfaction the users achieve when using any software or interactive application (c.f. (Nielsen, 1999)). Applied to personalised information services that is, effectiveness is ensured by optimal results of the filtering process, efficiency is ensured by requiring the users to perform as less as possible steps to reach their goal, and satisfaction is ensured by making the use of a personalised information service a pleasing experience.

3.2 Characteristics of Functioning Personalization Services

The question is what are the basic characteristics of the user interfaces, which fulfil the demand for effectiveness, efficiency, and satisfaction with personalised information services?

- **They are inviting, convincing novice users from the benefits of the personalization service.** PIS catch the users' attention and immediately reveal their benefits to the users as it is only a few moments that determine whether new users will consider a service valuable to further deal with or rather head on for the next one – which is always just a mouse-click away.
- **They convey credibility and trustworthiness.** Users get more and more concerned about the usage of their private data they are usually asked for when registering with a service. This includes that privacy statements are easy to understand. It gives users the feeling of being taken seriously and treated respectfully.
- **They are easy to set up.** People use personalised services because they want to make getting information easier, avoiding obstacles encounter them when dealing with several news and information resources, and thus save time and intellectual strain. Complex dialog processes for creating personal user profiles and customised interfaces strongly disagree to this claim of the users and make the entire concept appear not authentic.
- **They are accessible via different media.** To optimally fit to the users needs and interests personalised information services are accessible via different media such as cellular phone and personal digital assistant (PDA). At this, operating hand-held devices requires minimum user interactivity as all user preferences are set up by a PC workstation, which provides enough bandwidth as well as sufficient input and display facilities.
- **They are media-adequate.** User-friendly PIS take advantage of the interactive medium hypertext/hypermedia, that is several media such as text, video, and audio support the information where appropriate. Further, they support content-enriching features such as linking to additional sources that provide in-depth information or that correspond to the particular information topic, or support user-feedback, rate information quality and relevance for other users.
- **They are efficient in use.** Contents and information is clearly structured so that user can get their bearings and easily digest the provided information.
- **They are appealing and pleasing.**

4. Conclusions

The presented text showed that personalised information services have to be considered as an information commodity which creates added value for the provider as well as for the information seeker. With reference to the definition presented for personalised information services it became clear that publishers are in an ideal position to provide these kind of services. Nevertheless, it came up that the production of these services follow today an software engineering approach, cause there is no tool existing, which hooks into the well established value chain for the production of information goods. The paper proposed such a tool, developed by integrating several tools, which are already applied in media industry As glue between these application semantic analysis was proposed. Finally the paper stretched that high level usability of the personalised service is crucial for acceptance by the consumer and is thus an important precondition for all business models applicable for personalised information services.

5. References

Allen, Cliff *Personalization vs. Customization*. 2000 http://clickz.com/cgi-bin/gt/en/pm/pm.html
Bell, Timothy A.H. u. Moffat, Alistair. 1996. *The Design of a High Performance Information Filtering System*. Zürich:
Bender, W.; Chesnais; Elo, S.; Shaw, A. u. Shaw, M. 1996. "Enriching Communities: Harbingers of news in the future." *IBM Systems Journal* 35 (4&5):
Bender, W. 1996. "Community and personalization." *IBM Systems Journal* 35 (34): 367-368.
Berghel, Hal. 1999. "Value-Added Publishing." *Communications of the ACM* 42 (1): 19-23.
Glotz, Peter *Die Zukunft der Zeitung zwischen WAP und UMTS*. 2000 http://www.spiegel.de/netzwelt/medien/nf/0,1518,74766,00.html
Graham, Jeffrey *Creeping Personalization 101*. 2000 http;//www.clickz.com/cgi-bin/gt/cz/ems/ems.html?artcile=1087
Hermes, Peter.*Entwicklung eines Customer-Self-Service Systems im Technischen Kundendienst des Maschinenbaus*. Universität Stuttgart
Hess, Thomas. 1999. "Das Internet als Distributionskanal für die Medienindustrie - Entwicklungstendenzen im deutschen Markt." *Wirtschaftsinformatik* 41 (1): 77-82.
IBM Developer Works *Web site personalization*. 2000 http://www-4.ibm.com/software/developer/library/personalization/index.html
Kania, Deborah *Putting Personalization To The Test*. 2000 http://www.clickz.com/cgi-bin/gt/en/pm/pm.html?article=138
Luedi, Ariel F. 1997. "Personalize or Perish." *EM - Electronic Markets* 7 (3): 22-25.
Matzer, Michael. 2000. "Analysten streiten über Essentials bei der Verwaltung von Inhalten." *Computer Zeitung* (14): 17-17.
Middelhoff, Thomas. 1997. "Entwicklung einer Multimediastrategie für Medienunternehmem." *Die Betriebswirtschaft* 57 (3): 411-422.
Neuhold, Erich J. 1998. "Der Informationsarbeiter - heute und morgen." *Der GMD-Spiegel* 3/4 32-35.
Nielsen, Jakob. 1999. *Designing Web Usability: The practice of Simplicity*. Indianapolis: New Ryders Publishing
Nielsen, Jakob *Personalization is Over-Rated*. 2000 http://www.useit.com/alertbox/981004.html
NN. 1999. *Verleger haben nun weniger Angst vor der digitalen Autobahn*.
Palmer, Jonathan W. u. Eriksen, Lars Bo. 1999. "Digital Newspapers Explore Marketing on the Internet." *Communications of the ACM* 42 (9): 33-40.
Ryan, James. 1999. "Stop the press." *Business 2.0* (12): 196-209.
Sakagami, Hidekazu; Kamba, Tomonari; Sugiura, Atsushi u. Koseki, Yoshiyuki. 1998. "Effective personalization of push-type systems --- visualizing information freshness." *Computer Networks and ISDN Systems* 30 (1--7): 53-63.
Sander, Jörg u. Kröger, Carsten. 1998. "Content Management: Intranets richtig aufsetzen." *Diebold Management Report* (12): 14-18.
Shapiro, Carl u. Varian, Hal R. 1998. *Information Rules*. Boston: Harvard Business School Press
Varian, Hal R. 1991. *Grundzüge der Mikroökonomik*. München: R. Oldenbourg Verlag GmbH

6. Biographies

Dipl.-Inform. Thomas Ritz , born 1971 studied computer science and economics at the University of Bonn and obtained his degree in computer science in 1997. Since 1997 he is scientific employee at the University of Stuttgart IAT and the Fraunhofer IAO. He has a long standing experience in publishing industry and focuses his research activities on online communication and information. In several research projects he designed and implemented solutions for electronic information exchange, online communication in virtual communities, branch specific information portals and electronic commerce. Mr. Ritz acts as project manager in the DISMED project (funded by the European Commission in FP 4 Innovation program RSE 067) and in the PEACH project (funded by the European Commission in FP 5 IST programme IST-1999-11345). Besides he joined several public and industry funded research, consultancy and development projects.

*Electronic Publishing '01 –
2001 in the Digital Publishing Odyssey
A. Hübler et al. (Eds.)
IOS Press, 2001*

Metadata Usage in an Online Journal – An application Profile

Ana Alice Baptista
Altamiro Barbosa Machado[i]
analice@dsi.uminho.pt
Departamento de Sistemas de Informação
Escola de Engenharia
Universidade do Minho
Portugal

Abstract

In a chaotic environment like the Internet, data are not enough anymore. The description of resources is fundamental in order to keep some structure and make Internet services more efficient and more effective Metadata is, basically, data about data. However, metadata per se is also insufficient: with different kinds of services and software using different metadata and metadata structures, the problem persists. As it happens in other areas, standardization is a keystone to the metadata usage and implementation.

Dublin Core (DC) and RDF are two recommendations from two different initiatives: DCMI (Dublin Core Metadata Initiative) and W3C (World Wide Web Consortium).

In order to be widely used, the DCMI opted for broadly defining the DC semantics, while leaving the syntax issues open and undefined. This is the reason why RDF and DC match so well: RDF brings the syntax rules on which DC can be embedded.

The RDF schema, on its turn, makes it possible to design and implement, in a consistent way, project specific metadata vocabularies not covered by DC or other standard metadata vocabularies.

In this paper we will illustrate the use of DC, RDF and RDF Schema in the context of an online journal project: Informattica Online. An evaluation of this approach will also be presented.

0. Introduction

In a chaotic environment like the Internet, data are not enough anymore. Although indexing and information retrieval systems are more and more sophisticated, relevance and precision in user queries have not yet reached satisfactory levels.

In order to enhance information services' efficiency and effectiveness, semantic metadata needs to be used. However, with different kinds of services and software using different metadata and metadata structures, the problem persists. As in other areas, standardization is a keystone to the effective usage of metadata.

The Dublin Core Element Set (DCES) is a recommendation from Dublin Core Metadata Initiative (DCMI) and it consists of a core vocabulary of fifteen elements drawn specifically for the description of resources. Almost all of these elements have element refinement qualifiers, and/or encoding scheme qualifiers already approved by the Dublin Core Usage Committee (DCUC).

Element refinement qualifiers are, as the name suggests, other terms of the vocabulary that further specify the meaning of a given element. "A refined element shares the meaning of the unqualified element, but with a more restricted scope" (DCMI-DCQ, 2000). For instance, the element Date has as element refinement qualifiers the terms Issued, Created, Modified and Valid.

Element Encoding Scheme qualifiers, by their turn, "identify schemes that aid in the interpretation of an element value" (DCMI-DCQ, 2000). For instance, the same element Date, has as Encoding Scheme Qualifiers the W3C-DTF[1] and the DCMI[2] Period schemes.

Because DCMI is concerned with semantic issues, the DC needs a foreign syntax to be expressed. When DC is embedded in the Extensible Markup Language (XML) documents, the syntax chosen is, many times, the RDF/XML syntax. This is an XML application to express the Resource Description Framework (RDF) model (Lassila and Swick, 1999). The RDF Model is nothing but a set of triples (subject, predicate, object or resource, property, value). An RDF statement makes statements about resources using a property and having as a value the result of that property applied to the given resource. A statement can be seen as a triple composed of three elements: resource (subject), property (predicate) and value (object). A resource can be anything identifiable by a Uniform Resource Identifier (URI) (Harold 1999) pp.632.

The RDF Schema, in its turn, makes it possible to design and implement, in a consistent way, project specific metadata vocabularies not covered by DC or other standard metadata vocabularies. The RDF Schema Specification is a candidate recommendation since 27th March 2000 that "defines a schema specification language. More succinctly, the RDF Schema mechanism provides a basic type system for use in RDF models. It defines resources and properties such as rdfs:Class and rdfs:subClassOf that are used in specifying application-specific schemas" (Brickley and Guha, 2000).

In Informattica Online (IO) we used three vocabularies embedded in RDF syntax in order to fully describe our documents: DC[3], vCard[4] and IO[5]. To describe the vocabularies usage we created an RDF Profile (Heery and Patel, 2000) that will be presented in section 3.

In next section, we describe the contextualization in which we use the vocabularies. Then, we describe the general profile of Informattica Online and, afterwards, we draw some conclusion on the usage of these technologies, mainly RDF and RDF schema. Some glances over future work will follow.

1. Contextualization

Informattica Online (Baptista, Rodrigues et al., 1999) comprises the following document genres (Levy and Marshall, 1994): Scientific Article, Brief News, Comment, Anonymous Comment, Editorial, Revision, Revision Comment. Roughly, they are related as shown in Fig.1.

---

[1] http://www.w3.org/TR/NOTE-datetime
[2] http://dublincore.org/documents/dcmi-period/
[3] http://dublincore.org/2000/03/13/dces
[4] http://www.w3.org/2001/vcard-rdf/3.0 and ftp://ftp.isi.edu/in-notes/rfc2426.txt
[5] IO is a vocabulary namespace schema created by us using RDF schema. It can be found at http://www.dsi.uminho.pt/io/schemas/io-schema

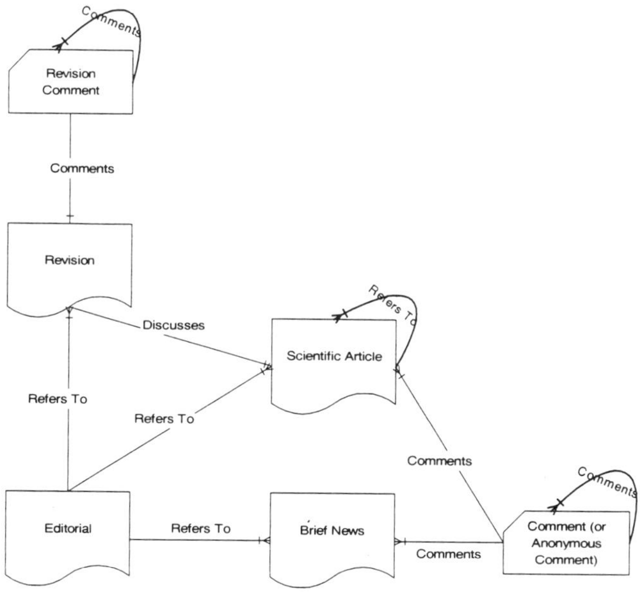

Fig. 1 – Relation between Informatica Online documents

For compatibility reasons, we decided to use widely used vocabularies as much as possible. Nevertheless, there were some specific semantics we needed that were not covered by them, leading us to create our own vocabulary and namespace schema using RDF schema. More specifically, we created the following terms:

- **Document Genre** - The Document Genre. This can be one of the following: Scientific Article, BriefNews, Comment, Anonymous Comment, Editorial, Revision and Revision Comment.
- **Document State** - The Document State within the system. This can be one of the following: underReview, underModification, forPublishing, forArchival, Archived, Published.
- **Approval** - Property to be used in the Revision Discussions Document. It can have four different values: Approved, Not Approved, Under Review, Under Modification
- **Version Number** - The version number of the document.
- **Document Code** - A code given to a document, independently of version, i.e., the document is considered to be always the same, whichever version it has.

2. IO General Profile

"Application profiles consist of data elements drawn from one or more namespace schemas combined together by implementors and optimised for a particular local application." (Heery and Patel, 2000). The Application Profile shows, in RDF, all terms and vocabularies and their specific meaning used in the scope of a specific application.

Application profiles are not the same as namespace schema. In fact, a namespace schema contains "all those elements defined by the managing body or registration authority (whatever that might be) for a particular namespace" (Heery and Patel, 2000) while an application profile is tailored for a particular implementation and "will typically contain combinations of sub-sets of one or more namespace schemas" (Heery and Patel, 2000).

In order to build the general application profile of Informattica Online (see Fig. 2), we used the Schemas vocabulary (smes namespace[6]) being developed under the Schemas Project[7] .

Each document genre needs a specific set of semantic metadata and therefore one profile, accordingly to its usage within the system. By making a union of these sets, we obtained the general set of vocabulary terms used in the overall system. Table 1 shows the terms and respective vocabularies used.

Table 1 – Vocabulary and respective terms used in Informattica Online

Vocabulary	Element	Element Refinement	Encoding Scheme
DC	Title	Alternative	
DC	Creator		
DC	Subject		
DC	Description	Table Of Contents Abstract	
DC	Publisher		
DC	Contributor		
DC	Date	Created Valid Issued	W3C-DTF
DC	Type		DCMI Type Vocabulary
DC	Format	Extent Medium	 IMT
DC	Identifier		URI
DC	Source		URI
DC	Language		RFC 1766
DC	Relation	Is Version Of Has Version Is Part Of Has Part Is Required By Requires Is Referenced By References Has Format	URI
DC	Rights		
vCard	FN		
VCard	EMAIL		
VCard	URL		
VCard	ORG		
IO	Document Genre		
IO	Document State		
IO	Approval		
IO	Version Number		
IO	Document Code		

6 http://www.schemas-forum.org/registry/schemas/SCHEMAS/1.0/smes

7 http://www.schemas-forum.org/

```
<rdf:RDF xmlns:rdf="http://www.w3.org/1999/02/22-rdf-syntax-ns#" xmlns:rdfs="http://www.w3.org/2000/01/rdf-schema#"
xmlns:dc="http://dublincore.org/2000/03/13/dces#" xmlns:dcq="http://dublincore.org/2000/03/13/dcq#"
xmlns:vCard="http://www.w3.org/2001/vcard-rdf/3.0#" xmlns:smes="http://www.schemas-
forum.org/registry/schemas/SCHEMAS/1.0/smes#">
    <smes:ApSchema rdf:about="http://www.dsi.uminho.pt/io/schemas/io-genProfile">
        <smes:isProfileOf rdf:resource="http://www.dsi.uminho.pt/io/semantics/general.html"/>
        <dc:title>The Informattica Online General Application Profile v1.0</dc:title>
        <dc:date>2001-04-12</dc:date>
        <dc:identifier>http://www.dsi.uminho.pt/io/schemas/io-genProfile</dc:identifier>
        <dc:creator rdf:parseType="Resource">
                <vCard:fn>Ana Alice Baptista</vCard:fn>
                <vCard:email>analice@dsi.uminho.pt</vCard:email>
                <vCard:URL rdf:resource=" http://www.dsi.uminho.pt/~analice"/>
                <rdfs:label>Ana Alice Baptista</rdfs:label>
        </dc:creator>
        <dc:publisher>Universidade do Minho</dc:publisher>
        <dc:type>Text</dc:type>
        <dc:language>en</dc:language>
        <dc:source rdf:resource="http://www.dsi.uminho.pt/io/semantics/general.htm"/>
        <smes:uses rdf:resource="http://dublincore.org/2000/03/13/dces#title"/>
        <smes:uses rdf:resource="http://dublincore.org/2000/03/13/dces#creator"/>
        <smes:uses rdf:resource="http://dublincore.org/2000/03/13/dces#subject"/>
        <smes:uses rdf:resource="http://dublincore.org/2000/03/13/dces#description"/>
        <smes:uses rdf:resource="http://dublincore.org/2000/03/13/dces#publisher"/>
        <smes:uses rdf:resource="http://dublincore.org/2000/03/13/dces#contributor"/>
        <smes:uses rdf:resource="http://dublincore.org/2000/03/13/dces#date"/>
        <smes:uses rdf:resource="http://dublincore.org/2000/03/13/dces#type"/>
        <smes:uses rdf:resource="http://dublincore.org/2000/03/13/dces#format"/>
        <smes:uses rdf:resource="http://dublincore.org/2000/03/13/dces#identifier"/>
        <smes:uses rdf:resource="http://dublincore.org/2000/03/13/dces#source"/>
        <smes:uses rdf:resource="http://dublincore.org/2000/03/13/dces#language"/>
        <smes:uses rdf:resource="http://dublincore.org/2000/03/13/dces#relation"/>
        <smes:uses rdf:resource="http://dublincore.org/2000/03/13/dces#rights"/>
        <smes:uses rdf:resource="http://dublincore.org/2000/03/13/dcq#alternative"/>
        <smes:uses rdf:resource="http://dublincore.org/2000/03/13/dcq#tableOfContents"/>
        <smes:uses rdf:resource="http://dublincore.org/2000/03/13/dcq#abstract"/>
        <smes:uses rdf:resource="http://dublincore.org/2000/03/13/dcq#created"/>
        <smes:uses rdf:resource="http://dublincore.org/2000/03/13/dcq#valid"/>
        <smes:uses rdf:resource="http://dublincore.org/2000/03/13/dcq#issued"/>
        <smes:uses rdf:resource="http://dublincore.org/2000/03/13/dcq#extent"/>
        <smes:uses rdf:resource="http://dublincore.org/2000/03/13/dcq#medium"/>
        <smes:uses rdf:resource="http://dublincore.org/2000/03/13/dcq#isVersionOf"/>
        <smes:uses rdf:resource="http://dublincore.org/2000/03/13/dcq#hasVersion"/>
        <smes:uses rdf:resource="http://dublincore.org/2000/03/13/dcq#isPartOf"/>
        <smes:uses rdf:resource="http://dublincore.org/2000/03/13/dcq#hasPart"/>
        <smes:uses rdf:resource="http://dublincore.org/2000/03/13/dcq#isRequiredBy"/>
        <smes:uses rdf:resource="http://dublincore.org/2000/03/13/dcq#requires"/>
        <smes:uses rdf:resource="http://dublincore.org/2000/03/13/dcq#isReferencedBy"/>
        <smes:uses rdf:resource="http://dublincore.org/2000/03/13/dcq#References"/>
        <smes:uses rdf:resource="http://dublincore.org/2000/03/13/dcq#hasFormat"/>
        <!--vCard-->
        <smes:uses rdf:resource="http://www.w3.org/2001/vcard-rdf/3.0#FN"/>
        <smes:uses rdf:resource="http://www.w3.org/2001/vcard-rdf/3.0#EMAIL"/>
        <smes:uses rdf:resource="http://www.w3.org/2001/vcard-rdf/3.0#URL"/>
        <smes:uses rdf:resource="http://www.w3.org/2001/vcard-rdf/3.0#ORG"/>
        <!-- io -->
        <smes:uses rdf:resource="http://www.dsi.uminho.pt/io/schemas/io-schema#documentGenre"/>
        <smes:uses rdf:resource="http://www.dsi.uminho.pt/io/schemas/io-schema#documentState"/>
        <smes:uses rdf:resource="http://www.dsi.uminho.pt/io/schemas/io-schema#approval"/>
        <smes:uses rdf:resource="http://www.dsi.uminho.pt/io/schemas/io-schema#versionNumber"/>
        <smes:uses rdf:resource="http://www.dsi.uminho.pt/io/schemas/io-schema#documentCode"/>
    </smes:ApSchema>
</rdf:RDF>
```


Fig. 2 - General Application Profile of Informattica Online

3. Conclusions

Although we tried to avoid creating a new vocabulary, we still needed some specific semantics not present in other vocabularies. Therefore, we created IO and defined a specific namespace using RDF Schema, which has shown to be very useful.

By their turn, DC, vCard and RDF syntax fit well and, although the characteristic verbosity of XML, the description of resources seems to be not only machine-understandable, but also human-understandable. The RDF profile of the application was also easy to develop.

Nevertheless, we have to say that the RDFMS Specification (Lassila and Swick, 1999) and the RDFS Specification (Brickley and Guha, 2000) are not easy to understand at first. However, this happens with almost all computer languages: after some experience their usage is straightforward.

Regarding RDF Namespace Schemas and Application Profiles, we expect that their usage and registry can bring some structure to the area.

4. Future Work

This project is an output of a PhD work in the field of Electronic Publishing. After having finished building the Application Profiles of all document genres, we intend to close the metadata definition part of our project.

Then some thoughts will have to take place to decide if this work should go on and implemented in a larger project with national and international partners.

5. References

Lassila O. and Swick R. R. (Eds). (1999). Resource Description Framework (RDF) Model and Syntax Specification. W3C Consortium.

Brickley D. and Guha R. V. (Eds). (2000). Resource Description Framework (RDF) Schema Specification. W3C Consortium.

DCMI-DCQ. (2000). Dublin Core Qualifiers, DCMI.

Baptista, A. A., E. Rodrigues, et al. (1999). Online Publishing as a Support for Scholarly Communication in Dynamic Knowledge Communities. ICCC / IFIP Conference on Electronic Publishing'99, Ronneby - Sweden, ICCC Press.

Harold, E. R. (1999). XML Bible. Foster City, IDG Books Worldwide, Inc.

Heery, R. and M. Patel (2000). "Application Profiles: Mixing and Matching Metadata Schemas." Ariadne(25).

Levy, D. M. and C. C. Marshall (1994). Washington's White Horse? A Look at Assumptions Underlying Digital Libraries. The First Annual Conference on the Theory and Practice of Digital Libraries, Texas - USA.

---

[i] Professor Altamiro Machado, my PhD supervisor and Head of the Information Systems Department at Universidade do Minho passed away on the 23rd March 2001 due to a heart attack. Because he was my supervisor and was aware of all my work, I decided to keep his name as an author in all documents we had in hand at the time he passed away.

Electronic Publishing '01 –
2001 in the Digital Publishing Odyssey
A. Hübler et al. (Eds.)
IOS Press, 2001

Converting heterogenous cultural catalogues and documents to XML - strategies and solutions of the COVAX project

Francisca Hernández(1), Peter Linde(2), Bob Mulrenin(3), Robin Yeates (4)

(1) Residencia de Estudiantes, Spain - fhc @interlink.es
(2)Blekinge Institute of Technology, Sweden – peter.linde@bth.se
(3) Salzburg Research Forschungsgesellschaft m.b.H., Austria – bob.mulrenin@ salzburgresearch.at
(4) London and South Eastern Library Region, United Kingdom - robin@viscount.org.uk

Abstract. COVAX (Contemporary Culture Virtual Archive in XML) [1] is an IST (Information Society Technology) funded project, launched as part of the IST first call, corresponding to key action 3 (Multimedia content and tools: cultural heritage and digital content) in the action line III.2.3 (Access to scientific and cultural heritage) under the European Community Fifth Framework for research and development. The main objective of COVAX is to test the use of XML to combine document descriptions and digitised surrogates of cultural documents to build a global system for search and retrieval, increasing accessibility via the Internet to electronic resources, regardless of their location. The project duration is 24 months. It started in January 2000 and the partners include content owners (memory institutions) and technological partners (developers: public RTD centres and private companies)[2]. COVAX's approach to achieving its objectives is based on the conversion of existing records to homogeneously-encoded document descriptions of bibliographic records, archive finding aids, museum records and catalogues, and electronic texts and on the application of XML (eXtensible Markup Language) and the various Document Type Definitions (DTDs) currently being used for library resource descriptions (MARC DTD), archives finding aids (EAD), museum materials (AMICO DTD) and electronic versions of cultural texts (TEIlite).

COVAX is designed to form a network of XML repositories as a distributed database. This will be accessed as a single database and will act as a meta-search engine, offering access to book references, finding aids, facsimile images, museum items, and other resources. COVAX is constructing a multilingual user interface to access such data. The project does not intend to create standards but to rely on the adoption of existing standards and concepts (XML, DTDs already in use, http...), using the Z39.50 protocol as a conceptual basis for communication between the multilingual user interface and the meta-search engine and Dublin Core Metadata Element Set elements as cross-domain access points. The conversion process has proved to be a crucial one in the COVAX-project and we therefore try to concentrate, in this article, on questions concerning our experiences of converting mainly library catalogues of different MARC or proprietary formats to XML.

1. COVAX OVERVIEW

The first stages of the COVAX (Contemporary Culture Virtual Archive in XML) project have been concerned with the definition of a COVAX architecture.

The purpose of COVAX is to analyse and draw up the technical solutions required to provide access through the Internet to homogeneously-encoded document descriptions of archive, library and museum collections based on the application of SGML/XML. The project will demonstrate its feasibility through a prototype containing a meaningful sample of all the different types of documents to build a global system for search and retrieval. It is based on the assumption that in libraries, archives and museums an enormous number of descriptions could be made available over the Internet by converting existing records or by creating new ones using specific SGML/XML DTD's.

1.1 User point of view

In the internet era, new challenges are constantly presenting themselves, and each new improvement in technique ends with a potential improvement in the functionality available to end-users. Sometimes these are founded on technical features such as speed, and sometimes on accessing new information resources. COVAX is expected to cover new challenges from this second perspective, transferring information resources to final users in a more adequate way, taking advantage of new XML technologies.The figure below gives an idea of what COVAX is expected to provide. End users, through the internet, will be able to access documentary information thanks to new XML paradigms.

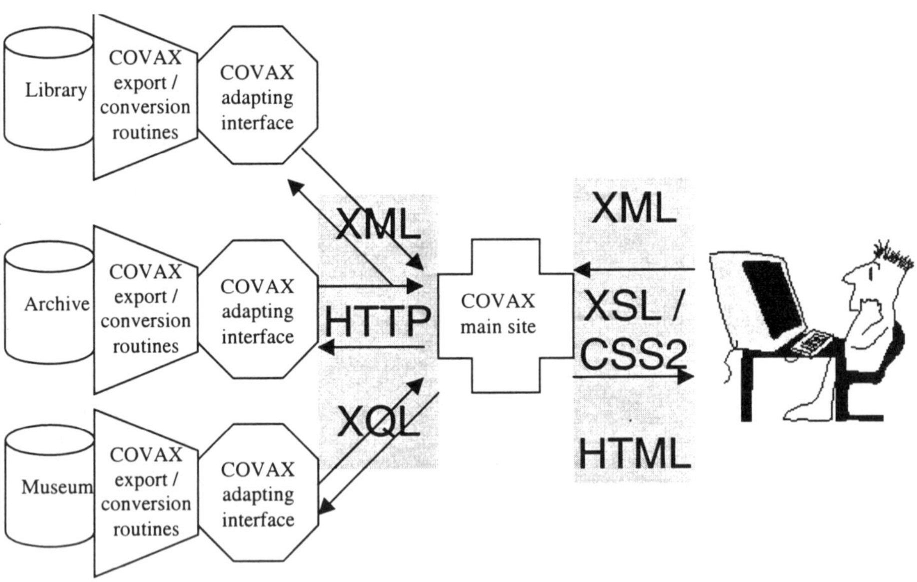

Fig. 1 - COVAX overview

The innovative aspect of COVAX is located in software layers that are invisible to the end user. The ability to obtain data from heterogeneous repositories, using emerging XML techniques, is where COVAX has to spend the maximum effort. Superficially, users will not notice any great difference from existing tools that access document databases.

1.2 Architecture design

The figure below shows, at the top level, the http client, which is the starting point of the COVAX system from the client side. At the next level, which might be called the servers level, at least two kinds of host will support COVAX: the COVAX web server, dealing with the main search and report capabilities; and the partner web server, specialising in the storage and indexing of information. Finally, at the bottom level, an off-line activity is shown, which is particularly important for the COVAX project: the conversion of current documentary data formatted for the XML databases.

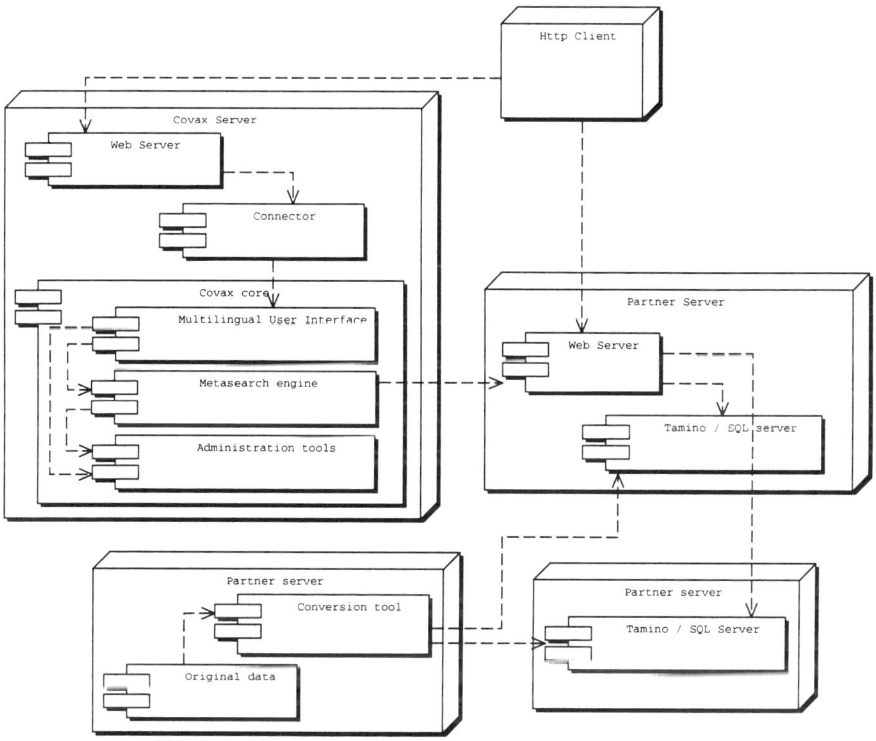

Fig. 2 - COVAX deployment diagram.

Physical architectural details as firewalls and external servers are not represented since the COVAX architecture is not dependent (it does not have to be dependent) on particular installations. It has to be adaptable for most typical environments, and this philosophy guides the design of the whole system. As currently defined, each partner system will be able to distribute the components of COVAX, without any requirement beyond accessibility to the internet.

1.3 Client

On the client side, there are two connections, one pointing to the main COVAX web server, and one pointing to the partner server. The user will access the main functionality of the system through the first connection. The second connection, directly to the partner server, is at present a possibility rather than a clearly defined function. We have envisaged the possibility of direct calls from downloaded HTML result pages to well-known sources. This connection is designed to allow this.

1.4 COVAX server

The COVAX server consists of three components: Multilingual User Interface, Metasearch Engine and Administration Tools. These provide the functionality expected from this system, comprising the core of the COVAX product:

> **Multilingual User Interface.** Its role is "*developing the multilingual interfaces to access the main COVAX functionality*".
> **Metasearch Engine.** It will "*develop the metasearch capabilities of COVAX, that will offer the following functionalities: in general, handle all the interaction with the COVAX individual library sites; and resolve COVAX-global queries*"
> **Administration Tools.** Their role is "*development of the Administration Tools as required by the COVAX main site ("access server") being the middle-ware component as well as the user related and content provider related components*".

Control of the COVAX system resides in the Interface component. It is supposed in this approach, that each time the Interface is called, it will determine the functionality required (through service components such as the Metasearch Engine and Administrative Tools), and it will generate the corresponding required web page response. The Metasearch Engine will provide information needed by the Interface, and will obtain, from available resources, the information required by the user.

1.5 Partner server

On the partner server side, at least two valid configurations have to be taken into account, as shown in the figure. One or more nodes can be used to provide the partner functionality. Only one requirement has to be met: to provide an XML front end (capable of being queried in XPATH) accessible from the internet.
The conversion component is also shown, as an independent node. It makes available current information that is not directly accessible from an XML perspective. Records that have to be converted to XML format will be transformed in this component. It is represented as a different node for clarity, but no special architectural requirements regarding this have been detected.

2. CONVERSION SO FAR

The conversion process has proved crucial in the COVAX-project. We therefore think it valuable to share the problems we have encountered and the solutions we have implemented during the project so far - both general aspects and specific issues -for anyone wanting to convert documents and catalogues to XML for easier retrieval and interchange.

The first parts of the project were devoted to the design of the system, the conversion of existing records, and the software development for version 1 of the COVAX prototype. The first design tasks were to define a coherent sample of records and documents from content owner partners; to analyse existing DTDs and select the appropriate ones; and to propose a common information structure.

A comprehensive dataset for the prototype was selected containing a wide variety of documents, descriptions, formats and databases: standard and non standard bibliographic records (including five different MARC formats), four different structures for archive and museum finding aids and information in six different languages (Catalan, Italian, English, German, Spanish, Swedish). The following excerpts from several content-owner partner returns gives an idea of the diversity of records and catalogues chosen for conversion:

Residencia de Estudiantes, Madrid - the union catalogue of bibliographic materials (monographs, serials and other) and archive documents held in 5 institutions (containing 75.000 records, mostly printed monographs, 1000 serials and 50 electronic publications, 100 videotapes and 100 sound recordings). Interchange formats: IBERMARC (USMARC – like). Archive finding aids: Over 36 personal and family archives from writers, scientists, painters, etc. related to Spanish contemporary culture. 3 archives from Spanish educational institutions. Some of the archives (10) are also described at catalogue level (20.000 records). In this case the format used is IBERMARC. During 2000 all the inventories will be converted to EAD and XML.

Angewandte InformationsTechnik Forschungsgesellschaft mbH, Graz - Swiss poster collection focussed on international contemporary posters from 1895 to date with about 200,000 records

Interchange format: USMARC/MARC21.

Universitat Oberta de Catalunya, Barcelona - Library catalogue, with a special emphasis on distance education, and virtual typology. Interchange format: CATMARC.

Blekinge Institute of Technology -The research document catalogue containing about 700 records, most of them with attached PDF-files for viewing the fulltext-document, administrated in a Lotus Notes Database. No standard Interchange format.

The library catalogue for the Naval Museum of Karlskrona containing about 2500 records. Interchange format: ISO 2709 Libris-Marc. Database: CDS-ISIS, version 1.0. Windows. Blekinge Institute of Technology is also providing about 30 full text XML-documents tagged according to the TEI-lite DTD. These documents are either museum-related or Swedish fiction.

LASER (London and South Eastern Library Region) - operates a union catalogue containing 4.27 million bibliographic record titles, in support of regional and inter-regional interlibrary loans and resource sharing. Interchange format: All records are held in UKMARC

Salzburg Research – Museum object inventory and multimedia product archive. Both collections are based on a proprietary format. The museum inventory is from "Museum in der Fronfeste" leather collection stored in a Macintosh FileMaker database. FileMaker is often used by many small museums in the Salzburg area. The multimedia product archive is derived from the Europrix multimedia contest rights publication database. This database had already been converted to XML based upon a proprietary DTD and subsequently stored in an XML database server, Tamino from Software AG. Both collections include references to multimedia content, images and videos.

During the past 6 months all the content-owner partners have put a lot of energy into trying to convert these very different catalogue records and documents into XML format according to the specified DTDs.

3. DTDs selection

In the system definition, a crucial point was the selection of DTDs to be used in the conversion process. The decision was made on the basis of the State of the Art studies[3] developed in the early stages of the project. From the beginning, the possibility of creating specific DTDs for COVAX was rejected, and the DTDs created by institutions with important standardisation capabilities were adopted (the above mentioned MARC DTD, EAD, AMICO DTD and TEIlite). The COVAX team has assumed that the influence, or even visibility of the project, was closely linked to the relevance of the standards adopted. The use of DTDs maintained by standardisation bodies also permits the use of a set of tools and procedures that will facilitate the adoption of XML by small or medium-sized Memory Institutions that do not have so many specialised staff or resources. All mentioned DTDs have been adapted to be converted from SGML to XML DTDs.

4. General Conversion issues

Once data structures to be used were defined, partners began conversion from original records, although there are differences between types of descriptions. Archival finding aids, museum descriptions and some of the electronic texts included in the prototype were created directly in EAD, AMICO or TEIlite. The main problem lies in the conversion of bibliographic records presented in up to five different MARC formats (IBERMARC, UNIMARC, UKMARC, CATMARC, LIBRIS-MARC). It has been necessary to plan different conversion processes: from original formats to MARC 21 (the basis of MARC DTD) using tools owned by the partners or by means of USEMARCON. In other cases, conversions were made directly, producing adequate code from original data structures using the MARC DTD. A free script provided by the Library of Congress, MARCCONV, was used to transform records to USMARC using the MARC DTD.

As explained in the previous section, unified DTDs have been selected to provide a common standard for transformation processes. These DTDs are the last structure that the records selected will show. Looking at the source data, one or two transformations are required.

We will use an example to explain the process of transformation from original data to the final XML documents. We consider the process for a non USMARC Bibliographic record. The correspondence with other possible formats is clear. The original non USMARC Bibliographic record has to undergo two transformations:

- To be semantically translated to USMARC.
- The semantically USMARC record, has to be converted to an XML structure.

These two steps can be performed in a single process, but the two 'logical' translations have to be carried out. Records in USMARC format will only require effort to translate them to the new XML format, without semantic considerations.

A small component diagram is shown below for a generic transformation process. The phase for adapting to USMARC format, is represented by one component representing the adaptation from any proprietary format to USMARC format. This proprietary format refers to any other non USMARC formats. The bottom component represents the structural transformation process in the case that the semantics are achieved. Three main formats have been considered as possible inputs for this component.

- ISO 2709, easily generated for most common bibliographic databases.
- Some installations can produce direct XML formats or even, raw data in XML format.
- Finally, proprietary formats that will require ad hoc developments.

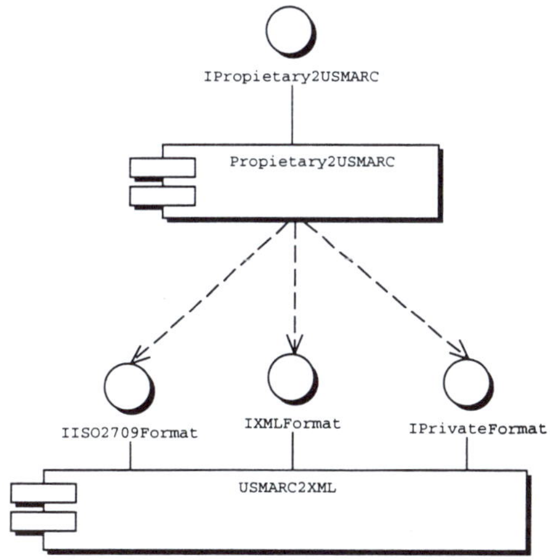

Fig. 3 - Migration component diagram

Interfaces represent the various detected input formats for this second step in the migration process. Once the record structure is achieved, it can be supported by records in ISO2709 format, XML format or any private proprietary format. For each input format, a different process has to be performed in order to obtain the common output: XML records with USMARC content.

4.1 Conversion types

As mentioned already, there are two ways to provide XML data. One is to have a front end translating on the fly some non XML data to an adequate XML format. The second is to store data in pure XML format, providing it in such an XML format when asked. We call them: adaptation and migration.

Adaptation.

Some partners in the COVAX consortium will investigate this approach. Taking advantage of records in relational databases, they will adapt the front end of the Data Base Management System to deliver results in adequate XML format.

Work on this kind of repository focuses on the appropriate configuration of front-end software, based on mappings between current data and the selected XML DTD.

Migration.

In this case, the data itself are stored in XML format. Work for this conversion involves the transformation of data from one structure to a new format. It requires a similar mapping to the previous method, but all transformations are made offline.

Data conversion will take place in several steps. As a result, converted data needs to be an XML representation of the underlying data. It might be adequate to transform the data into an internal representation (e.g.: XML with an proprietary DTD), which is then transformed using a target DTD. The conversion process can be detailed as shown in figure 4.

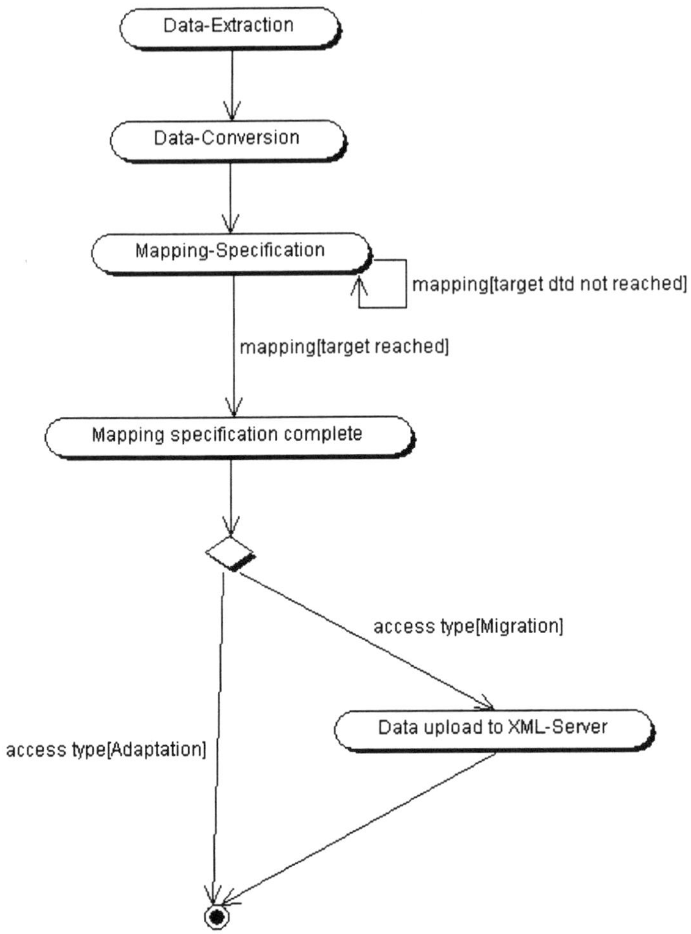

Fig. 4 – Data conversion process

4.2 Data-Extraction

The data needs to be available in an appropriate manner e.g. over a JAVA-Interface or in a text file. The data extraction activity therefore describes efforts to extract data from proprietary data stores such that other tools can use this data.

4.3 Data-Character-Conversion

Data-Character-Conversion takes place when the data does not support an appropriate character set. The mapping between different character sets is achieved in this step. Further discussion is needed to clarify if this step is part of the conversion tools or will be a service within the multilingual user interface.

4.4 Mapping-Specification

As the proprietary XML-representation may not be directly converted into the target format, multiple iterations of XML-mappings might be necessary.

4.5 Mapping-Specification Complete

When the target XML-representation is reached, it must be decided whether the conversion tools will implement an "adaptation" or "migration" strategy.

4.6 Software tested

Some efforts have been devoted to finding available tools on the web free of charge whenever possible to support migration or adaptation of records. Some success has been achieved. The most interesting tools tested are described.

Depending on the record format generated by the current information repository, different possibilities will be considered for the migration task. As previously defined, there are three different possibilities, according to the source format. Different tools can be considered for such formats.

4.7 Migration from ISO 2709

This is the most common format generated by document handling tools. Various tools on the web use this format for input:

Medlane Software. The Medlane project [MEDLANE] focuses on migrating ISO 2709 sources to XML records in Lane Medical Library. In addition to advancing XML as a representational format for document information, the Medlane work team has delivered a ISO 2709 to XML converter tool. There is a general tool to generate XML documents, from an ISO 2709 set of records, using any XML DTD as final structure. This implies that new DTDs can be used and applied during the transformation process. Another input represents the mapping between the original ISO 2709 contents and the final DTD structure. The tool is provided free of charge, and since August 2000, it can be used even in commercial systems.

Some experiments have been carried out using this tool, and minor successes have been obtained so far. We have completed some mapping between ISO 2709 input and the COVAX USMARC DTD, achieving partial success in the tests. We are in contact with a Medlane person responsible for help regarding this issue.

USEMARCON. User controlled Generic MARC converter [USEMARCON]. This is a tool converting ISO 2709 records between different formats:

UNIMARC to UKMARC (Bibliographic)
UKMARC to UNIMARC (Bibliographic)
UKMARC to UNIMARC (Authorities)
USMARC to UNIMARC (Bibliographic)
UNIMARC to USMARC (Bibliographic)

It has been tested with two sets of data: supplied test data and an ENEA sample of 100 records. The USEMARCON program installed and ran successfully with the supplied sample data. The ENEA sample was tested, but the default configuration is probably unsuitable for this data, as the program was unable to read past the first record. Further technical investigation is required to determine the exact cause of the problem.

BiblioML. BiblioML and AuthoritiesML [BiblioML] are XML-based formats for the interchange of UNIMARC bibliographic and authority records between applications. It is specific software for the translation of records from UNIMARC to some XML records following the structure described by two DTD's: biblioml_030.dtd and authoritiesml_030.dtd. We have not considered use of this tool due to the very specific nature of its approach.

MARCCONV. The Library of Congress provides a free tool [MARCCONV] that we have tested successfully. This tool translates MARC records from the ISO 2709 format to the published SGML DTD for bibliographic records. The pure XML requirements of the COVAX system have required some simple adaptations to the tested software, that have ended in the generation of XML documents (records) from several test records. More experiments are required with this tool before we can adopt it as a solution for translating bibliographic records in the context of COVAX.

The MARCCONV tool uses for reference a DTD (SGML) that is the SGML version of the XML DTD adopted by the COVAX consortium. This means that even if it is not possible (not easy at least) to adapt the software to new DTDs, the tool itself uses the same DTD structure as COVAX, or, rather, COVAX uses the same DTD as this tool.

5. Migration from XML

XSL (Extensible Stylesheet Language) is a standard (draft) [XSL] defining transformations of XML documents to other SGML formats. The typical application of such XSL definitions is the transformation of XML documents to HTML pages, in order to make the former more appropriate for user interfaces. The engine performing the transformation is called the XSLT (Extensible Stylesheet Language Transformations) processor.
The right combination of an XML source, for example UNIMARC XML records, and the appropriate XSL mapping the translation between UNIMARC XML to, for example, USMARC XML, would be considered another way of migrating records from one representation to another. The advantage of this method is the use of free and very common (each day more) tools. For instance software may include components like those proposed by [APACHE XML], such as Xalan (XSLT processor), Xerces (XML processor), and Cocoon (XML publishing and delivery components), and custom software, if desirable, to generate the XSL Stylesheet from templates and DTD mappings. The tools evaluated by COVAX partners are:

XML Translator Generator at IBM Alphaworks
This tool may be useful for converting XML documents based on one DTD to another DTD without using XSLT directly. This tool is a Java based XML processor (IBM XML Parser) that automates the translation of XML documents based on one DTD to another without the need for writing XSL scripts or program code. It uses examples of the same data in the two DTDs for generating a translator that can then be subsequently used for translation.

Tools to upload XML content to XML repositories (after conversion)
Following the conversion of data to XML, it will be necessary to bulk load the XML repository. Software AG [SAG] provides a new bulk loader, Java and Perl, with the Tamino 2.1 XML server

Adaptation from relational records
When the original data is located in relational databases, and no tools generating intermediate formats (ISO 2709, XML, ...) are available, we consider as a potential

solution direct reading of database records themselves. This can be done by ad hoc software or using existing tools. Tools considered are shown below:

XML Spy

[XML Spy] is a general tool useful for accessing and importing data from flat files or databases, including Microsoft Access. An XML document can be created when importing data and then transformed to the final XML document based on a COVAX DTD. Once an XML format is generated, if it does not conform to the COVAX DTD selected, it can be transformed using the Migration from XML tools.

5.1 XML migration XSLT combined with any data extraction tool

Data conversions from proprietary database formats or from non-standardized content are problematic. Mapping must be done to a DTD that may not be representative of all data in the source data. Furthermore, export tools and export formats may be completely non-standardized as well. What further complicates this situation is that the most current DTDs are not yet stable, especially for Museums. How does a content provider build a bridge to an XML repository?

5.2 Proprietary DTD and XML conversion document

One approach is to first build a proprietary DTD representing the database or a database view. The goal is to maintain an intermediate proprietary XML conversion document, although to create a new DTD is not a trivial task. We could, however, build our XML document without a DTD. The key is to export data with the database field names included within the source data. Using the database field names, we can build XML tags to encapsulate a particular field's data. One may visualise this process by using XML Spy to import a CSV (comma separated fields) file. Using this tool, we simple tell it to use the first row's labels as the column headers in the XML Spy table. Our XML tags are now defined. What we call column headings have become the XML elements of our intermediate XML document. XML Spy is one alternative for generating a proprietary XML document from a text file or database. Others exist, including specialized Perl scripts and Java programs.

Many database systems can generate CSV files with the first row containing the field names. FileMaker databases, found at many museums, can be exported as a *.mer file.

6. Why build an XML Conversion Document?

The conversion document represents the closest representation of the source data. From here, we have the ability to use XSLT stylesheets to transform our conversion document to an XML document based on a particular DTD. This DTD may be experimental or the most desirable at the moment. Many content providers will be participating in XML projects, each perhaps with standard or experimental DTDs. Our XML conversion document is our starting point.

6.1 Transformation of one XML document to another

We talked about an XML conversion document. Now we need an XSLT conversion stylesheet based on the target DTD (e.g. Amico-2in1, MARC DTD, etc) and our XML conversion document. For example, a simple sample XSLT stylesheet can be generated from the target DTD by using TIBO's XML Authority. With this tool we create a sample XML document from the DTD and turn it into an XSL stylesheet that includes XSLT (transformation instructions). Our goal is to transform the proprietary XML conversion document into an XML document based on the standard DTD. In our case, the transformation from proprietary DTDs to the museum DTD, Amico-2in1, was used for three museums.

Lastly, our greatest difficulty in conversion is handling encoded data for which there is no standard, e.g. subject or classification coding scheme. During our conversion steps, should we retain the original non-standard coding scheme or attempt to map to another coding scheme? This is a major effort and requires a more sophisticated conversion tool with defined lookup tables that cross-map to a standard coding scheme.

What makes matters worse among heterogenous XML repositories is that most search engines must be aware of the various coding schemes found in the various DTDs. We can be sure that MARC coding schemes are known for each library, but encoding schemes for museum data vary widely. For now, we must wait for the data collection software used by museums and archives to achieve standardization in their metadata formats and encoding schemes.

7. SPECIFIC CONVERSION EXAMPLES

7.1 Converting IBERMARC bibliographic records

As stated earlier, one of the key points of the system definition has been the assumption of DTDs on which the corresponding databases are to be configured. During this definition process at Residencia de Estudiantes in Madrid, both existing initial database records and specific characteristics of the used formats and cataloguing policies have been carefully taken into account. In fact, bibliographic record conversion from IBERMARC to MARC DTD will need some pre-processing in order to make some field contents match MARC DTD definitions.

This is as a result of slight differences between IBERMARC and USMARC formats and of the evolution process of the MARC 21 format itself. This format is the result of two complementary processes: Integration format, which integrated into one single code the application variants of some fields in terms of the described material; and the unification process of formats in use by the major bibliographic agencies. Since 1999, MARC 21 has actually replaced USMARC, CANMARC (maintained by the National Library of Canada) and UKMARC (used for the British National Bibliography) formats and has thus become the most widespread format, used in far more records than any other MARC family format. At the same time there has been no updating or revision process of the IBERMARC bibliographic format (maintained by the National Library of Spain), resulting in the fact that these slight differences have been increased. In spite of this, these differences are not especially significant. They are stated here in order to show the profundity reached in the conversion process:

- Codes affecting positions 29, 30, 31 & 33 of control field 008 (fixed-length data elements) need to be modified.
- Contents of field 019 (Legal Deposit) are moved into field 017 (Copyright Information Number).

Repeatability of field 080 (Universal Decimal Classification) needs to be modified, because at MARC DTD, sub-field $a is repeatable, but the field is not. At IBERMARC it is just the reverse: the field is repeatable, but the sub-field is not.

- Contents of sub-field $j of field 650 (subject) are moved into sub-field $v.
- Contents of sub-field $v of field 852 (localization) are moved into $z (public note).

The figure below shows the process and an example of the conversion process results for a single record:

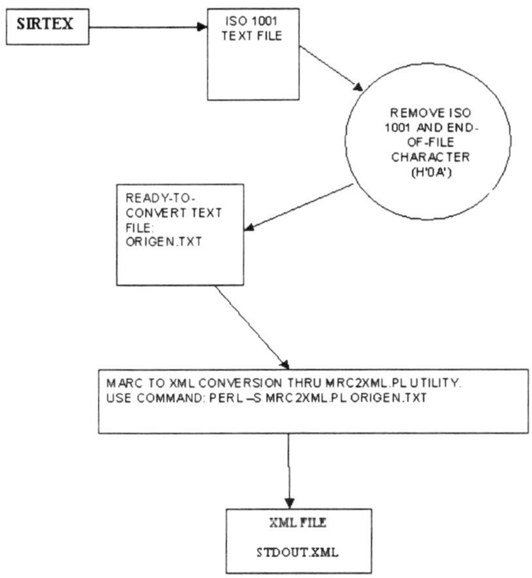

Fig. 5 XML Transformation process

Original Record:

```
00534nam  22001811  45
0010015000000050012000150080041000270350018000680400023000860800017001091
0000370012624500460016325000110020926000370022030000180025744000160027585
2006100291-AVC19990001281-19991122141-990701s1952    arg
spa d-  aMAXBI99000129-  aS(C)-FMAbspacCDM- 0a860-4"18/19"-1 aMenéndez
Pidal, Ramónd1869-1968-10aEstudios literarioscRamón Menéndez Pidal-  a7ª
ed.-0 aBuenos AiresbEspasa-Calpec1952-  a274 p.c18 cm- 0aAustralv28-40-
aS(C)-FMAbBMAjBMA/183zTiene algunas páginas subrayadas- 00607
```

Converted Record:

```
<?xml version="1.0" encoding="ISO-8859-1"?>
<mrcbfile>
<mrcb format-type="bd">
<mrcbldr bd>
<mrcbldr-bd-05 value="n"/>
<mrcbldr-bd-06 value="a"/>
<mrcbldr-bd-07 value="m"/>
<mrcbldr-bd-08 value="blank"/>
<mrcbldr-bd-09 value="blank"/>
<mrcbldr-bd-17 value="1"/>
<mrcbldr-bd-18 value="blank"/>
<mrcbldr-bd-19 value="blank"/>
</mrcbldr-bd>
```

```
<mrcb-control-fields>
<mrcb001>AVC1999000128l</mrcb001>
<mrcb005>1999112214l</mrcb005>
<mrcb008-bk>
<mrcb008-bk-00-05 value="990701"/>
<mrcb008-bk-06 value="s"/>
<mrcb008-bk-07-10 value="1952"/>
<mrcb008-bk-11-14 value="blank"/>
<mrcb008-bk-15-17 value="arg"/>
<mrcb008-bk-18-21 value="blank"/>
<mrcb008-bk-22 value="blank"/>
<mrcb008-bk-23 value="blank"/>
<mrcb008-bk-24-27 value="blank"/>
<mrcb008-bk-28 value="blank"/>
<mrcb008-bk-29 value="blank"/>
<mrcb008-bk-30 value="blank"/>
<mrcb008-bk-31 value="blank"/>
<mrcb008-bk-32 value="blank"/>
<mrcb008-bk-33 value="blank"/>
<mrcb008-bk-34 value="blank"/>
<mrcb008-bk-35-37 value="spa"/>
<mrcb008-bk-38 value="blank"/>
<mrcb008-bk-39 value="d"/>
</mrcb008-bk>
</mrcb-control-fields>
<mrcb-numbers-and-codes>
<mrcb035 i1="i1-blank" i2="i2-blank">
<mrcb035-a>MAXBI99000129</mrcb035-a>
</mrcb035>
<mrcb040 i1="i1-blank" i2="i2-blank">
<mrcb040-a>S(C)-FMA</mrcb040-a>
<mrcb040-b>spa</mrcb040-b>
<mrcb040-c>CDM</mrcb040-c>
</mrcb040>
<mrcb080 i1="i1-blank" i2="i2-0">
<mrcb080-a>860-4&quot;18/19&quot;</mrcb080-a>
</mrcb080>
</mrcb-numbers-and-codes>
<mrcb-main-entry>
<mrcb100 i1="i1-1" i2="i2-blank">
<mrcb100-a>Menéndez Pidal, Ramón</mrcb100-a>
<mrcb100-d>1869-1968</mrcb100-d>
</mrcb100>
</mrcb-main-entry>
<mrcb-title-and-title-related>
<mrcb245 i1="i1-1" i2="i2-0">
<mrcb245-a>Estudios literarios</mrcb245-a>
<mrcb245-c>Ramón Menéndez Pidal</mrcb245-c>
</mrcb245>
</mrcb-title-and-title-related>
<mrcb-edition-imprint-etc>
```

```
<mrcb250 i1="i1-blank" i2="i2-blank">
<mrcb250-a>7ª ed.</mrcb250-a>
</mrcb250>
<mrcb260 i1="i1-0" i2="i2-blank">
<mrcb260-a>Buenos Aires</mrcb260-a>
<mrcb260-b>Espasa-Calpe</mrcb260-b>
<mrcb260-c>1952</mrcb260-c>
</mrcb260>
</mrcb-edition-imprint-etc>
<mrcb-physical-description>
<mrcb300 i1="i1-blank" i2="i2-blank">
<mrcb300-a>274 p.</mrcb300-a>
<mrcb300-c>18 cm</mrcb300-c>
</mrcb300>
</mrcb-physical-description>
<mrcb-series-statement>
<mrcb440 i1="i1-blank" i2="i2-0">
<mrcb440-a>Austral</mrcb440-a>
<mrcb440-v>28</mrcb440-v>
</mrcb440>
</mrcb-series-statement>
<mrcb-location>
<mrcb852 i1="i1-4" i2="i2-0">
<mrcb852-a>S(C)-FMA</mrcb852-a>
<mrcb852-b>BMA</mrcb852-b>
<mrcb852-j>BMA/183</mrcb852-j>
<mrcb852-z>Tiene algunas páginas subrayadas</mrcb852-z>
</mrcb852>
</mrcb-location>
</mrcb>
</mrcbfile>
```


7.2 Experiences converting small library and museum catalogues at BTH

As stated before, it is not unusual that small and medium-sized museums and archives keep their records in homemade MS Access-, FileMaker-, Lotus databases etc. Such was the case when the partners at Blekinge Institute of Technology during the conversion phase of the COVAX-project had to deal with several small catalogues in different formats for conversion to XML.

From our user network of museums, libraries and archives in the region we tried to pick a varied sample of catalogues and full-text documents. This included for example a municipal archival guide made in Access, a very simple database with only a few fields, that had to be converted into EAD-encoded XML records; the Research document database of Blekinge Institute of Technology created in Lotus Domino containing about 700 records in a no standard format; A museum object catalogue in FileMaker of about 20.000 records from Karlskrona Naval Museum; A sample of full-text documents from local archives, libraries and museums - exhibition catalogues, yearbooks, novels, maps, naval charts, to be converted from print to XML-markup according to the TEIlite DTD.

Unfortunately there are not very many relevant tools for converting material like the above to XML. Most of our conversion effort has been a very time-consuming manual effort since we had very limited access to programmers.

Converting the Access archival guide, we simply used two methods: generating new records with proper EAD-tags out of data from database tables using Access' own report generator, and using the XML-spy-editor. XML-Spy has an "import database records" function that allows import of Access records and conversion of field-labels into the corresponding EAD-tag. This type of conversion was done as has been described above in the section named "Proprietary DTD and XML conversion document".

Choosing a DTD for the full text documents was never really any great dilemma since the collection that is being built at BTH and the samples needed for the COVAX project are contemporary cultural text-documents from museums, archives and libraries. The TEI (Text Encoding Initiative)is an international project to develop guidelines for the encoding of textual material in electronic form for research purposes. The TEI project have developed a set of very comprehensive DTDs that today are being used as more or less standards for marking up and interchanging cultural texts with SGML and XML. Very soon we found that one of these, the TEIlite DTD, suited our purpose of converting cultural heritage documents to XML, very well.

We used XML-Spy as the preferred editor when working with tagging the full-text according to the TEIlite DTD. We found it quite easy to work with XML-Spy since it has all the basic functions needed such as DTD support, the possibility to validate files and good import and export functions.

Tagging is very time consuming, but a straight forward thing as long as you are clear over what DTD, character set and elements to use in your documents.

Converting the Lotus Notes database, the main task was to map all the relevant fields to the MARC DTD. One problem here was of course the discrepancies in the semantics between the original research document catalogue and the MARC DTD. Another minor problem was the uneven quality of the catalogue record data.

When the mapping was done a Lotus script program was written which processed each record in the research document database and so generated a valid MARC XML-record for every record.

7.3 Converting Library Catalogs at LASER

LASER is involved in a number of projects with its members to digitize materials for the web, but its current database consists of bibliographic data. LASER operates a large union catalogue from which sample data needed to be extracted for COVAX. V3 Online (4) contains 4.27m bibliographic record titles, in support of regional and inter-regional interlibrary loans and resource sharing.

The selections for conversion were designed to ensure a number of identifiable 'collections' from a general purpose database as well as to reduce the number of records that need to be handled for the trial, so that COVAX content is reasonably balanced across sources.

LASER has experience of conversions from UKMARC to USMARC, and is aware of a number of difficulties with them. For example, we know we have a problem with converting UKMARC tag 248 (second level and subsequent level title) to USMARC, because it does not support this nesting of tags. We propose not to select records with 248 fields, or to delete that tag before output. In general a pragmatic approach has been taken during the project that represents the most replicable solution.

Other problems involve the selection of records which include a wide range of possible problem characters, especially special character such as the UK pound sign or rare characters that might cause loading and conversion problems later.

Since we planned to use standard existing conversion tools where possible, it was not deemed necessary to create full test records containing all possible characters and tags, and because of MARC flexibility, the possible range of complexity in records would be almost impossible to achieve by generating imaginary data anyway. Our emphasis was on producing realistic trial data that was shared via an intranet with partners from an early stage.

8. Data extraction and migration strategy

LASER has spent much effort outside the COVAX project to develop a transaction management system for ISO standard interloans based on its V3 database. In order to optimise development on the two separate systems, a migration strategy was preferred, so that work on COVAX did not interfere with work on the live systems. LASER was responsible for converting data from several MARC formats into USMARC, including UNIMARC, CATMARC and UKMARC. USEMARCON proved to require special configuration, and in general we preferred to adapt source systems to generate USMARC or UKMARC where possible. Samples were sent to LASER for validation and conversion to XML which was performed by using import procedures to convert records to Libpac internal format then export routines already in use to produce a range of USMARC products for publishers and libraries in Europe.

9. Data and character conversion

Having taken the decision to use USMARC and convert that to XML using Library of Congress MARC-XML Conversion Utilities (MARCCONV) with the mrcbfile.dtd (see http://lcweb.loc.gov/marc/marcsgml.html) we used XML Spy (downloadable free trial at http://www.xmlspy.com/) to validate the results and resolve problems. This is a complex and powerful editor that can be used to created DTDs and XML instances, but is also capable of validating XML against a declared DTD or XML schema. It is suitable for use by most library technical support staff. The main difficulty was deciding which character set encoding to use for XML output. UTF-8 was selected, although a number of problems remain with the handling of certain rare characters observed in data converted using MARCCONV, which we are currently working on at the time of writing.

10. Mapping specification

By choosing to use Libpac and Library of Congress tools, we avoided having to perform full mapping of UKMARC to MARC21 and from MARC21 to Dublin Core. Mapping is simply needed to ensure that all local tags required are included where necessary, such as our holdings information. We also needed to ensure that mandatory fields that will be required by COVAX system software are present. These included the MARC 040 tag (Cataloguing source), which for our purposes needs to contain a library code for each COVAX partner. We considered using Library of Congress codes for this (see the database and registration system at http://lcweb.loc.gov/marc/organizations/) but for administrative reasons chose to use simple codes during the initial pilot, in our case 'LASER'.

For some UOC and LASER tags, LASER bureau processing will strip tags from the source data during conversion to XML, by modifying the MARCCONV Perl script as required, or by pre-processing where this is more practical.

11. Validation

XML validation is performed using XML Spy, but even when data validates fully against the COVAX MARC DTD, we have found that there may be problems with characters appearing in the data. For example, the Tamino XML repository software in use at LASER for the project rejected UTF-8 records, and we then need to trace back to determine which software is validating wrongly. At the time of writing this is not clear.

12. Conclusion

It appears that conversion via migration of legacy MARC data to MARC21 and then XML can be done using available tools with minor modifications. Outstanding issues of character set encoding and holdings standards are likely to be resolved as we share experiences with partners within COVAX and subsequently beyond, and as the tools available are improved. We have already noticed that great strides forward have been taken by the Library of Congress since the project began, in such a way that European libraries can benefit. The recent announcement of the British Library's intention to change from UKMARC to use of MARC21 will further encourage adoption of MARC21 and the development of suitable conversion tools to handle legacy data such as ours. The next step is to mount live larger samples of our data (6,000 records) so that we can assess results display and bulk loading issues mid 2001.

13. References

[1]. *COVAX Web site* URL: http://www.covax.org/
[2]. The Project Co-ordinator is Residencia de Estudiantes (Spain) and the partners Angewandte InformationsTechnik Forschungsgesellschaft mbH. and Salzburg Research (Austria), Blekinge Tekniska Högskola (Blekinge Institute of Technology, Sweden), Software AG España, S.A., Universitat Oberta de Catalunya and Biblioteca de Menéndez Pelayo (Spain), LASER (London and South Eastern Library Region, UK), and ENEA (Italian National Agency for New Technology, Energy and the Environment, Italy)
[3]. State of the Art studies. *COVAX Web site* URL: http://www.covax.org/public_docum/p_documets.htm
[4]. V3 Online. URL: http://www.viscount.org.uk/products/v3online.html

*Electronic Publishing '01 –
2001 in the Digital Publishing Odyssey
A. Hübler et al. (Eds.)
IOS Press, 2001*

Improving Information Retrieval Performance by Experience Reuse

Lobna Jéribi

*LISI (Laboratory of Information Science Engineering)
INSA Lyon France, 20 avenue A.Einstein, 69621 Villeurbanne
lobna.jeribi@lisi.insa-lyon.fr*

Abstract: The goal to build a knowledge base, making "permanent" the user evaluations experiences on search results, constitutes the main motivation of this paper. In information retrieval systems, an experience is a search instance, represented by a search context and a set of evaluated document results. In this paper, we propose a search context model, characterized by the user's profile and query. Similarity functions between users' profiles and search contexts are defined, on the basis of the proposed model. The reuse process consists in expanding the initial user query by the documents terms contained in the similar instances. In contrast with the *Rocchio* method, these documents are those validated beforehand by users, having "similar" profiles as the current user, and being in a "similar" search situation. Our proposition enables to reduce system interactions with the user during his/her search session. These features were carried out in the COSYDOR (Cooperative System for Document Retrieval) project, based on *Intermedia* (Oracle 8i). Tests and evaluations are carried out using the test corpus of TREC (Text Retrieval Conference). The results show, for first search iterations, a significant improvement of performance compared to that of *Intermedia*. This work is carried out within the framework of a regional project, in which the sight deficient users constitute our application case. This research represents a considerable contribution for these users, considering their use difficulties of current information retrieval systems (too interactive systems, accessibility problems, etc).

0. Introduction

"Personalized" information retrieval systems, exploit "information about users" during retrieval, or filtering (*NewT* [MAE 94]), or query expansion (*smart*, [BUC 98]), or navigation process (*WebWatcher*, [ARM 95]). The user knowledge generally used in these systems, is often limited to some key words representing user interests, or some documents relevant to the user. However, using this knowledge, without defining its ***context*** (search situation, search goal, user features, etc.), reduces significantly its contribution to improve information retrieval results.

In a study carried out on intelligent system architectures and machine learning approaches for information retrieval, such as rings architectures [JER 98b] and multi-agents systems [JER 98a] [JER 2000a], we were directed towards the reuse techniques and instance based reasoning [JER 2001b]. This approach, based on the user reasoning cycle (intention, action, acquisition, evaluation), allows to carry out reasoning, to evaluate the document results automatically, and to improve them. This approach is relevant, because the user knowledge used is very "reliable" since "lived" and "evaluated" by this user. Moreover, the reuse approach enables to minimize the user interaction, which has a significant advantage for users having particular difficulties of access to information. Furthermore, the field of experience reuse, offers methods to specify and construct the experience ***context***, so that the reuse is optimal [MIL 99].

We propose in this paper to build an instance memory of information retrieval instances. When the users search contexts are "similar", these instances are reused to improve user query formulation. The user profile is considered as a significant element of an instance search context. Thus we propose in this paper a formal representation of "user profile" model. We also define a representation of an information retrieval instance model, in order to evaluate the similarity between instances. The similarity evaluation enables to highlight candidate instances to be reused, from the instance memory.

Some related works of context definition and experience reuse were proposed in the early literature. RADIX project [COR 99] proposes the modeling of internet navigation sessions carried out by the user. These models are reused in order to suggest similar sessions to the user. CABRI-N [SMA 99] is a personalized image retrieval system. Smaïn proposes a modeling of user strategy during an information retrieval process. Retrieval sessions are memorized and reused to improve user strategy search.

In this paper, we present briefly a modeling study of the user during a search session, and a representation of a search instance or search situation. Then, we present our approach of instance reuse for query expansion. Afterwards, we expose our project context and our application case. Lastly, we present the results of our first tests and the prospects for evaluations.

1. Information retrieval instance Modeling

In this section, we firstly define the user profile model, representing a relevant feature of the retrieval instance. Next, a global information retrieval instance is proposed.

1.1 User profile Modeling

Intelligent information systems aim to automatically adapt to individual users. Hence, the development of appropriate user modeling techniques is of central importance. Algorithms for intelligent information agents typically draw on work from the information retrieval and machine learning communities. Both communities have previously explored the potential of established algorithms for user modeling purposes [BEL 97] [WEB 98]. However, "work in this field is still in its infancy" [BILL 99].

1.1.1 User knowledge

Intelligent systems for information access are typically aimed at assisting a user in his search for interesting or useful information. A large variety of agents that make use of machine learning techniques have been developed and presented in the literature (e.g. [PAZ 97]). Most of this work focuses on the acquisition of a precise model of the user information need. However, in order to build truly useful information retrieval systems we also need to be aware of the user's knowledge.

To define the specific user knowledge, that is exploited during a search session, we have exploited **cognitive approach** results [ALL 91]. We have classified the user knowledge into four ***knowledge categories***, ranked according to their *evolution* degree.

1. Cultural knowledge (features having *little* or *no evolution*)
2. Professional knowledge (features having *long term evolution*)
3. System knowledge (features having *mean term evolution*)

4. Search knowledge (features having *short term evolution*), related to the current search session. The Figure 1 shows knowledge user features.

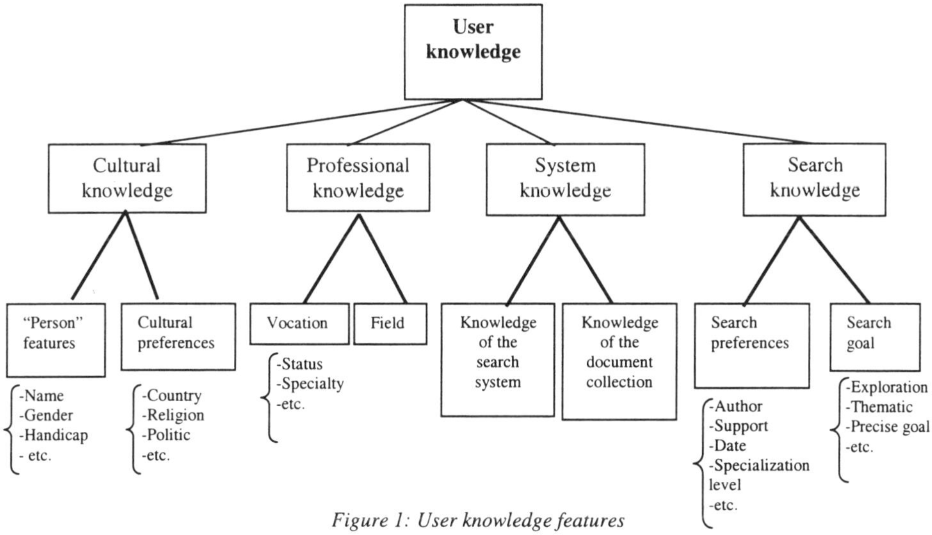

Figure 1: User knowledge features

Some features varies from an application case to another. These variations depend on the document, the search system and the user types. For example, in image retrieval systems, the search preferences include specific features as: plan, luminosity, contrast, colors, etc. Our specific model, concerning our use context, is presented in the next session (§4.1.2)

User knowledge features presented above, constitute a *generic model* of user profile, which *specific models* are related to the application cases used.

1.1.2 Representation formalism

The chosen representation formalism is the vector model. It is the formalism commonly used in both communities: information retrieval [SAL 86] and instance based reasoning [KOL 88]. The vector model presents several advantages in processing similarity between vectors.

Let $U=<U_1, U_2, U_3, U_4>$, be the vector representation of U, where U_i represents the ith category of user knowledge U.

$U_i = \{a_{i,j}\}$; $\forall j \in [1, n]$; $a_{i,j}$ represents the jth attribute of the category U_i;

$a_{i,j} \in \{v_k\}$; $\forall k \in [1, n]$; v_k represents the kth possible instance of $a_{i,j}$

We define then the space Γ_i with dimension n, of vector U_i as follows:

$$\Gamma_i = < (v_k^j)^{j=1\ to\ n} >; \forall k \in [1, m]$$

1.1.3 Similarity function

We propose to memorize user retrieval experiences, in order to reuse them, when users have "similar" profiles. Thus, our first goal of formalizing the user model, is to define the "distance" between user profiles. The expression (1) shows the similarity function S_U, between two user profiles U^i and U^p

$$S_U(U^i, U^j) = \frac{s_1(U_1^i, U_1^j) + \nu\, s_2(U_2^i, U_2^j) + \kappa\, s_3(U_3^i, U_3^j) + \lambda\, s_4(U_4^i, U_4^j)}{\mu + \nu + \kappa + \lambda} \quad (1)$$

Where:
U_p^i is the vector representing the pth category of U^j , which is the profile of the user j.
s_p: similarity function between vectors of the pth ***category*** of U
$s_p \in [0, 1]$; $\mu, \nu, \kappa, \lambda \in [0, 1]$
$\mu, \nu, \kappa, \lambda$, represent the parameters enabling to "contextualize" the similarity.
Details about the expression (1) are presented in [JER 2001b].

1.2 Search instance modeling

1.2.1 Search instance representation

The results of various studies on search instance [JER 2001b], make highlight of following features of a search instance:

- The user profile represented by ***U***
- The user information need expressed by a query, represented by ***Q***
- The documents solutions represented by ***D***
- The evaluations ***E*** of relevancy of the documents ***D,*** given by the user U

Referring to the problem resolution field, the initial problem in information retrieval system is represented by the user profile ***U***, and his query ***Q***. Collected documents ***D*** represent the solution to the problem, and ***E*** the solution evaluation.

We propose a formal description of a search instance, carried out by a user, during an information retrieval session, (vector representation) as follows:

Instance = <U, Q, D, E>

- ***U*****:** represents the user features during the search session: $U=<U_1, U_2, U_3, U_4>$
- *Q*: As defined in information retrieval vector model [SAL 94]; giving the space Γ including all the corpus terms: $\Gamma = <t_1, t_2, t_3, \ldots, t_n>$, Q is the weighted term vector representing the user query, in the space E: $Q = <a_1, a_2, a_3, \ldots, a_n>$; a_i corresponds to the weight of the ith term of the query
- $\boldsymbol{D} = \{d_i\}$; D is a set of documents d_i; $i \in [1, p]$; $\boldsymbol{p}$: number of documents evaluated by the user; $p = |D|$; $\boldsymbol{d_i} = <b_{i.1}, b_{i.2}, b_{i.3}, \ldots, b_{i.n}>$; $\boldsymbol{d_i}$ is the vector representation of a document in the defined space Γ_{corpus}; $\boldsymbol{b_{i,j}}$ represents the weight of the jth term of the document d_i. $\boldsymbol{d_i}$ is the weighted term vector representing the document (or a part of the document) that the user have chosen and evaluated.
- ***E*** represents the evaluation given by the user U of the relevance of D according to Q

1.2.2 Instances similarity function

Giving the current instance represented by: $I_{current} = (U_{current}, Q_{current}, D_{current}, E_{current})$; We define the similarity function S_I between $I_{current}$ and another memorized instance I as shows the expression (2).

$$S_I(I_{current}, I) = S_U(U_{current}, U) * S_Q(Q_{current}, Q) \quad (2)$$

S_U was defined previously (§2.1.3)
Next we present the similarity function S_Q.

1.2.3 Similarity between queries and thesaurus use

The similarity of a query in a search instance, with the current user query, constitutes a discriminating criteria of choice of the instance to be reused. The question is how to quantify this similarity? As the queries are expressed in a vector space, to define their similarity, one is based on the functions of similarity suggested in the vector model in information retrieval field [SAL 94]. More precisely, the function of the cosine will constitute the basis of proposed similarity function.

The cosine function for similarity process consists in highlighting the joint terms of the two vectors, and making the sum of the products of the joint terms weights (expression (3)). The major disadvantage of this similarity function is that it is limited to the joint terms, and ignore "close" terms expressed in two vectors. This problem represents the major drawback in the Vector Space Model.

In order to mitigate the terms independence problem in the vector model, we propose to enrich the queries with their ***linguistic contexts***. The linguistic context enables to define the "semantically" related terms to the query terms. The linguistic context terms issue from a ***thesaurus*** (or linguistic knowledge base specialized in the application field), allowing to highlight semantic links between the terms. In the case of the thesaurus, it has three principal types of link: synonymy, hierarchy and neighborhood .

Giving the current user query Q_c, let us define
$Q_c = \langle a_{1c}, a_{2c}, a_{3c}, \ldots, a_{nc}\rangle + \langle \mathbf{a}_{(n+1)c}, \mathbf{a}_{(n+2)c}, \ldots, \mathbf{a}_{(n+m)c}\rangle$ (Linguistic context)
$\langle a_{1c}, a_{2c}, a_{3c}, \ldots, a_{nc}\rangle$ represent the weights of terms of the corpus space Γ_{corpus}
$\langle a_{(n+1)c}, a_{(n+2)c}, \ldots, a_{(n+m)c}\rangle$ represent the weights of terms of the thesaurus space $\Gamma_{thesaurus}$
Supposing t $(t = n+m)$ is the dimension of the total space terms, the simplified expression of Q_c is: $Q_c = \langle a_{1c}, a_{2c}, a_{3c}, \ldots, a_{tc}\rangle$; where $a_{ic} \in [0,1]$
$Sim(Q_r, Q_c)$ is the similarity function between the current query Q_c and another query Q_r; where $Q_r = \langle a_{1r}, a_{2r}, a_{3r}, \ldots, a_{tr}\rangle$, represented in the same space terms.
The proposed similarity function, based on the Cosine product, is expressed as follows:

$$Sim(Q_r, Q_c) = \frac{\sum_{i,j=1}^{t} a_{ic} a_{jr}}{\sqrt{\sum_{i=1}^{t} a_{ic}^2 \sum_{i=1}^{t} a_{ir}^2}} \qquad (3)$$

$Sim(Q_r, Q_c) \in [0,1]$; $Sim(Q_r, Q_c) = 1$ when $Q_r = Q_c$

1.3 Confidence degree of a search instance

The search instance (judged similar to the current one) is reused with a confidence degree. The concept of "confidence" is inspired by the multi-agents approaches. It is taken into account during the communication and the co-operation inter-agents [SHE 93]. It depends on the agent "performance". The performance is calculated on the basis of the evaluation results of agent contribution [MOU 96]. This implies a system tractability, and a global evaluation of an iteration success or failure. The agents confidence degree also intervenes in the system maintenance, in order to eliminate non-active and non confident agents.

In our context, we enrich the instance case, by a confidence degree which reflects the relevance of the instance.

The confidence degree of the instance is a function φ which depends on:

- S_I: the distance between the current instance and the useful instance. φ decreases when the S_I distance increases.

- The session date of the instance. Considering the fast evolution of the fields of user interest and his search profile, we consider that a "recent" case is more "useful" comparing to a "non recent" instance. Thus, φ increases when (current date - date session) decreases.
- The instance performance: To each instance, we assign an index of performance which will reflect its rate of contribution to improve the results of retrieval. After the reuse phase, the similar instance having contributed to the reasoning will see its performance to increase or decrease according to the quality of the documentary answers (principle of reward / penalty). In our case, since the relevance feedback is not obligatory for the user, it is difficult to evaluate the success or the failure of an iteration. In order to simplify this study, we propose to carry out an average of the evaluations E given by the user, to evaluate overall results of the search iteration.

2. Experience reuse for query expansion

Before presenting our proposition of query expansion based on experience reuse, we introduce in the next paragraph the classical approaches of query expansion based on relevance feedback.

2.1 Relevance feedback for query expansion

2.1.1 Relevance feedback

Query based information retrieval is a sequential process. It is rare that the initial search retrieves exactly what the user is looking for, therefore he or she can generally benefit from submitted a revised query based on what has been learned about the topic from the initial set of relevant documents. This process is known as relevance feedback [ROC 71]. One can modify the query by adding or deleting search terms and/or modifying term weights. Clearly, manual query construction and revision is a relatively arduous and complex task. Given a relevant document, it is difficult to determine what terms to add to the query and which terms are more or less important. Therefore, the most desirable approach is to develop an automatic relevance feedback process so that the system does the work of revising the query.

An automatic relevance feedback system can be designed like this: the system processes the initial query and returns a list of documents ranked in order of their predicted relevance to the user. The user examines a few of the highest ranking documents, determines whether or not they are relevant, and sends this information back the system. The system uses the analyzed documents to automatically construct a revised query and produces a new ranking of the remaining documents in the collection. The user can examine more documents and repeat the relevance feedback process as often as desired.

2.1.2 Feedback using the Vector Space Model: Rocchio

The VSM is ideally suited for automatic relevance feedback since it accepts free text input for the query. Therefore, we can simply incorporate some or all of the text from the relevant documents directly into the query. Non relevant documents can be utilized in a similar fashion. One of the most successful relevance feedback strategies was developed by *Rocchio* [ROC 71], and works as follows:

$$Q' = \alpha Q + \beta\left(\frac{1}{|D_r|}\sum_{d_i \in D_r} d_i\right) - \gamma\left(\frac{1}{|D_n|}\sum_{d_j \in D_n} d_j\right) \quad (4)$$

$\alpha, \beta, \gamma \in [0,1]$; d_i is weighted term vector representing a collected document
$|D_r|$ cardinality of relevant documents set
$|D_n|$ cardinality of non-relevant documents set
This strategy simply adds a weighted sum of the relevant document vectors and subtracts a weighted sum of the non relevant documents from the query. Relevance feedback using this strategy produces a very large improvement in retrieval performance (from 20-80% or more, depending on the collection) [SAL 86] [HAR 92] [AAL 92].

Adding the full document text directly into the query does have its drawbacks. The number of terms in the query grows rapidly with the addition of evaluated documents, causing searches to take longer and longer. A full search must be repeated for each iteration of relevance feedback. Since relevance feedback is supposed to be an interactive process, the system must be able to return feedback results in a relatively short period of time.

2.1.3 Drawbacks of Rocchio method based on relevance feedback

Although relevance feedback has proven to be an effective way to improve information retrieval performance, it is rarely used in practice [NIE 96]. This mechanism has been incorporated into several online search engines, but few users actually use it. Nie thinks that an important reason is the short term effect of a relevance feedback. A user has to make great efforts in evaluating documents, but the evaluation only has an effort on a single query. Once a new query is input, new evaluations have to be made. From the user's point of view, it is simply not worth the effort. However, we think users are ready to make the effort when the effect is permanent. Therefore, we will suggest a way to adjust the system's knowledge according to relevance feedback.

2.2 Knowledge base for relevance feedback

2.2.1 Relevance feedback and Instance reuse

Our proposal is based on the *Rocchio* method of query expansion. The principle approach of the proposed solution, consists on "completing" the documents used for the query expansion issued from the current relevance feedback, by the evaluated documents extracted from the previous search instances. On the basis of these documents -coming from both sources-, we apply the *Rocchio* approach of query expansion, as illustrated in Figure 2. Thus, terms added to the user query could result from the instance base documents, evaluated previously by the user or other users being in similar search contexts, and having similar profiles.

However, these two document sources (showed in Figure 2) are not independent, since the documents evaluated during the previous search iteration (Relevance feedback) represent also an instance contained in the memory of instances.

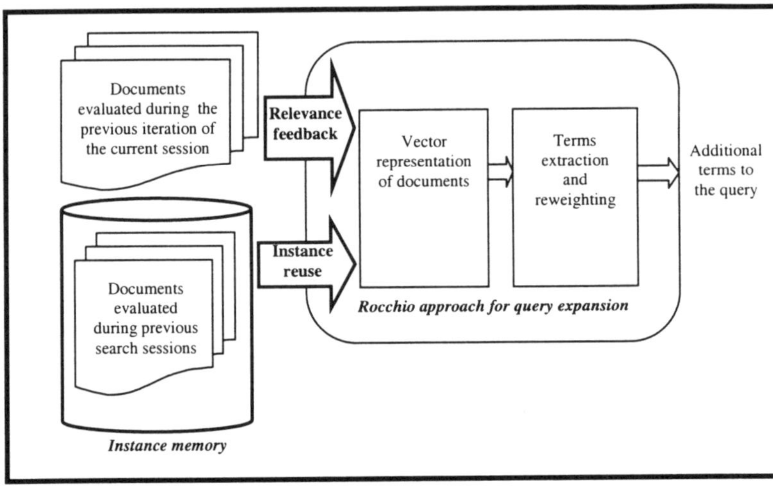

Figure 2: Instance reuse as complement to relevance feedback for query expansion

The interest of our proposal is primarily justified when no relevance feedback is made by the user during his search session. In this case, the reuse of the instance base constitutes an interesting alternative for the query expansion. Moreover, this enables to give a certain "freedom" to the user, because he doesn't have to evaluate documents relevancy to obtain system help to express his query.

Nevertheless, the instances reused cannot contribute in the same way for query expansion. For this, we propose to weight this contribution, according to the "confidence degree" of the reused instance. This concept will be detailed in the following paragraph.

2.2.2 Adapting Rocchio method for query expansion based on experience reuse

Giving the current instance represented by: $I_{current} = (U_{current}, Q_{current}, D_{current}, E_{current})$;

Instance$_{similar} = (U_{similar}, Q_{similar}, D_{similar}, E_{similar})$: the most similar instance to the current one ($\boldsymbol{I_{current}}$), with the confidence degree $\varphi_{similar}$.

$D_{similar}$ is a set of documents d_i; $\boldsymbol{d_i}$ is the weighted term vector representing the document (or a part of the document) that the user have chosen to evaluate; $\boldsymbol{d_i} = <b_{i.1}, b_{i.2}..., b_{i.n}>$;

$E_{similar}$ represents the evaluation given by the user, on the relevancy of $D_{similar}$ according to $Q_{similar}$.

The proposed expression of query expansion of $Q_{current}$, consists on adapting the *Rocchio* approach, by reusing the evaluated documents $D_{similar}$ extracted from the instance $I_{similar}$.

$$Q'_{current} = \alpha \times Q_{similar} + \varphi_{similar} \times \beta \left[\frac{1}{|D_{similar-r}|} \sum_{d \in D_{similar-r}} d_i e_i \right] + \varphi_{similar} \times \gamma \left[\frac{1}{|D_{similar-n}|} \sum_{d \in D_{similar-n}} d_i e_i \right] \quad (4)$$

$d_i \in D_{similar}$; $e_i \in E_{similar}$; $e_i \in [-1, 1]$; e_i corresponds to the evaluation of d_i

$\alpha, \beta, \gamma \in [0,1]$; α, β, γ are coefficients defined in the *Rocchio* expression (3).

$\varphi_{similar} \in [0,1]$; $\varphi_{similar}$ *confidence degree of* $I_{similar}$

$D_{similar-r}$ represent relevant document set of the instance $I_{similar}$
$D_{similar-n}$ represent non relevant document set of the instance $I_{similar}$
The new expression for query expansion is based on documents extracted from the instance base. The added terms result from documents evaluated by users when they were in similar search situations. However, we give more importance to the contribution of the instance coming from a relevance feedback compared to those coming from the instance memory. Hence, we propose to decrease by φ *(confidence degree of the similar instance)* the contribution of this instance in the proposed expression (4).

Nevertheless, when the used instance corresponds to a relevance feedback (documents evaluated by the same user during the same session of search), the confidence degree of this instance is maximal ($\varphi = 1$). In this case, the expression enables to apply the classical *Rocchio* approach.

2.2.3 Combining learning to the Rocchio approach

As presented above, our system allows two types of learning:
Long term learning thanks to the instance memory. The reuse approach and instance based learning allows the user to benefit from the aid of the system without having to interact and evaluate during each session, the collected documents (contrary to traditional methods of query expansion based on relevance feedback).

However, our solution is optimal when the number of instances of the instance base is significantly important. In the opposite case, the system functions, as *Rocchio,* are based on relevance feedback. The effectiveness of the instance base is well exploited when the user population using the system have common interests and carry out more exploitable common searches then other users. This is a classical constraint in the co-operative systems.

- ***Short term learning*** thanks to the training by reward / penalty of the search instances. The system evolves according to the failure / success of the proposed solutions.

3. Application case: sight deficient users

3.1 Project context

This research is carried out within the framework of a project of the Rhone-Alpes department. The project is entitled: "pedagogic information access systems for sightless users: use of speech and sound". From existing virtual libraries specialized in engineering sciences (scientific documents), the goal of this project is to produce an "intelligent" tool of information retrieval, adapted to the visually defective users. At this level, we are interested on the one hand in the design of an information retrieval system allowing to help the user to better formulate his information need on the one hand, and to offer to him a better access to the documents.

These specific users have particular information access difficulties, which is added to the traditional constraints of information retrieval (query formulation difficulties, irrelevant answers, etc). These accessibility difficulties are accentuated in the context of scientific documents (Braille transcribing and/or voice synthesis). This work concerning the accessibility aspects (Design of accessible IHM, transcribing Braille and/or vocal), was carried out in collaboration with the other partners of the project, and is detailed in [JER 2000b]. A work in close collaboration with "sight deficient" scientists enabled us to note that it becomes crucial for these users to have dedicated systems, taking in account their use profile. It becomes tiresome to these handicapped users to exploit the current information retrieval. This is due not only to the accessibility problems, but also to the imposed use logic of these systems (too interactive system, visual criteria, navigational logic, etc).

3.2 Sight deficient user profile

In this work, we applied the user model (§ 2) to the specific case of the sight deficient users, under a university context using scientific documents. In a study on the behavior of these users [BER 98], we highlighted the following features:

- The visual user group *(U_1)*: Sighted, Sight deficient, blind user
- The user category or function *(U_2)*: Student, Teacher, Researcher, Engineer
- The field of interest *(U_2)*: Mathematical, Natural science, Biology, etc.
- The knowledge about the system *(U_3)*
- The documentary preferences *($U_{4.1}$)*: restitution preferences (Braille, vocal), abstract extraction, document support, etc.
- The finality or goal of the search *($U_{4.2}$)*: bibliographical synthesis, technological survey, project study, etc.

These features are taken into account to evaluate the similarity of user profiles, by our prototype COSYDOR.

4. Experiments and evaluations using test corpus

4.1 COSYDOR prototype presentation

Our prototype COSYDOR (Cooperative SYstem for DOcument Retrieval) is based on *Intermedia* de Oracle 8i. We enriched *Intermedia* by an intelligent layer (developed in java) enabling the users query expansion and the management of the instance base (Figure 3).

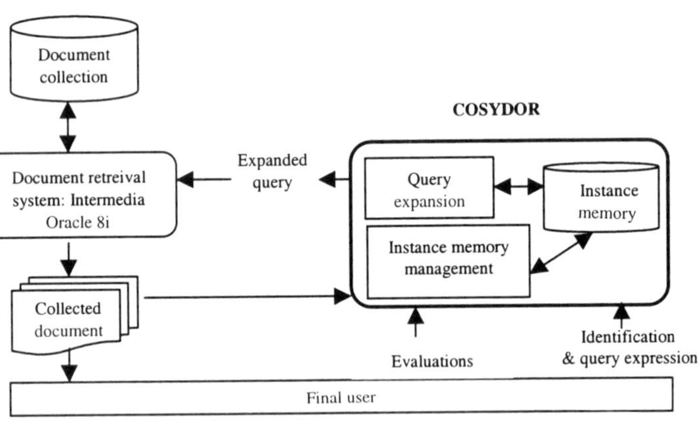

Figure 3: COSYDOR prototype

Intermedia is a textual DBMS, using linguistic tools (thesaurus, lexicon, etc.) for documents and queries representation. The choice of this tool results from a comparative survey on several information retrieval systems [JER 2001a]. *Intermedia* proved to be most relevant in our context. One of its advantages, is to offer paragraph extraction functionality, enabling to present document "views" during the document restitution to the user. This makes the user evaluation more precise on the one hand, and makes easier the access to the long documents for the sight deficient users on the other hand.

4.2 Test and evaluations

4.2.1 TREC test corpus

In order to test and to evaluate the contribution of our system, we have used a TREC corpus of test. TREC[1] (Text Retrieval Conference) is an American organization which provides a corpus of tests and common procedures of analysis of performance. Among this base of tests, we used and indexed a whole of 7000 documents, in format HTML, relatively long (approximately 600 mots/document) and specialized in the biomedical field. We reused the examples of search provided by TREC, and calculated the various indices of performance of our system: the rate of precision (a number of collected relevant documents / a total number of collected documents) and the rate of recall (a number of collected relevant documents / a total number of relevant documents of the documentary corpus).
In this base of tests, we used the expansion possibilities of our system to note our work contribution and improvement, compared to the *Intermedia* results. Our procedure of tests consists on iterations of retrieval, where query expansion are evaluated by "initiated" users. For each iteration, the rate of recall and the precision of the answers are processed.

4.2.2 Evaluations

In the carried out tests, we note that the rates of precision/recall are improved comparing to iteration 0, which corresponds to *Intermedia* performance. Thus, our solution enables to optimize *Intermedia* results. The experimental average of precision/recall rates for information retrieval is generally around O,3 [NIE 96]. These rates are often antagonistic, which justifies the shape of the obtained curves (Figure 3). We noticed that this is related to the type of expansion carried out. Indeed, we noted that the positive query expansion (terms extracted from relevant documents) causes a significant increase in precision rate (iteration 2 and 4). However, negative expansions were less effective.

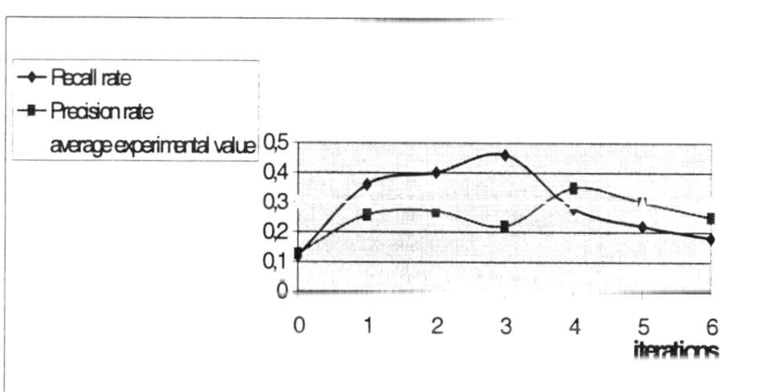

Figure 4: Performance evaluation of COSYDOR

Beyond the fourth iteration, we observed that the rates of recall / precision decreased. This is due to the length (a number of terms) of the query. Indeed, beyond a maximum number of added terms (5 terms in our context), the performance of expansion falls.

---

[1] http://trec.nist.gov

Moreover, the quantitative tests results enabled us to note the significant contribution to the system performance, of the weights assigned to the terms of the initial query.

The first evaluation results, although very encouraging, must be moderated by the limited number of tests (ten queries). Moreover, the users who contributed to the tests have very close profiles, and were previously initiated to the system use. It would be interesting to carry out these tests on a broader sample of users, having different profiles and having a visual handicap.

The second part of our evaluation consists on the comparison of COSYDOR performances versus other information retrieval systems using manual and automatic query expansion. The results of these systems were provided to us by TREC. First experimentation of these comparative tests are currently carried out in our laboratory.

5. Conclusion

The goal to build a knowledge base making "permanent" the user evaluations on search results, represents our first work motivation.

The search instances memory offers several improvements, compared to the *Rocchio* method of query expansion based exclusively on the relevance feedback.

The first advantage of the memorization consists to present an alternative solution to the *Rocchio* method, so that the user can be offered the system aid, without having to interact and to evaluate the collected documents, during each retrieval session. In fact, traditional methods of query expansion based on relevance feedback, are applied only after user interaction and after an evaluation of the retrieved documents relevancy. This approach "ignores" all knowledge chunks of the former search situations made by the user or by other users having "similar" profiles, and being in a close search situation.

The second advantage of the instance memory, is to enable the system to learn progressively, with experience acquisition. Indeed, the query expansion based on relevance feedback methods, constrain the system to make the same training during each session of search, from a search iteration to another, in order to arrive to an optimal query. Whereas, it would be interesting to avoid these repetitive stages, by memorizing the search instances and their corresponding evaluations.

The third advantage is related to user psychology. It will be much easier to get user to invest in the effort of evaluations, if they know that these will be permanent and reusable. This "reluctance" constitutes a real obstacle in the use of systems based on relevance feedback [NIE 96].

However, memorizing and reusing evaluations is a difficult task. It requires the ability to reproduce all the context of documents evaluation carried out by users, so that the memorized knowledge is representative of the moment, and the reuse is suitable. This justifies all the effort of contextual representation and modeling of search instance, presented in the first part of this paper.

These features were carried out in the COSYDOR system, implemented in Java, based on *Intermedia* (Oracle 8i). Tests and evaluations are carried out using the test corpus of TREC (7000 documents in the biomedical field) and their common procedures of performance analysis. The results show, for first search iterations, a significant improvement of performance compared to that of *Intermedia*. However, our sample of users is not sufficiently representative. Thus, an obvious direction for further research is to widen the sample of users in the experimental tests.

This work is carried out within the framework of a regional project, in which the sight deficient users constitute our application case. This research represents a considerable contribution for these users, considering their use difficulties of the current information retrieval systems (too interactive systems, accessibility problems, etc).

6. Acknowledgments

We thank Robert Laurini, Beatrice Rumpler, Abraham Alvarez for their reviewing and remarks.

7. References

[ALL 91] Allen N. Cognitive Research in information science: implication for design. *Annual review of information science and technology,* 1991, vol. 26, pp. 3-37

[ARM 95] Armstrong, R.; Freitag, T.; Joachims, T.; and Mitchell, T. WebWatcher: A learning apprentice for the World Wide Web, *In Proceedings 1995 AAAI Spring Symposium on Information Gathering from Heterogeneous distributed Environments*, AAAI Press.

[BEL 97] Belkin, N. Kay, J., Tasso, C. Special issue on User Modelling and Information Filtering . *User modelling and User adapted Interaction*, 1997, vol 7(3), pp. 313-331.

[BER 98] Bergère, T., Portalier, S. (1998). Modélisation du comportement de l'utilisateur déficient visuel. Workshop NTI SPI & santé. Chassey le Camp (France).

[BIL 99] Billsus, D., Pazzani, M. A hybrid User Model for New Story Classification. *Proceedings of the Seventh International Conference on User Modelling (UM'99),* Banff, Canada, 20-24 Juin 1999.

[BUC 98] Buckley, C., Mitra, M., Walz, J., Cardie, C. Using clustering and superconcepts within SMART: TREC 6. In E. M. Voorhees and D. K. Harman, editors, *The Sixth Text REtrieval Conference (TREC-6).* NIST Special Publication 500-240, 1998.

[COR 99] Corvaisier, F., Mille, A., Pinon, J.M. – Recherche assistée de documents indexés sur l'expérience (RADIX): Mesures de similarité des épisodes de recherche sur le WEB. *IC'99 Ingénierie des connaissances.*

[JER 2001a] Jéribi, L., Rumpler, B., Pinon, J.M. Recherche et traitement documentaire: Etude comparative d'outils existants. To apprear in : Techniques et Sciences Informatiques review, Edition Hermès.

[JER 2001b] Jéribi, L., Rumpler, B., Pinon J.M. Système d'aide à la recherche et l'interrogation de bases documentaires, basé sur la réutilisation d'expériences., *InforSID 7-9 juin 2001, actes des conférences, XIXème congrès,* 2001.

[JER 2000a] Jéribi, L., Rumpler, B., Pinon J.M. Personalised information retrieval in specialised virtual libraries. *New Library Worl review,* MCB press, VOL 101 N° 1153, 2000, p21-27.

[JER 2000b] Jéribi, L., Rumpler, B., Pinon J.M. Intelligent System for document retrieval and access to scientific documents for visually deficient users. 12-14 Avril 2000. *Conférence internationale de Recherche d'Information Assistée par Ordinateur, RIAO'2000: Accès à l'information multimédia par le contenu*, Paris (France). ISBN 2-905450-07-X, p 870-884.

[JER 98a] Jéribi, L., Rumpler, B., Pinon J.M. Intelligent retrieval in virtual libraries for education and training. 20-22Avril 1998. *ICCC/IFIP International Conference on Electronic Publishing: Towards the information rich society.* Central European University, Budapest (Hungry). p 144 – 157.

[JER 98b] Jéribi, L., Rumpler, B., Caelen J., Pinon J.M. COSYDOR. CO-operative SYstem for DOcument Retrieval. Application Case: Access System to Scientific Document for Sightless Users. 08-10 Décembre 1998. *MCSEAI'98: 5th Maghrebian Conference on Software Engineering and Artificial Intelligence*, Tunis (Tunisia). ISBN 9973-831-00-4, pp. 77 – 91.

[KOL 88] Kolodner J. L. (édité par). – *Workshop on case-based Reasoning, DARPA 88*. Clearwater, Florida, Morgan-Kaufmann, San Mateo, 1988.

[MAE 94] Maes, P. Agents that reduce work and information overload; *CACM*, 37 (7): 31-40,146-147

[MIL 99] Mille, A., Fuchs, B., Chiron, B. Raisonnement fondé sur l'expérience en supervision industrielle. *Revue d'Intelligence Artificielle* 13, 1999, p. 97-128.

[MOU 96] Moukas, A. G. Amalthaea: information discovery and filtering using a multi-agent evolving ecosystem. *In Proceedings of the conference on Practical Application of Intelligent Agents and Multi-agent Technology.*

[NIE 96] Nie, J, Y., Brisebois, M., Lepage, F., (1996). Information retrieval as counterfactual, *The computer journal*, 38(8): 643-657.

[PAZ 97] Pazzani, M., Billsus, D. (1997). Learning and revising user profiles: The identification of interesting web sites. *Machine learning* 27: 313-331.

[ROC 71] Rocchio, J,J. Relevance feedback in formation retrieval. In Gerard Salton editor, *The SMART retrieval system: Experiments in Automatic Document Proceedings,* pages 313-323. Prentice Hall, 1971.

[SAL 86] Salton, G. Text-retrieval systems, *Communication of the ACM*. July 1986, n° 7, p. 648-655.

[SAL 94] Salton, G., Allan, J., Buckley, C. Automatic structuring and retrieval of large text files, *Communication of the ACM*. February 1994, vol 37, n° 37, p. 97-109.

[SHE 93] Sheth, B., Maes, P. Evolving Agents for Personalised Information Filtering. In Proceedings of the Ninth IEEE Conference on Artificial Intelligence Applications.

[SMA 99] Smaïl, M. Recherche de régularités dans une mémoire de sessions de recherche d'information documentaire, *InforSID 2-4 juin 1999, actes des conférences, XVIIème congrès*, 1999.

[WEB 98] Webb, G. Special issue on Machine Learning for User Modelling. *User Modelling and user Adapted Interaction*, vol8 (1-2), Kluwer Academic Publishers.

*Electronic Publishing '01 –
2001 in the Digital Publishing Odyssey
A. Hübler et al. (Eds.)
IOS Press, 2001*

Print to Electronic: Measuring the Operational and Economic Implications of an Electronic Journal Collection

Carol Hansen Montgomery, Ph.D.
Linda S. Marion

*W. W. Hagerty Library
Drexel University
3141 Chestnut Street
Philadelphia, PA USA 19104
http:www.library.drexel.edu*

Abstract: As digital libraries move from demonstration projects to the real world of working libraries, it is critical to assess and to document the impact of the shift. This paper reports the methodology and initial results of an Institute for Library and Information Studies (IMLS) funded research study of the operational and economic impact of an academic library's migration to an all-electronic journal collection.

Drexel Library's entire print and electronic journal collections and associated staff are the test bed to study three key research questions:

(1) What is the impact on library staffing needs?
(2) How have library costs been reduced, increased and/or re-allocated?
(3) What other library resources have been affected?

We are using quantitative and qualitative methods to answer the research questions operationalized in the following tasks:

(1) Measure the staff time, subscriptions costs and other costs related to each activity required to acquire and maintain print and electronic journals.
(2) Compute the per-volume, per-title, and per-use costs of acquiring and maintaining print and electronic subscriptions.
(3) Study all impacted library services, including changes in reference service, document delivery, and instructional programs.

Initial results of measuring staff time indicate Information Services and Systems Operation departments constitute the majority of personnel costs for electronic journals. Technical Services and Circulation account for the majority of staff costs for print journals. Per title subscription costs appear to be substantially lower for electronic titles obtained through aggregator collections.

0. INTRODUCTION

The transition from the traditional mission of *building and archiving* a physical collection to *providing_access* to remote, globally dispersed electronic resources represents a fundamental paradigm shift for libraries. But does the traditional mission make sense in the global web-based information environment now used regularly by the overwhelming majority of the academic community? Our users want (*and expect*) easy, anytime, anywhere, access to information, and in 2001 this means delivery via the web to networked computers. In this model storing information in thousands of local library files does not make economic sense. Indeed, it is not even economically feasible. We must rather depend upon the formation and maintenance of central depositories by large organizations and publishers.

The tension between the paradigms is particularly salient in collection development of scholarly journals in academic libraries. Libraries made the transition, gradually and with minimum anguish, from collecting print abstracting and indexing resources to providing electronic access to them; however, the idea of replacing print with electronic journals is a source of much concern (Edwards, 1997; Hurd, 1999; Stewart, 2000; Keyani, 1999; Okerson, 2000). Several factors contribute to this concern. First, the pace of change is very rapid. For abstracting and indexing the transition took place gradually over nearly 30 years, but publication of electronic journal equivalents of important print journals accelerated dramatically three years ago and could be nearly complete in two more years. Second, new, reputable electronic-only journals are becoming commonplace. Finally, archiving is critical because journal literature is the primary scholarly record. Abstracting and indexing services are surrogates for the scholarly record, and thus presumably perceived as less necessary to archive.

In 1998 the staff of the W. W. Hagerty Library, Drexel University decided to make the transition to an all-electronic journal collection as quickly as possible. Print counterparts of electronic journals, with few exceptions, are not maintained, even when we must pay for them. This decision was based on several assumptions:

1. The electronic format serves our users better than print.
2. A critical mass and eventually the majority of scholarly journals of interest to our users would become available electronically within the next few years.
3. Maintaining a print collection takes significant resources that can be better used elsewhere.
4. Appropriate organizations would step forward and assume responsibility for archiving these journals.

Thus far, the first two assumptions have proven correct, and there is considerable evidence that our prediction about the last one was also right.[1] We are investigating the third assumption with the assistance of a grant from the Institute of Museum and Library Services. This paper describes the methodology used for determining personnel costs and preliminary results of that study.

This transition is happening faster at Drexel than at most, if not all, academic libraries in the United States. For 2001 renewals, the library subscribes to about 300 print journals and provides access to approximately 6,000 electronic journals through subscriptions and access to full-text databases. We expect to eventually have only a small browsing collection of about 100 titles in print. See Montgomery (2000) and Montgomery and Sparks (2000) for a description of the factors leading to this decision, and the collection policies and acquisition procedures.

Drexel is a technologically oriented urban university rated Research Intensive in the Carnegie classification, with strengths in engineering, computer science, information science and technology, design arts, and business. Current enrollment is 10,600 undergraduates and 2,500 graduate students. Full-time faculty members number just under 500. The largest colleges are Engineering and Business.

All library services are centralized in the W.W. Hagerty Library, an attractive, stand-alone modern facility of about 100,000 square feet. The print collection is approximately 370,000 volumes. The staff is comprised of 13 professional librarians, four systems staff, 23 support personnel, and seven graduate students from the college of Information Science and Technology who work half time in the Library in return for a stipend and tuition remission. Library patrons utilize Drexel University's new gigabit wired network along with Lucent Technology's local area wireless network. Thirty laptops, which are circulated, and Public Access Workstations consisting of 100 desktop computers are available for patron use. The Library manages its own web site and related servers.

1. LITERATURE REVIEW

Assigning costs to library services has always been a complicated process, and the advent of electronic resources has only compounded the process. Library managers and researchers have struggled for some time to develop appropriate and accurate models for measuring the economic consequences of the shift to electronic resources. The National Information Standards Organization (NISO), which recently sponsored a forum to discuss performance measures and statistics for libraries, concluded there is a critical need for systematic data collection as well as the development of new tools and approaches for practical application by the library community. Participants at the NISO forum acknowledged the difficulties of measuring and collecting data, particularly of electronic resources in the absence of standards (National Information Standards Organization 2001).

Several researchers have looked at methods for analyzing library costs (Abels 1997; Abels, Kantor, & Saracevic 1996; Saracevic & Kantor 1997; Kantor 1986). These authors, in a series of studies, investigated library services from the standpoint of unit costs, or functional cost analysis. Kantor and Saracevic identified two difficult problems in cost allocation for library services: allocation of salaries and the allocation of shared resources.

Abels (1997) advocated the use of sophisticated measures, such as Activity Based Costing, to determine costs. This method provides an analysis of what an organization or unit does over a period of time and the associated costs. Activity Based Costing concentrates on detailing all activities related to the focus of interest and assigning the time to particular cost centers. Through periodic samplings of time and related costs, information is gathered for use in determining staffing and resource allocation. These methods are adaptable to service organizations (Abels 1997; Danilenko 1994; Berts & Kock 1995).

ARL, in its New Measures initiative, is also supporting the development of statistics and performance measures to evaluate electronic information services (Association of Research Libraries 2000a,b). ARL is leading an effort to identify high impact library functions that call for economic study. These functions, known as cost drivers, offer library managers a focus for reducing source costs. At a brainstorming session at the American Library Association Midwinter meeting in February 2000, participants from various academic institutions identified potential cost drivers and recommended criteria for assessing them. The identified cost drivers are located in all departments of the library (Association of Research Libraries 2000c).

ARL is also sponsoring a Technical Services Cost Study (also known as a Time and Cost Study), in which five institutions, Cornell University, Iowa State University, Vanderbilt University, University of California at Santa Barbara and University of Missouri at Kansas City, are currently gathering data within their Technical Services Departments. The methodology uses a longitudinal approach and time sampling. All staff time is tracked for a seven day sample week. Four to six weeks are sampled annually, providing ongoing data (Association of Research Libraries, 2000d).

One model study for research on costs is the landmark Interlibrary Loan Cost Study sponsored by the ARL and the Research Libraries Group (Roche 1993). Survey results from seventy-six academic libraries were used to establish benchmark data on the costs of borrowing and lending materials. Information on direct costs included both staff and equipment costs but did not include indirect costs of major library functions or general overhead.

2. RESEARCH QUESTIONS

Drexel Library's entire print and electronic journal collections and associated staff are the test bed to study three key research questions related to the migration from a print to an electronic journal collection:

(1) What is the impact on library staffing needs?
(2) How have library costs been reduced, increased and/or re-allocated?
(3) What other library resources have been affected?

We will use both quantitative and qualitative methods to:

(1) Measure the staff time, subscriptions costs and other costs related to acquiring and maintaining print and electronic journal collections.
(2) Similarly determine the per-journal cost of acquiring and maintaining print and electronic subscriptions.
(3) Study all impacted library services, including changes in reference service, document delivery, and instructional programs.

This paper reports preliminary results from the initial phase of this research which includes an analysis of staff and subscription costs.

3. METHODOLOGY

The cost analysis we are conducting at Drexel follow the approach of the ARL/RLG Interlibrary Loan Cost Study (Roche 1993) and the ARL Technical Services Study. We are identifying the operational cost elements associated with journals in both print and electronic formats, including capital and operational components, and are looking at their contribution to the cost of maintaining the two journal collections.

We are developing two perspectives on Hagerty Library's transition to electronic journals: (1) a comprehensive comparison of the current costs of print and electronic journals; and (2) an assessment of overall changes in library costs since 1998, just prior to introduction of electronic journals. We use a number of different strategies to capture cost-related data. Personnel related costs amount to almost fifty percent of the library's operating budget. Therefore, in order to calculate the comparative costs of print and electronic journals, it is crucial to assess the amount of staff time spent on journal related activities. Staff time is tracked according to the tasks performed during sample weeks. The hourly salary of each employee is then multiplied by task time to arrive at task costs for each activity. Task times and costs are aggregated by library department.

Developing the instrument, Staff Activity Logs, and the data collection process took approximately six weeks. The project researcher (second author) met with staff members to formulate detailed lists of their journal related activities. We developed the activity checklists from the "ground up" for several reasons. First, we were unable to find any previously constructed lists of activities except for the Vanderbilt University Technical Services Cost Study, which unfortunately, investigated only Technical Services. Second, we believe that staff members are the individuals most knowledgeable about their jobs and the details of how their time is spent. Third, staff cooperation is critical in obtaining reliable, accurate and meaningful data. Our belief is that staff members will more readily support the goals and methods of the study if they have some ownership of the content and process in which they are participating. Fourth, we hope to provide a resource for future research. Lists compiled by Hagerty Library staff obviously differ in particular details from staff activities in other libraries; however, we expect that most of our staff's activities are generalizable across academic libraries. The conceptual model we presented to the staff was that of an organization in which professionals are asked to assign their billable time to various accounts. In this case, time spent on billable activities was assigned to pre-established categories for either print or to electronic journals.

The scope of the study is comparing print and electronic *journals*, not electronic and print *resources*. This distinction is crucial because we did not collect data on databases, only on journals. The scope made defining terms such as *databases* and *electronic journals* difficult because aggregators often include both abstracts and full text for some articles. We chose to define electronic journals as including both titles to which we acquire explicit and deliberate access through individual or group subscription and also those that are available through licensing full text databases (aggregators). We defined databases as resources with *only* abstracts or citations.

The process of assigning time to print and electronic journals called for staff members to view their jobs in a new way. Some staff found it difficult to separate the details of their activities because of their holistic view of their jobs. For example, an information services librarian focuses on finding the appropriate resource to respond to a patron's information need. That librarian sitting at the reference desk might spend some time working with print or online indexes as well as with online journals available through an aggregator. Technical Services workers similarly reported that their time with print and e-journal activities is commingled.

It is essential that the project be clearly endorsed by the Dean of Libraries, who is also the project's principal investigator. Although staff found the process of formulating the activity logs and recording the data time consuming and tedious, they also expressed interest in learning whether their perceptions about job changes wrought by the advent of electronic journals were, in fact, accurate.[2] The researcher translated results from interviews and meetings into checklists of activities. The checklists or Activity Logs were reviewed by staff and revised through an iterative process that occurred several times until the lists were defined adequately. We constructed a Data Dictionary containing definitions for the categories on the Activity Logs. The dictionary serves as a staff resource to prevent conceptual drift over time and will hopefully also become a model for future research.

Data collection officially began in mid-February 2001 and continued for eight weeks. Staff completed a daily Activity Log in which they recorded the number of minutes spent on a particular activity. Sampling will continue throughout the year by collecting data the first week of every month. Journal related activities in Hagerty Library follow a cyclical pattern, depending on renewal times and the academic calendar. Thus, we expect that this initial data collection period will show the smallest amount of journal related activity occurring during the year and will serve as a baseline or "steady state".

4. ANALYSIS OF RESULTS

4.1 STAFF TIME AND COSTS

The project research assistant collected completed Activity Logs daily and entered the data into Excel spreadsheets. See Table 1 for the major activities in each department[3]. The Table includes most staff and departments that work directly with journals. Administrative personnel, the Interlibrary Loan/Document Delivery Department and most of the Library

Systems Department are included in overhead expenditures, which will be reported at a later date.

Table 1: Major Journal Related Staff Activities By Department

Department	Journal Related Activities
Circulation	Reshelving current and bound volumes
Information Services	Information literacy workshops Liaison & communication with faculty & students Reference services Collection development
Technical Services	Vendor related activities, including ordering, renewing, canceling, claiming Current periodical activities, including check-in, processing, binding
Systems Operations	Maintaining E-resources web page Support for staff web pages Assist faculty/students with access problems Resource development Maintaining existing resources Problem troubleshoot Liaison with other staff

See Table 2 for staff time and annualized costs, derived from multiplying staff time by the total salary *and benefits* for each worker. Individual totals were aggregated by department. The relationships among departmental costs are presented in Graph 1 and Graph 2. Several observations are immediately apparent. Total staff costs associated with print are considerably higher than staff costs related to electronic journals in this low activity period. This ratio will change when we measure activity during the journal renewal period which takes a great deal of the time (categorized as Collection development) of the Information Services Department.

Not surprisingly, there is a large departmental difference in the amount of time and costs associated with each journal format. The Information Services staff and part of the Systems Operations staff constitute the major categories of staff costs for electronic journals. Information Services staff are on the "front lines" in the library, working with students and faculty, demonstrating how to access electronic journals as well as answering reference questions. The Systems staff is responsible for making the electronic journals available and accessible via the library's web site.

*Table 2: Annualized Print and E-journal Costs by Staff Category**

	Print		Electronic	
	Hours	Costs	Hours	Costs
Circulation	1,139	$15,800	0	$0
Information Services	379	$8,241	830	$19,082
Technical Services	2952	$51,326	73	$1,709
Systems Operations	-	$0	779	$23,401
Total	4,470	$75,367	1,682	$44,192

** Annualized from eight weeks of data. Note that these numbers represent a period of low staff activity for journals.*

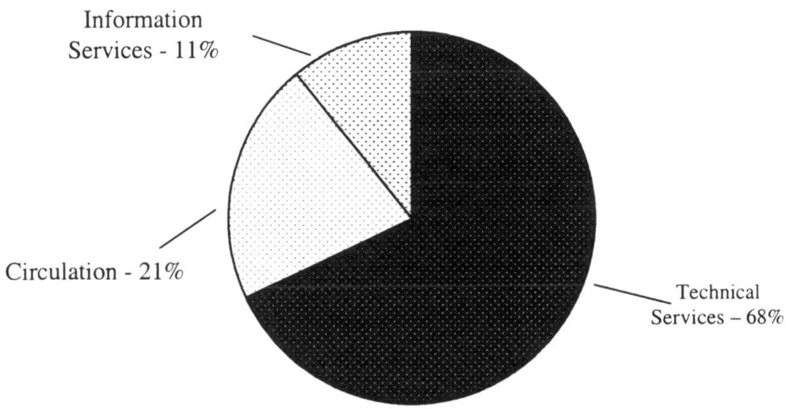

Fig.1: Print Journal Costs by Staff Category

Print journals, on the other hand, present a very different constellation of staff costs. Technical Services and Circulation staff, who do shelving, represent almost ninety per cent of the staff costs for print journals. It is important to note that the Interlibrary Loan/Document Delivery, which works exclusively with print journals, is not included in this preliminary analysis.

These ratios do not include either non-personnel costs, such as equipment maintenance and bindery or capital costs, such as for computer hardware and software or the capital building costs. They will be included in the final analysis at the end of this study.

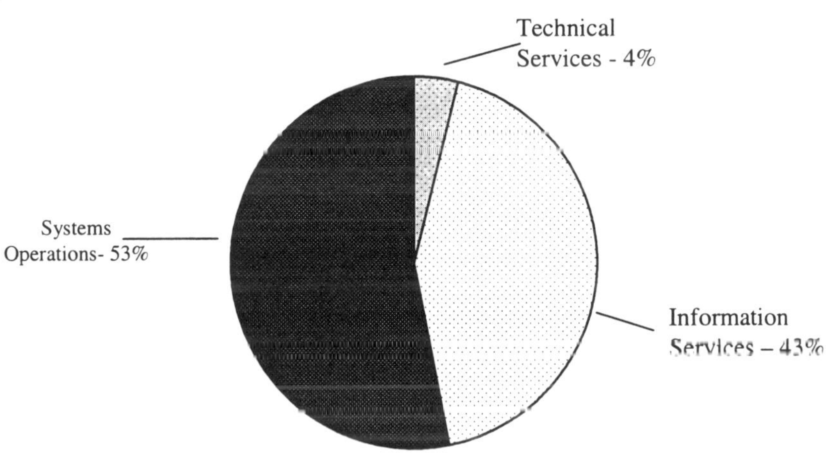

Fig. 2: Electronic Journal Costs by Staff Category

4.2 SUBSCRIPTION COSTS AND USE

Table 3 shows the range of costs associated with journal formats subscribed to by Hagerty Library. Print "only" are those titles which have no electronic counterpart. Titles for which we must subscribe to the print in order to receive the electronic versions are counted in Electronic Subscriptions. We define Electronic Subscriptions to be titles for which we have a subscription to the individual title with a persistent URL. We may purchase these titles individually or in groups from a single publisher or individually through a vendor such as OCLC. Aggregator Databases are services such as ProQuest or Lexis/Nexis that contain a mix of abstracts and the full text or partial full text of journals.

Table 3: Per Title Cost Information Spring 2001

Format	Number of Titles	Ave. Cost per Title
Print "only"	300	$120/title
Electronic Subscriptions	2,800	$196/title
Aggregator Databases	3,500	$ 12/title

These numbers are a snapshot in time (Spring 2001); Electronic Subscriptions and Aggregator Databases are a constantly moving target. The number of titles changes continuously in aggregator databases as titles are added or dropped without consultation with users and, often, without any notification. Our current small print collection includes about one-third general interest browsing journals, with most of the other print journals in the humanities, art and social sciences. On average, these titles are much less expensive than science and engineering journals. The latter have been leaders in converting to digital format and, along with business publications, form the majority of the Electronic Subscriptions collection. On the other hand, both types of electronic journals frequently come with several back years for the same price, a factor which makes these journals less expensive on a per volume basis. A comparison by volume would lower the cost of electronic publications compared to print.

Overall, these numbers cannot be generalized to other libraries' situations as they reflect Drexel's particular "deals" with vendors. Nevertheless, it is safe to say that on a simple title-by-title basis the journals in the aggregator databases cost far less than those from the other two sources. But all journals are not the same, and the title-by-title comparison does not reflect relative value. Both the print and E-Subscription titles are selected carefully to match the needs of our students and faculty. We have access to them for the subscription (i.e. calendar) year. Libraries subscribe to the Aggregator databases and the electronic journals in them as a whole ("what you see is what you get") and this can change from day to day. Also, coverage of titles may be partial in aggregator collections and often tables, illustrations and figures are not included.

Table 4 shows use data for the Drexel library's print journal collection in 1998/99 and 2000/01 (extrapolated). Several factors confound this data. The number of discontinued print titles is 3427, far greater than the number of current subscriptions in either time periods. The library had about 130,000 bound journals volumes in 1998/99 and, after extensive weeding, about 95,000 in 2000/01. For about five years preceding 1998/99 Drexel's print journal subscriptions were stable, but then decreased dramatically from 1999 to 2001. Cost per use cannot be calculated without accounting for these factors.

Table 4: Print Journals Use and Cost

Year	No. of Titles	Uses	Total Cost	Cost/Title
98/99	1,710	45,305	$375,203	$219
00/01*	300**	26,435	$36,000	$120

*Cost figures are given for the calendar Year 2001, while use covers 07/00-06/01 (extrapolated), and includes counts for titles that were cancelled in 2001.
**2001 subscription year titles only

Table 5 shows electronic journal use and cost data for several types of suppliers in 2000/01. The use data comes from publishers and is defined here as a view of a full-text file or download of a PDF file. Unfortunately, we cannot compute use data for all our electronic journals because it is not available from all publishers.

Table 5: Sample Electronic Journal Use and Cost (00/01) (Extrapolated)

Type of Publisher	No. of Titles	Uses	Total Cost	Cost/Title	Cost/Use
Society Publisher	32	4,352	$ 21,980	$687	$5.05
University Press	134	9,742	$ 6,000	$ 45	$0.62
Commercial Publisher	1,174	54,199	$123,960	$106	$2.29
Commercial Aggregator	1,791	106,000	$ 20,263	$ 11	$0.19

One very clear conclusion can be drawn from these numbers: *Electronic journals are used more heavily than print journals.* Even taking into account that the University has grown in the last three years, and that the print counts are *per-volume* while the electronic counts are *per article* which would make them somewhat higher, the differences are startling. Two of the sample electronic collections shown in Table 5 were used more than all the 1710 current print titles and 130,000 [est] bound volumes held by the library in 1998/99. There is significant variation in the cost per title and cost per use for these sample publishers. The Aggregators is the least expensive, but all are far less expensive than, for example, obtaining an article via Interlibrary Loan.

5. NEXT STEPS

To determine the average unit cost of print journals compared to the unit cost of electronic journals we will continue to record staff time throughout the year. Because of the increase in time taken by the renewal process in early Fall, this is the only way to obtain an accurate picture. We will also complete measurement of the non-staff, non-subscription capital and operations costs to provide a picture of the true cost of each journal format. To do this, adjustments must be made for major complexities not accounted for above, such as length of journal runs and age of journal volumes. Ultimately we will compare costs on three units of measure: per-volume, per-title, and per-use.

6. FOOTNOTES

1. A number of major archiving initiatives have begun. They include:
Library of Congress - http://memory.loc.gov/ammem/amhome.html.
Association of Research Libraries (ARL) - http://www.arl.org/preserv/index.html.,
Council on Library and Information Resources – http://www.clir.org/diglib/preserve/criteria.htm,

The JSTOR Project - http://www.jstor.org/,
Online Computer Center Library (OCLC) -http://www.oclc.org/oclc/presres/,
Open Archives Initiative (OAI) – http://www.openarchives.org,
UK Digital Preservation Coalition - Joint Information Systems Committee (JIDC) – http://www.jisc.ac.uk/dner/preservation/dpcintro.htm,
The British Library Digital Library - http://www.bl.uk/.
2. Staff members will also be interviewed about their perceptions of the job changes occurring with electronic journals. The results of these interviews will be reported separately.
3. Detailed lists of activities is available in the Data Dictionary, which can be found at http://www.library.drexel.edu/facts/imls/default.html.

7. REFERENCES

Abels, E. G. (1997). Improving reference service cost studies. *Library & Information Science Research, 19(2)*, 135-152.

Abels, E. G., Kantor, P. B., and Saracevic, T. (1996). Studying the costs and value of library and information services: Applying functional cost analysis to the library in transition. *Journal of the American Society for Information Science, 47(3)*, 217-227.

Association of Research Libraries. (2000a). ARL statistics and measurement program. Retrieved April 4, 2001 from the World Wide Web: http://www.arl.org/stats/index.html

Association of Research Libraries. (2000b). ARL: A Bimonthly report on research library issues and actions from ARL, CNI, and SPARC. Retrieved April 4, 2001 from the World Wide Web: http://www.arl.org/newsltr/210/emetrics.html

Association of Research Libraries. (2000c). Investigation of cost drivers. Retrieved April 4, 2001 from the World Wide Web: http://www.arl.org/stats/newmeas/costdriver.html

Association of Research Libraries. (2000d). Technical services cost study. Retrieved April 4, 2001 from the World Wide Web: http://www.arl.org/stats/newmeas/tcs_overview.html

Berts, K. & Kock, S. (1995). Implementation considerations for activity-based cost systems in service firms: The unavoidable challenge. *Management Decisions, 33(6)*, 57-63.

Bowen, W. (1998). JSTOR and the economics of scholarly communication. *Journal of Library Administration, 26(1/2)*, 27-44.

Danilenko, G. (1994). Activity based costing for services: The corporate information center. *Special Libraries, 85(Winter)*, 24-29.

Edwards, J. (1997). Electronic journals: Problem or panacea? *Ariadne, 10.* Retrieved April 4, 2001 from the World Wide Web: http://www.ariadne.ac.uk/issue10/journals/

Hurd, J. M. (1999). Serials management: Adrift during a sea change? *Journal of Library Administration, 28(2)*, 77-89.

Kantor, P. (1989). Library cost analysis. *Library Trends, 38(2)*, 171-188.

Kantor, P. (1986). Three studies of the economics of academic libraries. *Journal of Library Administration, 5*, 221-286.

Kantor, P. & Saraceivic, T. (1999). Quantitative study of the value of research libraries: A foundation for The evaluation of digital libraries. *Proceddings of the 62nd ASIS Annual Meeting.* Washington, D.C. October 31-November 4, 1999. Medford, NJ: Information Today, 407-419.

Keyhani, A. (1999). Coping with the digital shift: Four of the thorniest issues. *The Serials Librarian, 36(1/2)*, 149-162.

Montgomery, C. H. (2000). Measuring the impact of an electronic journal collection on library costs. D-Lib Magazine, October. Retrieved April 4, 2001 from the World Wide Web: http://www.dlib.org/dlib/october00/montgomery/10montgomery.html

Montgomery, C. H. & Sparks, J. (2000). Framework for assessing the impact of an electronic journal collection on library costs and staffing patterns. Retrieved April 4, 2001 from the World Wide Web: http://www.si.umich.edu/PEAK-2000/montgomery.pdf

National Information Standards Organization. (2001). Report on the NISO forum on performance measures and statistics for libraries. Retrieved April 11, 2001 from the World Wide Web: http://www.niso.org/stats-rpt.htm

Okerson, A. (2000). Are we there yet? Online e-resources ten years after. *Library Trends, 48(4)*, 671-693.

Roche, M. (1993). *ARL/RLG Interlibrary Loan Cost Study.* Washington DC: Association of Research Libraries.

Stewart, A. (2000). Choosing between print and electronic resources: The selection dilemma. *The Reference Librarian, 71*, 79-97.

Vanderbilt University. (2000/2001). Vanderbilt University library technical (and related) services time and cost study 2000/2001. Retrieved April 4, 2001 from the World Wide Web: http://staffweb.library.vanderbilt.edu/admin/CostStudy/Intro.htm

Electronic Publishing '01 –
2001 in the Digital Publishing Odyssey
A. Hübler et al. (Eds.)
IOS Press, 2001

A year without print at Princeton, and what we plan next

David Goodman
Princeton University Library
Princeton, NJ, USA
dgoodman@princeton.edu

Abstract: Princeton has begun to receive some major titles as electronic only, beginning with the 2000 subscription year. We are doing this in appropriate cases where we have confidence in the stability, archiving, and performance of the publisher, and where the financial advantage is significant. Not only have there been no complaints, but there have been almost no comments. Apparently users now look for current journal articles online , using the paper versions only if online is not available.

0. INTRODUCTION

Among large American research universities, only Princeton has begun to receive some major titles as electronic only. Drexel has done the same, but it is a technologically-oriented small university with the special benefit of a library school, and is part of a program to rapidly provide library resources primarily in electronic form in conjunction with a campus equipped for overall wirêless access. At Princeton, we do not plan such a rapid change, but rather a continuous series of changes in the way library services are requested and delivered.

This discussion represents the author's personal view, and should in no sense be taken as the official position of the Princeton University Library. Rather, it represents his interpretation of current trends in the thinking of himself and many of his fellow librarians. Even when I refer specifically to our policy, it represents my understanding of what the administration and staff of the library jointly intend--but still is not to be taken as an official statement. Certain possible developments of our system will be discussed, but no guarantee whatsoever is given that any of the possibilities will actually reach fruition.

1. BACKGROUND

Princeton is relatively small for an American research university, with an enrollment of about 4600 undergraduates and 1700 graduate students; there are about 900 faculty and 800 professional and technical staff. This is a much higher faculty/student ratio than usual in American universities, and a greater emphasis is placed upon undergraduate education than at larger research universities. But the main difference is that there are no professional schools except small ones in architecture and public affairs: no business school, no medical school, no law school, no school of education, no schools of natural resources, agriculture, or forestry.

The Princeton library is not the largest or richest among American university libraries, but because of the small student body, is by far the most expensive per student: the acquisitions budget alone is over $1600/student; with a comparably very high staff/user ratio. This permits us to offer a very personal level of library service; good American college libraries, many of which give the same individual attention, do not generally attempt to maintain as complete a research collection. The library has great depth in all the classic departmental areas of the humanities, social sciences, and sciences; it has much less strength in applied, interdepartmental, or newly arising subject areas. We have very ample storage facilities, and a general policy of never discarding any item in usable condition unless a duplicate.

2. E-JOURNALS AT PRINCETON

When we first began to get e-journals at Princeton, we, like everyone, got them as supplements to the print.[1] Our first experiments without print were, as typical, with databases. We quickly observed that the students would use only the electronic versions. I remember during one network failure of our *Medline*, trying to get some of the students to ise the printed *Index Medicus* along the wall of the same room; they all preferred to wait until the next day if necessary. After a few experiences like that, we discontinued print versions. We do make a careful distinction of those services like *Ulrich's*, where the online version shows only the current year's data, and maintain a continuing complete set of the print.

At the Biology Library we made a brief count of unbound journal usage for two months in the fall of 1999. As we had suspected, only a very few titles were used significantly in that format, even those that were used very heavily as bound journals. People apparently read through or even browse a very small range of titles, compared to the wide range they use for articles to read. At the same time, as more and more journals became available electronically, we realized that we should offer them in that format if at all possible.[2]

For many years, Princeton's general policy had been not to join plans like IDEAL or ScienceDirect. For the titles we owned, paying a 20% surcharge did not seem attractive, considering the second rank level of a good many of them. For the ones we did not own, we would have bought a few if we had the money, but most would have been of so little use that document delivery of some sort was a preferable solution. Nonetheless, our patrons very much wanted the easy availability from their desktops, and the e-journals were at that time not available except as part of a complete consortium package.

At the end of 1999, we were offered an end-of-the-year opportunity to join IDEAL as part of the NERL (North East Research Libraries) consortium. Of course, by that time we had already spent almost all of the science funds for the 1999-2000 year on our regular subscription renewals. By various administrative tricks, we were able to find just enough money to pay the necessary charge to continue them--but to continue the electronic only, and to begin with only the 1999 subscription year, not the full 1993+ backfile. Any individual selector who thought worthwhile had the option of paying the

---

[1] The best printed summary of the state of the art in electronic journals is. C. Tenopir and D. K. King, *Towards Electronic Journals: Realities for Scientists, Librarians, and Publishers.* New York, Special Libraries Assoc., 2000.

[2] D. Goodman , "Should scientific journals be printed: A personal view." *Online Information Review* 24(5): 357-363 (2000).

25% surcharge for print. In the event, we paid it for only 9 of the 112 titles, mostly in mathematics. We also obtained electronic versions only for the three biology titles from Rockefeller University Press, which were priced so that electronic and print together cost twice as much as either one alone, and the 6 titles from the American Physiological Society, which were voluminous in paper and offered a 10% discount. For the 2001 subscription year, we added another small group of titles from American Society for Microbiology and from the Society for Plant Physiology. We are still not a member of Elsevier's ScienceDirect, but if we ever join, we will certainly continue only very few titles in print. Many of the titles not continued in print are by no means marginal titles, and in some cases leading titles in their fields.[3]

Many universities have received special funding for electronic resources . If we had had such funding, would we still have discontinued the print? We chose not to get both versions of the biological society journals, though the cost would have required only the cancellation of one or two additional commercial titles. We consider this justified where the financial advantage is significant, where browsing use is trivial, and where we trust the stability and performance of the publisher. We are driven by two different considerations: the desire to anticipate inevitable future developments, and the financial advantages. Many universities are willing to adopt electronic-only but just for marginal titles, and universities joining plans like IDEAL are automatically accepting it for the additional titles made available. In general research universities are continuing to receive major core titles in print--even when it costs double. Naturally, many smaller institutions are adopting electronic-only to varying degrees, and in their case it seems an even more obvious strategy.

3. ACCEPTANCE AND USABILITY

Before proceeding with IDEAL, some selectors did obtain the specific approval of all concerned faculty--or at least of the ones who spoke up. Others, including myself, did not made a formal survey, or ask the faculty or other users as a whole, knowing from continuing discussions that our users would find it desirable. Several faculty members in various departments, who in past years had expressed their total unwillingness to consider such projects, now said some version of "well, I guess the time has come."

This seems to have received total acceptability at Princeton, where we have now been without print copies of these journals since January 2000. Our Voyager online catalog shows the print and online status, and we have an electronic journals page on the web, but we have otherwise deliberately made the minimum of formal announcements. At the Biology Library, we initially obtained electronic tables of contents from the publishers for all titles received in electronic form only. They were placed in binders, on the shelf where the unbound issues had formerly been, but, as they received very little use, we have now discontinued them. One user expressed his unhappiness at not having the printed contents, but was delighted when we explained how he could get tables of contents e-mailed directly from the publisher, which he considered a much superior solution. Now we retain only signs reminding them of the situation.

There have been no complaints; even more significantly, there have not even been any comments. Users in the sciences and corresponding social sciences now look for current journal articles online first, using the paper versions only if there is no online available. We think they generally do this directly from databases like PubMed or

---

[3] A complete list is available on our web site (http://www.princeton.edu/~biolib/serials/ap)

Inspec or from citations in other articles, more than they look for the journal specifically. They do not yet do this for earlier years, although an increasing number of titles are now available. In the humanities, where few titles are currently available, some of the most important have backfiles available from J-STOR and similar projects, and these receive heavy use. Over the next two years we will be studying the relative use of the print and online version of these titles, in order to decide whether they should be transferred to a storage area.

Users have been quite forgiving of occasional difficulties. There was one period where the Academic Press titles were unavailable for almost a week due to failure of their server. Patrons, somewhat to my surprise, accepted this: they were in almost all cases indeed looking for an individual article, and the situation was just the same as if the issue had been unavailable at the periodical bindery. What they really complain about, is when a title once available becomes totally unavailable--as with *Nature*.[4]

Asides from this, the very first complaint occurred this spring in a special context. One of the biology graduate students had the responsibility of scanning certain current titles for her group. Her complaint was that she found both the online tables of content on the publishers web site, and the emailed contents from the publisher, much less compact and readable than the printed version.

This is a valid complaint. No publisher or distributor has yet found an adequate information-dense way of presenting the contents of a journal issue in browsable form. The actual articles are no problem, since no human reads them on the screen, but rather prints them out and then reads them. This is probably a function of current screen resolution; tech-nological progress in this area has been very slow as compared to other aspects of computer technology. Some of it may be biocultural adaptation. I find that I (and others) have an expectation based on format: something on screen is something to be read quickly--a source of immediate current information. Something on paper is to be studied. Furthermore, like most librarians I am very rapid at scanning printed material. I am much slower with online material--but over the last two years I have found myself getting faster at it, as my mental and visual circuitry adapts.

Another distinction is that I myself, and an increasing number of users, do not store the paper printouts. I read them and discard them. I myself usually save the PDFs or other images on my computer: hard disk space has become extremely inexpensive and we have automatic central backup and archiving. I am much more likely to locate a paper by the criteria in an electronic search than in a physical filing cabinet. Those more advanced than I do not even store the images: they know they can find the item again from the original source if they have the need.

4. ARCHIVING AND STABILITY

We are aware that this is in advance of the full development of the technology. Distrust of the stability and permanence of electronic publishing enterprises can cause rational hesitancy. There are several levels to ensuring availability. The most basic level is that a journal work consistently, with essentially 100% uptime. This should even include Jan.1, where the journal should work without the need to re-register or re-verify the subscriptions. The technical requirements are known: a competent business office, competent technical support, advance notification of changes and downtime, a sufficient

[4] D. Goodman. "*Nature* and others: Restricted electronic access as financial discrimination" " *Proceedings of the 22st National Online Meeting*. N.Y. Information Today, 2001, in press.

number of reliable mirrored servers with automatic switchover--not just for the journal content but for the auxiliary files like the subscriber list--all in at least two separated locations, with redundant internet connections and no single point of failure.

The next level is that a library must retain ownership and access to what it has purchased. The simplest way for this, with the lowest administrative costs, is the current proposal to make all content free to the world after 6 or 12 months. Alternative acceptable routes all have significant administrative costs, which the library that has cancelled can expect to pay.

The third level is long term rights availability. Unless the rights become public after 6 or 12 months, this requires that the publisher possess either ownership of the electronic rights to the material, or a perpetual and non-revocable license, and a commitment to making the material available though an acceptable and reliable source such as OCLC, regardless of business or technical changes. Many commercial and university publishers are publishing journals for scientific societies, and the societies own the rights. This is not acceptable unless the publisher has at the least a non-revocable license to the years already published if the society should change publishers. It is also not acceptable for a publisher to sell a journal to another publisher, without retaining the electronic rights to the years published, or making equivalent or better arrangements. Now that we are aware of this, all contracts should provide not merely that the publisher use his best efforts, but that he guarantee: what he sells when he sells the journal is under his control.

The fourth level is long term technical availability--the conventional meaning of electronic archiving. The standards are known, and will not be discussed now. They include the commitment to transfer the material to new media as it develops, to use long-lived standards, and to rely on a permanently existing non-commercial agency that can guarantee this--preferably a national library. Personally, I think that this should be supplemented by additional dimensions of protection, and that the major scientific societies, and major universities should replicate the preservation process. The free availability of the rights obviously facilitates this.

The fifth level is very long term survival, possibly past the demise of technological civilization. The simple answer is short-run printing, on paper, microform, titanium, or granite. Given a large enough comet, the preservation of *BBA* or even *Cell* will be the least of our worries.

5. MEASURED USE

It has been generally observed in a very wide variety of situations that the use of a journal electronically is about 5 to 10 times the use of the same journal in print at the same institution. Part of this is measurement error: one cannot capture every print use; one can in the right circumstances capture each electronic use. The difference is partly the substitution of direct electronic access for indirect access, such as lending someone a copy. But it is partly the actual true increased use of the information. I am not aware of any adequate studies of these factors; interviews with my users suggest that the increase in true use is a factor of about 2. This is not as startling as the apparent factor of 10, but it is a real major difference: it corresponds to a doubling of circulation.

Some studies have found that users will use anything in electronic format, even material that is of no apparent value, would not be used in print, and would not be requested on interlibrary loan. This is sometimes called the Ohio paradox, as it first became apparent in the analysis of the Ohionet data. Typically, it is found that if an institution obtains electronic access to all the journals of a publisher, those that the institution had not previously subscribed to are used almost as much as those it had. The cynical explanation is that selectors can't tell the difference, and select based on tradition rather than usefulness. I am aware of such examples at Princeton, and I assume it occurs in Ohio, but the general level at most universities is better than that.

Table 1 reports the data for Princeton's experience with Academic Press, as compared to the reported figures from Ohio State University. For our users, mere availability of the additional titles did not result in their extensive use, thus showing that the electronic format can be a delivery system for increasing appropriate use, not a way to encourage the patrons to use articles they don't need. The data from the two universities are not strictly comparable: Princeton's data is for IDEAL only, the OSU for both IDEAL and ScienceDirect. Princeton's availability covered only 1 to 2 years of each title; Ohio's covered 5 years or more. The Ohio project was promoted extensively; ours was not, and any novelty effect of electronic journals had worn off in the two years before Princeton's project. OhioNet and others will surely report more data for subsequent years, and it will be possible to determine the cause of the initial anomaly. I predict that their use will come to resemble the Princeton data.

Table 1. Use of E-Journal Articles From Owned And Unowned Titles

	Titles Previously Held	Articles Read From Titles Previously Held	Titles Not Previously Held	Articles Read From Titles Not Previously Held
Princeton	60%	93%	40%	7%
OSU	56%	72%	44%	28%

6. FUTURE PLANS

6.1 Additional journals

One might think that the obvious course of action is for us to expand this to other publishers. For some publishers there has been no question of the value of the material to us, and we have added the electronic versions under contracts providing access to additional titles. Unfortunately, these publishers' contracts are often such that we would get little or no savings from discontinuing print. Worse, they often also do not yet provide the guarantees of third party continuation of material that Academic Press and Elsevier provide. When both conditions are met, we will gladly drop our print to the same extent as for Academic Press. It is true that even if there were no savings in price, there would be a cost savings from the lack of the need to process and store the print, but we do not regard that as sufficient financial incentive, for the purely chauvinistic reason that this savings does not come from the acquisitions budget. We similarly have blanket order plans with many scientific societies, most of which similarly offer no cost savings.

For some publishers, the question here has been the value of the material. Many of my colleagues question whether the intrinsic quality of their journals is worth the price; even if they provide all their journals in electronic form, many of my colleagues think it is still not worth the price. I do not always agree. Though the content for many titles is objectively not of great use, the additional accessibility does increase what usefulness there is, and the only readily apparent way of getting the accessibility is to pay the cost, outrageous as it is. We have the obligation to reform the system for future users, but I am very aware of our obligation to provide currently needed material for the present users. If our non-participation could change the system, I would support not participating, but that unfortunately does not seem to be the case. We are currently attempting to resolve the situation by exploring various subject options as now offered. But it is certain that, if we were to participate in additional plans, for those publishers with assured third-party backup, we would continue only a very few of the journals in print--probably about one-tenth, as for Academic Press.

6.2 Non-journal material

We are very interested in the various e-book schemes. With current display technology, we do not see using them for our basic copy of any material, except perhaps some relatively ephemeral items. But we want them as second copies, and we especially want them for electronic reserves. So far we have been limited by the willingness of the publishers to publish current academic and research material in this format. The most popular service any university library can offer, as far as its undergraduates are concerned, is electronic reserves. At present we are photocopying most of the material ourselves under license, and find the photocopying is even more burdensome than the licensing. For those subjects that require whole books, rather than selections, we will wait until the publishers make them available.

The most truly revolutionary use of electronic publishing is in making archival material and primary sources generally available. Like other major universities, we are engaged in a number of these projects. This of course also applies to scientific material whose use will remain too scattered for formal publication, and much biological data is beginning to appear is this format only.

7. FUTURE CATALOGS

7.1 E-journals, indexes, and the catalog

Our Voyager online catalog has the potential to incorporate other Z39.50 data sources. This would permit us to offer searching the Princeton catalog together with Medline, or Inspec, or other indexes. This would have obvious advantages: the user would directly retrieve references to books and articles on his subject at the same time. The distinction between journal articles and books in even obvious cases has long been very unclear to users, and consequently poses a problem to librarians. In the sciences, where almost all research is published in short items that are either articles in journals, chapters in books, or short books in long series, the distinction can be unclear even to specialists; this makes for the relative invisibility of many items. This is accentuated by the lack of consistent handling by both indexing services and libraries. We are not convinced that this step is not yet appropriate: the users, we fear, will find this more confusing than helpful. This will change when all such sources are available electronically. At that point, they will all be reachable by the same route, and the distinction between indexing services and catalogs will disappear.

E-journals are of course integrated in our Voyager catalog, complete with the exact holdings. They are if possible entered as a copy, not a separate entry, and the sequence of copies is adjusted so the electronic version or versions appear at the top. In those cases where e-journals are accessible for only a limited period, or only after a time delay, they are entered in the catalog if the subject selector considers it worthwhile. We do not currently list journals available in electronic form from aggregators such as Proquest or Lexis because such services cannot guarantee the availability of their journals in future years, and not all the articles actually contain the full page-by-page content. These services are useful as a general purpose source of a wider array of material, but not for scholarly purposes. If we could list them in a way that does not confuse them with the real thing, we would.

If the articles were listed equally with the books, we would have a catalog growing at the rate of 1,000,000 entries a year, not 60,000. Students find great difficulty selecting relevant material from 5 million cataloged items. How would they manage with 500 million? I do not think that the present generation of indexing techniques is capable of dealing with this. It is not just selecting the relevant material, but the high quality material. Currently, *Science Citation Index* is our most popular index--the usefulness of citation techniques is not hard to understand. On the web, those indexes using citation techniques seem to perform better than others, at least from the perspective of materials wanted in an academic library.

We foresee that as the use of informal publication on web-based servers increases, either in place of or supplementary to the regular journals, the indexing services will be forced to include this form of publication or gradually become useless. This will further complicate the situation, especially as this too becomes integrated into the catalog.

Some of us--including even some in technical services--are realizing that there must be an alternative to the catalog for finding things. We are currently planning a document delivery service, which will be a new service at Princeton. The interface for it will have the usual choices: Item owned by Princeton, Item from storage, Interlibrary loan, etc. It will also have the usual selections: Book, Book chapter, Journal article, Dissertation, etc. And it will have, as appropriate, the usual entry boxes for Title, Author, Date and the like, and the opportunity to cut and paste in a citation. But it will also have a label "GET ME THIS:" followed by a big empty box for input. A highly experienced paraprofessional will then screen all the items, including those where the patron specified exactly what was wanted, and will divide them into streams for routine processing, and a stream for professional manual intervention. I call this "Imitation Artificial Intelligence." It's better than waiting for the real thing: it should be in place in September 2001, not September 2020.

7.2 The personalized library catalog

I do not seriously expect that any user except the most sophisticated will be able to navigate a truly complete integrated catalog successfully. This obviously provides a great field of opportunity for reference librarians like myself. Most users will not consult a librarian unless desperate; if they did, the librarians would not be able to handle the workload. My university has one librarian in most subject areas; if everyone who needed help asked for it, we would need ten times that number. Devices like those suggested in the last section will intercept some of this need; if widely used, they will pose the same problem of staffing.

An equal problem is that the students' working hours do not correspond with ours. Reference service is available in the main library till 10PM, and in the branches till 5 or 5:30 PM. The students, especially the undergraduates, seem to do most of their work from 9 PM to 2 AM. We could not obtain librarians willing to work these hours. Even if we did, the users are as much more likely to be working from their rooms or labs than from the library. The common solution offered is telephone, e-mail, video, or chat based serviceS. We provide a little of this on a uncoordinated basis, and plan to do much more, but I do not think that even librarians working from home could match the students' hours. Rather, I see us developing interfaces that will guide the students--and the faculty. The process of library research, like academic life, is relatively standardized. An undergraduate using the library is doing the assigned reading and writing the expected papers for the courses being taken. A faculty member is engaged on one or more research projects, and knows what areas need be followed. A person investigating a new subject for personal interest will do best with a relatively predictable approach. These will not meet all situations, but should cover most. And there will always be the box: "JUST TELL US WHAT YOU WANT:"

8. IS THERE A CONTINUING ROLE FOR PAPER?

Will there be a continuing role for paper? Only in special cases. First, it will be a long time until all research materials are converted into electronic format. There is quite a bit of material, relevant for special historical purposes, that may never be. (Five hundred years after the invention of printing, not all previously written manuscripts have in fact been printed.) More essential, there will always remain a role for the paper as artifacts. A digitized drawing is not the same as the drawing; a digitized folio of Shakespeare is not the same as the book itself. And the backup preservation role of print has already been mentioned.

In addition to all this, there is in my opinion a wide range of material for which print will long remain the preferred format--for which it meets the necessary conditions of size, weight, readability, and lack of technological complications. My empirical test is whether it fits into a jacket pocket.

Electronic Publishing '01 –
2001 in the Digital Publishing Odyssey
A. Hübler et al. (Eds.)
IOS Press, 2001

The Roquade project: an infrastructure for new models of academic publishing

Natalia Grygierczyk
Bas Savenije

Abstract
Due to a number of problems the traditional scientific journal has become an obstacle for efficient scientific communication. Many initiatives have been started for realising alternative ways of scientific publishing thereby using information technology. In various disciplines, however, a relatively large number of scientists are still reluctant to make use of completely new ways of publishing.
The extraordinary aspect of the *Roquade* project is marked by the fact that it offers a variety of possibilities. Together they constitute an expeditious way for gradually changing the publication behaviour of scientists. This project, initiated by the university libraries of the Dutch universities of Delft and Utrecht, aims at creating an infrastructure that encompasses the swiftness of publication which hitherto could only be realised by grey publishing, with quality judgement without the serious delay of the traditional review procedures.
Roquade offers a wide number of facilities to a broad audience, based on a common organisational and technical infrastructure. So far already 18 journals and other types of scientific work have been published within the Roquade infrastructure - and the project continues until 2002.
In the paper, both project philosophy and organisation are described, as well as the preliminary results, experiences and best practices, technical XML based choices, web marketing and of course the needs and demands of authors and readers. The advantages of co-operation and the role of the university library in facilitating scientific communication are dealt with too. An outline of the Roquade business model after the project stage will also be presented.

Structure of the paper:
1. The breakdown of scientific communication
2. Roquade: its philosophy and organisation
3. Roquade: first results
4. Roquade: business model
5. Concluding remarks
6. References

1. The breakdown of scientific communication

1665. The first issue of *Journal des Savants*, the first scientific magazine is published. A year later it is followed by a second journal, *Philosophical Transactions*. Both appear not in Latin but in the vernacular language, a quite unusual phenomenon during those days. What were the reasons to start these endeavours? A major factor was the rising number of researchers. Similarly important was the influence of Francis Bacon who had been successfully advocating the use of systematic and empirical scientific inquiry and who had emphasised the significance of exploring written sources. In order to stimulate the process of building on each other's findings as well as to avoid duplication of efforts scientists needed to be informed on the results achieved and collected by their colleagues. Bacon aimed at comprising library, laboratory and fieldwork.

Of course, there were books. But as a carrier for scientific information they had some disadvantages. Their main drawback - an aspect related to their volume - was their delay in appearing, due to precious time lost in producing them. Books also featured a definite character. Therefore, they tended to be less suitable for discourses on detailed investigations. Especially if the facility of additions, comments and reply was useful. It was these aspects that were of great significance to Bacon and his colleagues. Objections to the book as an inflexible medium for distributing concise, relevant information were first expressed by physicists, physicians and technicians. Increasing international contacts among scientists required a platform on which the results of their research could be revealed and discussed. What these scientists basically wanted was to trust their rather unstructured correspondence to a medium that was neither a book nor a letter. The answer was the scientific journal. At first, the *Journal des Savants* was even a weekly magazine. The ensuing growth in various scientific periodicals was indicative for their need.

As such, this very need for communication among scholars has always been the very raison d'être of the scientific magazine. Editors were appointed to judge the quality of the contributions and their results. Due to differences in evaluations, a hierarchy was gradually emerging. Some editors proved to be more critical than others since they had decided to introduce stricter selection conditions. Thus, a number of journals were acquiring a better reputation than others. Consequently, scientists started deriving their stature from the reputation of the journal to which they contributed. Increasingly, readers were becoming aware of the difference in quality. This difference even led to emergence of a ranking system. Finally, the ranking system resulted in playing a significant role in the evaluation of scientific papers and articles. A role that is now firmly established. So-called citation indexes are important tools in the evaluation of articles. These indexes refer to the citation frequency of articles as well as to the reputation of the magazines in which the articles are cited. The composition of the indexes even evolved into a new discipline, bibliometry, in which these indexes constitute a basic element. As a result, scientific journals have become a distinct factor in evaluating academic research programs. Oddly enough, the same people who favour the current scientific journal consider this factor as the main argument for continuing its existence. But do we really have any reason to be satisfied with its present form?

'Publish or perish' is an adage that we are all familiar with. It is mirrored by the growth in the number of scientific papers. As a consequence of this growth, the existing publishing system is troubled by considerable problems.

1. Publishing is sluggish: it takes at least six months, sometimes up to a year and a half, before a submitted paper actually appears in print.
2. There is growing doubt about the system's trustworthiness, particularly since reviewers may take advantage of their prior knowledge.
3. The system is becoming unaffordable because of vast price increases, which are often higher than the general price index. These rises lead to the cancelling of subscriptions, which in turn cause new increases, eventually evolving in almost monopoly-like situations held by the publishers.
4. Furthermore, we must be aware of the fact that, in addition to these price increases, universities have to pay for these publications more than once, since they also pay:
   - the salary of university staff members who write the articles and papers;
   - the salary of the reviewer who, at the request of the publisher, judges whether the articles are suitable for publication;
   - the publication's purchase price;
   - the archiving of the publications.

We can no longer deny it: the current scientific magazine can hardly be called a communication medium if we consider the amount of time between submission and publication of an article. Fortunately, scientists are also beginning to acknowledge this. They have started publishing their pre-prints on the Internet. In fact, their article's eventual publication in a magazine has become more of a formality, a procedure in which a quality certificate is assigned *afterwards*. Our conclusion must be therefore that the scientific journal in its conventional form can no longer play an essential role in the process of scientific communication. Moreover, this fact undermines its very raison d'être.

2. Roquade: its philosophy and organisation

Currently, an author who wants to publish his article sees himself confronted with a dilemma. If he is after speedy publication, he has to seek refuge into so-called grey literature. On the other hand, if quality is more important he must address a traditional publisher, thereby accepting a lingering publication process.
Modern information and communication technology can solve this dilemma. However, many scientists seem to be a little squeamish when it comes to publishing their results. Naturally, this is partly understandable, because of the crucial role traditional journals play in quality assessment procedures. To a large extent, scientists derive their reputation from the journal's reputation. Nevertheless, their reservations towards alternatives cannot only be explained by this aspect. As strange as it appears, scientists are reluctant to participate in innovative experiments which in their eyes are risky. They tend to be more interested in projects that have a certain resemblance to the traditional publishing process, like an electronic version of a traditional journal.

Unsurprisingly, the traditional commercial publisher is not anxious to stimulate certain innovations that could change the established process of scientific communication. Traditionally, the publisher has been engaged in core activities like gathering, quality certification, registration and distribution. In the value chain spanning between information producer to information consumer, the publisher's added value is mainly in certification and distribution. The distribution of electronic documents is a process that is fairly similar to the library's function of providing access to information, especially if this task is combined with conservation and storage. In the past, the distribution of information was not considered a task of the library. It presupposed a marketing-orientated view, a requirement which libraries could only meet to limited extent. Moreover, it was thought of as an uncertain business, an aspect which subsidy funders tended to dislike. However, the distribution of information in digital form, though, is regarded as a different matter. From a financial point of view, it is seen as a less hazardous operation, because it makes use of an existing infrastructure, i.e. the academic community's electronic network.
As to quality certification, the peer review is now done by academics and organised by publishers. There are two obvious organisational alternatives to this process:

- It could be organised by publishers who do not act as information owners but as service providers hired by the university;
- It could be organised by libraries.

One of the advantages of the latter alternative is the possibility of immediate contact between library and scholars and their personal networks. For the present we may therefore safely conclude that in future the publisher's added value may no longer be self evident.

Two years ago the university libraries of Utrecht and Delft, joined forces with the library of the Royal Netherlands Academy of Arts and Sciences to change this situation. It was the starting point for the *Roquade* project. The project aims at setting up an infrastructure for electronic publishing. Its mission is the enhancement of scientific communication by offering scientists a wide variety of facilities and organisational structures, helping them to gradually change their publishing manner. The project is directed towards all disciplines and concerns Dutch publications as well as international initiatives.

Roquade is distinguished by two aspects of electronic publishing support.
The first involves supporting institutional open archives. Its priorities are storing, conservation and providing access to the university's scientific output (e.g. its own publications). If every academic institution were to organise the scientific information it produces, this would result in a world-wide network of servers making full-text scientific information accessible on-line to everyone. The next step would be to order the information by subject within various knowledge domains. The essential objective of these tasks is creating a digital archive that contains the scientific output of the university, as well as preserving this information and making it accessible to the academic community.
The second aspect is more discipline-oriented. It emphasises the necessity of new publishing models that stimulate scientific communication, accelerate the exchange of research results and organise open discussions within knowledge domains. Researchers can place their papers on the website of their department or set-up electronic journals. Furthermore, they are provided with facilities for publication servers and new peer-review models. The initiative for these activities, of course, comes directly from researchers within departments, from research institutes and learned societies. But in realising them they are supported by back-office processes and facilities, including the organisational and technological capacities.

For both aspects of electronic publishing *Roquade* provides a flexible infrastructure. The scientists and research institutions can use the type of publishing process they prefer: one that entirely meets their actual needs or the one that they are up to. The reason for offering extensive and limited options is that many scientists are not yet ready to use fully new ways of publishing in order to make the issuing of their research results independent from the monopoly of commercial publishers. These scholars are provided with an infrastructure that facilitates a gradual transition from traditional publishing to highly sophisticated models.

2.1 The main structure of the project

The general idea behind the *Roquade* project is that it consists of a set of basic components, i.e. services to scientists. For instance an editorial board can select not only a certain type of service but also one, two or all the components of the publishing process depending on his wishes or his computer literacy. Naturally, the selected components also depend on the publication type.
This general idea is reflected in the project structure and its activities.
The main structure of *Roquade* project consists of:

- Satellites: a number of subsidiary projects with a variety of possibilities:
  1. electronic substitution for traditional publishing
  2. a publication site with experimental peer review systems
  3. open archives facilities:
     - a moderated pre-print service
     - re-print service
- Generic Roquade infrastructure: a subsidiary project aiming at a technical and organisational infrastructure that is common for all satellite projects.

Roquade's satellites and infrastructure form an undivided entity. On the one hand, these satellites use the (intermediate) results of the *Roquade* infrastructure projects. On the other hand, these results are tested, refined and further developed within the satellites projects.

In the first type of satellites, which can be described as electronic substitution for traditional publishing, two categories of publications can be distinguished:

- dissertations and conference collections
- scientific journals

Two subsidiary project types are concerned with scientific journals:

- Publishing new and existing electronic journals: this involves supporting editors who prefer the traditional form of electronic publishing. In this case, the electronic journal is an electronic 'copy' of the traditional paper journal (even when the journal is e-only: it should have the look-and-feel of an existing paper journal).
- Co-publishing: setting up a series of digital publication services for publishers, e.g. for electronic versions of existing paper journals.

Similar to many scientists most editors who are interested in setting-up an electronic journal also want to start in a more or less traditional way mainly involving text and pictures. The concept of volumes and issues – typical of the paper journal – is maintained during the start-up phase and, as in the case of traditional paper journals, peer review takes place before publication. Gradually, an broad range of additions, modifications and alternatives is possible:

- the concept of separate issues will eventually become obsolete. Articles are published as soon as they are ready for publication;
- research data can be appended;
- communication and discussion facilities can be added;
- multimedia can be used to enrich the publication.

The second type is a publication site with peer reviewing. Its main feature is a series of pre- and post-publication peer reviewing processes. They are based on experience and knowledge gathered in traditional and digital academic publishing processes. Subsequently, the traditional process of peer-reviewing is transformed into several new types preserving the traditional advantages as much as possible. In this variant it is possible to achieve speed without omitting the time-consuming peer review process by delaying peer reviews until after publication. This variant also offers the possibility of experimenting with different forms of quality assessment, e.g. an open and public (not anonymous) peer-review discussion.

The third type consists of pre-print and re-print open archive service. There are two functions which are particularly useful from the authors' point of view in this respect:

- Long-term preservation, including guarantees for permanent accessibility, readability, integrity and authenticity (with respect to the transition from one medium and/or format to another).
- Broadening of the readership by making the publications traceable via various Internet channels. Here, advanced methods of archiving and indexing play a crucial role, as do the options for self-ordering and ordering in knowledge domains. The use of the publications is further promoted by employing usual library tools in modernised form (such as user-friendly and accurate search engines, alerting and filtering systems and well-organised presentation of the publications on the web).

These types contain the main objective of the *Roquade* project: a gradual transition from less to more innovative solutions.

The generic part of the project is a subsidiary project that aims at a technical and organisational infrastructure common for all satellite projects. This core project generates for all the different types of publications the tools, services and know-how. They all have a modular structure, so it is not necessary to use the whole range of services and tools.

2.2 The phases of the project

In the project the following phases can be distinguished.

1. The preparation phase (May 1999– July 2000)
2. The start-up phase (September 2000 – December 2001)
   a. Setting up the generic infrastructure for various publication variants
   b. Satellite for each publication variant
   c. Financing
   d. Evaluation
3. The development phase (January – July 2002)
   The objective of this phase is to adapt and further expand the organisation on the basis of the experience acquired in the satellite projects.
4. Expansion phase (July – December 2002)
   The objective of this phase is scale enlargement of available publications and the audience.

At this moment the project is in its start-up phase, in which the infrastructure is being built and tested in satellite projects.

3. Roquade: the first results

The current *Roquade* satellites are:

- Electronic substitution for traditional publishing:
  - Scientific Journals:
    - *International Journal of Integrated Care*
    - *International Shipbuilding Progress*
    - *European Journal of Transport and Infrastructure Research*
    - *Kronos - Journal of Cape History*
    - *Veterinary Sciences Tomorrow*
    - *Ars Disputandi*
    - *Ancient Narrative*
    - *Neerlandistiek.nl (Dutch Philology)*
    - *Cahiers voor Geschiedenis en Informatica (Journal of History and Computer Sciences)*
  - Journals in co-publishing
    - *Pedagogiek (Pedagogy)*
    - *Tijdschrift voor Hoger Onderwijs (Journal for Higher Education)*
    - *The Veterinary Quarterly*
  - Dissertations:
    - *LOT Dissertations (PhDs from The Netherlands Graduate School of Linguistics)*
  - Grey Literature:
    - *Newsletter Historia & Informatica*
    - *Unitwin Series for Namibia*
- Publication site with experimental peer review systems:
  - *Design Research Internet Magazine*
  - *Interactive Publication: European Journal of Transport and Infrastructure Research*
  - *Syntactic Microvariation*
- Open archives:
  - *Institutional open archive in Law (Utrecht University)*

The core of the Roquade project: a technical and organisational infrastructure common for all satellite projects has a modular structure. The components are at this moment, during the project phase, divided as follows:

- author management concerns the communication with (and between) authors and editorial boards. This module concerns the complex of rules, conditions, requirements and tools that are at the disposal of author and/or editorial board during the production and sending-in of an electronic article (with possible appendices or attachments).
- editorial workflow. It concerns rules, conditions and requirements, as well as the choice or construction of tools for publishing and peer review processes sec.
- progress administration concerns the administration (and a supporting system or tool) of all activities that need to be carried out from the moment that an article is sent in for publication to its technical processing, including the persons responsible for these actions.
- storage, archive and distribution module refers to the tools and services regarding the process phases from processing the final editorial product (including metadata) to medium-neutral storage as well as selection and extracting medium-neutrally stored information for processing into final product(s).
- website module refers to the producing of various models and templates for optimal layout as well as functionalities of diverse types of online publications.
- customer relationship management module refers to the management (and a supporting system or tool) of contacts with the authors, editors, peer reviewers and readers of electronic publications.
- marketing module concerns the relation with (potential) readers and authors. It mainly focuses on promoting *Roquade* publications via various new e-marketing methods and channels.
- support module regards instructions for using services and tools that have been developed in other modules.

This division into components is based on a pragmatic division in assignment of activities to the project partners. It does not yet reflect the exact division of the definite modular products and services of *Roquade* after the project stage. This division will be based on an already initiated survey scanning the needs of authors and editorial boards.

During this project stage, the most important, tested and transferable results are:

- a storage, archive and distribution module: an XML-based semi-automatic conversion system. The input is a publication (at this moment only in MSWord, later also in other text and media formats) manual provided with various structure- and meta-data codes. The meta data concern both disclosure and information in view of long term preservation.
  This publication is automatically converted into XML and then automatically inserted into the corresponding style sheet that publishes it on-line:
  - in HTML for on-line reading
  - and PDF for printing-and-binding-on-demand option.
- website module: model and tools for ergonomical lay-out and functionality for an e-journal, an e-dissertation and an institutional open archive. This model is based on user surveys as well as web publications analysis.
- marketing module: a checklist and instruction set for e-marketing methods and channels.

4. Roquade business model

As has become obvious, it is *Roquade*'s mission to facilitate e-publishing within the academic community without the traditional intermediary role of the publisher. It should be clear, however, that it is not *Roquade*'s ambition to evolve into a publisher. In other words, *Roquade* helps the academic community, its members and its institutes to become publishers themselves. They can make use of all the *Roquade* facilities or only part of the available modules.
Its ultimate goal is that all the facilities and tools are used by the academic community with a minimum of intermediary support.
This is an essential point of departure for *Roquade*'s business model. It implies that *Roquade* must not evolve into a strong intermediary organisation, because such an organisation sooner or later will have its own existence and future viability as an important goal. There is a danger that, instead of facilitating, it would then deteriorate into an obstacle for "self-publishing".

4.1 Organisational transfer

The Roquade project is managed by a steering group, which consists of the library directors of the Dutch Royal Academy, and the Universities of Delft and Utrecht, plus a general project manager. After the project phase, the Steering Group is transformed into a *Managing Board*, responsible for *Roquade's* facilities and exploitation. They form the *Roquade Consortium.*
Roquade makes a clear distinction between back office and front office.

- The *back office* consists of the technical infrastructure: software and hardware, as well as maintenance, expansion, upgrading and innovation. The back office is managed by a co-ordinator with the help of a specialist team recruited from the consortium libraries. The users of these facilities are so-called *satellites* of Roquade: these are autonomous publishing initiatives and projects. However, they do not make a direct use of these technical facilities, but do so with the support of the front offices of Roquade.
- The *front offices* are franchise holders of the *Roquade* brand. These front offices can also use the Roquade facilities (for example Delft University Press) or support other organisations who want to make use of the facilities. The consortium members form front offices themselves, but other front offices will also be recruited, especially in other countries.

Thus, the satellites form in fact the clients of the front offices.
The front offices are co-ordinated by a *co-ordinating front office*, which is the central contact point of *Roquade* and which directs new satellites to the front offices. The support given by the front offices can vary depending on the organisation's or project's request for support. This support can cover all technical facilities, as well as project management for setting-up new publications and implementing the project results. However, it can also be limited to a simple helpdesk function. On the basis of their experiences, the front offices play an important role in the feed-back and evaluation of the tools that are offered by *Roquade*. The co-ordinating front office also controls the fulfilment by the front offices of a number of constraints that are necessary conditions for the franchise of the *Roquade* brand. Among these constraints are:

- requirements concerning the quality (control) of the publication's content;
- requirements as to the quality of support given by the front office;
- principles concerning cost calculation for using the infrastructure and the front office services;
- the way the *Roquade* brand is mentioned in the publications.

Co-ordinating the exchange of information, experiences and feed-back is the task of the co-ordinating front office. The front offices collaboration could be seen as a network organisation.

The organisational structure can be represented as follows.

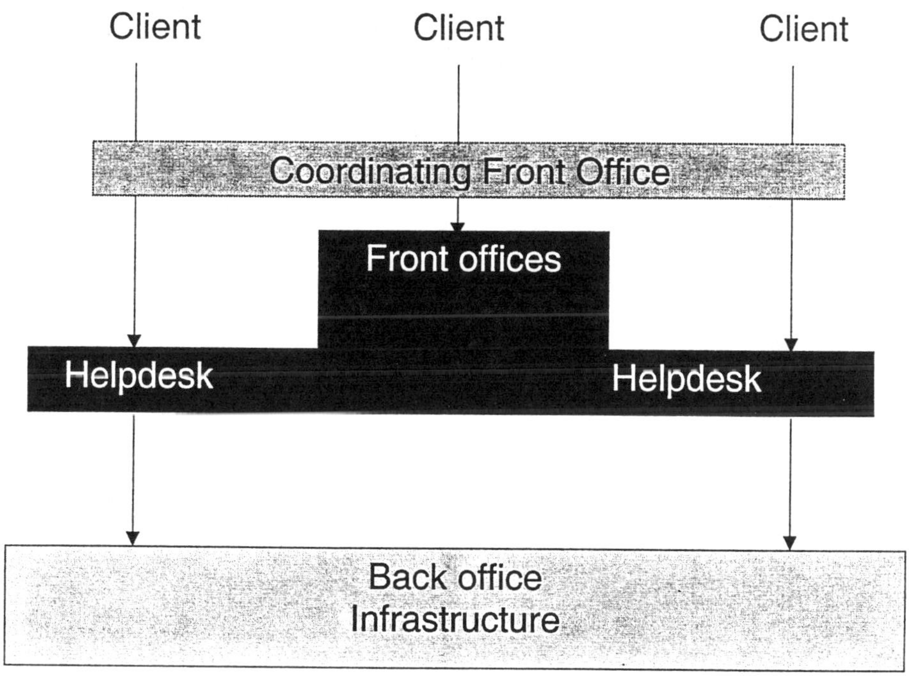

fig. 1: organisational structure

5. Concluding remarks

The experiences with the *Roquade* project thus far show that there is a new and real challenge for university libraries to become engaged in the support of electronic publishing. It is a true challenge because projects like *Roquade* are not initiated solely on the basis of a strategic analysis by the library management. They have reason for existence because scientists within our universities appeal to the library asking for support and assistance in making a successful transition to electronic publishing and new publishing models.

It is difficult to predict the future for academic publishing. Furthermore, we would be short-sighted if we were to prescribe a standard for what the future should look like. Therefore, it would be unmindful to impose a preferred model onto scientific communication. The academic community should initiate the flexible facilitation of new structures in scientific information processes that are advantageous to the academic

community itself. *Roquade* is an initiative that has this ambition. It holds benefits for the academic community as well as for the libraries that take the initiative.
Its benefits for the academics (both authors and readers) can be summarised as follows:

- Rapidity
- Quality
- Transparency of the reviewing and publishing process
- Positive attitude of scientists towards digital publishing
- Technological innovation
- Fair price
- Usage statistics

The benefits for the library are:

- Opportunities for applying gained experience of digital publishing and for exploiting the existing infrastructure in order to support the information and communication requirements of researchers.
- Better position in negotiations with publishers active in all fields in order to slow down the rising of subscription rates as well as improving financial benefits for the academic community in the long run.
- International co-operation.

6. References

- Harnad, S. (2001) For Whom the Gate Tolls? How and Why to Free the Refereed Research Literature Online Through Author/Institution Self-Archiving, Now. At At Workshop on the Open Archive Initiative and peer review journals in Europe. Geneva, 22-24 March 2001: http://www.cogsci.soton.ac.uk/~harnad/Tp/resolution.htm
- Savenije, J.S.M. & Grygierczyk, N.J. (1999). The *Roquade* project: a gradual revolution in academic publishing. Proceedings of the 23rd International Online Information Meeting. Learned Information Europe Ltd, pp.211-216.
- Savenije, J.S.M. & Grygierczyk, N.J. (2000). The role and responsibility of the university library in publishing in a university. Paper presented at the LIBER Annual Conference. Copenhagen, 27-30 June 2000.
- Savenije, J.S.M. (2001). The Roquade Project. The library as a catalyst of change in scholarly publishing. At International Conference on Scholarly Communication and Academic Presses. Florence, 22 March 2001.
- Savenije, J.S.M. (2001). The Dutch Roquade Project. At Workshop on the Open Archive Initiative and peer review journals in Europe. Geneva, 22-24 March 2001.
- Open Letter Online Public Libraries of Science: www.publiclibraryofscience.org
- Open Archives Initiative: www.openarchives.org
- Waaijers, L. (1996). The science and art of information and libraries: Practical implications. Interdisciplinary Research Conference on Information Science. Delft, December 1996.

Electronic Publishing '01 –
2001 in the Digital Publishing Odyssey
A. Hübler et al. (Eds.)
IOS Press, 2001

Electronic publishing in Brazilian academic institutions: changes in formal communication, too?

Sely Costa, PhD
Wagner A. A. Silva
Marcos B. Costa

Departamento de Ciência da Informação e Documentação
Universidade de Brasília
Campus Universitário Darcy Ribeiro, Brasília, DF - Brazil
selmar@unb.br

Abstract
The use of electronic facilities for informal communication amongst academic researchers is a common place already. That is, according to a number of studies in different disciplines around the world, the adoption and use of electronic communication in the informal stages of the scholarly communication system is prevalent. Nevertheless, the same studies that testify such a ubiquity of the informal electronic communication in the academic world also show that the adoption of these media in the formal stages of the communication process, though occurring, has been slow and cautious. The reasons for that are many and have also been extensively discussed. In reality, these studies point out that the adoption and diffusion of electronic media for formal communication are in progress and therefore needs to be assessed in order to see to what extent, and in which way it has been occurring. The study discussed in this paper aims to provide a picture of the adoption and use of electronic facilities for scholarly publishing in Brazil within the academic environment. As an exploratory research, the study aims to see whether there have been electronic publications being produced by academic institutions – universities and learned societies- and, if so, which sort of publications have been mostly provided, what are their major features in terms of format, content, availability, accessibility, etc. and whether they can provide any basis for the identification of disciplinary differences in publication patterns. Since none of the sampling frames available from departments and institutes within the Ministry of Education and the Ministry of Science and Technology hierarchy, a number of procedures have been applied in order to define the sample. It actually consists of those academic institutions that have produced scholarly electronic publications - namely books, journals, serials, annual proceedings and secondary sources such as abstracts, reviews, etc. Some partial results show that so far, there has been electronic publications being produced by Brazilian academic institutions, but the adoption of pure electronic formal communication amongst academic researchers seems to be far from become ubiquitous, as can be observed in relation to the informal communication.

0. Introduction

This paper presents partial results of an ongoing research project that has been carried out in Brazil. The research constitutes an exploratory study of electronic publications produced by Brazilian academic institutions, namely universities and learned societies. Its main aim is to see to what extent scientific and scholarly publications such as journals, books and conference proceedings have been produced and made available by those institutions either on the Internet or CD-ROM. The study also aims to analyse and describe, in the light of some insights from the literature on scholarly publishing, the main features of those publications from the perspective of both the project researchers and the editors of a small sample of the publications identified.

The research motivation came from three basic assumptions. Firstly, it has been assumed that technology infrastructure has increasingly been made available within those institutions environment and it might have an effect on the will for using it, as stated by the technological determinism approach. Secondly, electronic media has already become ubiquitous for informal communication amongst academics world-wide and it is time to see to which extent this adoption has migrated to the formal stages of the communication process, too. Finally, production costs of electronic publications have increasingly dropped over the past few years and it may also have an influence on the use of electronic media to provide research information.

As an exploratory research, the methodological procedures used for carrying it out was a tentative, and loose-jointed one, especially in terms of the construction of the research sample. It has been oriented by the qualitative paradigm in the sense that the study looks for identifying data from the publications identified themselves, which can be then analysed and used to describe them in terms of a selected set of features. It is expected that data from both the publication analysis and from the publishers points of view will contribute to some understanding of the use of electronic media for formal communication within the academic world in Brazil.

It is important to notice that it is largely known that electronic media have already been increasingly used for scholarly publishing. Most of the major printed scholarly journals, for example, are also available in electronic format, along with a number of other purely electronic ones, as well as a growing number of other electronic publications such us conference proceedings and some initiatives with monographs. However, a number of studies have pointed out that, although electronic media has been commonly used by academics for informal communication, its adoption as a formal medium for both publishing and reading research results still seems to be a matter of time (e.g. Costa, 2000; Hurd, Weller and Crawford, 1996). Nevertheless, changes in technology and its use grow quickly and need to be followed closely. This has been the foremost commitment of this study.

1. Background from the literature

It has been predicted by Richardson in the late 1980s that computer-mediated communication would soon be commonplace in organisations which have significant members of knowledge workers as members, such as higher education institutions (Richardson, 1990). In fact, the policy of universities over the past decade in most countries in the world has been towards provision of networked computers for all researchers. One can therefore state that Richardson's prediction has been fairly accomplished. As a result, there has been an increasing use of electronic communication amongst academics world-wide, despite the difficulties faced in Third World countries. In this regard, it is interesting to point out recent results from a study carried out amongst Brazilian academic researchers from the social sciences, which did not find significant differences between those researchers and their colleagues from the UK in terms of the use of electronic facilities for research communication (Costa & Meadows, 2.000).

In fact, over the last seven years or so -that is, mostly from Schauder (1994), which seems to be a sort of seminal work in this theme, as his work has received many citations in the literature so far- a growing number of studies have highlighted the increasing use of computer-mediated communication within the scholarly community. Such a growing use of computers and electronic networks for communicating research, however, has been mainly driven to the informal stages of the process, from the initial discussion with colleagues to the submission of manuscripts to publishers (See Costa, op. cit.; Vorbij, 1999; Kaminer et al, 1998; Lazinger, 1997; Cohen, 1996; and others).

What about the formal stages, i.e., final publication? Well, there is plenty of evidence in the literature of the growing efforts in the use of electronic media for publishing scientific and scholarly literature, too. It appears to be an inexorable trend. There has been a sort of a slowly replacement process taking place, although there are differences related to both, the stages of the communication process and the type of publication. Accordingly, such a substitution can be observed regarding a continuum that ranges from books to conference proceedings. The print-on-paper production of the latter seems to have already been almost totally replaced by the electronic media (though there still is a co-existence of the electronic and the print-on-paper versions amongst those who can afford both) while in relation to the former such a substitution seems to be far from happen. In the middle there are the journals, which have shown a growing, yet slowly trend in this replacement process though, again, the same co-existence of print-on-paper and electronic versions are observed. In reality, so far it appears to be more appropriate to talk about complement than to consider substitution.

It is interesting to draw attention to the fact that, as any other issues regarding technology use, there are enthusiasts and adversaries of electronic publishing. Amongst the formers, it has been highlighted that

> "Although printing has for three centuries been an agent of change in scholarly communication, we should remain mindful that central values of scholarly communication ... pre-dated the first learned journals; so, too, can they post-date the paper paradigm. The journal as we have known it was successful because it was the best technology available to do the job. This is no longer the case." (Morton, 1997)

From the latter group there is a counterclaim that 'there is an apparent reluctance within the academic community to accept a replacement to paper-based journals' (Elliot et al, 1997).

Although such a debate relates to journals, it can easily be extended to other types of formal communication such as books. In relation to books, however, the reluctance is by far and large greater than that regarding journals and it seems that it is not the case of conference proceedings at all. In any case, what counts is that electronic publications have been increasingly produced and it directs the debate to issues regarding technology adoption and adaptation, as proposed by Borgman (2000, p. 9), who reminds everyone that 'underlying the design of any information technology are assumptions about how and why people use it'.

The adoption of information technology has been extensively studied and reported by Rogers (1995), who presents his results according to a model consisting of five stages. First, there is the knowledge stage, which consists of awareness of the existence of a new technology. Second, there is the persuasion stage, regarding a sort of assessment process developed by each individual in terms of technology characteristics and benefits. Third, the decision to accept or reject technology forms the stage that would allow going ahead in this adoption process, or not. Fourth, if, and only if accepted first, there is the implementation stage; and finally, there is the commitment to use (a confirmation to continue to use, if considered sufficiently useful). As highlighted by Borgman (op. cit.), in the case that the technology innovation is rejected (third stage), it is likely that the individual still may revisit the decision and adopt it later.

Informal communication amongst academics provides a good arena to observe the completely adoption of electronic media for scholarly communication purposes. The use of email, for example, has become pervasive and this may reflect a 'global' adoption process that have already achieved its fifth stage. As regarding formal communication (publishing), however, the actual picture shows a slower adoption process than that relating to the informal. In this sense, one could dare (because without empirical evidence) to state that, taken in general terms, the process can be seen as in its third stage since it has still been rejected by many (keeping in mind differences relating to the type of publication stated above), while has found some acceptance in terms of the number of initiatives already implemented world-wide. That is, it does not yet show sufficient evidence of large scale implementation and confirmation to use (fourth and fifth stages of the adoption process), despite the apparent irreversible trend of this technology to prevail. Therefore, the majority of those involved in this discussion hitherto recognises that there will be (for some time to come) a co-existence of electronic and print-on-paper media.

As a provoking argument then, let us just go back to the last sentence in the paragraph before last and simply consider that those who have rejected electronic publishing so far, may revisit the decision and adopt it later. It actually would anticipate how the future might look. However, before such a scenario takes place, the amount of electronic publications produced and available can be taken as one way of looking at the level of adoption of computers and electronic networks for publishing research results to date. This, in turn, provides a feasible arena upon which studies have been carried out. In fact, electronic publishing constitutes an extraordinary topic for research, since it brings about paradigm shifts and, as such, challenges some of the (well) established issues in information science, at least.

One of these issues refers to the peer review process, which has appeared as an invariable question in a number of studies of the scholarly communication process in terms of changes brought about by the introduction of new technology within the academic environment. One example is that, although the information technology available allows free distribution of completed research reports, it is the classical model of the peer review process that has still mostly driven both their acceptance as 'scholarly work' and concerns regarding the recognition/reward system. This, in turn, has kept the communication process as a whole a hybrid one, in the sense that it has been partly based upon the print-on-paper paradigm and partly based upon the electronic/digital paradigm. Harnard, Varian and Parks (2000) and a number of other authors have contributed to a heated debate that shows how significant this topic is to be followed-up in any research that focus on electronic communication amongst academics.

Technology itself constitutes another (obviously) relevant issue in studies of electronic publishing. Changes in technology always bring about new discussion, by the extent to which it leads to changes in the research communication environment, too. Besides that, the endeavour for keeping abreast of technology innovations gives rise to a great dynamism in the process, which, in turn, produces more research interest. As a result, the use of technology is a mandatory issue in the study of electronic publishing. Questions like digital image production (see Chapman & Comstock, 2000), information extraction software (see Adams, 2001), metadata models such as the Dublin Core Metadata Initiative (see Weibel & Traugott, 2000), authors/institutions self-archiving models such as the Open Archives Initiative (see Van de Sompel, 2000) and a number of others are relevant to take into account in the study of electronic publications that have been made available.

In summary, the study of the literature in electronic publications brings insights to the discussion about changes in the scholarly communication systems in terms of its formal stages, and constitutes a fertile ground for discussion. It takes account of issues regarding adoption versus rejection of technology, the ethos of the scholarly communication environment, especially in terms of the peer review process and the rewarding/recognition system and, as a mandatory question, developments in information technology.

2. Methodological procedures

Studies of the use of electronic facilities by academic researchers have dominated the literature in information science over the last decade. A number of methodological procedures have been used in these studies, according to the focus chosen, the context involved, the theoretical foundation and, obviously, the nature of the problem investigated. In this study, which relies amongst the pioneers of this type in Brazil, an exploratory design has been chosen. The main reason for that was the lack of previous results upon which some analysis and discussion could be done. A qualitative approach has been adopted, since the data collected and analysed constitute a simple description of the main features of the publications identified from the perspectives of the project researchers via assessment of the publications themselves, and of a small sample of editors interviewed via email.

The theoretical approach: models of the communication process and use of technology

The study of electronic publications in information science constitutes one of issues encompassed in the body of knowledge in scholarly communication. In this sense, it can be looked according to any model of the scholarly communication process. One of these models has been proposed by Garvey & Griffith (1979) who have studied a variety of channels by which scientific information is communicated and ended up with a model that has been used as a basis to a variety of studies across the physical and social sciences. Throughout the 1990s, when the focus on scholarly communication has been driven by the use of technology, a number of investigations that looked at such a use of information technology for communication purposes within the academic environment have based the analysis in Garvey & Griffith communication model.

In this regard, Tenopir & King (2000) observes that, 'electronic alternatives ... can affect and be affected by the communication channels and distribution means'. In reality, the introduction of information technology into the academic environment has brought about changes in the scholarly communication process at all its stages, from the most informal to the most formal. Some of these changes have been the focus of the investigations carried out by Hurd (1996), who proposed new models that emerged from the Garvey & Griffith one, namely the 'no-journal' model, the 'unvetted' model and the 'collaboratory' model, all of them entirely electronic-based. Accordingly, the authors suggest that the scientific communication will, and should, evolve from a printed-based system to an electronic system. They highlight, however, that this evolution will be gradual, and acknowledge that print and electronic information sources are likely to co-exist for some time to come, although major changes in the scientific publication sector will probably occur.

Taking into account this co-existence, a hybrid model has been proposed by Costa (2000), in which the informal stages of the communication process are almost entirely electronic-based whereas the formal ones have still been mostly print-based, yet gradually evolving into an electronic one. In this sense, according to some of the results of Costa's study, this scenario stands for a complementary picture of these media rather than for a substitution process. Therefore, as the pervasiveness of the electronic media in the informal communication has been widely recognised, it seems needful to track changes in the formal communication, too.

The universe of the study and sampling procedures

The research reported in this paper aimed to identify and analyse, in the light of a set of selected features, the occurrence of electronic publications produced by academic institutions in Brazil in the fields of biology, physics, sociology, economics, linguistics and philosophy. The main reason for including these disciplines was to have the three divisions of knowledge represented in the sample. It was decided to include two disciplines of each division in order to look for probable differences between and within each division. The universe of the study consisted of two types of establishments: higher education institutions which offer courses in these six disciplines, and learned societies comprising each of them.

Two kinds of initiatives have been initially, and simultaneously, tried in order to sample this universe. The first one was to look for a site on the Internet where an inventory of every course in the disciplines offered by academic institutions in Brazil could be available. It aimed to answer the question, 'how many and where are the university departments which offer courses in these disciplines'? These answers could then be used to contact them and ask about the occurrence of electronic publications produced in their compass. One government site provided the first results: the *Prossiga*[1] ('go ahead', in Portuguese) project, from CNPq (National Scientific and Technological Development Council), but, as the data available were both incomplete and out-of-date (in terms of the URLs and email addresses available) other government sites were tried, mostly from the Ministry of Education hierarchy. The *Scielo*[2] page also offered some hits, but all these data were either incomplete or out-of-date.

The second initiative consisted of inquiries made upon search engines in general sites such as Yahoo! Brasil, Google and Alta Vista by searching each discipline as a specific term (sometimes combined with terms such as 'department' or 'society'.) in order to identify both learned societies and university departments. This, obviously, provided some results, especially up-to-date URLs that led directly to the sites looked for. However, again, it did not give a complete inventory.

A personal inquiry was then decided to be made via telephone to the Higher Education Secretary, within the Ministry of Education. (It had been tried via email before but the reply was misleading because it did not take into account the six disciplines, only). As a result of this inquiry, an Excel file containing the inventory of every course offered in Brazil on the six disciplines investigated was sent to the research co-ordinator through email. As this inventory was arranged by discipline, and each university offer different courses, either at different levels or in different sub-disciplines, it contained around 2.250 entries. The file was therefore 'cleaned', in order to eliminate all duplications in terms of institutions. This allowed to end up with a inventory of 426 entries. From this list, a number of inquires were made upon search engines on the Internet to identify the specific, up-to-date URL of each institution, visit their sites, and contact them. Although it has not been a straightforward task, it allowed to send a message to all 426 institutions selected asking for information about either the department of interest (if not available on the institution web site directly) or the occurrence of any electronic publication (if there was a link to departments). The process described above was evidently iterative and, at the end, provided a final sample of 76 electronic publications, comprising 53 journals/serials, two books and 21 conference proceedings, all available on the web.

Because of many technical problems with electronic communication throughout the process of sampling, the chaos that has been found in this medium, the lack of 'computer intelligence' that can be observed in the construction of web sites in the country in many senses, etc., etc., it does not constitute a reliable sample. It can in fact be seen as the most that could be achieved, given all the difficulties found. It does not include publications on CD-ROM, either. None of the replies from university departments referred to publications

---

[1] *Prossiga*, http://www.prossiga.gov.br, is a government project from the Ministry of Science and Technology that aims to be a discussion forum for scientific and scholarly information.

[2] Scielo (Scientific Electronic Library Online), is a Brazilian digital library, http://www.scielo.org.br, which aimed to build and make available an electronic collection of Brazilian scientific and scholarly journals.

on CD-ROM. However, it is well known that there has been a growing number of conference proceedings on that format, and this required a different approach, which was towards searching a database on scholarly events that is made available by the Nuclear Information Centre, from the National Committee of Nuclear Energy. As the availability of this information on the database depends on libraries that belong to a consortium on this, another strategy has been to contact those libraries individually in order to identify which proceedings are available on CD-ROM format. As an alternative approach, it has also been decided to contact researchers from the university to which this project researchers belong to, in order to ask them about the occurrence of CD-ROM conference proceedings in their disciplines. These procedures are underway and the results obtained will be described in the oral presentation of this paper during the conference.

3. Analysis of the preliminary results

3.1 General criteria, applied to all types of publications

The analysis presented here is a coarse one, in the sense that it has not yet been completed. Besides this, data obtained by asking editors have not yet been analysed, since these procedures are still in progress. This section therefore just presents the results of a first glance at the data collected from the publications themselves, up to now. Nevertheless, it does provide a suggestive general picture of scientific and scholarly electronic publishing in Brazil.

The results described below have been based on the criteria used to analyse general features of the publications identified. They actually offer a rough overview of the electronic publications made available by academic institutions in Brazil, only, and are expected to provide a basis for further analyses that are intended to be done.

Form of access

This feature has been analysed to allow having a picture of the predominant form of access to electronic publications that has been produced in the country. That is, whether the electronic publications produced by academic institutions are available, paraphrasing Harnard and his colleagues, for free or for fee (S/L/P, i.e. subscription, site license, pay-per-view). So far, the totality of the publications identified are freely available.

Handling mechanisms

This refers to mechanisms available for handling the content of the publication in terms of downloading as a file, directly reading on/printing from the screen, searching the content, and interacting with other publications eventually cited through links within it. Here a mixture of all these options is found. However, most of the searchable publications are those journals available on the Scielo site. Only very few publications identified include links to other publications cited either in the body of the text or in notes and references. Most of them are either downloadable PDF files or text files displayable on the screen, and that can be printed out.

Idiom of the content

The Internet offer a great opportunity of visibility for authors. However, there is a language barrier for those who do not publish in English. Therefore, it appeared important to see whether there has been an influence of this on the scientific and scholarly Brazilian electronic publications. The data analysed so far showed that, although the majority of publications are available in Portuguese, there are a number of journals, mostly in the sciences, i.e. Biology and Physics, and which are amongst the most prominent journals in those disciplines in the country, published originally in English.

Type and structure of content

This relates to whether the information provided is a full text document or the abstract only. There is a mixture of forms in this regard, too. In terms of the major journal titles available, the majority are full text documents. The two books included in the sample also comprise full text files. However, a number of links to publications available on some university sites refer to a sort of propaganda. That is, what is made available is the book cover (photograph) and summary, only, information for subscribing to journals, journals' table of contents, etc. There are also a number of journals that provide only the abstract and keyword of the articles. Some of the conference proceedings identified provide the full text of papers. The great majority of the publications consist of a sort of image file of a printed model, without any navigation tool.

Sponsor institution/Publisher

Most of the publications identified are published by a university department or institute. However, there is also a number of publications found that have been published by a learned society, especially those in biology and physics. According to the literature, the new information technology allow university presses to (re)take their function of delivering research information generated in their environment. However, according to the small number of electronic publishing initiatives found, universities in Brazil are not yet benefiting from this. As pointed out by Stumpf (1997), some universities have created their own journals, assuming an important role in the scholarly communication system. Within this context, individual editors have been key participants in the production of the Brazilian university journals and are often prominent researchers in their fields. It is expected that data collected from them will certainly contribute to complement, and better explain, this situation.

Web site

There is a great number of journals available on the Scielo site. Others, alongside the conference proceedings identified, can be found in universities or learned society sites. Nevertheless, the way of building these web pages or of just putting up the journal/conference proceedings, not always allow to find them by entering those sites. Here, a sort of lack of computer knowledge or 'intelligence' can be clearly observed.

Peer/Publisher review procedures

This information is available in part the publications found, only. In fact, some of them do not provide any information to authors and readers about the publication, its policies, norms, etc. However, all the scientific and scholarly journals available on the Scielo site are refereed, as well as a few of other journals, with plenty of information about review procedures. The two books found do not have any information about this, neither the conference proceedings.

Format

This relates to whether the publication is available either on CD-ROM or online (the Internet). As stated in the methodology section of this paper, publications analysed here comprise only those available online on the Internet.

Technology

This criterion of analysis relates to the sort of software used for digitising the content. It also aims to identify the language and format used to deliver the content of the publications, e.g. if it is html, xml; pdf, doc; etc. As stated above, most of the publications are PDF files. A number of others are available in Word for Windows or other text formats. Again, a poorly technology usage is observed. It will be the editor's interview, however, that ill allow better understanding.

3.2 Criteria applied to journals/serials only

Version

This criterion has been applied in order to see whether the journal or serial is electronic *ab initio*, a previously print-on-paper journal that has migrated to electronic media, or a hybrid one: printed-on-paper and electronic. As this information is mostly neglected in the journals identified, it has been left to the editors interview that will be analysed later on.

Interval of publication

Since the majority of journals identified appear to be electronic versions of print-on-paper ones, the majority is based upon this kind of publication model. Accordingly, most of them are made available at regular intervals.

Organisation of the content

Because of based upon the print-on-paper model, most scientific and scholarly journals are organised in terms of volumes/issues. None appeared to have adopted the deconstructed model proposed by Smith (1999) up to what this analysis has allowed to find.

Type of information

The majority of journals found publish articles, and only articles. Others are informative only, in the sense that they only publish news. A number, which have not been looked for, have been identified, and those publish secondary information only: abstracts and/or references and notes.

3.3 Criterion checked against books only

The only criterion used to analyse books is that concerning authorship, whether it is individual or organisational. At the individual level, there is also the observation of the occurrence of team work. The two books found are co-authored.

3.4 Criteria checked against conference proceedings only

Two arbitrarily selected criteria have been used to study conference proceedings. The time for delivery, whether before or after the conference itself, and, depending on the case, whether it includes discussion, video record of the speeches, or other complementary information.

4. Some remarks

There is a gradual adoption of electronic media in the formal stages of the communication process within the academic environment in Brazil. As a result, electronic publications, especially scientific and scholarly journals, have been increasingly, though slowly, made available. In terms of the peer review process, most publications that provide information about it are those scientific and scholarly journals available on the Sicelo site. In fact, the Scielo Project represents a milestone in Brazil in terms of electronic publishing initiatives.

Nevertheless, there still is a great need for technology development which is necessary to this sort of initiative in the country. Even the information technology internationally available for handling metadata, building self-archives, extracting information, marking up documents, constructing (intelligent) homepages etc., especially those which need to be translated to Portuguese, appears to be poorly adopted and used so far.

Apparently, there has been a great need for computer intelligence. The chaos found in this environment, particularly in terms of intelligently delivering information on the Internet, must be a result of this lack of expertise in all these matters. There has been government initiatives within the Ministry of Education, the Ministry of Science and Technology, and a number of Universities. However, they need to grow fast, otherwise the country will be kept behind.

5. References

Adams, Katherine C. The web as a database: new extraction technologies and content management. *Online*, 25(2), pp. 27-32, 2001. Available at: http://www.onlineinc.com/onlinemaq/OL2001/adams3_01.html, accessed on April 12, 2001.

Borgman, Christine L. *From Gutenberg to the global information infrastructure*: access to information in the networked world. Cambridge, MA> The MIT Press, 2000.

Chapman, Stephen and William Comstock. Digital emerging production services at the Harvard College Library. *RLG DigiNews*, 4(6), December 15, 2000. Available at: http://www.relg.org/preserv/diginews/diginews4-6.html#feature1, accessed on April 12, 2001.

Cohen, Joel. Computer mediated communication and publication productivity among faculty. *Internet Research: Electronic Networking Applications and Policy*, 1996, 6 (2/3), pp. 41-63.

Costa, Sely and Meadows, Jack. The impact of computer usage on scholarly communication among social scientists. *Journal of Information Science*, 26 (4), pp. 255-262, 2000.

Costa, Sely. Changes in the information dissemination process within the scholarly world: the impact of electronic publishing on scholarly communities of academic social scientists. In: Peter Linde, John W. T. **Smith and Elena Emelianova**. *Electronic Publishing in the Third Millennium*. Proceedings of na ICCC/IFIP Conference held at the Kaliningrad State University, Kaliningrad/Svetlogorsk, Russia 17-19 August, 2000.

Elliot, G., S. Polovina, G. Rourke and T. Tyrell. Breaking the barriers of resistance to electronic journal entry: experiences of BIToday. In: ICCCC/IFIP Conference, 14-16 April 1997. *Electronic publishing 97: new models and opportunities*, Canterbury: University of Kent at Canterbury, 1997. Preliminary version.

Harnard, S. Academic publishing in the online era: what will be for-fee and what will be for-free? Culture Machine 2. Available at: http://culturemachine.tees.ac.uk/frm_f1.htm, accessed on April 12, 2001.

Hurd, Julie M. Models of scientific communication systems. In: Susan Y. Crawford, Julie M. Hurd and Ann C. Weller. *From print to electronic*: the transformation of scientific communication, Medford, NJ: Information Today, 1996, pp. 9-33.

Hurd, Julie M., Ann C. Weller, and Susan Y. Crawford. The changing scientific and technical communication system. In: Susan Y. Crawford, Julie M. Hurd and Ann C. Weller. *From print to electronic*: the transformation of scientific communication, Medford, NJ: Information Today, 1996, pp. 97-114.

Kaminer, Noam and Yale M. Braunstein. Bibliometric analysis of the impact of Internet use on scholarly productivity. *Journal of the American Society for Information Science*, 1998, 49 (8), pp. 720-730.

Lazinger, S. L., J. Bar-Ilan and B. C. Peritz. Internet use by faculty members in various disciplines: a comparative case study. *Journal of the American Society for Information Science*, 1997, 48 (6), pp. 508-518.

Morton, B. Is the journal as we know it an article of faith? an open letter to the faculty. *The Public Access Computer Systems Review*, 1997, 8 (2). (URL:http://info.lib.uh.edu/pr/v8/n2/mmort8n2.html), 14 Aug. 1997.

Richardson, John. The limitations to electronic communication in the research community. In: M. Feeney and K. Merry (Eds.) *Information technology and the research process*. Proceedings of a Conference held at Cranfield Institute of Technology, UK, 18-21 July 1989, London: Bowker-Saur, 1990, pp. 190-209.

Rogers, E. M. *Diffusion of innovations*, 4. Ed., New York: Free Press, 1995.

Schauder, Don. Electronic publishing of professional articles: attitudes of academics and implications for the scholarly communication industry. *Journal of the American Society for Information Science*, 1994, 45 (2), pp. 73-100

Smith, John W. T. The deconstructed journal - a new model for academic publishing. *Learned Publishing*, 1999, 12 (2), pp. 79-91.

Stumpf, Ida R. C. Revistas universitárias brasileiras: barreiras na sua produção. *Transinformação*, 9(1), pp. 45-57, 1997.

Van de Sompel, Herbert. The Santa Fe convention of the Open Archives Initiative. D-Lib Magazine, 6(2), 2000. Available at: http://www.dlib.org/february00/vandesompel-oai/02vandesompel-oai.html, accessed on April 10, 2001.

Voorbij, Henk J. Searching scientific information on the Internet: a Dutch academic user survey. *Journal of the American Society for Information Science*, 1999, 50 (7), pp. 598-615.

Weibel, Stuart L and Traugott Koch. The Dublin Core Metadata Initiative: mission, current activities, and future directions. *D-Lib Magazine*, 6(12), 2000. Available at: http://www.dlib.org/dlib/december00/weibel/12weibel.html, accessed on April 12, 2001.

Electronic Publishing '01 –
2001 in the Digital Publishing Odyssey
A. Hübler et al. (Eds.)
IOS Press, 2001

Embracing the Museum Publication

Eckhard Stasch, Michael Reiche, Arved Hübler, Klaus Kreulich

Institute for Print and Media Technology
Chemnitz Technical University
D-09126 Chemnitz, Germany
eckhard.stasch@mbv.tu-chemnitz.de
http://www.tu-chemnitz.de/pm

This paper deals with a document management application which is being devoloped for and implemented in the Industrial Museum of Saxony.

Whereas most of the common museum documentation projects focus on the issue of collection management, this project is content-centered. It intends to establish an XML-based visitor-information-system, which enables the museum to provide on-sreen visitor information "on-the-floor" and in the internet as well as print-output (PoD) automatically from the same data source.

The paper will sketch the system's architecture and take a closer look at the conception and development of the document models, meta-data and stylesheets, which allow to create rich and diverse multimedia presentations. The discussion will outline some key demands of a publication system which is tailored to the needs and expectations of museum visitors as well as the museum staff.

0. Introduction

This paper presents the concept of an information system for museum visitors which provides online information as well as printed information from the same digital document source. This system is based on XML.

Establishing an XML application still is complex and time-consuming. It requires a thorough examination of the material which has to be handled and processed, and a conception of the system functions, tools and workflows. It also has an effect on the environment where it is implemented. Establishing an XML application involves the staff and their routines. In the case of the Chemnitz Industrial Museum, documentation and publishing practises will have to be reorganized and tuned to a new overall strategy. And, most obviously, the first period of such a project takes quite a number of meetings with little 'visible' outcome and it can be challenging to keep the staff involved. Establishing an XML application is real effort. Thus, it must be justified by a reasonable vision of the utility and advantage of the designed system.

1. Tailoring a Concept

The visitor information system outlined in this article will be implemented in the Chemnitz Industrial Museum. The museum was founded in 1991. Its origins are closely related to the historical context of the collapse of the political and economic system in former Eastern Germany. On one hand, this situation was auspicious for gathering a collection of industrial history when hundreds of companies shut down and gave away their remains for free. On the other hand, this radical turnround called for an institution like an industrial museum. Chemnitz had been a center of engineering and textile industries for about 200 years and it was bad enough for the people in the region to see their working equipment rendered in items of cultural heritage. The Chemnitz Industrial Museum preserves (and reflects) the reminiscence of a cultural identity many people have lived with.

This close link to the roots and fate of a region led state and municipal politicians to giving the museum more prominence. Therefore, they funded the reconstruction of an old foundry building which will be the new site of the museum. It is due to re-open in 2003 with a broader mission as the Industrial Museum of Saxony.

When the museum executives asked the Institute for Print and Media Technology to support them in establishing a visitor information system in their new residence they already had designed the framework of the exhibition concept.

First, the new exhibition will be grouped into seven topic areas.[1] Second, the exhibits are intended to be the predominant physical objects on the exhibiton floor, presented in a very purist manner without decorative wrapping or furnishing. This vision, which is inspired by the idea and appearance of an art exhibition, goes that far that it does not want to have information displays, charts or text boards along with the exhibits except from very small tables which only give a short description of each exhibit. All other information should be condensed into POIs (*Points of Information*) which are placed prominently in the center of each of the seven topic areas of the exhibition (*landmarks*). The POIs were expected to be multimedia kiosks, which present rich and diverse information and tell the whole 'museum story'.

Given this determination to rely on electronic information, we had to consider the following issues:

1.1 Information should be available and accessible

In the second place, this does concern the physical measurements and design of the kiosks and their devices. In the first place visitors will have to find a kiosk which is not occupied by someone else.

We recommended to the museum not to think of *stand-alone* kiosks which display one certain presentation related to their neighbourhood, but rather to establish an overall museum *information network*: the kiosks, no matter where they are located should give access to the entire information bases. The relation towards a topic area could be displayed according to a fish-eye principle: the 'default' presentation on every kiosk will focus on the topics of the area where it is located but all other branches of the thematic structure can be reached through some clicks of navigation.

With kiosks as outlets of a coherent Visitor Information System (*VIS*) we hope to make sure that users will disperse smoothly across the whole exhibition floor.[2]

1.2 Information should be rich and multiple

As the presentation of the exhibits is deliberately purist and sober the information supplied through the kiosks would have to be rich, manifold and compelling. It should not only describe the exhibits but also give a lot of additional and contextual information. In a nutshell, it should 'tell the story' of industrial development and culture in Saxony.

Information should be attractive for different types of visitors in terms of different ages,

---

[1] These are: The Saxons, the working people, the entrepreneurs, the family, the creators, the people from Karl-Marx-Town and the consumers. The design of the topics express the intention of the Museum not to focus on technology but on people in different roles and classes.

[2] The museum stats show that more than 70 % of visitors come in groups, 50 % of the visitors are pupil classes. Consequently, the occupation of the POIs will have peaks whenever two or more groups arrive at the same time. This tendency stresses the importance of a coherent network solution.

interests, educational levels, and different familiarity with electronic information devices. Therefore, we outlined a dual level structure of mainstream and deepening.

The *mainstream* is the core sum of information we intend to bring about to most of the visitors. On the surface level it presents a movie-like trailer for each of the seven topics of the exhibition; this trailer is presented in the default loop of every kiosk, so that a very unexperienced user can follow them without even touching a single button. Next, the mainstream presents a nicely narrated walkthrough of five to seven aspects of each topic, often in the form of portraits of people (*historical agents*). The mainstream orients towards a level of *common understanding* and makes intensive use of multimedia (graphics, audio, video, interactive games and models). The mainstream is organized horizontally like a guided tour, which leads the user from one issue to the next. Every narrative in the mainstream should appear as 'complete in itself' and give the visitor the opportunity to come to an end.

The *deeper level* contains all kind of further information: the description of special aspects, details, documentation. This level addresses to visitors with special interests or educational purposes. It is accessible through reference and navigation, but also through request and retrieval. The quantity of documents on the deeper level is virtually infinite.

To sum up, the VIS will contain more documents than the user can consume and comprehend within a visit. User tests measured the average time spent at a POI ranging from 3 to 7 minutes.[3] This will just be enough time to go through two or three mainstream articles.

From here it was close at hand to think of a print option. We proposed to implement a 'print basket' where the visitor can drop documents during his museum tour when he intends to read them later. These documents are compiled on an account and form a personal sample. At the end of his museum tour the visitor can sort his account, widen or narrow his sample and finally trigger a print job. After a minute he can take away his personal museum catalogue for deeper reading.[4]

1.3 Information should also be offered in the WWW

This demand seems only too reasonable. Today, internet pages play a crucial role for a museum's aiming to reach and maintain a broader public. The only issue discussed with the museum team was whether all inhouse content should be brought to the internet as well. The question was if a complete internet presentation would satisfy the users' interest so much that visiting the museum online is worth enough and makes a real visit seem to be redundant.

We argued that this was quite impropable. Just the contrary, we are convinced that a rich and profound internet site is an indicator of the museum's substance and expertise and will rather awake the desire to see the place behind it.

1.4 Re-usable content

The wish to supply museum visitor information via different output devices could not be fulfilled without the concept of re-usable content.[5] This concept became more prominent

---

[3] Annette Noschka-Roos (1999): Evaluation der Neuen Medien im Museumskontext – Befunde und Konsequenzen. Unveröff. Manskript des Vortrags zum Konferenzthema 'Zauberformel Interaktivität', Heinz Nixdorf Museumsforum, Paderborn, 16.11.1999.

[4] The opportunity to print electronic documents is strongly recommended by user tests which state that electronic displays are the appropriate medium for presenting dynamic information but that readers prefer paper copies for comprehensive reading. See: Andrew Dillon (1994): Designing usable electronic text. Ergonomic aspects of human information usage. London 1994: 30 ff.

with the rise of XML which is based on the idea of seperating form from content. In our project the strategy of a trifold use of the same content (kiosk, internet and personal sample print) was justification enough make a deeper approach bv implementing an XML application.

Another pre-condition encouraged this appraoch. The museum, founded in 1991, is a very young institution and does not have too many legacy systems or records which will have to be inherited in the new system. The new information system will be installed in a new museum building from the very beginning. Thus, the concept and design of an XML document repository could start from scratch and did not have to tackle the difficulties of migration. Indeed, the museum team rather has got a spirit to create 'something new' on the occasion of above mentioned fundamental reconstruction of its residence.

2. Developing a Museum-DTD

After scetching the different functions of the visitor information system we had to work on the document structure which is the backbone of the application. An XML application allows applying different formats to one single content entity and the merging of different entities within a new document or publication 'on the fly' in case the elements which have to be gathered and formated are known. The application of abstract formating rules re quires an abstract content model, the DTD.

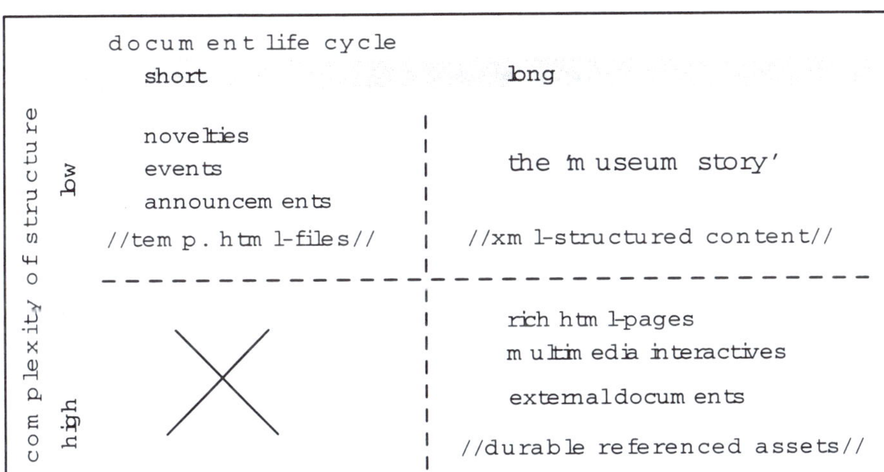

fig. 1: matrix of museum content types

At first glance, narrative content appears to be very diverse and manifold, and it seems a bit discouraging to align it with an abstract schema. It is either possible to tailor the schema to the various types of content which renders a DTD painfully complex. Or one can submit

[5] This is true given the limitations of most museum institutions who have to fulfill very diverse requirements with very little ressources. Writing and editing content is only one aspect of the museum business.

the content to a more concise DTD at the risk of creating a schematic application with little appeal. We tried to avoid both extrems.

An analysis of the range of the museum content formed a matrix with to axes: Once, the document lifecycle could be short or durable. Second, the degree of complexity of the content structure could range from very much individual presentations to rather schematic content types. [see fig. 1]

We estimated that about 80% of the content within the VIS would be longlived and schematic. This is where we marked the claim of the content DTD. And we allowed two exceptions to occur: the permanent flow of short-lived information which occurs in the form of genuin html-pages, and the case of non-structured or non mark-up content which will be incorporated into a structured document container as a plug-in. Besides these two exceptions, the majority of documents represents more or less a discoursive or narrational text and illustration type of content.

2.1 General content structure

In structuring this text and illustration type of content we did not go into very deep. On the top level we subdivide our document page into the sections of head, index, and content. Within the content, we separated the illustrations ('visuals') from the text ('chapter').

```
<!ELEMENT content
        (title, visuals, chapter*)>
```

The integration of text and illustrations is a task that can spoil any abstract formatting very easily – just think of the occurance of pictures with a vertical or horizontal orientation. We rid ourselves of this problem by defining an area of preview images which occurs on top of each chapter. These preview images all have the same height and vary only in width; if necessary we allow ourselves to crop the original picture. The preview images are linked to fullscreen views of the same graphics which can be switched into the page by the user. In some cases we will use the fullscreen area to display a multimedia type of content, which we handle as a subset of 'visuals'.

2.2 Text structure

Within the structure of the text area ('chapter') we identified three entities with specific conditions: the firstPara, the anyPara and the lastPara element.

```
<!ELEMENT chapter
        (firstpara, anypara*, lastpara?)>
```

We chose a flat structure for the text content because we wanted to allow the authors to write in a 'natural' manner without a mark-up headache. All other distinction of document and content types is accomplished by different subclasses of the firstPara element and by document meta-data. Furthermore, firstPara and anyPara provide some format options like quotations, lists or tables, as well as stressed, highlighted or colored sections.

In the default chapter the firstPara is only of presentational use: it is the section which will be highlighted in the layout and which delivers an introduction or opener for the rest of the chapter. In addition to the default chapter, we identified five special content types, which seemed to occur on a regular basis: the description of an exhibit, of a person or institution ('agent'), a 'location', a 'date' or an event, the definition and explanation of a 'keyword', and the presentation of a document, an asset or illustration as 'source'. In these cases, the firstPara contains different sets of obgligatory elements such as 'name', 'place' and 'date' of 'birth' and 'death', and 'occupation' for 'agents'.

The anyPara element is meant for any further description and discourse.

The lastPara element is specified to contain document information and relational links. Elements of the lastPara are creator and contributor, the date of creation and the copyright info, the list of quoted sources, and references towards related or recommended documents for further reading.

```
<!ELEMENT lastpara
(chaptersources?, copyrights?, references?)>
<!ELEMENT chaptersources
(chaptersource*)>
<!ELEMENT chaptersource
(% content;)>
<!ELEMENT copyrights
(copyright*)>
<!ELEMENT copyright
(copyrightitem, copyrightowner, copyrightyear)>
<!ELEMENT copyrightitem
(% content;)>
<!ELEMENT copyrightowner
(% vcard;)>
<!ELEMENT copyrightyear
(#PCDATA)>
<!ELEMENT references
(reference*)>
<!ELEMENT reference
        (% uri;)>
```

2.3 Referencing external documents

A last issue which required some reflection was the handling of keywords. When we surveyed existing museum information systems we decided rather quickly not to apply a typical hypertext structure. We felt that hyperlinks embeded in the text interrupt the flow of reading and confront the readers with a distracting decisions to either maintain reading or to track the link. In the early conceptual stages we even wanted to ban all hyperlinks from our content and postpone them to the end of each article (see the 'reference' element in 'lastPara').

This seemed to work perfectly with all references to related our deeper reading. We only felt uncomfortable with keyword definitions at the end of the article because readers do ask for a definition at the moment when a keyword occurs. Therefore we decided to list keywords appearing throughout the text in the index area of the page and allow the readers to switch in definitions if they want. For switching we use the firstPara element of a keyword definition article and display a short description of the issued term. for deeper reading the reader will then find a link to the full article at the end of the document.

To conclude with, our DTD for the content of visitor information aims to balance flexibility and structure. We allow exceptions from the XML-structured content at the expense of loosing the print-option for those documents. Our content DTD is flat enough to support a natural manner of writing,[6] and it works with documents of any lenght which can even consist of nothing else than the firstPara element (i.e. for keyword definitions). A

[6] The flat structure also makes it easy to apply the DTD to documents from external authors because most text can be dropped into the DTD structure with little copy and paste effort.

deeper structure would only make sense if we wanted to handle and process documents in a more modular way. This was not necessary because our documents are coherent units.

3. Document Meta-Data

In the VIS application meta-data have three basic functions: they supply the description of a document, they support retrieval and they serve for the ordering and grouping of documents.

The first question was where the meta-data should be derived from: the existing *museum catalogue* or the new visitor information system. The museum catalogue already contains data-records on about 7.000 exhibits, 3.600 bibliographic items, and about 1.500 photographs, graphics and illustrations. In the future it will be used for digital asset management as well. Could these meta-data from the catalogue be re-used ?

3.1 Interrelating internal and public repositories

When we examined the existing catalogue records for their applicabilty within the VIS we had to face the different nature of these two systems: The VIS is designed as a repository for the public, the catalogue was not. This does not only mean that some of the fields of catalogue records have to stay hidden from the public, it also means that records were not gathered intending public usage.

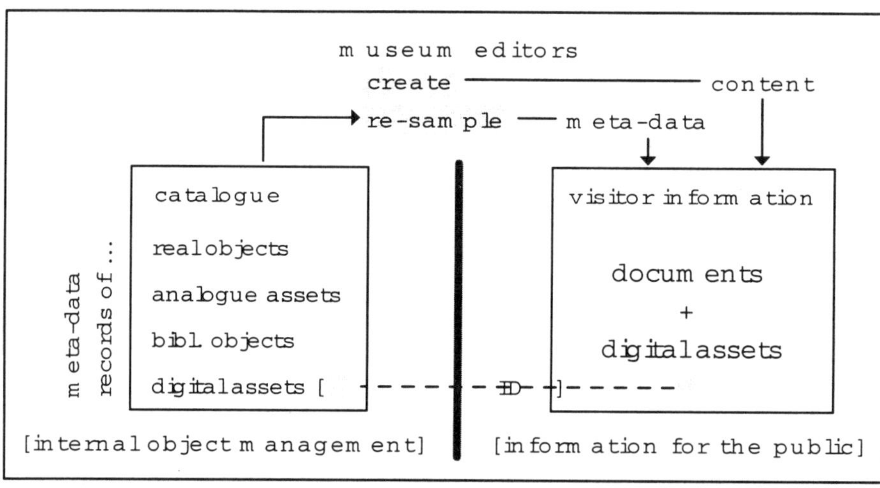

fig. 2: the interrelation of internal and public repositories

For many of the object descriptions the quality of records is too poor and cryptic to be displayed in the visitor information system. Exhibits are documented with pocket camera pictures, descriptions use staff specific abbreviations and
expressions. All in all, the quality and style of the catalogue records is based on *'good enough'* and *'you know what I mean'* criteria.

Second, we were decided to align our publication meta-data neatly with the Dublin Core set of elements as the most widely shared standard. Obviously, the designers of the catalogue had not thought of D.C.: some of their fields were kind of identical to D.C. elements, but had a different name, some others were completely missing. For publication it would have been necessary to transform some of the existing records and to supplement others.

Instead of thinking about filtering and transcription mechanisms, we decided not to connect the two systems and to establish the VIS as an independent repository seperated from the catalogue. [see fig. 2] The only bridge between the catalogue and the VIS will be the continuity of unique identifiers which have to be consistent throughout the museum.

With this separation we make the editors responsible for the style and quality of any information which is displayed for the public.

3.2 The set of meta-data

In the VIS we apply a set of Dublin Core meta-data extended by some own, museum specific (*'imc'*) elements. We present the designed set of meta-data grouped according to their functions.

3.2.1 Naming and description of documents

DC.Identifier, DC.Title; DC.Description, IMC.Mode, DC.Ressourcetype, DC.Language, DC.Format; DC.Creator, DC.Contributor, DC.Date, DC.Rights, DC.Source, IMC.Printcharge

The elements for the naming and description of documents will be displayed to a different degree in different situations. For tables of content rendering the title element will be sufficient. A description is helpful together with the presentation of surch results. 'DC.Description' offers a very short abstract of the content, while 'IMC_Mode' and 'DC.Ressourcetype' specify the manner how the content is presented. 'IMC_Mode' refers to the way how a document can be experienced by the user, its distinguishing features are text, audio, video, image, model and multimedia. 'DC.Ressourcetype' characterizes the way in which a matter is treated or approached, it presents a genre-like term, such as 'essay, portrait, interview, table etc ...', according to a list of expressions. Together with the 'DC.Language' element these description items help the users to refine their choice within a list of search results.

The 'DC.Format' element will mainly occur in the internet. It is relevant when the content has a multimedia format such as movie, audio or director files. Internet visitors need to know which plugins are required, and they like to know how long it will take to load the file. These issues don't count in the controlled environment of the museum. Here, we will only tell the users the running time of an audio or video file.

3.2.2 Grouping and listing of documents

Meta-data elements are *IMC.Parent* and *IMC.Predecessor.*

For *grouping and indexing* documents we have to handle two major classes of content, the *'museum story'* and the *'apparatus'*. Within the 'museum story' every document has a unique and specific occurance in the hierarchy and sequence of the whole narrative. The *'apparatus'* is our term for those documents which cover a single aspect or item and can occur in different relations, such as the description of a person or institution, the definition of a keyword etc. These documents will mostly be listed in alphabetical or numerical order.

Documents which are assembled within the museum story all derive from one root - the museum homepage and they are knitted through horizontal or vertical paths. Besides that, every document which leads to subordinate child documents can be regarded as a 'root' too. We decided to define all vertical relations 'bottom up', so that child documents refer to their specific root by referencing it as 'parent'. Horizontally, documents with the same 'parent' reference occur on one level. We define their sequence through a backward reference, so that every document refers to its 'predecessor'.

These two elements, 'parent' and 'predecessor', allow the complete description of a tree structure. [see fig. 3] This structure is easy to maintain, even if documents have to be inserted into an exesting sequence. In this case you would only have to redefine the 'predecesor' reference in the following document. Through its abstract order it even allows to create coherent numbered indexes for personal print samples. By refering to the orginal index of the complete museum story the gaps of 'missing' documents can be closed easily.

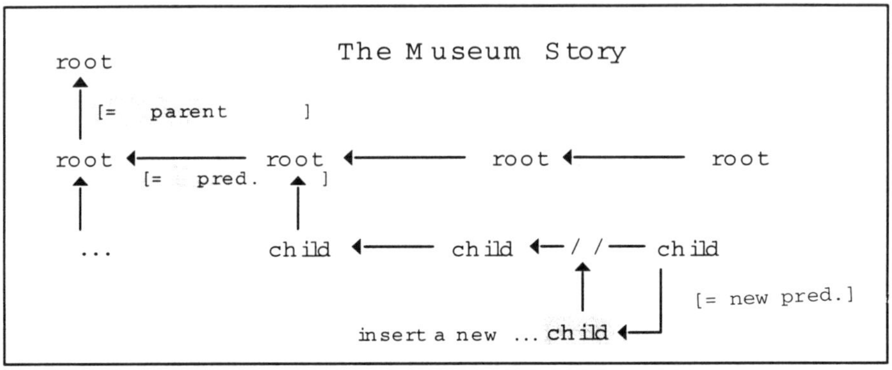

fig. 3: an abstract tree structure referenced back- and upwards

3.2.3 Retrieval of documents

DC.Subject_exhibit, _agent, _date, _place, _keyword; DC.Coverage_exhibit, _agent, _date, _place, _keyword; IMC.Context

When designing the retrieval options for the VIS it was important to remember the target audience. Museum visitors are most likely to ask for comprehensive information, they like overviews and get involved into short guided tours. Others focus primarily on the museum highlights and scan the site for the most spectacular exhibits or the 'coolest' multimedia presentations. Some visitors will further like to explore the range and character of the collection and the information system. But most museum visitors are neither experts nor researchers.

Therefore, retrieval had to be easy and understandable rather than refined and sophisticated. We provide three modes of access to the museum content: Overviews and TOCs, different lists for browsing and a free search mode.

Most users will certainly navigate the information system along with the thematic and narrational structure of the content. They will find 'tableaus' for each of the seven topic areas: nice graphic menues for overview and quick access to the mainstream highlights.

Next, users will find different types of lists. The most prominent list leads to the description of exhibits and will be close at hand throughout the information system. Besides that, we expect many visitors to look for certain types of media, mainly movies or interactive multimedia to play with. Some others will probably look for documents related to people or institutions, places or dates, often because they are related with their personal history. A third type of users will certainly like to browse the list of keywords in order to see what the story is about. The applied set of meta-data elements is designed of support the listings of documents according to these issues. Choosing the name of a person from the list of historical agents triggers a retrieval process which will deliver a list of all documents that relate to the requested person.

The applied set of metadata makes it possible to identify three levels of relevance within search results: they can be rendered as

document 'a' *treats* search-term 'b' [based on 'DC.Subject']
document 'a' *covers* search-term 'b' [based on 'DC.Coverage']
search-term 'b' *occurs in* document 'a' [based on full text search]

Finally, the design of the retrieval option allows a free search request. But we estimate this mode not to be used very frequently. Indeed, we did not support the retrieval of a wide range of qualified hits. Most results for a free search will probably derive from the full text search procedure. In order to make our system coherent we narrowed the variety of items occurring as 'subject' or 'description'. With the element subsets _agent, _date, _place and _keyword we rather try to enforce multiple hits for one list item instead of a wide spread of single results.

4. StyleSheets

The generating of various output from one single XML source is based on XSL Style Sheets. Printable output format from the VIS will be PDF. For screen displays we transform XML files to HTML. In the controlled environment[7] of the museum we apply StyleSheets in a rather sophisticated manner. We will also make use of high-quality images and multimedia. For the WWW we will have to check our StyleSheets for browser compatibility and replace our highres-assets with some more compressed versions.

The most tricky issue was the transformation of screen-design into print layout. Here, we held on to the principle of seperating the pictures from the text. In the printed version we will present the pictures of a chapter above the text, too. Instead of switching keyword definitions into the page, we will make use of footnotes in the print-version.

A deeper look at StylesSheets and different layouts would go beyond the scope of this article.[8]

5. Discussion and future opportunities

The conception and design of the visitor information system (VIS) for the Industrial Museum of Saxony tries to balance the expections and requirements of both parties who will live with it. On the input and maintenance side, the basic concept of re-usable content makes the work of the museum editors very effective. A flat DTD allows them a natural manner of writing, and the amount of meta-data to be maintained seems reasonable and bearable.

On the output side the application had to be structured without appearing schematic and dull. This could be fulfilled by establishing a body of xml-structured content which allows the occurance of non-structured up to date information as well as sophisticated multimedia. Rich, various and compelling multimedia content will be crucial for the public acceptance of the information system.

The outlined print option is a prototype application in a museum context. Thus, it is difficult to estimate its acceptance. But within an xml-based information system, this feature

[7] As the kiosk browser, at the moment we prefer the Internet Explorer because it supports CSS very satisfyingly.
[8] Some examples will be shown during the conference presentation.

can be established at very low entrance costs. It requires little extra effort but an additional stylesheet and a digital printing device.

At the beginning, the opportunity to print a personal sample of the museum content may be regarded as a nice but unfamiliar gadget by most of the museum visitors. What is more, the PoD sample does not intend to replace the official museum catalogue or other high gloss publications: it will be printed in greyscale and the finishing will be more or less simple.

We rather do conceive the print option of the VIS as a node of plant which has the potential for growing. The idea is to establish a platform for different kinds of niche publications. These are some scenarios and pathways for future development:

5.1 Special interest groups

The origins of the Chemnitz Industrial Museum go back to the initiative of a group of ardent enginieers who are very much interested in the technical aspects of production lines and machinery. Organisized as a board of museum companions, they have formed several working groups for the inquiry and documentation of technological development in different branches of the local industries.

Whereas the mainstream of museum visitor information orients towards a level of common understanding, the print plattform will be able to host all the deep and specialist documentation produced by the engineering working groups. The museum encouraged these working groups to develop and maintain their own edition of essays on technological issues.

5.2 Cooperation with schools

School classes represent about 50 per cent of the total visiting party of the museum. Many of them see their museum trip as a day off and it is a challenge for the museum guide to keep pupils involved during a tour.

The general idea for the educational role of a museum is to support and complement the work that is done in school. Therefore, it will be useful to offer schools material for preparing and resuming their museum visit. This material can range from background information on certain aspects of the exhibition, over guides and games which help to explore the exhibition, to documents about regional aspects of industrial development which are underestimated in the exhibition but can help to tranfer and apply pupils knowledge from one sphere to another. This kind of material is due to be gathered and developed in close cooperation with school teachers to make sure they can find what they need. The vision for this branch of the print repository is a tollbox where every teacher can find the right stuff to make a sample for her purpose.

Beyond this, it might be nice for pupils to bring their fruits of learning back to the museum. The print repository could also have a branch of essays written by pupils. These essays could certainly encourage other pupils to explore aspects of industrial society 'their way'.

5.3 Reprints of editions from third parties

The museum is in contact with the informal network of researchers in the field of industrial history. These researchers edit or contribute to publications on different occasions. One phenomenon with scientific publications is that they circulate within very narrow paths. First editions often count less than a thousand copies, and many journals can only be found in special libraries.

The print repository can become an archive for scientific articles and essays. Researchers and institutions will be invited to deposit their publications in here in order to keep them available. Print on demand makes this service attractive in two ways: reprint is cost effective with only one copy, and articles from a volume can be supplied as modular issues and merged from different original sources. Such a 'digital library of industrial history' will not only attract scientific users. Hosted in a museum it can also serve as a gateway towards common visitors.

5.4 Internet access

Any of the different editions and branches of the print repository should be accessible via internet. It should also be possible to mingle any documents from the VIS with documents from the print repository. Users can choose if they want to have their samples printed in the museum and delivered via mail or if the want a PDF file for their home desktop printer.

Internet access will certainly broaden the number of users of the print service. It will also raise the question of a business model. At least, the museum will have to establish an accounting system. It will be a strategic decision whether to run print on demand as a commercial activity or to keep it on the level of a usefull museum service.

6. Appendix: Project information

The presented application will run in the Chemnitz Industrial Museum from the date of its new opening in 2003.

Address: Chemnitz Industrial Museum
Zwickauer Str. 119 – 125
09112 Chemnitz, Germany

Homepage: www.saechsisches-industriemuseum.de
eMail: chemnitz@saechsisches-industriemuseum.de

Electronic Publishing '01 –
2001 in the Digital Publishing Odyssey
A. Hübler et al. (Eds.)
IOS Press, 2001

SyDoM: A Multilingual Information Retrieval System for Digital Libraries

Catherine Roussey, Sylvie Calabretto, Jean-Marie Pinon

LISI – INSA de Lyon
Bâtiment Blaise Pascal
7, avenue Jean Capelle
69621 Villeurbanne Cedex
France
Tel: (33) 4 72 43 88 94
Fax: (33) 4 72 43 87 13
catherine.roussey@lisi.insa-lyon.fr, sylvie.calabretto@lisi.insa-lyon.fr,
jean-marie.pinon@lisi.insa-lyon.fr

Abstract: In this paper, we present a multilingual information retrieval system based on knowledge representation model. This system allows document indexing and information retrieval in a multilingual document collection where documents are written in different languages, though each individual document may contain text in only one language. The underlying model permits to describe the semantic of document in a multilingual context. This model, called semantic graph, is an extension of the Sowa's model of conceptual graphs where different vocabularies are available. Indeed, in this model two kinds of knowledge are identified:

- Domain knowledge organises domain entity in two hierarchies of types (concept types and relation types),
- Lexical knowledge associates term, belonging to a vocabulary, to concept type or relation type.

Then, a same semantic graph can have different representations depending on the vocabulary chose. For example, the French representation of a semantic graph uses the French labels of types to display each graph component and the English representation of the same graph uses the English labels of types to display the graph.

Our proposition has been validated in the logical information retrieval system SyDoM. The system is dedicated to the needs of virtual libraries for managing XML documents. Thanks to the semantic graph model, SyDoM develops several functionality for multilingual information retrieval. This first evaluation gives better results than traditional information retrieval system.

Keywords: Multilingual Information Retrieval, information modelling, XML document, knowledge representation, Conceptual Graph, Digital Libraries

0. Introduction

Doc'INSA is the library of a scientific and technical university called INSA (National Institute of Applied Sciences) located in Lyon. This library offers various types of scientific and technical documentation and provides students and researchers with local resources in the engineering sciences: 85,000 books and 1,740 periodicals. The collection is divided into different topics such as computer science, mechanics, etc. Currently, Doc'INSA is working on the design of a Digital Library that allows its subscribers to retrieve and consult documents alongside the Internet network.

The indexing method in Doc'INSA involves a librarian in building manually a bibliographic record for each document. This bibliographic record is composed of several fields: the title of the document, the authors' name, the publishing date, keywords and an abstract. The keyword field contains a list of keywords describing the document content. Later, the librarian writes an abstract, which will be displayed after the retrieval procedure in order to obtain a more accurate description of the document.

The Information Retrieval system of Doc'INSA uses a Boolean model where a query is composed of keywords associated by Boolean operators. All bibliographic records whose keywords field matches the Boolean query, are retrieved and displayed.

Unfortunately, this indexing method has several limitations:

- Firstly, a document is represented by a list of keywords. Therefore, this method does not provide an accurate and precise description.
- Secondly, there is no control of keyword assignment which means that two documents dealing with the same subject could be indexed by a different set of keywords. Consequently, librarians can not handle correctly the vocabulary evolution.
- Finally, this indexing method is monolingual and builds only French indices. French indices are not adapted to the needs of a multilingual collection of documents. For example, a translation process is necessary to query in English these French indices.

In order to improve the indexing method of Doc'INSA, we propose a semantic graph model adapted for multilingual information retrieval (IR) purpose. This model combines domain knowledge and lexical knowledge, used to present domain knowledge in several languages such as French or English. Indices will be written in a language independent way thanks to the domain knowledge.

First of all, we present in chapter 2 a review of conventional Multilingual Information Retrieval approaches. Next, in chapter 3, we propose a formal presentation of our semantic graph model, following by our research algorithms (chapter 4). As shown in chapter 5, this graph model permits to develop several functionality for our multilingual information retrieval system SyDoM. And finally, we compare SyDoM with the Doc'INSA information system.

1. Related works

The major part of Cross-Language Information Retrieval approaches translate a query into target languages, using bilingual dictionaries [1], [8], bilingual corpora [4] or Machine Translation systems [12]. These approaches use monolingual Information Retrieval system, so they still deal with monolingual indexing.

Dumais & Co [5] have proposed a method of language independent indexing based on parallel corpus. They have used a matrix reduction technique called Latent Semantic Indexing (LSI) to extract langage independent terms and document representations. Unfortunately, parallel corpora are not common in general, tending rather to be restricted to specialised domains like legal domain of multilingual country (Switzerland, Canada).

P. Vossen & Co [17] describe a language-independent indexing on the basis of the multilingual database EuroWordNet (EWN). A Wordnet is a network of word meanings and one Wordnet per languages is created (English, Dutch, Spanish, Italian, German, French, Czech and Estonian). All Wordnets are connected by the Inter-Lingual-Index (ILI) which contains a set of universal concepts called ILI records.

Their aim is to index documents and queries in terms of language-independent ILI records. Unfortunately, the French wordnet is still under development.

In conclusion, we are aware of only few methods using real language-independent indexing methods. Moreover these methods represent documents as a traditional vector. So indices are a linear combination of terms. We proposed a semantic graph model in order to improve the document representation in a multilingual information system.

2. Semantic graph model

Our proposition takes Conceptual Graph approaches into account [6], [7], [11], by proposing a graph matching function optimized for the information retrieval needs. First of all, we present a graph formalism allowing the document description in a multilingual context. We have transformed the conceptual graph formalism to be closer to a documentary language. Concepts are limited to generic concepts because descriptors represent notions and not individuals or particular objects. We consider that processing a graph is equivalent to processing its normal form, in which a concept node appears only one time per graph. Thus, the number of possible indices for a document is limited.

2.1 Semantic thesaurus

We proposed a formalism in which two kinds of knowledge are identified:

- Domain knowledge organises domain entity in two hierarchies of types (concept types and relation types). This knowledge is formalised in a support. Domain knowledge are considered to be language independent entity.
- Lexical knowledge associates term, belonging to a vocabulary, to concept type or relation type. Lexical knowledge displays domain knowledge in an understandable way for human users.

Domain and lexical knowledge are associated in a semantic thesaurus. This thesaurus defines a multilingual documentary language.

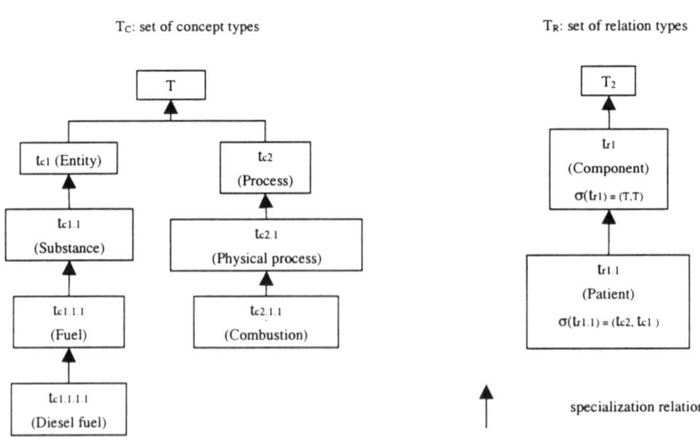

Fig. 1. An example of support.

2.1.1 Domain conceptualization or Support

A support S is a 3-tuple $S = (T_{C,} T_{R,} \sigma)$ such as:

- T_C is a set of concept types partially ordered by the specialization relation, noted $\leq$, and it has a greatest element, denoted T.
- T_R *is a* set of binary relation types[1] partially ordered by $\leq$ and it has a greatest element, noted T_2.
- σ, called *signature*, is a mapping which associates with any relation types the greatest concept type of its arguments. In a semantic graph, for any $t_r \in T_{R,}$ the type of the kth argument of t_r should be more specific than the type of the kth argument of $\sigma(t_r)$. The ith argument of $\sigma(t_r)$ is denoted $\sigma_i(t_r)$. The figure 1 contains two examples of signatures.

2.1.2 Semantic thesaurus

A semantic thesaurus, noted M, (composed of P languages) is a 4-tuple $M = (S, V, \lambda_C, \lambda_R)$ such as :

- S is a support composed of a set of concept types T_C , a set of relation types $T_{R,}$ and a mapping σ which associates signatures with relation types.
- V is a set of vocabularies, split into set of terms belonging to the same language (a vocabulary). $V = V_{L1} \cup V_{L2} \cup \ldots \cup V_{Lj} \cup \ldots \cup V_{LP}$ such as V_{Lj} is a set of terms belonging to the language Lj.
- $\lambda_C = \{ \lambda_C^{VL1} \ldots \lambda_C^{VLj} \ldots \lambda_C^{VLP} \}$ is a set of P mapping such as $\lambda_C^{VLj} : T_C \rightarrow V_{Lj}$ is a mapping $\lambda_C^{VLj}(t_c)$ which associates a term of the language $Lj \in V_{Lj}$ with a concept type $t_c \in T_C$.
- $\lambda_R = \{ \lambda_R^{VL1} \ldots \lambda_R^{VLj} \ldots \lambda_R^{VLP} \}$ is a set of P mapping such as $\lambda_R^{VLj} : T_R \rightarrow V_L$ is a mapping $\lambda_R^{VLj}(t_r)$ which associates a term of the language $Lj \in V_{Lj}$ with a relation type $t_r \in T_R$.

[1] In general, a type of relation can have any arity, but in this paper, relations are considered to be only binary relations like case relations or thematic roles associated with verbs [11].

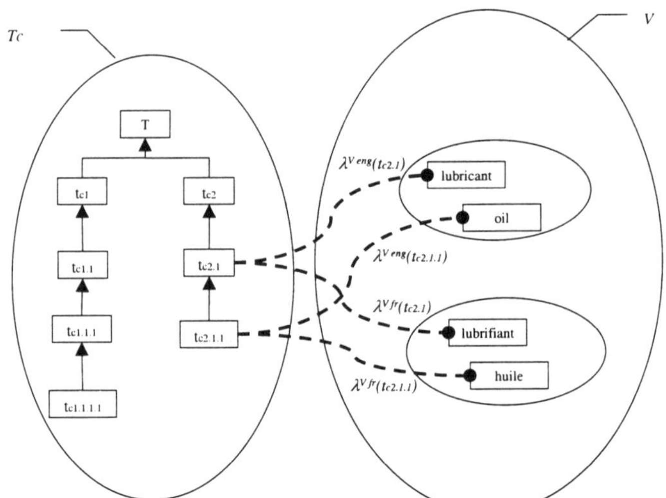

Fig. 2. An example of semantic thesaurus.

The figure 2 presents an example of mapping λ_C , in which V is composed of two vocabularies: an English vocabulary, denoted V_{eng} , and a French vocabulary , denoted V_{fr}. Each concept type is linked to a term of each vocabulary. For example, the type of concept $t_{c2.1} \in T_C$, is linked to the English term $\lambda_C^{Veng}(t_{c2.1})$="*lubricant*" and it is also linked to a French term $\lambda_C^{Vfr}(t_{c2.1})$="*lubrifiant*".

From this semantic thesaurus defining domain knowledge and lexical knowledge, our formalism, called semantic graph, is defined. A semantic graph is a set of concept nodes connected to each other by relations. Comparing to conceptual graph, the accent is made upon relations linking concepts. That's why we define the notion of arc as a couple of concept nodes labeled by a relation type.

Semantic graph

A semantic graph is a 6-tuple $Gs = (C, A, \mu, labelC, \nu, labelR)$ related to a semantic thesaurus M, such that :

- C is a set of concept nodes[2] contained in Gs.
- $A \subset C \times C$ is a set of arches contained in Gs. For each arch $a= (c, c') \in A$; the ith concept node of a (also called argument of a) is denoted a_i: $(a_1 = c$ and $a_2 = c')$.
- μ: $C \rightarrow T_C$. μ is a mapping which associated for each concept node, $c \in C$, a label $\mu(c) \in T_C$, $\mu(c)$ is also called the ***type*** of c.
- $labelC$ is a set of mappings $labelC = \{ labelC^{VL1}, ..., labelC^{VLj}, ..., labelC^{VLP}\}$ such that the mapping $labelC^{VLj}$: $C \rightarrow V_{Lj}$, associates a concept, $c \in C$, with a term of the language Lj, $labelC^{VL\,j}(c) \in V_{Lj}$. $labelC^{VL\,j}(c)$ is called the ***label*** of c for the language Lj.
- ν: $R \rightarrow T_R$. ν is a mapping, which associated for each arch, $a \in A$, a label $\nu(a) \in T_R$. $\nu(c)$ is also called the ***type*** of a.
- $labelR$ is a set of mapping $labelR = \{ labelR^{VL1}, ..., labelR^{VLj}, ..., labelR^{VLP} \}$ such that the mapping $labelR^{VL\,j}$: $A \rightarrow V_{Lj}$ associates an arch, $a \in A$ with a term of the language Lj. $labelR\,(a)^{VL\,j} \in V_{Lj}$. $labelR^{VL\,j}(a)$ is called the ***label*** of a for the language Lj.

---

[2] In this article, "concept node" and "concept" are equivalent expressions.

A semantic graph fulfils some constraints :

1. *A* fulfils the constraints fixed by the mapping σ, defined in the semantic thesaurus *M*. For each $a \in A$ such that $a = (c, c')$ and $\nu(a)=r$ then $\mu(a_i) \leq \sigma_i(r)$ so $\mu(c) \leq \sigma_1(r)$ and $\mu(c') \leq \sigma_2(r)$. For example, the relation type *Patient* defined in the Figure 4 has a signature such that $\sigma(Patient)=(Process, Entity)$. So all the relation typed by *Patient* should have a first argument, which concept type is more specific than *Process,* and a second argument, which concept type is more specific than *Entity*.
2. *LabelC* is the association of two mappings μ and λ_C. So, for all $c \in C$, $labelC(c)= \lambda_C(\mu(c)) =\lambda_C \circ \mu(c)$.
3. *labelR* is the association of two mappings ν and λ_R. So, for all $a \in A$, $labelR(a)= \lambda_R(\nu(a)) =\lambda_R \circ \nu(a)$.

Thanks to previous definition there exists different representations for the same semantic graph depending of the label used.

1. The first representation of semantic graph labels each graph component with its type. For example, in the semantic graph presented in the figure 3, the first concept node c is labeled by its type $\mu(c)= t_{c2.1.1}$. This type is defined in the support of the figure 1.

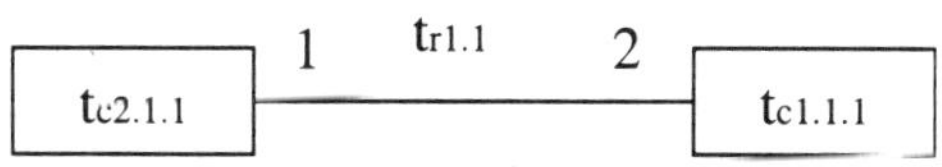

Fig. 3. An example of semantic graph labeled by types.

2. The second kind of semantic graph representation labels each graph component with a term chosen in a vocabulary defined in the semantic thesaurus. For example, if the language used is English, only the terms belonging to English vocabulary, noted *Veng* (cf Fig. 2), are used to label the graph component. So for a concept node *c*, its label is $labelC^{Veng}(c)= \lambda_C^{Veng}(\mu(c))$. Indeed, there exists several representations of the same semantic graph depending of the vocabulary chose. The figure 4 presents two representations of the semantic graph defined in the figure 3. In the first one, all the graph components are labeled by French terms and in the second representation, graph components are labeled by English terms. As a consequence, index composed of semantic graph can be displayed in different languages.

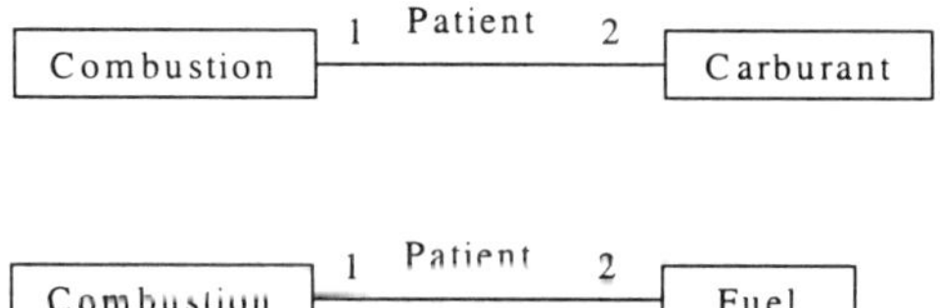

Fig. 4. Examples of semantic graph labeled by terms.

Now, we presents the similarity function between graphs used as a matching function in our multilingual information retrieval.

Similarity functions

Information retrieval systems based on Sowa 's Conceptual Graph use the projection operator as a matching function between index graphs of documents and query graphs. But this operator gives boolean results: projection between graphs exists or does not exist. To use this operator as a matching function in a IR system, the projection operator should better returns a float value (ranging between 0 and 1) thus making it possible to order the results. To this end, we will present various similarity functions used to define a similarity function between graphs. Each similarity function (between types, arches, graphs) returns a normalized float value ranging between 0 and 1.

First, from specialization relation presented in the semantic thesaurus, similarity functions between types will be defined.

2.1.3 Similarity function between types

The similarity function, noted *sim*, between types is an asymmetrical function. *sim* is defined as follows:

$sim: T_C \times T_C \cup T_R \times T_R \rightarrow [0,1]$

- If two types are not comparable then the similarity function returns a value equal to 0.
- If two types are identical then the similarity function returns a value equal to 1.
- If a type t_1 generalizes another type t_2 directly, i.e. there is not intermediate type between t_1 and t_2 in the type hierarchy, then the similarity function returns a constant value lower than 1 equal to V_G. V_G is fixed arbitrarily.
- If a type t_1 specializes another type t_2 directly, i.e. there is not intermediate type between t_1 and t_2 in the type hierarchy, then the similarity function returns a constant value lower than 1 equal to V_S. V_S is fixed arbitrarily.
- If a type t_1 specializes or generalized another type t_2 not directly, i.e. there is an intermediate type t between t_1 and t_2 in the type hierarchy then the similarity function between t_1 and t_2 is the product of the similarity functions between (t_1, t) and (t, t_2).

According to similarity function between types, we defined similarity function between arches and graphs.

2.1.4 Similarity function between arches

The similarity function between two arches, noted Sim_A is defined as follows:

a_H is an arch such as $a_H = (c_H, c'_H)$ and $\nu(a_H) = t_{rH}$ and a_G is an arch such as $a_G = (c_G, c'_G)$ and $\nu(a_G) = t_{rG}$.

$$Sim_A(a_H, a_G) = \frac{sim(\nu(a_H), \nu(a_G)) + sim(\mu(a_{H1}), \mu(a_{G1})) + sim(\mu(a_{H2}), \mu(a_{G2}))}{3}$$

Or

$$Sim_A(a_H, a_G) = \frac{sim(t_{rH}, t_{rG}) + sim(\mu(c_H), \mu(c_G)) + sim(\mu(c'_H), \mu(c'_G))}{3}$$

Sim_A computes the average of the similarity between each type of arch component.

2.1.5 Similarity function between graphs

The similarity function, noted sim_G, between a graph $H = (C_H, A_H, \mu_H, labelC_H, \nu_H, labelR_H)$ and a graph $G = (C_G, A_G, \mu_G, labelC_G, \nu_G, labelR_G)$ is a function returning float value ranging from 0 to 1.

$$sim_G(H,G) = \frac{\sum_{a_H \in A_H, a_G \in A_G} Max(sim_A(a_H, a_G)) + \sum_{c_H \in C_H, c_H \in C_G} Max(sim_C(\mu_H(c_H), \mu_G(c_G)))}{|C_H| + |A_H|}$$

sim_G computes the average of the similarity function between each graph component (arch and concept node) of H and a graph component of G. Because a graph component of H can have several comparable components in G, we take the maximum of the similarity function between a component of H and a component of G.

3. Information retrieval algorithm

After introducing our semantic graph formalism, we shall concentrate on the implementation of the matching function between graphs. Search algorithms find documents indexed by a semantic graph, called **index graph**, comparable with the query graph.

The semantic graphs are composed of arches and concept nodes. So there are two types of indexing entities (arches and concepts). Thus the document content is represented by two different indices: a list of arches and a list of concepts, from which the index graph of a document can be rebuilt.

Following the works of Ounis [11], our algorithms are based on the association of inverted files and acceleration tables. The inverted file groups in the same entry all the documents indexed by an indexing entity. This means that, given an indexing entity, we can immediately locate the documents indexed by it. The acceleration tables store, for each indexing entity, the list of comparable entities as well as the result of the similarity function between the comparable entity and the indexing entity. The construction of the inverted file and the acceleration table is done off-line, as part of the indexing procedure.

Our database is divided in two parts depending of the indexing entities used.

1. In the first part of the database, only arches of semantic graphs are taken into account. Each document is indexed by arches contained in its index graph. This part of the database is composed of an inverted file denoted *InvertedFileArc* and several acceleration tables denoted *FirstArgValue, SecondArgValue, RoleArgValue.*
2. In the second part of the data base, only the concept nodes of the semantic graphs are taken into account. Each document is indexed by the list of concepts contained in the index graph. This part of the database is composed of an inverted file, denoted *InvertedFileConcept* and a acceleration table, noted *ConceptValue.*

We present the principles of the search algorithm about arches. The search algorithm about concepts follows the same principles.

VARIABLES

GraphReq is a query graph composed of **nbArc** arches, noted **ArcReq,** and of **nbConcept** concept nodes

ListDocResult is a list of documents weighted by the value of the similarity function between the query graph **GraphReq** and the index graph of document.

ListArcIndex is the list of **ArcIndex** (arch indexing document) weighted by **WeightArc** the value of the similarity function between **ArcReq** and **ArcIndex**

ListDoc is the list of document **Doc** whose index contains **ArcIndex**

ListDocArc is the list of document **Doc** weighted by the value of the similarity function between **ArcReq** and their index graph.

```
ALGORITHM
ListDocResult ← empty
For each arch ArcReq of GraphReq do
   ListArcIndex ← empty
   ListDocArc ← empty
   ListArcIndex ←FindArcComparable(ArcReq)
   For each(ArcIndex, WeightArc) of ListArcIndex do
      ListDoc ← empty
      ListDoc ← FindListDoc(ArcIndex)
      // For an ArcReq, the document weight is the max
      of the similarity between ArcReq and an arch of
      document index
      For each Doc of ListDoc do
         If ListDocArc.Belong(Doc)
         Then
            Weight ←ListDocArc.FindWeight(Doc)
            NewWeight ← max(Weight, WeightArc)
            ListDocArc.ReplaceWeight(Doc, NewWeight)
         Else
            ListDocArc.Add(Doc, WeightArc)
         Endif
      Endfor
   Endfor
// Compute the final Weight of document.
   For each (Doc, WeightArc) of ListDocArc do
      If ListDocResult.Belong(Doc)
      Then
         Weight ← ListDocResult.FindWeight(Doc)
         NewWeight ← Weight + (WeightArc / (nbArc + nbConcept))
         ListDocResult.ReplaceWeight(Doc, NewWeight)
      Else
         ListDocResult.Add(Doc, WeightArc)
   Endfor
Endfor
```

FindArcComparable**(ArcReq)** returns a list of arches **(ArcIndex)** comparable to **ArcReq**, weighted by the value of the similarity function between **ArcReq** and **ArcIndex**, noted **WeightArc**.

In the search algorithm, the result documents are obtained in polynomial time, because most parts of the algorithm consist in union and intersection. Usually, the cost of a mapping between graphs is prohibitive because, in graph theory, it is equivalent to find a morphism between indefinite structures. To overcome this problem, we have limited the graph structure: we consider that a concept node is unique in a semantic graph.

4. The SyDoM prototype

We have developed a logical information retrieval module based on semantic graph. This module is a component of the documentary system called SyDoM (Multilingual Documentary System) [13]. SyDoM is dedicated to the needs of digital libraries for managing XML documents. The system is implemented in JAVA on top of the relational database system Access. The semantic thesaurus is the core of our system. Its goal is to formalize the conceptualization of the librarian's point of view for a particular domain. This thesaurus is then enriched by the various vocabularies contained in the document collection. This specific conceptualization will be presented to the various users in the language of their choice. SyDoM is composed of three modules:

1. The **semantic thesaurus module** manages the documentary language (addition of new vocabulary or new domain entity). Documentary language is used for indexing and querying a multilingual document collection. Actually the semantic thesaurus can be displayed in different languages (French and English).
2. The **indexing module** indexes and annotates XML document with semantic graphs using a set of metadata associated to the semantic thesaurus.
3. The **retrieval module** performs multilingual retrieval. The users introduce their queries through the query interface presented in figure 8. This figure corresponds to the French query "*modèle de combustion*" (combustion model).

Indexing module

Our indexing method enrichs XML documents with two types of metadata:

1. XML documents are annotated in order to identify significant terms. Annotations have two functions: first of all, language dependent expressions are linked with domain concepts, that is to say terms are identified as labels of concepts and is used to update one of the vocabulary of the semantic thesaurus. Secondly, the set of annotations generates an index composed of a list of concepts.
2. Starting from the annotation index, librarians refine it. This new index is composed of concepts linked by relations. This index is a precise and short description of the document content. Users can estimate the purpose of the document when reading it, and compare it to their information needs.

4.1 Document annotations

The document annotations specify the expression of particular concepts inside the document. So, a new XML element called **term** is added inside the XML structure of the document. For example, we want to annotate the XML document whose title is "A practical approach to jet engine lubricant evaluation". This XML document is:

```
<Document>
<Title>A practical approach to jet engine lubricant evaluation</Title>
<Introduction>
<Title>.... </Title>
<Paragraph>...</Paragraph>
</Introduction>
...
</Document>
```

Fig. 5. An XML document dealing with « *A practical approach to jet engine lubricant evaluation* »

After annotation, the XML document becomes:

```
    <Document>
    <title>A practical approach to <term conceptkey="TC1.1.1.1.1.5"
xml:lang="en-GB" status="1">jet engine</term>
      <term conceptkey="TC1.1.2.1" xml:lang="en-GB"
status="1">lubricant</term>
      <term conceptkey="TC2.1.3.1" xml:lang="en-GB"
status="1">evaluation</term>
     </title>>
    </Document>
```

Fig. 6. An annotated XML document

The **term** markup has three attributes:

1. The first one called **conceptkey** is the type of the concept. Indeed, the expression, contained in the mark-up, references a concept. This concept is characterized by its type.
2. The second one, called **xml:lang** defined in the XML standard, indicates the language used.
3. The third one, called **status,** indicates the preference degree for the annotator. If the annotator think that the expression should the a label of the concept type **status** equals 1 otherwise **status** is less than 1.

The semantic thesaurus is automatically updated by parsing annotated documents that is to say to link an expression with a concept type. So document annotations enable to take into account the vocabulary evolution. The users interface of SyDoM displays the semantic thesaurus in the user's native language, to facilitate the annotating process.

4.2 Document index

After annotating a document, the librarian has a list of concepts referenced inside the document. These concepts can be displayed in any language belonging to the semantic thesaurus. The librarian selects the most important concepts and link them by relation. He could also add other concepts, he judges relevant for the document. Indeed, he builds a semantic graph where relations connect concepts. This indexing graph is transformed into a set of XML elements. In order to be language-independent, types, rather than labels, identify each component of the graph. Three kinds of mark-up are used:

- <Role type="TR1">...</Role> identifies a relation and its type.
- <Argument number="1"> </Argument> identifies arguments of a relation and its position in the list of arguments (number = 1).
- <Concept type= "TC2.1.3.1"/> identifies a concept and its type.

These markups are encapsulated in an index one added to the beginning of the document. Let us point out that none of these mark-ups has any word content so they do not alter the document presentation. These mark-up provide meta information about the document content.

```
<index>
    <role type="TR1.1.2.2.2.2">
        <argument number="1">
            <concept type="TC2.1.3.1"/>
        </argument>
        <argument number="2">
            <concept type="TC1.1.2.1"/>
        </argument>
    </role>
    <role type="TR1.1.2.1.2.1">
        <argument number="1">
            <concept type="TC2.2.1"/>
        </argument>
        <argument number="2">
            <concept type="TC1.1.2.1"/>
        </argument>
    </role>
    <role type="TR1">
        <argument number="1">
            <concept type="TC1.1.1.1.1.1.5"/>
        </argument>
        <argument number="2">
            <concept type="TC2.2.1"/>
        </argument>
    </role>
</Index>
```

Fig. 7. XML Index of a document dealing with « *A practical approach to jet engine lubricant evaluation* »

Retrieval module

4.3 Query formulation

The users introduce their queries through the query interface presented in figure 8. To formulate his query, the user goes through the semantic thesaurus presented in his native language to choose concepts and relations.

For example, a French user wants to query the mechanical collection of DocINSA. He is looking for documents dealing with combustion model. Thanks to the visualization of the French ontology, he builds the graph presented in the next figure:

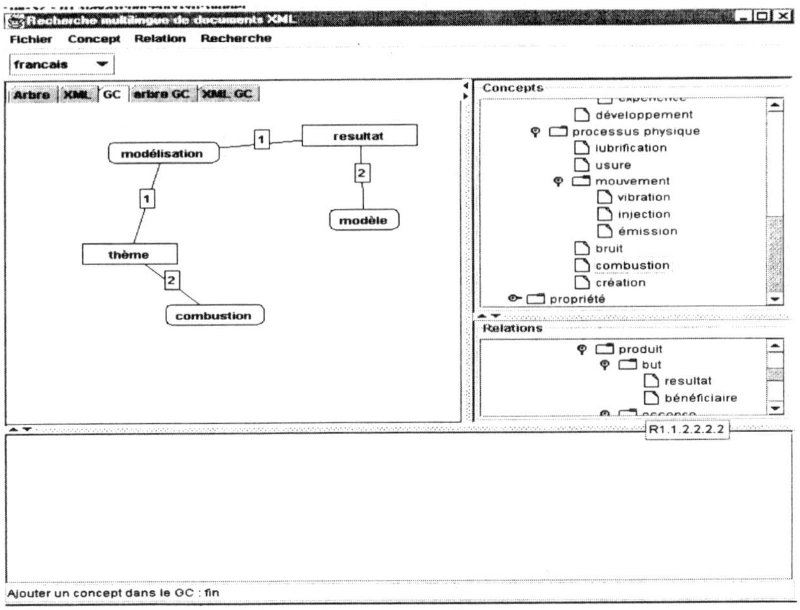

Fig. 8. SyDoM interface

As shown in Figure 9, this graph is transformed (French labels are replaced by types) to generate a language-independent query.

[TC2.2.5]→(TR1.1.2.2.2.2)→[TC2.1.3.3]←(TR1.1.2.2.1.1)←[TC1.2.1.2.1]

Fig. 9. A language-independent query graph

4.4 Visualization of result documents

Result documents could have different presentations depending on the user's choice. First of all, if the user wants a brief description of document centers of interest, he could see the index of the document written in his native language. As shown in Figure 10, this index is composed of concepts connected by relations where types are replaced by terms (labels of concept) thanks to semantic thesaurus.

Relation theme:
- Argument 1: évaluation
- Argument 2: lubrifiant

Relation instrument:
- Argument 1: lubrification
- Argument 2: lubrifiant

Relation composant:
- Argument 1: moteur à réaction
- Argument 2: lubrification

Fig. 10. The French index of the document dealing with "A practical approach to jet engine lubricant evaluation.

Next, if he believes that the document is useful, he could visualize the whole document. If the document is written in a foreign language, the document is translated partially. That is to say that every expression of concept, identified by annotation, is replaced by term in the user's native language.

Title: A practical approach to jet engine lubricant evaluation
...

Fig. 11. The English document

Title: A practical approach to (moteur à réaction) (lubrifiant) (évaluation)
...

Fig. 12. A partial translation of the English document

5. Evaluation

The library Doc'INSA gives us a test set of English articles. These articles deal with mechanics and they are called *pre-print of the Society of Automotive Engineers (SAE)*. The first step of the experiment was to build a semantic thesaurus for mechanics. Thanks to a mechanical thesaurus, we selected around one hundred mechanical concepts to supply our semantic thesaurus. On top of the concept hierarchy, we added the thirty-five relations proposed by Sowa in his Knowledge Representation Book [15]. During manual indexing, only titles are taken in account. For our first experiments, we have manually indexed approximately fifty articles and performs ten queries. The average index graph consists of four arches and the average query graph consists of two arches.

To evaluate our system, we compare it to the IR system used at Doc'INSA. In this system, documents and queries are represented by a list of keywords. The matching function between documents and queries evaluates the number of common keywords. The indices of this system were generated automatically from the index graphs of SyDoM, to avoid to take the index variability into account. The next figure presents the comparison of SyDoM with the Doc'INSA system. We compute the average precision for ten recall intervals. The constant value of similarity function are arbitrarily fixed[3] (V_G = *0.7 and* V_S= *0.9)*. The trend of the curve can be explained by the fact that our collection size is small. Therefore, most part of the queries deals only with few documents. Because these documents are retrieved with an important weight (more than 0.8), the precision is good whatever the recall could be. We can notice that relation processing and hierarchy inference improve significantly the quality of the answer even for manual indexing.

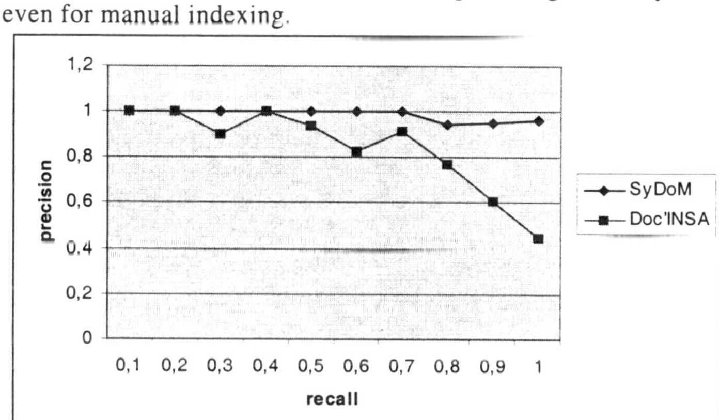

Fig. 13 Evaluation of SyDoM and Doc 'INSA system

[3] We chose the same value as [3]

6. Conclusion

In this paper, we propose a solution to the challenge using complex knowledge representation formalism for information retrieval purpose. Moreover, we present a graph formalism used to describe the semantic of document in a multilingual context. This formalism is an extension of the Sowa's formalism of Conceptual Graphs. Starting from recent works, we propose a new comparison operator between graphs taking the specific information retrieval needs into account. Our operator is based on the generic model suggested in [9] by considering the graphs in normal form. This choice enables us to decrease the complexity of the search algorithm. Our proposition is validated by the SyDoM prototype dedicated to digital libraries. SyDoM is a multilingual information retrieval system with several useful functionalities. It has been evaluated using an English collection of articles. We have already noticed that SyDoM gives better results than traditional documentary system.

7. References

[1] L. Ballesteros, W.B. Croft. « Statistical Methods For Cross-Langage Information Retrieval », *Cross-Language Information Retrieval*, Chapter 3. G. Grefenstette (ed.) Kluwer Academic Publishers, Boston, 1998.

[2] L. Bourrelly, E. Chouraqui. « Le système documentaire SATIN1: description générale et manuel d'utilisation ». *Centre National de Recherche Scientifique*, Paris, 1974, 398 pages.

[3] P.D. Bruza, M. Lalmas. « The use of logic in information retrieval modeling ». *Knowledge Engineering Review*, 13(2):1-33, 1998

[4] M.W. Davis. « On The Effective Use Of Large Parallel Corpora In Cross-Langage Text Retrieval », *Cross-Language Information Retrieval*, Chapter 2. G. Grefenstette (ed.)Kluwer Academic Publishers, Boston, 1998.

[5] S.T. Dumais, M.L. Littman, T.K. Landauer, T.A. Letsche. « Automatic Cross-Language Retrieval Using Latent Semantic Indexing », *Working Notes of AAAI Spring Symposium on Cross-Language Text and Speech Retrieval*, Stanford, CA, 1997. http://www.ee.umd.edu/medlb/filter/sss/papers/dumais.ps.

[6] D. Genest, M. Chein. « an experiment in Document Retrieval using Conceptual Graph ». Proceeding of 5th ICCS Conference, Washington, USA, p 489-504, august 1997.

[7] D. Genest. « Extension du modèle des graphes conceptuels pour la recherche d'information ». PhD Thesis, Montpellier University, Montpellier, France 2000.

[8] D.A. Hull, G. Grefenstette. « Querying Across Languages: A Dictionary-Based Approach to Multilingual Information ». *Proceedings of the 19th ACM SIGIR Conference in Research & Development in Information Retrieval*, Zurich, 1996, p 49-57.

[9] P. Martin, P. W. Eklund. « Knowledge Retrieval and the World Wide Web ». IEEE Intelligent Systems (Special Issue on Knowledge Management and the Internet) 2000.

[10] J.Y. Nie. « un modèle logique général pour les systemes de recherche d'informations. Application au prototype RIME ». PhD Thesis, Joseph Fouriei University, Grenoble, France 1990.

[11] I. Ounis, M. Paşca. « RELIEF: Combining expressiveness and rapidity into a single system ». Proceeding of 18th SIGIR Conference, Melbourne, Australia, p 266-274, august 1998.

[12] K. Radwan, F. Foussier, C. Fluhr. « Multilingual Access to Textual Databases ». Proceeding of the Conference on Intelligent Text and Image Handling RIAO91, Elsevier, avril 1991, p 475-489.

[13] C. Roussey, S. Calabretto, J. M. Pinon « Un modèle d'indexation pour une collection multilingue de documents». Proceeding of the 3rd CIDE Conference, Lyon, France, p 153-169, July 2000

[14] J. Sowa. « Conceptual Structures: information processing in mind and machine ». The System Programming Series, Addison Wesley publishing Company, 1984.

[15] J. Sowa. « Knowledge Representation: Logical, Philosophical, and Computational Foundations ». Brooks Cole Publishing Co., Pacific Grove, CA., 2000.

[16] C.J. van Rijsbergen. « A new Theoritical Framework for Information Retrieval ». Proceeding of the 9th SIGIR Conference, Pisa, p 194-200m septembre 1986.

[17] P Vossen, W. Peters, J. Gonzalo. "Towards a Universal Index of meaning". Proceedings of the ACL-99 Siglex Workshop, University of Maryland, 1999.

Electronic Publishing '01 –
2001 in the Digital Publishing Odyssey
A. Hübler et al. (Eds.)
IOS Press, 2001

Human and Economic Impacts of Electronic Publishing at the NRC Research Press : A Case Study

Scott Mellon and Aldyth Holmes

NRC Research Press
Canada Institute for Scientific and Technical Information
National Research Council of Canada
Ottawa, Ontario K1A 0S2 Canada

Abstract

The NRC Research Press has a seventy-year history of provision of high-quality scientific journals, currently totalling 14 titles in various areas of science and technology. These titles were made available to our clients electronically in 1996, [see http://researchpress.nrc.ca] and we are currently engaged in a second phase of what will likely be an ongoing process of technical evolution. This paper focuses on the impacts of such rapid change on our organization and people, and discusses change management principals, which have been found to be effective. Such impacts include the recruitment, and retention of appropriately qualified staff and the costs associated with each; and the design of space to facilitate new working styles. We will explore the "build-or-buy" conundrum and present our current philosophy on this issue. Strategies such as matrix management and out sourcing for managing technology workers in a hitherto non-technical operation; and techniques for learning and transferring technology to and among staff will likewise be addressed. This paper will also discuss our co-evolution with our clients, the journals' readers, authors and editors, and ways in which their development and changing expectations have informed our products, systems and processes.

0. Introduction

The National Research Council of Canada (NRC) began publishing journals in 1929 in response to a perception that the work of Canadian scientists was not being adequately disseminated because Canadians had limited access to the scientific journals of the time. The situation of a country new to original scientific research was much like the situation that new disciplines find themselves in today, viz. lack of an appropriate venue for publication. The major journals have never had more than very limited interest in new disciplines or in the science that is perceived to be only of regional interest. From those early beginnings, the NRC has grown in stature and become a recognised major research institution on the world stage. As NRC grew in international prestige so did the journals being published by them. Today the NRC publishes fourteen internationally recognised journals and is launching a fifteenth this fall. These journals attract authors from around the world and are distributed both in paper and electronically to over 12,000 subscribers world wide.

One of the factors that has given us a unique view of the world for a not-for-profit publisher is that we publish journals in a wide variety of disciplines. As we will show, the different disciplines have exhibited quite different behaviour patterns in their acceptance of electronic journals.

The decision to become an electronic publisher was made in 1994 and implemented over a three year period. It was recognised at the time of the initial decision to produce electronic versions of the journals, that the technology available at the time would not meet all the suggested possibilities for enhancing the journals and that any choices of technology would necessarily be transitional to new better technologies as they became available. The decisions made had to be justified from a business perspective and the implications for staff had to be taken into consideration.

0.1 An outline of the changes (background)

In 1994 our production process was to receive hard copy of a manuscript previously accepted and peer reviewed by our external editorial offices, and then assign a scientific copyeditor who marked up the changes to improve the quality of the English, removed any ambiguities in the text (querying authors as necessary), and changed the style to conform to the house style. This would include for example the use of SI units and the use of italics in conformance to the standards for the various disciplines we publish in. (Council of Biology Editors standards for expression of taxonomies, IUPAC for naming of chemical compounds etc.) The marked up paper was then sent to a typesetting house, and a galley proof was generated and sent to the author. The author and the copyeditor then proofed the galley. The authors' changes were reviewed by the copyeditor and transferred with the copyeditors corrections to the typesetter. This marked up document was sent to the typesetting company and final page proofs produced. These were then sent to the printer who used camera (or in some cases, electronic files) to produce the plates for the press and the blue lines for the copyeditors to review.

The first electronic versions of the journals were produced from PDF files created in-house. That is to say we replaced the contracted out typesetting function by an in-house group. When we established this group we asked authors to send us diskettes of the accepted paper to reduce our need to re-key whole papers. We were surprised to find that we were able to get the disks from nearly all authors, wherever they were in the world. We did have some interesting conversion challenges in the early days. But we could nearly always at least get the ASCII code for the text of the paper if not for the mathematics. Today we have far fewer problems. There are better conversion programs available and authors are tending to use a limited range of major software packages to prepare their material.

Our choice of software was pragmatic, based largely on what staff would find easiest to work with. WordPerfect was selected for on screen editing because it was the NRC office standard at that time. In fact that changed less than a year after we began the project when our parent organisation switched to Microsoft Word. WordPerfect had the added advantage that the tags added by the copyeditor could be displayed on screen and if necessary deleted, leaving the copyeditor with a sense of control over the text.

Our decision on a layout package was equally pragmatic. We had researched various packages including Ventura and Quark Express, but our final decision was driven by the arrival of an NRC employee whose job in another part of the organisation had disappeared; they were available and they were expert in Ventura, which we felt was adequate. The choice of Ventura saved us training dollars and when Corel acquired WordPerfect we thought we would probably have two packages that would work together well.

1. Impacts of Change

1.1 Human Impacts

Staff working in our current production system have a much greater variety of tasks in each job than they did in the manual system. Essentially the tasks of pre-marking, and page layout merged. We have worked to reduce the number of times a paper goes around the review/author approval cycle - it had been as many as four, but is now seldom more than one. We have also shortened the approval process by FTP'ing PDF files to authors instead of relying on surface mail.

Copyediting is still a separate function because of the requirement for scientific knowledge. However due to the multi-disciplinary nature of our journals, and inevitable staff changes, the level of such knowledge is not high enough to allow for substantive editing. (Our process assumes that any substantive editing required has already taken place within our volunteer community editorial office as an adjunct of the peer review process.) Still there was a major shift in workstyle by copyeditors, for whom working on screen was new, and to some unsettling.

We struggled initially with the correct supervisory structure. We introduced the program with a Head of Journals and three Senior Copyeditors who were responsible for the production of clusters of journals in related subjects. As we added staff to replace the contracted out typesetting, they reported to the senior copyeditor whose journals they worked on. Initially we added a layout person who handled the final page layout and the graphic images and another position called pre-marking. The pre-marker converted the author's version of the accepted paper to WordPerfect, stripping out all formatting and began re-formatting to our house style before passing it to the copyeditor. That is to say senior copyeditors supervised staff who did purely technical tagging and layout. This was felt to be ineffective use of their time, and has since evolved into a separate Production Unit with its own Head and structure.

We have also struggled with the correct structure for technical support. NRC Research Press is fortunate in being part of the National Research Council of Canada, and of the Canada Institute for Scientific and Technical Information, so that access to leading-edge technologies is readily available. But how to manage it in this particular situation? After some experimentation, we have determined that our computer support is best managed outside the Press, which while still within the Council, effectively means, outsourced. This has several advantages: we are able to obtain access to fractions of people with a wide variety of skill sets, and the people involved are professionally managed by other computer professionals. This latter issue implies that they have a career path, a succession plan, and hopes for promotion.

Our ready access to technology can sometimes be a two-edged sword however, as the technology has occasionally threatened to become our driver. That is to say, we sometimes need to fight off a "Technology for the sake of technology" syndrome, and in particular, the infamous "Not-Invented-Here" syndrome. We constantly need to remind ourselves and others that we are in the business of publishing, and not the business of software-for-publishing. In general, our bias is to buy technical solutions whenever possible.

1.2 Economic Impact

Electronic publishing was introduced for 2 journals in 1996. Five further journals were converted to this process in 1997 and the remaining 7 journals in 1998. The following table shows our cost breakdowns by function from 1994 to 2000. The most interesting changes are in the indices for copyediting, printing and overhead.

Table 1
Index of Average Publishing Costs per Page for 14 Journals

	1994	1995	1996	1997	1998	1999	2000
Copyediting	100	82.55	88.77	118.80	128.21	102.43	87.42
Peer Review	100	112.14	115.43	127.23	137.12	135.98	135.53
Printing	100	120.07	92.16	110.23	68.35	48.95	61.38
Overhead	100	83.83	141.25	107.96	181.77	184.06	166.31
pages	100	103.24	102.84	96.40	92.47	104.04	109.95

Copyediting: The cost of copyediting actually increased in the first two years of electronic publishing and is now sinking back to previous levels, even though more of the actual production process is now done at this stage, and even though no adjustment was made for salary increases. We believe that this is evidence of the cost of the "learning curve". The transition can be clearly seen in 1998 when all journals were finally being produced electronically.
Printing: Printing costs appear to have dropped dramatically; however this is in part a statistical illusion. Prior to the introduction of electronic publication the typesetting function was contracted to the printers and appears as part of the printing index. Once the process was re-engineered and the production of the electronic file was done in-house the costs became part of the copyediting budget. The increase in printing cost in 2000 is most probably attributable to two factors: the reduction in print runs as electronic subscriptions began to replace paper subscriptions which tended to increase the average cost per page; and the change in policy for two journals which began to offer free colour for authors. This had the result of significantly increasing the amount of colour published with a corresponding impact on the average cost.
Overhead: Increases in overhead costs in 1998 and 1999 are attributable to technology upgrades.

1.3 Impact on Production Time

Similarly, as the following table shows, our average production time also typically increased in the first year or two of our new system, before any real long term improved could be detected.

Table 2
Average Days per article spent in production process

(Year electronic)	1993	1994	1995	1996	1997	1998	1999	2000
Journal 1 (1996)	124	124	121	118	115	186	119	94
Journal 2 (1997)	189	176	191	157	196	256	293	220
Journal 3 (1998)	131	143	135	149	155	199	214	115

Journal 1 was a monthly biomedical journal and was one of two journals used as prototypes to develop the processes for electronic production. Additional staff were employed and trained on the layout as part of their training to work on other journals. This explains the drop in time in the year the new processes were introduced, additional staff training on this title continued the following year but the benefits of the first years leaning show clearly in the second year of electronic production. However when the staff allocated to this title were reduced to normal levels i.e. no new staff assisting in its production as part of their training, the time peaks and then recovers as learning is consolidated.

Journal 2 was a bimonthly engineering journal with more complex graphics than the two prototype journals but again a similar pattern emerges. As additional staff have been previously trained on journal 1 are assigned and a new staff added to train for this title the time increases and when the more experienced staff member is withdrawn and reassigned the learning curve goes up sharply to begin declining the following year.

Journal 3 is a large prestigious monthly biology journal. The pattern repeats itself.

The implications of these data are that delays or increase in production time could have been reduced by acknowledging that it took not one but two years for staff to reach an acceptable speed of work with the new technology. This implies that the transition was under-resourced, and that inadequate funds were available to double staff positions for that length of time.

1.4 Technology Impacts

There was much discussion when the decision to pursue electronic publication was taken as to the appropriate software packages to consider and the desirability of using SGML. Two studies were undertaken two years apart asking the question how much would it cost to go to an SGML base workflow and what would be the benefits from it. In both cases the cost of introducing SGML did not justify the benefits. The underlying problem for any science journal was the difficulty of handling mathematics in SGML and the cost of developing DTDs and all the associated staff retraining for implementation. While we could see the potential value of having SGML tagged files in the long term in terms of the ease with which they could be converted to newer technologies and could be archived we could not find short term benefits from the perspective of the author and reader. The original decision was, therefore, to go with a PDF format recognising that this would be transitional to some other format at some future date. This responded to the clients needs at that time. Scientists five years ago did not want to read on screen. They wanted to locate the article and have it delivered to the desktop where they wanted to print it out so that they could read it and annotate it just as they had done with paper. We fully expected this behaviour to change as the nintendo generation joined the research community but we did not know what the time scale for the changed demands from authors would be. Moreover, we could not afford to be financially exposed by investing in unproven technologies. We were content to observe the major scientific societies who had deeper pocket experiment and observe the behavioural impact on the scientists of these experiments. At first we thought the need for full text search capability would force us to abandon PDF very quickly but early consultations with our colleagues in NRCs Institute for Information Technology assured us that full text searching within PDF would be available very quickly. They were correct. By the time we had the first seven titles in PDF the products were on the market.

2. Lessons Learned

It is clear that we underestimated the cost of the learning curve, and the time required for staff training and development. In fact the "learning curve" which was originally seen as mostly a matter of learning software, ultimately included a significant change in both corporate culture and required skill sets. Editors in particular have had to learn a new language, and they need much more technical knowledge of the production process, including, for example, text and graphics formatting. The change has also required an ongoing search for process and workflow improvements. The effect of that underestimation was seen in publication delays, and consequently in dissatisfied authors and editors. Any future major changes in our production systems will need to take this into account, and appropriate resources found.

Another important lesson, we feel, is that our re-engineering has brought us benefits which we would not have been able to predict. For example, our new ability to send PDF files to authors has significantly reduced time-to-publication, even though it was invented for quite another purpose. Similarly we are seeing intangible but very real benefits which flow out of our improved position within the Canadian publishing community in particular, and hope to be able to share the benefits of our experiences with those colleagues.

3. Next Steps

Five years after the original decision to go electronic we are starting to see the behavioural changes that we predicted. Scientists are acquiring higher quality monitors which make reading on screen less demanding. Along with better desktop technology for the subscribers came increasing pressure to make more use of the electronic world. Furthermore, expectations of readers and authors have continued to evolve, and many features not possible in PDF files, from reference linking to Virtual Reality simulations, have become quite normal in some disciplines. We have therefore launched a major project to update our production system yet again. Our goals for this project are first, to continue to shorten the production cycle in response to continuing pressures from some of our communities; second to add value to our online products by giving us the capabilities available through HTML, and ultimately online XML articles; and third, to "future-proof" our archival data by storing them in formats which will have long term reliability. In so doing the lessons of our first major foray into electronic publishing will be very valuable to us, and I hope, to others.

Electronic Publishing '01 –
2001 in the Digital Publishing Odyssey
A. Hübler et al. (Eds.)
IOS Press, 2001

Introducing electronic books at Göteborg University

Mats Cavallin
Carin Björklund
Göteborg University Library
Box 222
SE 405 30 Göteborg, Sweden
Mats.Cavallin@ub.gu.se
Carin.Bjorklund@ub.gu.se

Göteborg University Library has signed a contract with netLibrary providing users on the University's network access to 500 copyrighted electronic books. These electronic books represent "the third wave" at our Digital Library- the earlier "waves" of resource networking were bibliographic databases and electronic journals. The project is funded by the university board and was started in 2001 after testing and preparations during the fall of 2000. The only realistic alternative for the library was found to be netLibrary. The process started with a collection evaluation resulting in the creation of a list of titles appropriate for acquisition. Negotiations with netlibrary followed and a contract was signed in February 2001. The service was launched over the University's network in March 2001. After the local introduction of the netLibrary electronic books at the library the project work will continue with forming a eBook consortium. A study of other e-book alternatives will also be carried through. The current project will be evaluated on the basis of end-user experience.

Introduction

In February 2001 Göteborg University Library signed a contract with netLibrary providing access to 500 copyrighted electronic books for users on the University's network. Göteborg University Library has 7 libraries with a total of about 3 million volumes and serves Göteborg University, which is located in the southwestern part of Sweden, with a student population of some 36,000 and almost 3,000 teaching staff and researchers.

The eBook project, which is being funded by the University Board, was started in January 2001 after testing and preparation during the autumn of 2000. The project is run by the Digital Library[1], which is a part of the University Library. The project has three main goals; to acquire netLibrary titles as appropriate; to study the effects of eBooks on library work and user acceptance; to consider other library suppliers of eBooks; and to test various forms for future library consortia.

The process of introducing copyrighted electronic books beyond the freely available texts is complicated and very educative for a library. Being one of the first libraries in Europe to accomplish this doesn't make it easier. In this paper we want to present our work on establishing an eBook service at Göteborg University Library. Our presentation will not focus on the grand theories but is just a simple account of what it was like and how we acted. To this will be added some general thoughts on the nature of a collection of eBooks and on all the rethinking and adjustments that have to accompany the transition from the world of print to the digital world.

Our experience as a netLibrary customer is not very extensive. After periods of testing in 2000 the Library started the eBook selection process in December 2001, negotiated in January 2001, got access later in the same month, carried out staff training in February –March, imported eBook records into our OPAC in March and launched the service on 20th March.

Private eBooks or library net collections?

The first decision to make was if we should consider supplying eBooks through different kinds of reader devices and hand-held computers. Since we were looking for a general library solution, the supply of eBooks through specialized eBook reader hardware would not be an acceptable method for our users. The only realistic infrastructure is the web and ordinary PC's. These two tools are the most frequent ones at hand (with no library intervention) for students as well as researchers.

Negotiation process

Viewed in this perspective choosing netLibrary as our first supplier was one of the easiest parts in purchasing eBooks, since there were no other library alternatives available. Contract negotiations were begun in January 2000, and the contract was signed in February.

All negotiation was conducted with the head office of netLibrary. During this process a European office in London and recently also an agency for the Scandinavian market were established. Testing and negotiating with a company which until recently had only Mountain Time office and support hours did have some disadvantages for a customer in Europe.

Conditions

In order to distribute eBooks to libraries there must of course be systems for the protection of copyright and the commercial interests involved. An eBook may be used by only one person at a time. If there are too few copies available, further copies will have to be bought. The texts are encrypted. There are technical obstacles against copying or downloading more than a few pages.

Services

NetLibrary has developed standard solutions for eBooks concerning a wide range of service offers. This is a pioneer work that has shown that there are ways of distributing modern academic literature from well-known publishers breaking the distrust of publishers against electronic publishing in libraries.

The main services are listed below:

- Pricing: A standard price list based on list prices and options for two models of payment.
- Lending: An eBook may only be used by one person at a time.

- Access: Accessing is IP-filtered, and when you are in a netLibrary accessible address you will be directed to the netLibrary collections your library has acquired.
- Collections: About 30,000 modern titles in English only and 4,000 copyright-free titles.
- Searching: Conventional searches can be carried out on author, title, subject etc., but also in full text.
- Catalogue: MARC records can be delivered and easily transferred to a local OPAC.
- On-line reading: May be done through an ordinary web browser.
- Offline reading: Can be done through a client (PC's only). The client has added some services (notes, underlining etc.) that are not implemented in the web browser reader.
- Administration: The lending system server is situated in USA. Library administrators can set parameters on loan periods, rights of staff and users etc.
- Backup: The system has backup facilities for the customers in cooperation with OCLC in case the company should cease to operate.

Choosing titles

To be a netLibrary customer you have to buy 500 titles to start up. A group of experienced acquisition librarians made their choices among the 30,000 titles available. We were a bit disappointed that we were not allowed to use the total netLibrary book database for that purpose. The librarians had to work with different types of lists, which were distributed by netLibrary or downloaded from their site.

The process of rethinking and readjusting the acquisition criteria normally applied for printed books to adequate ones for eBooks was certainly a very educative experience. Should we buy books we already own? Which books should be hired for an annual fee, and which should be permanently acquired?

Cataloguing eBooks

NetLibrary provides full-level MARC records for every eBook in the netLibrary collection. The company uses the paper book MARC record to create an eBook MARC record in MARC21 format.[3] When netLibrary began cataloguing eBooks, they identified issues that had not been addressed by bibliographic standards and formats such as Anglo-American Cataloguing Rules, 2nd ed Rev and MARC Bibliographic Standards. NetLibrary and OCLC therefore petitioned the Library of Congress to make changes in the rules for cataloguing eBooks, resulting in LCRI1.11A (Library of Congress Rule Interpretations 1.11A) [3] The problems of defining electronic reproduction and eBooks as reproductions of printed books is a very controversial subject. [1]

Silipigne Connaway, Vice President of Research and Library Systems at netLibrary, describes the eBook cataloguing challenges and presents netLibrary solutions in a very informative conference paper "Librarians, Producers, and Vendors: The netLibrary Experience". Her paper ends with a promising future for the enhanced bibliographic record. A bibliographic record will include table of contents, links to book reviews etc. If publishers, technology providers and eBook providers work together they could map standards and schemes and, above all, integrate these into the MARC format. [5]

Göteborg University Library uses the Virtua library systems from VTLS, Inc. The process of integrating electronic book in our OPAC was surprisingly easy. We obtained records for our 500 electronic book titles directly from netLibrary's FTP site. There were no problems in the distribution via FTP to the Library, and the records were loaded correctly! Göteborg University OPAC currently uses the SweMARC format. Next year LIBRIS, the Swedish union catalogue of academic and special libraries, will convert to MARC21. Göteborg University Library and all other Swedish libraries will have to move to this format as well. The imported MARC 21 records for eBooks will need only minor changes, whereas the SweMARC records will have to undergo a more complex conversion.

In order to load eBook MARC21 records into our SweMARC OPAC, we shall have to modify the field for printed ISBN manually. The ISBN for the printed version comes in 020 $z. In order to make this ISBN searchable, we shall have to change the subfield to $a. We shall also have to add fields for the Swedish classification code (SAB) and for subject headings.

Since our OPAC already holds about 90 % of the records for the printed counterparts of our eBooks, the eBook record can be easily updated by copying and pasting tags for classification and subject headings in Virtua MARC editor.

Ellen Cannon and Beth Watson describe their experience of netLibrary project problems occurring in the cataloguing process.[6] They decided to remove the ISBN for the print version in order to avoid bad matches. We do not have this problem, because field 035 is the matching tag for record overwriting. Most important for the user is that the eBook MARC record has a tag (the 856) with the eBook´s URL. The user can go directly to the eBook at netLibrary by clicking the hyperlink. Cannon and Watson had to remove subfields in the 856 for the link to work. We had no problem with that.

For the moment VTLS has no cooperation with NetLibrary. Other library systems from Innovative, EPIXtech etc. have integrated the cataloguing module with netLibrary. The Millennium library system from Innovative will in the future also integrate the circulation modules. The possibility of queuing for a book is a service, which we should have been glad to offer to our users. Let us hope that this function will eventually become available to our library system as well.

Consortium

In USA, where most of the experience of netLibrary has been gained, there has been a trend to form large regional consortia.[7] When Göteborg University Library opted for netLibrary, we were planning to do the same. Göteborg University Library is now leading a consortium project funded by BIBSAM at the Royal Library in Stockholm. The consortium consists of 8 libraries and is focused on social sciences.

If you look at e-journal collections in libraries, you will find almost exactly the same journals in any well-equipped library around the world. This is of course a result of what is on the market, of the fact that no more than 20 % of all journal titles are needed to cover 80 % of the demand, and of various types of consortia.

When forming a consortium for monographs other rules than those for journals will have to be followed. The eBook in a consortium is an extremely swift inter-library loan where the cost of buying a book is spread out over all the consortium members. The main point is to bring about as much diversity as possible for the consortium titles. A very popular book could easily be purchased with several copies by the consortium or by a single member of it.

Evaluation

At this moment (April 2001) we really do not have a clue as to how our users will behave with our netLibrary books less than a month after the launching. Will they ignore them, or will their use sink the netLibrary server in Boulder?

There are already several studies concerning reading on the web[8], but they are mostly more concerned with the web as such and not with commercially available net libraries with amounts of books like netLibrary, Questia or eBrary.

In our project we will further on pose some very simple questions to our users on the basis of end-user experience. A master student from the Library School at Borås is to undertake the first evaluation. The study will contain a small interview study, later on to be followed up by a larger questionnaire. The most important questions are: *Will our users read a lot of text on the screen? What kind of texts do they want to read (ordinary monographs, reference material, textbooks)? How will they want to read/browse the literature?*

User statistics

The ordinary statistics to be had from an OPAC provides facts about the books and the users. netLibrary gives you facts about the books but not about your users. Invisibility increases when the supplier of the texts is on the Internet and not controlled by you. The same problems occur with user statistics of our e-journals. If the library does not run the server with the e-journals or eBooks those figures will just not be available.

The single eBook and the social net Book

The single eBook (The sequential text)

Ever since the invention of the codex the book has had its own status and ontology in the
world of science. The book is a closed piece of content with a beginning and an end. In the Eighties, when the PC:s arrived and the texts began to be digitized in a larger scale, the book market foresaw huge amounts of floppy-disk and CD books to be sold, but such predictions turned out to be false. Most of the expected users found reading on a computer uncomfortable despite the new opportunities to search through the texts. Publishers saw the CD-ROM as a good way of selling a "thing". With the technical breakthrough around the year 2000 of various specially adapted readers there have been tremendous hopes and plans for a new eBook era. This time they are based on new and refined cryptographic techniques, such as linking an eBook to a single computer. Nevertheless this is nothing but a typical old-fashioned ASQ (Automating Status Quo) – merely copying the advantages of a single printed book with the added value of a search facility covering the full text of the book.

The social net book (recognizing the non-sequential text)

For the moment we can't predict that the modern eBook on a single device will be a commercial failure but we can say that large searchable amounts of relevant texts will offer new opportunities for a user. That was clearly understood by the early fathers of hypertext theory V. Bush[9], T. Nelson[10] and J.C.R. Licklider[11]. They all saw the scientific book giving references to other sources and literature as a kind of hypertext in print.

The problems were the physical limitations and searchability of the book. Nelson called a printed book a sequential reading meaning that there is just one way to read a book from start to ending.

Licklider saw the future for a research information system as a fusion of computer networks and the libraries. Most of the predictions that were made in earlier decades have come through. Perhaps they underestimated the role of the future commercial actors expecting the scientific literature to be freely distributed without commercial bonds. A wish, that hasn't hitherto been fulfilled.

Studies of the use of large e-journal collections[12] give somewhat amazing results about the relationship between the use of journal titles already owned in print by a library and titles not owned in print. The titles not owned in print and therefore not earlier chosen by the library are being used just as much as or even more than the printed/chosen ones. Have we librarians got it all wrong? Over the last few years we have heard the complaints of our colleagues: "We must have the opportunity to choose the titles." Perhaps it is now the user's choice in an environment with large collections of titles and books.

Conclusions

What will our library be doing in the next few months? A lot of marketing has to be undertaken within the University. Plenty of work has to be devoted to classifying and adjusting our imported netLibrary catalogue records. The problem of how to handle free e-journals and e-texts in the OPAC will have to be considered. The evaluation project is to be continued during the autumn. The consortium process will go on and hopefully be up in September 2001. The library has applied for another project this year. If this will be granted we will focus on library solutions concerning price models and technology with suppliers of academic literature from Sweden.

What will happen in the future with eBooks? As mentioned above, there are some trends o consider – the single or social eBook. Will the eBook suppliers accept the security levels and price models for library use? What will the relations be like between libraries and suppliers that make hundreds of thousands of titles searchable? Will libraries put all the titles in their OPAC's or leave it all to the supplier? We already have a number of problems with a few thousands of journal titles, but how do we act with these masses of eBook titles that will arrive? Will the Z39.50 protocol be our saver? Will library eBook solutions prevail, or will it all boil down to individual micro payments in the end?

References

1 Electronic books. Digital Library Göteborg University Library. Available http://www.ub.gu.se/Gdig/ebok/index_eng.html [April 17, 2001]

2 netLibrary eBook MARC records Available http://www.netlibrary.com/eBook_News/marc.asp [April 17, 2001]

3 Draft LCRI 1.11A Non-Microfilm and Electronic Reproduction. Background to the Revision of LCRI 1. http://www.loc.gov/catdir/cpso/1_11A_cover.html [April 17, 2001]

4 The problems defining what an electronic reproduction is have been discussed in many cataloging groups. The concept of "reproduction" is also one of 12 changes in cataloging rules which according to Matthew Beacom are necessary to adapt to a digital networked communications environment. His paper at the Bicentennial Conference on Bibliographic Control for the New Millenium (Beacom, Matthew. Crossing a Digital Divede: AACR and Unadressed Problems of Networked Resources. Bicentennial Conference of Bibliographic Control for the Next Millenium. Available http://lcweb.loc.gov/catdir/bibcontrol/beacom.html [April 17, 2001]) ends with the list of changes he wants AACR2 to adapt. In number 4 on the list he points out that concepts such as "original" or "copy" may continue to be highly useful for analog materials but not for electronic resources.

His suggestion, "Re-define the concept of a "reproduction" in an age of digital networked materials", was accepted by the postconference Topical Discussion Group 4B "How can AACR become more responsive to Cataloging Networked Resources on the Web?" Available http://www.loc.gov/catdir/bibcontrol/ [April 17, 2001]

The discussion group decided to develop a package of rule revisions. These revisions are now put on the agenda for the Joint Steering Committee meeting in april 2001. (Joint Steering Committee for Revision of Angle-American Cataloguing Rules. Draft Agenda. Washington, DC, USA, 2-4 april 2001.
Available http://www.nlc-bnc.ca/jsc/0104ann.html [April 17, 2001]

5 Silipigne Connaway, Lynn. Librarians, Producers, and Vendors: The netLibrary Experience Bicentennial Conference of Bibliographic Control for the Next Millenium, Confronting the Challenge Of Networked resources and the Webb: sponsored by the Library of Congress Cataloging Directorate, November 15-17, 2000 Availabel http://www.loc.gov/catdir/bibcontrol/connaway_paper.html [April 09,2001]

6 Cannon, E & Watson, B. E-book technologies is moving fast.. Are You ready to get behind the wheel ? *Computers in Libraries*. March 2001

7 Cannon, E & Watson, B. E-book technologies is moving fast... Same as 6

8 Wilson, R. E-books for students: EBONI. Ariadne 27 (March 2001)
Available http://www.ariadne.ac.uk/issue27/e-books/ [April 17, 2001]
The article is an overview of a large project carried out by Centre for Digital Library research at the University of Strathclyde. The study is focusing on the experience of effect and design of web texts.

9 Bush, Vannevar As we may think. The Atlantic Monthly. July 1945. Available http://www.theatlantic.com/unbound/flashbks/computer/bushf.htm) [April 17, 2001]

10 Ted Nelson used the phrase "Hypertext" in a paper at the annual conference of the Association of Computing Machinery in 1965. This paper is however not included in the proceedings from that conference.

11 Licklider, J.C.R. Libraries of the Future. 1965. pp 4-7.

12 Luther, J, White paper on Electronic Journal Usage Statistics. October 2000. CLIR Reports 94. Available http://www.clir.org/pubs/reports/pub94/contents.html [April 17, 2001]

Electronic Publishing '01 –
2001 in the Digital Publishing Odyssey
A. Hübler et al. (Eds.)
IOS Press, 2001

Improving the Usability of a Digital Library

Harald Krottmaier
Institute for Information Processing and Computer Supported new Media
Inffeldgasse 16c, A-8010 Graz, Austria

Abstract

The Journal of Universal Computer Science (J.UCS) was introduced in 1994 and after more than 7 years of operation the service is still up and running. Articles published on the server are categorized in several ways (e.g. in the ACM Classification Scheme) to simplify browsing and finding articles again. Nevertheless users wants to create their own view on the material and their own categories. Traditionally a user creates some categories on the client-side in a bookmark-structure and stores the URLs of the according papers in this structure. But the use of bookmarks binds the user to a specific client on one single machine and so it is not possible to take full advantage of the restructured view. This is just one reason why it is helpful for the user to manage his personal view of the articles on the server-side. In this paper we introduce a personal workspace for registered users of the Journal of Universal Computer Science. It is possible to create and modify a personal view, add some personal and/or public comments of the articles and use the workspace as personal repository of published articles. We also show other advantages like personalized search scope, customization of the order of articles and some other useful features of the system.

Keywords: Hyperwave, Journal of Universal Computer Science, personalized content

1 Introduction

Typical digital libraries are static and passive systems. They do not adapt to users preferences, like colors and design of the interface, topic of interest, rearrangement of articles etc. Because every user is different in many ways, this issue must be considered in the design of an easy to use and helpful digital library. Passive in the context of digital libraries means that the user interacts with the system, but the system does not initiate an interaction with the user. This behavior can be omitted by sophisticated tools later described in this document.

There are several possibilities to address these two issues. To get rid of the static behavior, user preferences must be stored at some place. Due to the generic accessibility of one system, usually a standard web-browser is used to access and visualize the content digital library. Therefore preferences might be stored at the client-side, at a proxy-server or at the server-side.

Storing data at the client-side in some cookies (e.g. [Clarke, 2001]) is a problem when mobility, backup etc. is an issue. Just to address the problem of mobility: If one changes the client-computer due to failure or any other reason, the preferences are not accessible and therefore the server-system can't take these preferences into account when assembling the content of a page. Also if a user changes the type of browser on one single computer, the stored cookies for browser *a* are not accessible for browser *b*. These are just two reasons why it's not very reasonable to store personalized information.

A proxy-server is an intermediate server-system between client and server. If such a proxy is located at the intranet within some company, it will not be possible to access this intermediate server-system to get some user defined preferences. Therefore in some cases – e.g. for an exclusively company-wide digital library system this approach might be possible, but for an international, public available system only the following storage location of user preferences is proper: the server-side. All advantages (browser and client-computer independent access, central backup etc.) and disadvantages (failure of server implies unavailability of the service to all clients etc.) are immanent in this approach. But independent availability is a key-issue in our system [Maurer and Schmaranz, 1994] so the decision was to store all user defined preferences at the server-side. This paper is addressed to this storage location also know as workspace. Some requirements to the implementation of the workspace and some tools are described. These tools handle the problem of passivity of typical digital library systems. The following section describes the requirements for the workspace which will be implemented for the Journal of Universal Computer Science (J.UCS) to release the power of a digital library.

2 Requirements for a Workspace

As described above the workspace in our context is some storage place at the server. Another term for a workspace might be 'Homecollection' or 'Homepage' with some additional tools. Some parts might be accessible for all users or for some groups, other parts are private and therefore invisible for other users. Like in traditional libraries, there is a need for classification of the content. In J.UCS the categorization is done in several standard ways:

ACM Classification System: The first ACM classification system for the computing field was published in 1964. This system was developed several times to consider new topics in computer science [ACM, 1998] and makes it easy for a reader to access immediately the topic of interest without wasting time to find articles on a specific topic. For example, if one is interested in the topic of digital libraries, he will find related articles in category H (H...Information Systems), aspects of Information Interface and Presentation are found in category H.5, whereas the sub aspects of user interfaces in information systems are found in category H.5.2 User Interface.

By Time: Obviously newer articles are in some kind more interesting to users than old ones. There must be a simple distinction in the time-line of articles. Articles are published in monthly issues and are bound to a volume for each year. This makes it very easy for the user to recognize the time of publication of each article.

By Author: If one is interested in all papers published by one author, the related papers can be found simply by browsing to the corresponding collection. Due to the many articles already published in J.UCS, there is a need for further granulation of articles.

Please note that all these listings are generated on the fly and are therefore every time up to date. As a requirement for a private workspace, it must be possible to allow the users to create their own views on the material (i.e. articles, issues or volumes). If the user is interested in e.g. information systems (category H), why should the user see the articles of category F (Theory of Computation)?

To put that issue into practice users must define their topics of interest. This can be done in several ways: Either one user links the collection of category H to his assigned workspace, or the displaying routine for the category listing consider specific variables set by the user via some form. To take full advantage of the parent/children-relations of a Hyperwave Information Server (e.g. [Maurer, 1996], [Hyp, 2001]) it is clear, that the first approach (link some part – e.g. a paper or any other entity of the content – to the workspace) must be implemented. This can be either done automatically (via some cgi-script or some server-side Java Script) if the user fills out some form or manually by the user using some tools. If some user decides that his own categories should be available for other users, he simply assigns the appropriate rights to his own categories.

This approach immanently implements 'public bookmarks' and can be used in an background-library for some learning environment or web based training system. Note the big difference of that approach to the discussed possibilities described above. Unlike client-side bookmarks this workspace is not just available to other users (if the owner sets appropriate rights), but the structure is also available within *any* web-browser. Administrators are able to extract valuable information from the linking structure of the content and can thereby advise the editors about topics often viewed by users. A system explicitly implementing such a public/private bookmark-service is e.g. [MyB, 2001] but it is obvious, that a library system should implement this feature immanently to take full advantage of the system.

One can imagine that due to personal preferences and intention of some collection, the sort order of the linked entities may differ. To give an example: One may collect some articles in one collection *'History of Information Systems'* and therefore wants some sort order of the articles ascending in date of publication. Another user might create a collection with the same articles *'Latest Developments in Information Systems'*, but with another sort order (descending in date of publication). It is obvious, that no physical copies are allowed but simple transclusions (reference links, see e.g. [Nelson, 1987]) must be implemented.

If another arbitrary sort order of articles must be possible, context specific attributes to the articles must be implemented. This can either be achieved via specific container objects or via attributes in the parent collection of the linked articles. Another feature easily implemented with that technology will be a global history of what the user accessed on the server system.

One can see, that this kind of workspace has some powerful features and will make the life much easier for users of the library. The next step of implementation will allow to rearrange and collect material (i.e. everything addressable by an Uniform Resource Identifier (URI, [Berners-Lee et al., 1998]) not stored on the local Hyperwave Information Server but anywhere at the web [Krottmaier and Maurer, 2001].

As pointed out above a personal workspace can improve the usability of the library enormously. But so far, only the navigation through the material of the library and finding articles again is improved in comparison to static libraries. In the following section some improvements in existing functions and new functions provided by the library are described.

3 More than just Reading...

As mentioned in section 1, a user should work with the library and not just read articles in it. It is obvious that a personal workspace on the library server is just the first step to a useful environment.

Traditional features for adding some kind of value to the articles are annotations or comments to articles. J.UCS was one of the first systems implementing that feature. Nowadays nearly every electronic library system supports annotations in some way. Annotations are not necessarily 'Letters to the Editor' about some article but small comments to a specific part of an article. They should either be public or private. Special kinds of annotations may have a priceless value to the reader and the editor of the library. To give some examples:

Rating of Content: Annotations can be used to rate some article. If this feature is easy to use, users will work with it and after some users rated the article, a preselection of articles for other users will automatically occur. Several discussion systems like news server and appropriate clients already implement that kind of preselection of articles. One can see this rating process as a 'review' process of the users using the library.

Link to the Future: Comments are not just text based. HTML tags are also allowed in annotations and therefore links to some external sources (identified by some URL) are possible. If the system has access to some citation index these 'Links to the Future' can be created automatically by simply looking for documents referring to that specific paper. The question 'Who uses this paper?' can be answered by search engines and if the result of that question can be interpreted by the system, links might be inserted automatically. On the other hand if one article is cited in a paper on the same server system, the cited article might be linked to the reference section of the paper automatically and the user have direct access to the cite.

Highlight / Cancel: Several programs (e.g. PC-Bibliothek [PCB, 2001]) are supporting this feature of highlighting some text in some text-document. This is also a kind of annotation (an annotation probably without content but with several attributes like colors, rating, time of annotation etc.). Again, if this feature is easy to use and several persons highlight or cancel some text, an automatic summary can be generated by the system and reading speed will increase enormous! This human based text mining will be a powerful feature. Problems will occur when implementing this feature. One will be the lack of programming support of the different web browsers. When using Java Script as a common basis (supported by most of the browsers) it is possible to extract the value of the selected text part, but it is not possible to get the position information! Some tricks and assumptions must be performed (e.g. assume, that the reader is highlighting the article in some 'known' sequence) to get the exact highlighted part of the HTML document.

Another problem will be the handling of different formats of one article. In J.UCS one paper is published in different data formats like PostScript, PDF and HTML. At the moment there are tools available for annotating HTML documents. The annotation feature is not available in PostScript-format documents, but in PDF documents. Therefore it must be possible, if one annotates the HTML-document at some point that this annotation is also available to the user in the PDF document using e.g. Acrobat Reader. Due to the fact that HTML is not a page description language it will be difficult to determine the exact position of the annotation in the PDF document especially if graphics are included in the document.

Questions and Answers: A special type of annotation is a question/answer dialog. As mentioned in [Maurer, 2001] this kind of annotation enables the implementation of 'active documents', documents which are able to automatically answer questions. In [Heinrich and Maurer, 2000] the basic idea of these documents is described: "The basic idea is that in the future, users of documents in any networked system should not just be able to communicate with other users, but also with documents."

[Maurer, 2001] explains some requirements and shows the power of many users. If hundreds of thousands of persons are working with a document, many semantically equal questions will arrive. To give a description of the work flow: The document is published at the system and facilities are available to ask any question at any position in the document. Experts answers such questions. These answers and the related questions are recorded.

> Experimental evidence shows that no new questions (just may be old questions in a new form) are asked after some 500 - 1000 viewers. Thus, if a document is viewed within, say, a year by 200.000 users, experts to answer questions are only required for a short time (until the first 1000 persons have visited the document). After this, all other 199.000 users get their answer from the system, if only the system can tell whether two similarly looking questions are indeed semantically identical. ... In our example, only 0.5% of users get their questions answered by experts, the remaining 99.5% receive the answer instantaneously from the system, a good approximation to the vision mentioned, indeed!

As one can see the old idea of annotations is a powerful feature especially when many users are working with the library. Obviously the tools must be available for every user on any client system and as discussed above these tools must be as easy to use as a pencil. Annotations are not the only possible interactive feature. One can imagine links from some very specific technical terms in the text to some dictionary server. Some systems like the one used at Learning Network of 'The New York Times' [Lea, 2001] have already implemented this useful feature.

Some large dictionaries like PC-Bibliothek [PCB, 2001], Brockhaus Multimedia ([BMM, 2000], one of the largest available multimedia collections) are client-side implementations. If one wants to use a dictionary, he simply selects the unknown string, type a defined hot-key combination and the dictionary does its work. Therefore changing the laptop implies also changing of the desktop-environment and the loss of the installed dictionary (like in the traditional world, if one changes the office, all books needed must be transfered too...). The client/server paradigm makes the live more easier for some users.

Implementing links in the content to these dictionaries shows, that user preferences are an essential requirement to realize this feature. An example will clarify this statement: Imagine two users of the library, a novice student of computer science and a professor of computer science. It might be nice, if there is a link from the term 'Programming Language' to some basic computer science dictionary for the student, but it makes no sense to create such a link for the professor! On the other hand if there are some new developed programming languages which are maybe interesting for the professor, then a link will also be suitable for the professor, but the target is then obviously a different document as for the student. This implies, that not just 'skill/experience' (e.g. in a range from 1 to 5) but also 'interest' is a criteria for the link-creation tool. Either the entry of a dictionary or the whole dictionary as such must be classified in a similar manner, i.e. a 'Basic Dictionary Of Computer Science Terms' might be declared to be of interest for students (skill/experience $\leq$?) and for very interested people (interest ≥ 4). Note, that it is absolutely necessary to evaluate the response of the users and to classify the dictionaries properly.

Currenty the Dublin Core Education Working Group (DCEd) proposed a Working Draft to the Dublin Core Usage Committee of the Dublin Core Metadata Initiative (DCMI) to overcome this problem [Mason and Sutton, 2000] of describing the audience for some material. They introduced a element called 'dc-ed:audience'. E.g. the Education Network Australia (EdNA, [EDN, 2001]) is in the process of implementing some vocabulary. Various education-specific thesauri contain audience classification descriptors (e.g., the Thesaurus of ERIC Descriptors and the NICEM Thesaurus, to name but a few) [Mason et al., 2000]. A discussion about different kinds of links (reference links, glossary links etc.) can be found in [Schmaranz, 1996].

One interesting topic currently discused at the World Wide Web Consortium (W3C) is the Semantic Web [W3C, 2001]:

> The Semantic Web is a vision: the idea of having data on the Web defined and linked in a way that it can be used by machines not just for display purposes, but for automation, integration and reuse of data across various applications.

Several techniques are available to describe data. If there is a common sense of the semantic of that meta data a Semantic Web can be implemented. This web can be used to find related articles or a cluster of similar articles automatically. In J.UCS similar articles are clustered in different collections. As described above, the ACM-classification scheme is used for the clustering of documents stored on the same server system. If the Semantic Web becomes reality also documents stored on different systems can be clustered together and this would be a powerful feature for all users.

4 Conclusion and Future Work

There is a need for users to bias the layout and the content of a digital library. These user dependent preferences must be stored at some place. If these preferences are stored on the server-side there are enormous advantages. A workspace for a registered user of the Journal of Universal Computer Science (J.UCS) was introduced and some functions like rearranging articles, public and private bookmarks, and a global history were described. A digital library should not just be read, but a user should work with it. Links to the future, special annotations etc. are necessary tools to make full use of the power of many users. Reuse of existing material in terms of reference linking instead of cut-and-pasting is a key issue.

The next step is to redesign some existing annotation tools to make rating of content and other described annotation facilities possible and to implement some of the described functions. Articles are already described by some meta-data but these data are in a proprietary format and must be translated to a common format (like Dublin Core) to make the Semantic Web possible.

References

[BMM, 2000] (2000). Brockhaus multimedia. `http://www.brockhaus-multimedia.de`.

[MyB, 2001] (2001). `http://www.mybookmarks.com`.

[EDN, 2001] (2001). Education network australia. `http://www.edna.edu.au`.

[Hyp, 2001] (2001). Hyperwave information server. `http://www.hyperwave.com`.

[Lea, 2001] (2001). Learning network. `http://www.nytimes.com/learning`.

[PCB, 2001] (2001). Pc-bibliothek. `http://www.iicm.edu/pcbibliothek/home`.

[ACM, 1998] ACM (1998). Computing classification system. `http://www.acm.org/class`.

[Berners-Lee et al., 1998] Berners-Lee, T., Fielding, R., Irvine, U., and Masinter, L. (1998). Uniform Resource Identifiers (URI). RFC 2396. http://www.faqs.org/rfcs/rfc2396.html.

[Clarke, 2001] Clarke, R. (2001). Cookies. `http://www.anu.edu.au/people/Roger.Clarke/II/Cookies.html`.

[Heinrich and Maurer, 2000] Heinrich, E. and Maurer, H. (2000). Active documents: Concept, implementation and applications. *JUCS*, 6(12). `http://www.jucs.org/jucs_6_12/active_documents_concept_implementation`.

[Krottmaier and Maurer, 2001] Krottmaier, H. and Maurer, H. (2001). Transclusions in the 21st century. In *Proceedings of WebNet 2001, Orlando.* to appear.

[Mason and Sutton, 2000] Mason, J. and Sutton, S. (2000). Education working group: Draft proposal. `http://dublincore.org/documents/education-namespace/`.

[Mason et al., 2000] Mason, J., Sutton, S., and Co-chairs (2000). Education working group: Report of deliberations. `http://www.ischool.washington.edu/sasutton/dc-ed/Dc-ac/DC-Education_Report.html`.

[Maurer, 1996] Maurer, H. (1996). now hyperwave — the next generation web solution.

[Maurer, 2001] Maurer, H. (2001). Beyond classical digital libraries. In *Proc. NIT conference.*

[Maurer and Schmaranz, 1994] Maurer, H. and Schmaranz, K. (1994). J.ucs - the next generation in electronic journal publishing. *JUCS*, 0(0). `http://www.jucs.org/jucs_0_0/j_ucs_the_next`.

[Nelson, 1987] Nelson, T. (1987). *Literary Maschines.* Ted Nelson.

[Schmaranz, 1996] Schmaranz, K. (1996). Professional electronic publishing in hyper-g. In *Proceedings of WebNet 1996.* `http://curry.edschool.virginia.edu/aace/conf/webnet/html/130.htm`.

[W3C, 2001] W3C (2001). Semantic web activity. `http://www.w3.org/2001/sw`.

Electronic Publishing '01 –
2001 in the Digital Publishing Odyssey
A. Hübler et al. (Eds.)
IOS Press, 2001

How Dynamic E-journals can Interconnect Open Access Archives

Steve Hitchcock and Wendy Hall
IAM Research Group, Department of Electronics and Computer Science, University of Southampton SO17 1BJ, UK
Contact email: sh94r@ecs.soton.ac.uk

Abstract. Influential scientists are urging journal publishers to free their published works so they can be accessed in comprehensive digital archives. That would create the opportunity for new services that dynamically interconnect material in the archives. To achieve this, two issues endemic to scholarly journal publishing need to be tackled: decoupling journal content from publishing process; defragmentation of the control of access to works at the article level. It is not necessary to wait for publishers to act. It was predicted that, enabled by links, e-journal publishing will become more distributed. (Hitchcock *et al.* 1998) An editorially controlled new model e-journal that links material from over 100 distributed, open access sources realises that prediction. *Perspectives in Electronic Publishing* (PeP) combines the functions of a review journal with original materials and access to full-text papers on a focussed topic, in this case on electronic publishing, in a single coherent package that indexes and links selected works. The paper describes the main features of PeP and how it can be used, and considers whether PeP contributes to the scientists' objective of a dynamic and integrated scientific literature.

0. Introduction

Physicists are building it, mathematicians are heading towards it, computer scientists have the vision and the tools to automate it, while biomedical scientists are very keen to have it. What is it? A comprehensive collection of published research papers that can be efficiently indexed, searched, and linked: 'a dynamic digital archive' (Roberts *et al.* 2001). Ironically, biomedical scientists have the closest approximation to it with *Medline*, widely and freely available and used to link the biomedical journal literature, but in this case the 'archive' is a collection of abstracts acting as proxy for the full-text papers.

This paper is not about the form of the archive, whether it should be a single centralised repository or distributed and harvested archives as proposed by the Open Archives initiative (OAi). It is about the 'dynamic', the innovations and services we might begin to see if the content of the archive or archives becomes openly accessible to third-parties. In particular, it investigates the benefits when works are freely available to readers in some form. 'Unimpeded access to these archives and open distribution of their contents', Roberts *et al.* continue, 'will enable researchers to take on the challenge of integrating and interconnecting the fantastically rich, but extremely fragmented and chaotic, scientific literature'.

That statement encapsulates what this paper, and the model it promotes, contend are the vital features of any system of electronic scholarly communication, which must be:

- Integrated, making something accessible from something else
- Dynamic, computationally adding time-critical data services

The philosophy is equally well elaborated by Hellman (2001): 'The best way to add function is to do one function very efficiently, and through open standards allow other generic technologies and organizations to layer on added functionality.' Search services such as Google, and annotation services as were exemplified by Third Voice, are cited as examples: 'for a scientist, exposing an e-journal to Google indexing adds more value at lower cost to an e-journal than almost ANY of the innovative functions' of most e-journals.

Thus, to get to the proposed model we first have to deal with two issues endemic to the existing scholarly journal publishing system:

- Decoupling content from publishing process and function
- Reversing the fragmentation of the scientific literature

There are some significant cautions, however, concerning misconceptions about the likely impact of e-journals and the viability of e-journal models:

- Lower cost predictions for e-journals are unproven and insignificant: studies over 30 years reported by Tenopir and King (2000) show that it is hard to justify e-journals on economic arguments alone, especially if those e-journals mimic print journals in all important respects.
- Authors prefer established journals to new e-journals: studies indicate the continued preference of authors for established, i.e. print, journal titles (e.g. Anderson *et al.* 2001; Bjork and Turk 2000) despite findings that often these same people, as readers, want access to free Internet journals.
- Electronic publishing models are not universal: electronic publishing enthusiasts are warned against "a one size fits all" approach for modelling electronic publishing across academic disciplines. (Kling and McKim 1999)

1. Decoupling journal content from publishing process

The essential steps in the traditional process of journal publishing are:

1. Shape journal: define, design, target
2. Attract authors
3. Review and select papers
4. Production: subedit, format, collate
5. Market and delivery

The journal attempts to be more than the sum of its parts, that is, the journal framework is more important than any single paper, yet it has to control those papers that fall within the package. This is how it happens. It is well known to many, but is worth elaborating because it affects the analysis of decoupling content from publishing process.

The publisher leads stages 1 and 2. By stage 3 there is a third party, the author, whose interest is believed to be co-joined with the publisher. Successful review of a submitted paper assures the author that the paper is fit to be viewed by his or her peers. In fact, if fulfilled correctly, the journal review has principally established that the paper is consistent with the profile of the journal. Nevertheless, joint interests have been confirmed between publisher and author, and a small cost has been incurred.

What are the implications of the peer review process? The publisher has learnt from a non-contracted expert witness, the peer reviewer, that the work probably has some value in its market. That value may be imprecise, but it is something that can be exploited in the journal framework. In terms of the paper, the publisher so far has only a small cost to recover, but in terms of stages 1 and 2 a bigger investment needs to be recouped and the paper has to be able to make a contribution to those costs.

1.1 The pivotal point: assignment of rights

What happens next is pivotal. The publisher needs the author's consent to publish the work. For many publishers that is not enough and the author may be asked to assign all rights in the work, that is, transfer complete ownership and beneficial interest in the work to the publisher. In part this is not unreasonable. If the author's journal selection has been good and the review has strictly been associated with the journal, then that journal ought to be the most appropriate publication vehicle for the paper. In an era of multiple media, however, authors would be better off reserving some rights that journals alone cannot serve, as we see in the steps below.

With all rights acquired the publisher puts the paper into its journal production process, stage 4. This invariably incurs a larger cost than that of the peer review process and will be passed on to the end user. The end user is never consulted on the value of the production process. A journal may have especially high design and production standards, which can improve reading, but this is a sideshow. The main deal has already been done, and if the peer review has been effective the target end user needs to see the paper whatever the cost and effect of production. The evidence, presented by Tenopir and King (2000), is that while journals continue to be accessed at high levels, personal subscriptions to journals have been decimated over the last 30 years.

1.2 E-print archives prompt divisible rights

In print the journal publishing process is indivisible, but not electronically. Consider an author in a field that supports e-print archives. Prior to journal review the author deposits the paper in a freely-accessible archive. Within 24 hours the author's peers will have been alerted and are able to access and read the archive version of the paper. After review the author retains the right to self-archive the work and supplements the original e-print in the archive with a revised version that has satisfied the reviewers. The work - the words, the presentation - is entirely that of the author. The process of deposit in the archive takes a few minutes of the author's time so long as it was produced in a format that adheres to the requirements of the automated archive. Within 24 hours the author's peers are able to access the new version of the paper.

It is possible the purpose of the review might be diminished outside the scope of the journal. In practice the distinction is rarely made as a Journal-Ref, a note of the journal that has reviewed and accepted the paper, is added to the metadata for the paper in the archive.

The author benefits in every respect. Instant readership for the preprint is guaranteed in the archive; for the best papers the status conferred by the Journal-Ref tag assures continuing higher numbers of readings in the archive. (Harnad and Carr 2000)

The publisher feels short-changed. Should it? That status has been attained by its efforts over many years, but what the publisher is left with is a commodity, which is what the paper has become, of dubious value now that exclusivity has been lost.

This is not necessarily the case. In physics, the only discipline with a large, universal e-print archive, journal publishers have continued to thrive in exactly this scenario. Data on profit growth may be unavailable, but there have been no reports of exceptional fall-off in subscriptions to journals in physics since the archive was launched in 1991.

Other publishers in other fields are more sceptical. Physics is a special case, they argue. Some journals invoke an embargo at stage 2, denying consideration to papers that have been submitted elsewhere, such as e-print archives. Or, with all rights in hand, they could feasibly demand withdrawal of any archive versions prior to publication. Some publishers have set up preprint archives that make papers free-to-view, but only up to the point of journal publication. (Dessy 2000) It appears that non-physics authors might be denied the benefits of their physics colleagues.

Except authors can claim the prize for themselves, by doing exactly as the physics author does, and reserving the right to self-archive their own versions of their own works. Should authors feel any twinge of guilt towards the journal publisher they could surmise the following: if the journal has an appreciably high status - there seems little point in submitting if it has not - it has no doubt been achieved by fortune of exclusive publication to date and it no longer needs that advantage; also, that if publishing is difficult and the publisher adds significant value that the self-archiving author alone could not, then the publisher should be capable of competing with sources based on author self-archiving.

In effect, the paper has been decoupled not from the peer review process, which the author values most, but from the production process, a superficiality of less importance.

1.3 Theory and practice of decoupling

Other commentators have theorised on the process of decoupling and the consequent benefits. Describing the 'deconstructed' journal, Smith (1999) wanted to establish the idea that most of the activities involved in journal publishing are independent ('quality control activities are not concerned with distribution') and therefore that there is no obvious need for these roles to be controlled, and the resulting product owned, by a single publisher.

The Scholar's Forum proposal (Buck *et al.* 1999), which aimed to wrest control for peer review and publishing value-adding tasks from journals to a Los Alamos-like 'document database', seems to have been still-born but indicated the concerns of influential academics. Phelps (1998), a university vice-chancellor, similarly elaborated a national electronic archive as a means to introduce competition: 'we must find ways to introduce competition into every phase of the process that journals once performed as a bundled effort -- quality certification, editorial improvement, distribution, indexing, and archiving'.

2. Defrag: removing access controls

There can be few users of Windows-based personal computers who have not used the disk defragmenter tool, defrag. Performance degrades rapidly when hard disc storage space nears capacity. Logical organisation of information held on the disc begins to break down as new files are stored where space dictates, so speed of retrieval of these files suffers. Applying defrag can ameliorate the process, reorganising the files into some logical and accessible order.

A similar process of deframentation is underway in the online publishing space, reversing the process of specialisation forced on paper journals by page constraints and other factors, and the consequent stagnation in the ability of non-specialist users to access these works. The ACM saw that users wanted access to the whole corpus of its publications: 'The business model and marketing campaign ... de-emphasized subscriptions to individual journals in favor of a single, annual access fee for unlimited usage of our Digital Library'. Rous (1999) This has resulted in faster growth of individual subscribers, the ACM claims, reversing entrenched steep declines in personal subscriptions affecting most print journals (Tenopir and King 2000). The importance of integrating access to journals to offer comprehensive coverage within fields has been established in user studies (Borghuis *et al.* 1996) and seems to be the choice of scholars and librarians. (Bailey 1994)

The most vivid evocation of defragmented scholarly publication is 'skywriting' (Harnad 1991): 'just as if each contribution were being written in the sky, for all peers to see and append to'. Even this is but a step in the direction of Engelbart's (1975) remarkable NLS oNLine System, described as a 'workplace' for knowledge workers, supporting dialogue and collaboration as well as access to texts and information services: 'publication time is very much shorter; significant "articles" may be as short as one sentence; cross-reference citations may easily be much more specific (i.e., pointing directly to a specific passage); catalogs and indexes can be accessed and searched online as well as in hard copy; and full-text retrieval with short delays is the basic operating mode. The end effect of these changes is a form of recorded dialogue whose impact and value has a dramatic qualitative difference over the traditional, hard-copy journal system'.

Defragmentation has the flexibility to create new packages that build on journal branding but are not dependent on it. Examples of this are the subject-focus portals such as BioMedNet and more recently the so-called 'virtual journals' promoted in most cases by these portal operators. Virtual journals appear to offer new services to the user, notably personalisation, but in some cases are simply vehicles for pay-per-view. This is because access remains tied to the original journal or publisher, the journal that performed peer review and most likely obtained exclusive rights to publish.

At the journal level defragmentation is not new, and has been practised by journal aggregators and secondary (bibliographic) services for many years. Where they are able to provide full-text content as a third-party service or a supplement to their own data, however, that content has had to be delivered in the form of the original journal package. Subscriptions or site licenses buy access only to whole journals. Documents can be ordered individually but are typically delivered in a non-processable, non-enhanceable form such as a print facsimile.

As with the Windows example, we are concerned with the defragmentation of the *control of access to works*, in this case at the article level. In other words, dissemination of individual works need no longer be tied to single, exclusive journal packages. Without this distinction it could be argued that the e-journal model proposed in this paper is re-fragmenting the journal literature.

3. A new e-journal model

It would be premature to anticipate journal publishers accepting the need for decoupling and defragmentation in the form described above, as the various PubMed Central debates testify (Varmus *et al.* 1999, Butler *et al.* 2001). Fortunately it is possible to build a model based on these premises using works already available freely on the Web, from free e-journals, online conference proceedings, eprint archives and author-maintained pages, among other sources.

That model is part of a larger project than can be fully described here, but we can cover the essential features. First, a simple guided tour will show what the implementation can do. It is important to separate the general model from the specific implementation, but once familiar with the features we try to place this model among other emerging e-publishing models and judge whether it fulfils the criteria of a dynamic, integrated e-journal aspired to above.

3.1 Perspectives in Electronic Publishing (PeP)

PeP is a real service, not a hypothetical model, at http://aims.ecs.soton.ac.uk/pep.nsf. PeP is free. It can be used by anyone with a Web connection and browser, optimally with Microsoft Internet Explorer v5.x.

At the front page you are presented with a list of the papers most recently added to the service. These papers, all editorially selected and focussed on the theme of electronic publishing, can have been posted anywhere on the Web. To be considered for inclusion, in this implementation, papers must be freely accessible.

PeP covers all aspects of electronic networked publishing, with an emphasis on academic publishing and on journals. It covers the publishers, the publishing process and intermediary services. Coverage extends to research and technical development that will impact on publishing, including some aspects of digital libraries. Changes to the legal framework of publishing for the network environment are another important component.

When a paper is chosen for inclusion, a bibliographic record describing it is created in a database. This contains typical data on the paper - publication data, also versioning data, information on authors - as well as editorial comment and chosen extracts from the paper. Some of these data are to be presented to the user; a separate program that builds data for linking collects data from the record too.

At the time PeP was launched in the second quarter of 2001 the database described a few hundred papers, all accessible to the Web user. Users can find specific papers using search, or browse using an index. This index is presented in a second browser window, for reasons described below, so is referred to as the 'remote' index.

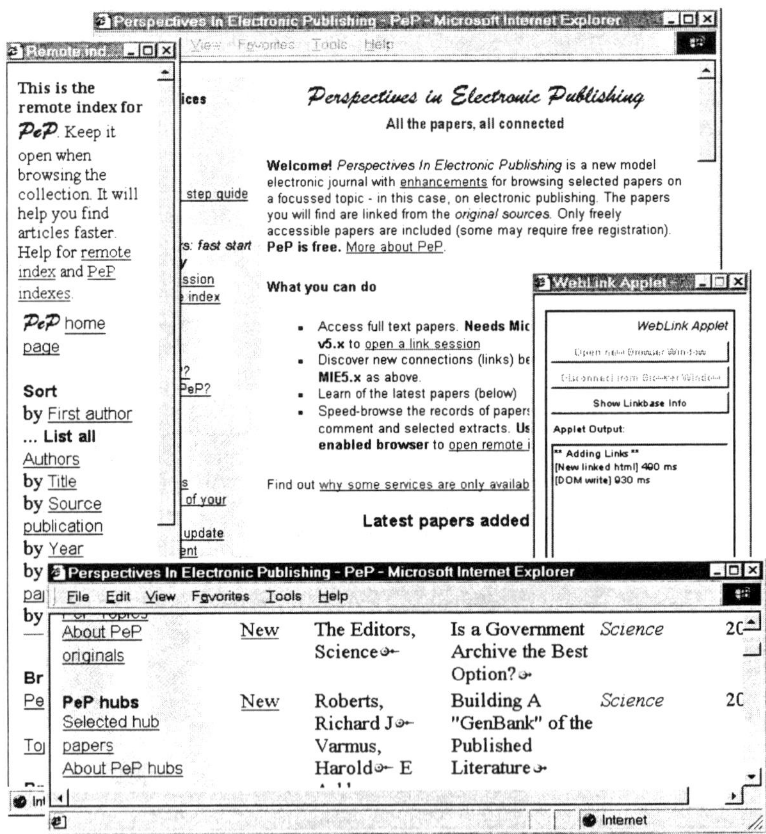

Figure 1: Full featured PeP service, showing the original Web front page, the linked version of that page with clickable link graphics added (enlarged view), the remote index (left) and the WebLink Applet

At this stage we have essentially a simple library-like catalogue. This is transformed by requesting the link data mentioned above. Technical constraints limit this part of the service to MIE5.x users. For those users, the browser downloads a link applet containing the link data. This WebLink applet interacts with pages subsequently downloaded by the user and attempts to insert links, which are displayed as small graphics to differentiate them from conventionally authored, underlined and coloured, text links.

There are two types of link:

- direct, pointing from PeP to the full text of the selected papers
- indirect, querying the PeP database for more information on the chosen subject, which may be an author name, or a key word or phrase

We now have the service shown in Figure 1, with the link applet window and a second text browsing window. The remote index remains open too.

Following the *PeP* or *New* link to the left of the listing in a contents page opens the PeP record for the chosen paper (Figure 2). Alternatively, the graphical link inserted beside the title of the paper retrieves the full text (Figure 3). Notice that although the paper is served from the originating site - it is not copied to PeP! - it also has added links. This is an example of a well-linked paper. The applet will try to add links to any page to be displayed in the linked browser window - it is not discriminating - but it is more likely to find text fragments matching link data, by definition, in a page with some relevance to electronic publishing.

It now becomes clear why the index is remote from the main text window. It would be inappropriate and potentially misleading to frame pages from sources other than PeP. Compared with a print journal the remote index can be seen to be acting as the permanent binding, or glue, of the journal.

Using the added links the user is able to explore the literature on a focussed topic from over 100 sources, one paper linked to another in a web-like form. Or, more likely for a small application, it could be viewed as a tree structure, using the index to return to the database when a web path leads nowhere. As the collection grows these paths should begin to reveal new insights and perhaps unanticipated relationships between works. No other service, as far as we are aware, presents such relationships between the full texts of papers.

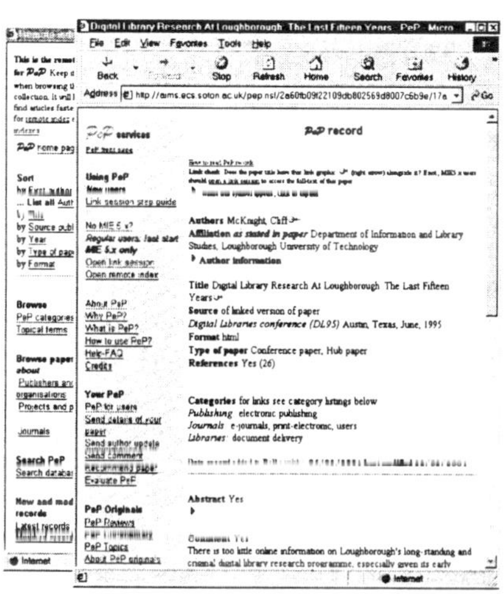

Figure 2: A record for every paper entered in PeP, with bibliographic details, comment and notable extracts, and a link to the full text.

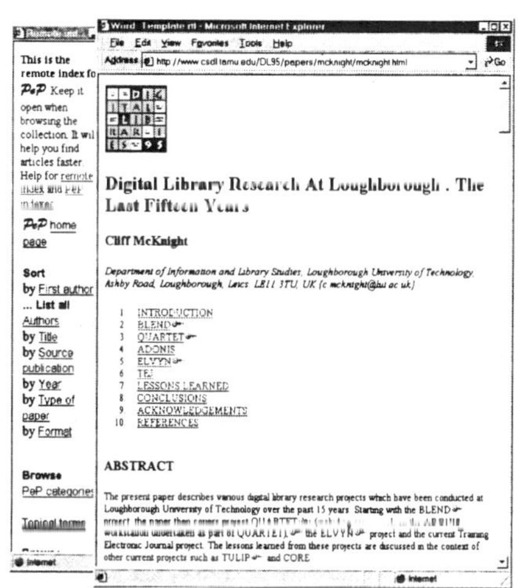

Figure 3: Original full text with added links, or return to PeP using the remote index (unlinked browser and applet windows both minimised)

3.2 What is PeP?

By adding links, what has PeP been transformed to? It has already been compared with a library catalogue, but it also has features in common with abstracting and indexing services such as ISI's Web of Science, and with portals or subject gateways. In fact, *PeP was designed to be a journal.* In this respect it is perhaps most closely aligned with review journals. It has one major distinction from all these services: the user has immediate access to the full text of all papers listed without the need of any other service.

As with many new Web applications, what PeP was designed to be and what it proves to be useful for may be different. That is down to users and is subject to ongoing evaluation. In this discussion PeP is considered to be a journal in its original and traditional sense:

Defn. journal:

> *a record of current transactions; an account of day-to-day events: a record of experiences, ideas, or reflections kept regularly for private use: a record of transactions kept by a deliberative or legislative body.*

3.3 Separating model from application

PeP is the application, not the model. There are two criteria that distinguish the model on which PeP is based: subject focus, and access. Specific features of PeP - the focus on electronic publishing, the condition of freely accessible papers, papers reviewed but not formally refereed - are not mandated in the model.

PeP could equally well be on another topic. Focussing on electronic publishing works well in this framework because it is a discursive topic, amenable to some informality and not dependent on formal peer review. It is also interdisciplinary, appealing to a broad constituency with widely varying degrees of commitment. Every researcher has a stake in the effectiveness of publishing as a communication channel for his or her work, more so at times of change like the present. So while relatively few researchers would see electronic publishing as their primary interest, many will contribute intermittently, and when they do they will usually address their own peers, not always the broader community. In other words it is a highly fragmented literature that PeP can act on to the benefit of researchers.

Another application could be based on commercial journal papers, with appropriate agreements, including only refereed papers, say, although this runs the risk of breaking the access criterion. Despite the best efforts of journal publishers - site licences, virtual journals, database service providers and journal aggregators, CrossRef, etc. - the journals industry is manifestly unable to achieve breadth and access together, because the fee-based journal structure fragments access and prevents this. Ultimately, the effective researcher who is happy to pay a fee or use a library-based subscription requires that those combined subscriptions cover all that he or she may conceivably need to access. The effective large research university, meanwhile, probably requires access to absolutely everything. Clearly impossible as long as the fragmented journal model continues, but distinctly feasible if the electronic environment is utilised effectively.

The ideal platform for the PeP model is distributed archives advocated by the Open Archives initiative. (Van de Sompel and Lagoze 2000) For PeP these will most constructively be e-print archives, although OAi aspires to encompass broader types of materials that might be found in digital libraries. E-print archives provide access to raw author-created data, the ideal foundation to encourage competition for compelling 'virtual journals' and PeP clones.

3.4 Comparing PeP with other models

PeP was inspired by more visionary systems, such as Memex (Bush 1945) and Xanadu (Nelson 1999), which were never fully realised. The real model on which PeP was based is Microcosm, a multimedia linking system also built at Southampton University (Davis *et al.* 1992). This is ironic because Microcosm was never a Web application. It has been adapted for the Web in various guises, notably as the Distributed Link Service (Carr *et al.* 1995), but these were effectively linking engines that discarded the editor and user interface in favour of a programming based approach. PeP re-invents the Microcosm interface for the Web and, although PeP also adopts the Microcosm 'generic' (link everywhere) link type, it does not use any part of Microcosm.

Microcosm was among the first systems to show that within digital information systems links can be managed as separate entities from the other information content. Long heralded by hypertext developers, this gave the capability to interconnect materials created independently and in different media. The potential has become more evident with the emergence of networked information services such as the Web where sites are frequently presented as self-contained 'islands' of information rather than interconnected webs.

PeP links were specified to be simple but editorially controlled, recognising that integration based on links needs to be focussed on content. An early motivation for this approach was outlined by O'Reilly (1996), founder of the eponymous books publisher, who saw how the core skill of non-fiction publishing, creating 'information interfaces', could be applied more powerfully on the Web: 'In the old model, the information product is a container. In the new model, it is a core. One bounds a body of content, the other centers it.' O'Reilly urges publishers to reinforce the fundamentals of the Internet, 'participation, access, communication'.

3.5 A dynamic and integrated e-journal

We can now assess whether PeP realises the self-proclaimed critical features of a system for electronic scholarly communication. Is it dynamic and integrated?

Links and search are the computational tools provided to support the online user. PeP's editorially controlled link service is the bridge between the computational 'overlay' and integration at the article level. Raney (1998) argues that citation and search should be seen as tools, not alternatives to journals, but in the design of PeP they are integral.

Links also fulfil the requirement for time-critical data services. Works are fixed in time but links added to these works can point forward or backward from that moment in time. Links are interactive, not just for the user. Inserting links enables PeP to interact with the texts selected for inclusion.

PeP is a primary example of decoupling journal processing tasks. As currently structured, it can include papers with much lower cost overhead than conventional journals, because it doesn't perform all the functions - refereeing, editing and layout, etc. - of those journals. PeP has limited scope but unlimited space, which it can fill faster than any conventional journal. This reinforces the integration feature, which becomes more powerful as the information space grows.

It could be argued that PeP is parasitic on journals that perform valuable services for authors. It is true that among the best sources in PeP are professionally published open access e-journals, but PeP supplements these with its own original content in the form of review articles, and adds additional services for the user that aren't available elsewhere, the link 'perspectives' of the title. This is a manifestation of Hellman's call to allow layers of functionality to be added to journals.

By including content from over 100 sources, PeP is a beneficiary of the defragmentation of access to both well-known and little-known sources. While selection of articles is a component of PeP, thereby recreating fragments from the whole of the freely accessible literature, it does not own the selected works and therefore does not compromise the benefits of defragmentation for other services.

PeP has adapted to the dynamic of the online environment without relinquishing the editorial coherence of the conventional journal in favour of wholesale automation.

4. Conclusion

Evaluation and user data on PeP are being collected at the time of writing. More models and user data will be needed to make a convincing case for the universal appeal of e-journals and derived models, which face a more sobering environment and greater challenges than were anticipated in the mid-1990s. Tenopir and King (2000) conclude that innovative electronic services 'may take considerable time to achieve acceptance, if ever'.

PeP is not unique in any single feature but is unusual in its combination of features. Its innovations may be less noticeable but ultimately more effective by responding to the needs of users.

What about the cautions outlined in the introduction? No economic arguments have been advanced for PeP as they haven't yet been evaluated. Whatever those arguments might be, they will not be that producing PeP is cost-free. Improved and cost-effective functionality for users will be the main determinant of the impact of PeP. It is less overtly appealing to authors in its present form, lacking formal refereeing and established identity, but unlike conventional journals it is not dependent on individual submissions but on the willingness of authors generally to make their works available from open-access journals or other freely accessible sources.

PeP is almost certainly not a universal model, but we have analysed why it works in this case and what features to look for in topics that might be amenable to similar treatment.

PeP is a journal for users today. It may prove to be built on an intermediate technology, but one that can embrace change. PeP is unlike other journals but recognises its debt to those journals and other publications from which it draws while adding its own original content and perspectives.

It may be presumptuous to draw parallels with Nelson's (1999) vision for a digital publishing system, but for all the reasons he expressed, PeP may not suit everyone: 'Those who see work as finished and closed, who see subjects as bounded and hierarchically related, who see research as final ... who don't worry about lost information, who don't worry about minority points of view, who don't see the need to express alternatives, who don't see a need for intercomparison, who don't see a need for literary continuity, have a great deal of difficulty with this paradigm.'

4.1 Acknowledgements

The WebLink applet used in this application was designed and built at Southampton University by Tim Miles-Board with support from Les Carr. Gareth Hughes manages the database Web server from which PeP can be accessed.

5. References

Anderson, K. *et al.* (2001) Publishing Online-Only Peer-Reviewed Biomedical Literature: Three Years of Citation, Author Perception, and Usage Experience. *Journal of Electronic Publishing*, Vol. 6, No. 3, March
Bailey, C. W. Jr (1994) Scholarly Electronic Publishing on the Internet, the NREN, and the NII: Charting Possible Futures. *Serials Review*, Vol. 20, No. 3, 7-16
Bjork, B.-C. and Turk, Z. (2000) How Scientists Retrieve Publications: An Empirical Study of How the Internet Is Overtaking Paper Media. *Journal of Electronic Publishing*, Vol. 6, No. 2, December
Borghuis, M. *et al.* (1996) TULIP Project Final Report. Elsevier Technical Report http://www.elsevier.nl/inca/homepage/about/resproj/trmenu.htm
Buck, A. M. *et al.* (1999) Scholar's Forum: A New Model For Scholarly Communication. Author's server, March
http://library.caltech.edu/publications/ScholarsForum/
Bush, V. (1945) As We May Think. *Atlantic Monthly*, July
Butler, D. *et al.* (2001) Future e-access to the primary literature. *Nature Web Debates*, 5 April
http://www.nature.com/nature/debates/e-access/index.html
Carr, L. *et al.* (1995) The Distributed Link Service: A Tool for Publishers, Authors and Readers. *Fourth World Wide Web Conference (WWW4)*, Boston, December
Davis, H. C. *et al.* (1992) MICROCOSM: An Open Hypermedia Environment for Information Integration. CSTR 92-15, Computer Science Technical Report, University of Southampton
http://www.bib.ecs.soton.ac.uk/records/1317
Dessy, R. (2000) Chemical E-Preprints: The Ostriches. *Trends in Analytical Chemistry*, Vol. 19
Engelbart, D. C. (1975) NLS Teleconferencing features: the Journal, and Shared-Screen Telephoning. *IEEE Catalog* No. 75CH0988 6C, pp.173 176
Harnad, S. (1991) Post-Gutenberg Galaxy: the Fourth Revolution in the Means of Production of Knowledge. *Public-Access Computer Systems (PACS) Review*, Vol. 2, No.1, 39 - 53
Harnad, S. and Carr, L. (2001) Integrating, Navigating and Analyzing Eprint Archives through Open Citation Linking (the OpCit Project). *Current Science Online*, Vol. 79, No. 5, 10th September
Hellman, E. (2001) Less is More! Re: Reader-Designated HyperLinking In/Between/Among E-Journals. Web4Lib Electronic Discussion Archive, 13 February
http://sunsite.berkeley.edu/Web4Lib/archive/0102/0218.html
Hitchcock, S. *et al.* (1998) Making the Most of Electronic Journals. *Computing Research Repository*, cs.DL/9812016, 14 December
Kling, R. and McKim, G. (2000) Not Just a Matter of Time: Field Differences in the Shaping of Electronic. *Journal of the American Society for Information Science*, Vol. 51, No. 14
Nelson, T. H. (1999) Xanalogical Media: Needed Now More Than Ever. *ACM Computing Surveys*, Vol. 31, No. 4, December
O'Reilly, T. (1996) Publishing Models for Internet Commerce. *Communications of the ACM*, Vol. 39, No. 6, June, 79-86
Phelps, C. E. (1998) Achieving Maximal Value from Digital Technologies In Scholarly Communication. *ARL Proceedings*, October
Raney, R. K. (1998) Into a Glass Darkly. *Journal of Electronic Publishing*, Vol. 4, No. 2, December
Roberts, R. J. *et al.* (2001) Building A "GenBank" of the Published Literature. *Science*, Vol. 291, No. 5512, 2318-2319, 23 March
Rous, B. (1999) ACM: a Case Study. *Journal of Electronic Publishing*, Vol. 4, No. 4, June
Smith, J. W. T. (1999) The Deconstructed Journal - a new Model for Academic Publishing. *Learned Publishing*, Vol. 12, No. 2, April
Tenopir, C. and King, D. W. (2000) Towards Electronic Journals: Realities for Scientists, Librarians, and Publishers. *Psycoloquy*, Vol. 11, Issue 084
Van de Sompel, H. and Lagoze, C. (2000) The Santa Fe Convention of the Open Archives Initiative. *D-Lib Magazine*, Vol. 6 No. 2, February
Varmus, H. *et al.* (1999) Journals Online: PubMed Central and Beyond. *HMS Beagle: The BioMedNet Magazine*, No. 61, September 3rd

Perspectives in Electronic Publishing was the principal tool used in the research and compilation of this reference list. The online version of this paper, when viewed using the PeP link service, will show direct links to the full text of every paper cited. The online version of the paper can be found in PeP.

*Electronic Publishing '01 –
2001 in the Digital Publishing Odyssey
A. Hübler et al. (Eds.)
IOS Press, 2001*

Disintermediation of Academic Publishing through the Internet: An Intermediate Report from the Front Line

Thomas Krichel,
*Palmer School of Library and Information Science
Long Island University, 720 Northern Boulevard, Brookville
New York 11548-1300, USA*
krichel@openlib.org

Simeon Warner,
*MS B285 Los Alamos National Laboratory
Los Alamos, New Mexico, 87545 USA*
simeon@lanl.gov

Abstract. There has been a lot of discussion about the potential for free access to scholarly documents on the Internet. At the turn of the century, there a major initiatives. These are arXiv, which covers Physics, Mathematics and Computer Science and RePEc, which covers Economics. These initiatives work in very different ways. This paper is the fruit of collaboration between authors working for both initiatives. It therefore reflects the perspective of people working to achieve change, rather than an academic perspective of pure observation.
We first introduce both arXiv and RePEc, and then consider future scenarios for disintermediated academic publishing. We then discusses the issue of quality control from an e-print archive point of view. Finally, we review recent efforts to improve the interoperability of e-print archives through the Open Archive Initative (OAI). In particular, we draw on the workshop on OAI and peer review held at CERN in March 2001 to illustrate the level of interest in the OAI protocol as a way to improve scholarly communication on the Internet.
This paper is available online at http://openlib.org/home/krichel/sants.html

0. Introduction

The exchange of contracts over the Internet is now commonplace. In the majority of cases, delivery of the merchandise occurs off-line. However, purely informational commodities--such as statistical data or pornographic pictures--can both be contracted upon and delivered over the Internet. That affords the holders of such commodities the opportunity to directly contract with customers in the way that was not possible off-line. The new medium thus provides an opportunity for disintermediation.

In the academic world, the debate about the possible extent of disintermediation has concentrated on the rôle of academic publishing. A large part of academic writing attracts no payment from publication. For the sake of simplicity, this paper deals exclusively with scholarly works for which the author receives no payment. These will be referred to as "research papers" or "papers" for short. It is further assumed that the advent of the Internet will not change the reward structure in the academic world. We assume that authors will still want to write without payment, with the exclusive aim of achieving peer recognition.

It has been proposed, most vociferously by Harnad (1995) and in many papers since, that the Internet will lead to free access to academic papers. In 1995 two large-scale initiatives were already well under way to work on realizing this vision. These were the arXiv archive for Physics, and the RePEc dataset for Economics. This paper has been written by people working within these initiatives. It is a contribution to the debate about "freeing the literature". The volume of papers on this topic is already quite large. What justifies a new paper on the topic?

The process by which the academic literature is to be freed is most often referred to as author-self archiving. This is somewhat of a misnomer, but we will stick with the term for a moment. This paper has been written by practitioners of author self-archiving. Thus it offers practical insight from the process that are often not available to the outside observer. More generally, we have also been involved in recent efforts to coordinate author self-archiving initiatives in the Open Archives Initative. We will therefore take a look beyond the day-to-day running of our work and propose some steps that would bring the process forward. Thus we bring two innovative perspectives to the literature, a practical perspective and a normative one.

The remainder of the paper is organized as follows. In Section 2 we introduce the arXiv archive, and in Section 3 we discuss the RePEc dataset. In Section 4 we suggest scenarios for future Internet-based publication. In sections Section 5 and Section 6 we discuss steps forward and setbacks for the author self-archiving movement. In Section 7 we discuss the question of quality control. In Section 8 we present recent work of the OAI. In Section 9 we offer a few conclusions.

1. The arXiv archive

The arXiv e-print archive is the largest and best-known archive of author self-archived scholarly literature. It is discipline-based and centralized, in that all submissions and the master database are at one site. Here we briefly review the history of arXiv and then discuss its place in the scholarly publishing environment.

The arXiv e-print archive, formerly known as xxx, was started in August 1991 by Paul Ginsparg. The first subject area was theoretical high-energy physics, 'hep-th' and it was initially little more than an email reflector for paper exchange. In 1992 an ftp interface was added and the archive expanded to other areas of high energy physics. Development since then has seen steady expansion of the subject areas to cover all of physics, mathematics, computer science and non-linear systems; and the addition of new interfaces and facilities as new technologies have become available. Significant developments have included: web interface (December 1993); automatic PostScript generation from TeX source (June 1995); PDF generation (April 1996); and web upload (June 1996). Recently, arXiv has been at the forefront of the Open Archives Initiative (OAI).

arXiv serves an estimated 70,000 users in over 100 countries. There were about 13,000,000 downloads of papers in 2000. There were over 30,000 submissions in 2000, and the number of new submissions is growing approximately linearly, with about 3,500 additional new submissions each year. The growth in submissions has had little impact on the administration of the arXiv although there is an increasing reliance on moderators to assure appropriateness. More that 98% of the submissions are entirely automated: 68% of them via the web, 27% via email and 5% via ftp. It is interesting to note that if just 15 minutes were required for each submission then a full-time staff of 7 people would be required to deal with new submissions. Instead, arXiv uses less than one full-time equivalent to deal with day-to-day operations.

The Los Alamos site is funded by the US National Science Foundation and the US Department of Energy. The 15 mirror sites around the world are funded independently, the cost is just a few thousand dollars for a new machine every few years and a small amount of system administration effort.

The high-energy physics community uses the TeX text formatting system almost exclusively, and this has been very convenient for arXiv. arXiv does not accept preprocessed TeX submissions, authors must submit the source. This allows generation of various types of output including DVI, PostScript in several flavors, and PDF. Expansion into other areas of physics means that there are now an increasing number of non-TeX submissions and this trend is sure to continue. Unfortunately, many common word-processing packages produce very inefficient and sometimes low-quality output unless used expertly. Experience shows that PostScript or PDF submissions require greater screening effort than TeX submissions. This is an example of how the physics and mathematics communities differ from other communities in a way that has favored author self-archiving.

Before 1994, archives for some new subject areas were started at other sites using the same software. In November 1994 the data from the remote sites were moved to the central site, and the remote sites became mirrors. The reason for this reorganization was the need for stability. While a distributed model is appealing, sites relying on a single person, who's main occupation is not the archive, are not stable on a time-scale of years. A user perception of stability is important for the success of an archive. arXiv is once again investigating a more distributed model but any new system will be robust to the disappearance of any site.

arXiv has not been an academic exercise, it was started from inside the community it aimed to serve. At all stages of expansion to cover a wider subject area, arXiv has been guided and promoted by members of the new fields. Nowadays, some commercial publishers tacitly acknowledge the legitimacy of arXiv by accepting submissions where the author simply quotes an arXiv identifier. Policies vary on whether the publisher permits the author to update the arXiv version to reflect changes made during the refereeing process. However, authors often ignore any prohibitions.

arXiv is by far the largest author self-archiving project. Some proponents of change in scholarly publishing have heralded arXiv as the single mode forward for the change of scholarly communication. While it is possible that the arXiv model could be successfully applied to all other disciplines, there are good reasons to question this. We will highlight two issues.

First, there have been attempts to emulate the success of arXiv by building discipline-based archives for other disciplines. Two working examples are CogPrints at the University of Southampton and the Economics Working Paper Archive. Both have been operating for more than four years, yet neither has grown beyond 1,500 documents. Why have they not been more successful? This leads us to question the applicability of the centralized scheme to other disciplines. It should be noted that both initiatives have been run by members of the community they serve. Therefore they can not be dismissed as failing because they are foreign to the discipline and not sensitive to its particular needs.

Second, even though arXiv has been successful in attracting submissions in several areas of physics and mathematics, an attempt to expand to computer science has had limited success. A high-level committee on the future of scholarly communication in computing entered an agreement with arXiv to run a Computer Science Research Repository (CoRR). This has, to date, received rather little attention from computer scientists in spite of various publicity efforts within the community. Are we to conclude that computer scientists care little about formal on-line dissemination of research papers? Are they simply happy to leave their papers on their homepages?

If current trends continue, arXiv will provide and increasingly complete free layer of primary research literature for the mathematics and physics disciplines. This leads us to ask whether it is likely that, over time, small-scale archiving, be it in departmental or homepage archives, will decline. There is certainly a trend for departmental archives in mathematics to migrate to arXiv. However, the Open Archives Initiative (OAI) has the potential to change the tradeoffs in the choice between centralized and decentralized archives. If cross-archive discovery and awareness tools exist for decentralized archives then institutional and department archives may become as effective as centralized archives such as arXiv.

2. The RePEc database

RePEc is much less known than arXiv and it is also less well understood. There are two reasons for that. First, it is limited to the economics discipline. Second its business model is more abstract.

Historically, RePEc grew out of the NetEc project. It was started by Thomas Krichel in February 1993. In April 1993 he opened a tiny collection of a electronic papers on an ftp server with a gopher interface operating at Manchester Computing. However, it was never the business plan of NetEc to become an electronic working paper archive for the discipline. Instead the idea was to collect data about printed and electronic papers as published by various sites so that they could be searched together on a single site. It was a library of bibliographic data rather than a archive. The project developed mirror sites in Japan (July 1996) and in the US (January 1997). In 1997, the RePEc dataset was created by the NetEc project, and two other projects that were active in the area, DEGREE and S WoPEc. These projects agreed to exchange metadata in a common, purpose-built format called ReDIF. This metadata can be harvested following a simple harvesting protocol called the Guildford protocol. Shortly after the implementation of the protocol, several user services appeared that were build on the data. Thus the RePEc project is a true forerunner of the Open Archives Initiative. In 1998, data about Economics institutions was In 2000, a personal registration service was opened. It allows persons to register associations between them and the document and institution data in the database. At the time of writing, it has over 160 different archives that contribute metadata, and eight different user services. There are about 40,000 downloadable paper cataloged in RePEc. The NetEc project received £129,000 funding from the Joint Information Systems Committee JISC, it now runs without any external funding. Running such a large-scale operation with volunteer power only is a remarkable technical and organization achievement.

RePEc is not only a database of papers in economics, but it also contains data about economics institutions and academic economists.

The registration of institutions is accomplished through the EDIRC project. The acronym stands for "Economics Departments, Institutions and Research Centers". This dataset has been compiled by Christian Zimmermann, an Associate Professor of Economics at Unversité du Québec à Montréal on his own account, as a public service to the economics profession. The initial intention was to compile a directory with all economics departments that have a web presence. Since there are many departments that have a web presence now, a large number are now registered, about 5,000 of them at the time of this writing. All these records are included in RePEc. For all institutions, data on their homepage is available, as well as postal and telephone information.

At the moment, EDIRC is mainly linked to the rest of the RePEc data through the HoPEc personal registration service. This service can be used by economists to register themselves as authors of the documents that are contained in RePEc. To date 6% of all papers have an at least one of the authors as a registered person. The HoPEc registrations will in the future be used for building a collection of papers held in the homepages of these authors. Already now, the collection is used to link from the papers of authors to their homepage and for the provision of current contact information. Clearly, current contact information may be quite different from the contact information in the bibliographic data.

Thus RePEc appears as a very ambitious project. In its end stage, every author, institution and document in economics will be registered in the database. What are the chances that this project be completed? Two remarks are on order here.

First, while RePEc have rejected centralization of papers as a means forward for the collection of grey literature, but it happens that RePEc has a commercial competitor in the "Economic Research Network" operated by "Social Science Electronic Publishing". Much of the offerings on their site are free. There is a substantial overlap with the contents of RePEc. At the time of writing, they have reached about 12,000 electronic papers. Thus they are still much smaller, but they seem to be expanding at a faster rate. There is two reasons for the success of the company. First, they have extensive statistical reports on download of papers, something that is next to impossible to collect in the context of a multi-service operation.

Second, the company has started cooperative agreements with departments who wish to sell the working papers that they produce. If this trend expands we will see under the Internet access to things that used to be free in the paper days. Second, while are some commercial publishers that already collaborate with RePEc, it is not easy to forecast that there will be wide-spread collaboration. There are two reasons for that. First in economics, no publisher holds a large amount of material. Many publishers produce economics journals, but for each publisher it is a small amount of their business. Therefore the cost to working with RePEc-specific bibliographic system is relatively high as compared to the returns. Therefore the contents of RePEc is still dominated by working papers.

3. Future scenarios of publication

In the introduction, we pointed out that the term "author self-archiving" is somewhat of a misnomer. In the arXiv scenario it is arXiv that do the archiving. In the RePEc scenario the archiving is performed by the intermediate providers like departments and research centers. To be quite precise, "author self-archiving" would be more appropriately applied to authors depositing their papers in homepages. However, this type of activity can hardly be classified as archiving because the concept of an archive suggests a long-run storage facility which is rarely the case with personal homepages.

Thus we would like to introduce the concept of academic self-publishing as a replacement for author self-archiving. By academic self-publishing we mean a trend for the academic sector to take over the publication of its own output. It should be noted that we understand "publishing" here in the wide sense of the word as "making public", rather than in narrow sense of "making public through an intermediate agent to whom copyright is being transfered". Both RePEc and arXiv fit this description.

Academic self-publishing of research material is currently being experimented with on a per-discipline wide basis. A useful discussion of same initiatives is Kling and McKim (2000). We agree with the basic message of their paper. There will be no unique method by which networked scholarly communication will be running across disciplines. Discipline-specific differences are likely to persist. For each discipline, it is most likely that evolution depends on

- the established communication patterns prior to the proliferation of electronic networks

- the presence or absence of entrepreneurial pioneers to stimulate change
- the political and financial environment of the discipline
- in that order. The persistence of discipline-specific features in academic self-publishing is the first assumption for our discussion here.

A second assumption is that authors will continue to write research papers. These are discreet accounts of individual research findings written by one author or a small group of co-authors. Thus we reject the idea that in the future, work of individual authors becomes dissolved in a global scientific hypertext net. It this case it would be difficult to trace the responsibility for the research results. Academic reward structures depend on precise knowledge of the authorship of research papers.

A third assumption is that the Internet will not go away. It will always be available as a medium for the distribution research papers. Therefore we assume that a free layer of research papers will always exist, even if sparsely populated.

A fourth starting assumption is that in all disciplines some form of toll-gated access to research papers will survive. This assumption can be justified by the idea that there is little chance that all the teaching material will be made freely available. In all disciplines authors of teaching material have always received a monetary reward. Since the border between research and teaching documents is fuzzy, it appears unlikely to us that there will ever be a free access to all research documents.

Having made these starting assumptions, we have two points still to determine

- the extent of coverage of the free layer
- the size of any quality gap between toll-gated and non-tollgate papers.

Here we propose three terminal scenarios. Individual disciplines may adopt one scenario or develop a mixture between scenarios.

In scenario one, there is a free layer of research documents deposited on the web by their authors. They may be withdrawn at any time. There is no bibliographic organization of these papers other than ones organized by machine. In addition, since these papers are in places where they can be modified by authors, it does not appear to be possible to base a certification system on these papers.

Papers in the free layer can be found through general Web search engines, or possibly through a specialized engine like inquirius. In addition, there will be a toll-gated layer of quality controlled, final publication. It will have a good bibliographic description but there will be no common catalog in the public domain. Thus there will be quality controlled libraries that be behind toll-gates.

Although this scenario may appear unlikely, it has been defended by Arms (2000). He imagines the co-existence of an expensive layer of a research library that is powered by humans, with the extensive quality control of the data, and a free layer that is essentially computer generated. Author pressure, he speculates, will make a lot of research papers openly available. But the bibliographic layer, since this is costly to produce, is not likely to be free. Some elements of the construction of the free interface can not be fully automated. This for example concerns the removal of duplicates, dealing with moved, changed or merged collections, maintaining a correct set of author data etc.

In scenario two there will be the free layer of research papers and there will be a free bibliographic system too. The layer of toll-gated and free papers will be decentralized. The bibliographic system will comprise both free and toll-gated papers and indications on which servers they live. The bibliographic layer may be centrally or decentrally organized. In a centralized system all providers of papers will submit to a central index of all papers.

It is an open question how such a server may be organized and funded. In a decentralized bibliographic system, all sites that provide papers will have a metadata layer that can be harvested through a machine interface. In this scenario the problem of funding a central agency does arise only to a small extend. The only central agency that we think will be needed is one that registers participants in the catalog exchange scheme. These participant may either be providers of catalog data or providers of services using the catalog data.

In scenario three there will be a large central site of papers, which comprises the vast majority of papers in a discipline. The quality control of the papers will be done in overlay services. These overlay service may contain links to papers on the central site that have been found fit for inclusion in the overlay service. It may also contain reviews of the free material. We would expect that most overlay services are free but that is not crucial to the scenario.

To compare the three scenarios, let us stress that we imply that there is an implicit quality ladder. Scenario 1 is the least controlled, scenarios 2 and 3 improvement upon this because they allow for better information retrieval and better facilities for quantitative evaluation of the research process. Scenario 3 improves over scenario 2 because it makes the long-run preservation of the archived data much more secure. A centralized system would be likely to find it much easier to implement format conversion than a decentralized system.

4. Steps forward

Having established terminal scenarios we will discuss steps that may lead to them. If nothing is done, by default, we will have scenario 1. The academic sector may find ways to implement scenarios 2 and 3, but it is not clear today what should be done. In this section, we make some suggestions.

First, we believe that change to the scholarly communication will be discipline community driven. Anyone proposing a new service should make sure that they receive the maximum backing of the community of the discipline that they are supposed to serve. The successful services have managed to do that. These statements may say the obvious, but there are examples where such elementary advice has not been followed. The most prominent is Varmus (1999), the initial call for the creation of PubMed Central. This call was clearly a simple translation of the principle of arXiv to the biomedical field. Little thought was given to adapting the arXiv business model to the needs of the biomedical community. Much of the negative reaction to the proposal would have never occurred if its discipline-specific implications would have been thought out before.

Second, proper attention has to be played on the motivation of contributors. Too many schemes have been proposed where a lot of effort has been spent on developing a user interface, but little effort is spent on population the services. This holds in particular for projects that are funded by the library community. Libraries are accustomed to address end-users, and therefore do not pay much attention to the question of contributors. There has been general agreement that public access to scientific documents does wonders to the exposure that these documents receive. But this additional exposure has to be demonstrated to contributors. If it can not be demonstrated, with figures at hand that organized contents is better than unorganized contents, then it is difficult to see much contents organization will taking place.

The first step forward must be the collection of contents. Any collection of contents that is organized with some metadata, as long as it is large enough, will stimulate interest. The problem with most of the existing attempts is that the contents is simply too thin. To stimulate the provision of contents, the collection must be conceived as an advertisement of the work of its contributors. To do that, the contributing person or institution must be at the center of the collection effort. Again, we need a break with the tradition of libraries. In a library setting, the work is at the center of the descriptive effort. In an academic self-publishing setting, the contributor, rather than the works created by the contributor must be the center of the collection effort.

For most disciplines, it should be possible to gather free research papers that are available on the Internet in a gateway catalog. All disciplines have some form of informal communication channel, and many of these papers in these channels can be made freely available if somebody is willing to "put them up". If a sufficient number of papers in a small discipline can be made available, this can really change the way the sub-discipline works. Such small-scale efforts, opened up to the wider academic word through on OAI compliant archives would be an important step forward. Unfortunately, the current climate in academic institutions is such that, while writing papers is valued, collecting and organizing them is often not valued so such work is not incentive compatible.

5. Steps backward

There are a number of failed collections whose ruin can provide valuable insights into why collection efforts fail. An interesting example is the NCSTRL collection of Computer Science Technical Reports. On that site, we read

> NOTICE: This site is being maintained on a legacy basis and support for it is minimal. As a result, some of the functionality is limited. We will be posting a message in the near future about the future status of this site. Posted 2000-03-05.

This message that was supposed to be forthcoming is not found on the site. Despite watching relevant mailing lists closely, the authors have not found that announcement. It seems that NCSTRL, if not terminated officially, is in serious crisis.

The failure of NCSTRL is worrying for two reasons. First it is a failure of work for the Computer Science area. Many digital library efforts find it very hard to access appropriate computing expertise at times when such expertise is in high demand by other sectors that have more financial resources. But such expertise should have been plentiful at Computer Science departments. Second, the failure comes after years of development and on a collection of considerable scale. NCSTRL started as early as 1993 and has about 10,000 papers available in electronic format. After arXiv and RePEc, this is the third-largest collection of freely downloadable documents.

We suspect that the failure is not of a technical but managerial nature. As outsiders, we can only make some speculations about what the problems are.

One possible explanation in the double nature of NCSTRL. It was conceived as a digital document collection and a digital library test bed. It those circumstances, there is constant experimentation. NCSTRL worked on an elaborate protocol called Dienst to run the collection. Dienst was a language with many instructions call verbs. To allow several versions of Dienst to run on servers, each verb in Dienst had a version number, and more recent versions of the Dienst software could still execute the old verbs. Nevertheless in order to install more recent versions of Dienst software, archives had to do extra work. NCSTRL could not simply be a service without research components without compromising the funding position of the collection. ArXiv has continued funding as a service, RePEc has no funding and is vulnerable because of that.

Another possible reason for failure may have been the NCSTL decentralized architecture. Many participating sites were staffed by graduate students. This implies discontinuities in archive management. This is also a problem for RePEc but the technical architecture of RePEc is much simpler, and therefore the problems are much smaller.

To sum up this discussion, it is crucial that the business plan for any collection effort is well thought out. Everything else depends on it. The problem with author self-publishing in academic circles is that many academic institutions do not have a good record of enterprise, in particular in cases where the activity is unlikely to generate much revenue.

6. The question of quality control

Defenders of the status quo in publishing defend the system because of the quality classification of standard papers that it affords. A free publication system must consider the feasibility of filtering in a world where anybody can publish anything.

To tackle the problem of quality control, our experience from managing self-publication systems suggest a simple model of paper quality. We defined just two levels of quality: standard and inadequate.

Inadequate papers are so poor that almost everybody with a Master's level degree in the discipline, who would read these documents would become aware that they simply do not contain scientific material as it is recognized within the discipline.

Standard papers are the remaining papers, the majority of which will be unremarkable. A few will be read by a sizable group, even fewer will be cited in the future, and still fewer will be considered seminal works.

We claim that it is trivial for a member of the appropriate disciple to separate inadequate papers from standard papers. We have a moderation process instead of the conventional refereeing process. On the other hand, distinguishing between different shades of quality in standard papers is very difficult and costly in terms of time and effort. In the next Section, we will show how the OAI protocols can be used to implement a technical infrastructure that would be useful for this process. In the remainder of this section, we will look at how the filtering of inadequate submissions can be automated.

The object of automated filtering is to reduce the cost of the moderation process which still maintaining sufficient quality control. One approach is to allow submission based on institutional affiliation; our experience shows that a paper from Cornell University is likely to meet the requirements of standard quality. In this approach might also assume some institutional responsibility for submissions. However, in the construction of such systems it is important to cater for cases where unaffiliated authors wish to submit work that meets the requirements of standard quality. It would be a retrograde step for the author self-publication movement to be more prejudiced than the existing system.

Another way to function is to construct registries of personal and registration information for academics who are allowed to publish on open e-print archives. Depending on the discipline these registries might be administered by scholarly societies, academic institutions or the archives themselves, with policies reflecting the views of the community. A system which avoided duplicate registrations would be labor saving for both maintainers or the registries and authors who would have to keep their information up-to-date. A shared registry would have several other benefits. It could contain contact data shared by several organizations in the academic sector, such as scholarly societies. At the moment each scholarly society maintains its own registry of members, with a shared set of personal data, a society would simply maintain the handles of it members in the shared personal dataset.

There could be a mix of these approaches where personal registration might be based partly on the affiliation of a person with a recognized institution.

7. The Open Archive Initiative

Stimulated by work of Van de Sompel, Krichel, Nelson et al. (2000), there have been recent moves towards improving the interoperability of e-print archives. This work is now called the Open Archive Initative (OAI). When the OAI started, there was little interoperability between e-print initiatives and cross-archive resource discovery was the focus of the initial meeting in Santa Fe. The scope of the initiative has expanded considerably since then.

The basic business model proposed by the OAI was inspired by the RePEc project. In particular, the Open Archives Metadata Harvesting (OAMH) protocol separates data provision and service provision as pioneered by RePEc since 1997. The OAMH protocol is a simplification of the subset Dienst protocol experimented with after the Santa Fe meeting. It was designed to provide a very a low-barrier to interoperability. Key features include: support for multiple metadata formats, requirement for Dublin Core (DC) metadata as means of global interoperability, use of Hypertext Transfer Protocol (HTTP) transport, and use of Extensible Markup Language (XML) encoding. There are four means to select between records

- Datestamp of a record
- Identifier of a record
- Metadata format(s) available for a record
- Sets, which are groups of records

There are three commands to support other protocol requests

- *Identity* gives basic information about an archive
- *ListMetadataFormats* shows the metadata formats that are supported
- *ListSets* shows the sets

There are the three other commands to access the records

- *ListRecords* returns records
- *ListIdentifiers* returns identifiers only
- *GetRecord* returns a single record

This protocol has attracted a lot of interest from digital library communities. It is hoped that it will provide a framework for the solution of many interoperability issues in digital libraries.

We conducted a survey of registered OAI repositories on 8 March 2001 to see how many data providers were operational less than 2 months after the OAMH protocol was announced. In the list below we show the name of the archive and the number of record identifiers returned from a *ListRecords* request.

name	*number*
arXiv	155522
OCLC Theses & Dissertations Repository	102762
NACA	6352

M.I.T. Theses	5196
Oxford Text Archive	1290
Perseus Digital Library	1030
CogPrints	1028
NSDL at Cornell	870
PhysNet	472
Humboldt University of Berlin	464
Resource Discovery Network	388
University of Tennessee Libraries	201
Linguistic Data Consortium	216
European Language Resources Association	183
A Celebration of Women Writers	142
The Natural Language Software Registry	78
California Digital Library	3

The OAI sponsored a workshop on OAI and peer review in Europe between March 22 and 24 of 2001. In was organized by the Access Division of LIBER, the Ligue des Bibliothèques Européenne de recherche. One working group, led by Herbert Van de Sompel, discussed ways in which the OAI framework could be used in the certification , by peer review or some other method, of academic works. We outline some of the ideas from this discussion in the remainder of this section. We hope that it will illustrate the potential of the OAMH protocols for more than just the resource discovery aspect of scholarly communication.

Let us first consider what certification means in the current environment of traditional paper journals. The type of certification is usually peer-review and the indication of this is publication in a particular journal. The journal reference is in essence a certification metadata for the work even if it exists somewhere other than in the journal, for example the author's homepage or in some other archive. We will not here consider the issue of whether this other copy is true to the certified version. The journal publisher provides, in addition to other things, a certification service.

The simplest scenario to consider is the certification of a paper that is first placed on an e-print archive. The certification process could be initiated by pull from the certification service or push from the archive, but is more likely to occur by direct author action (such as an e-mail). If the paper exists on an e-print archive then the certification service can retrieve it, and also harvest a metadata record using the OAMH protocol. After or during the certification process the certification service could expose certification metadata using the OAMH protocol. This could be harvested by the original archive and associated with the e-print provided it contained the identifier of the e-print. The American Physical Society (APS) already accepts submissions from arXiv (by quoting the e-print identifier). There was agreement between the APS and arXiv to test this scheme.

Given that some OAI data providers might then have records for both certified and non-certified papers, how could one harvest information about only certified records within OAI? Technically, there are several ways that this could be accomplished. One way is through multiple metadata sets, perhaps one for discovery metadata, one for the certification, etc. Using OAMH protocol, it is then possible to harvest metadata only for the certified records by requesting the certification metadata set (objects that do not have that metadata will not be returned). Another approach would be for the data provider to expose certified and non-certified sets which could then be harvested separately.

The group also discussed the contents of the certification record. It was thought that any certification metadata scheme (i.e. data `about the certification') should be applicable. across different communities. At the very minimum it must contain a link to the certified document (or a metadata record for it), information about the certification service (e.g. journal name), and a timestamp for the certification. It might also include a timestamp at which the original harvest too place, and an indication of the current status for an open certification process. There might also be an indication of the certification type. A controlled vocabulary would be desirable for this.

From the above discussion, it is clear that the OAMH protocol could be a very useful tool for the transformation of scholarly communication through the Internet. Using the OAI, we can accomplish new tasks in a collaborative way that are not possible in the established setup of essentially closed initiatives.

8. Conclusions

While there is more and more freely accessible academic content on the Internet, the organization of that content is much less useful than the organization of content in formal archives and libraries. The Open Archives Initiative (OAI) is well suited to develop protocols that improve on this state of affairs by permitting interoperability between archives.

It has been suggested that the OAI framework be used to support institution-based digital archives. These archives will contain research results produced in an institution and archived in the library. The ARNO project (Academic Research in the Netherlands Online) is a small-scale, but pioneering effort to do just this. It remains to be seen how successful it will be. For libraries to take on the rôle to archive, rather than to make material available that is produced by intermediaries outside academia, is a big step. It implies a change in their perceived rôle. It remains to be seen if libraries will take up that challenge.

It may be that the establishment of institution-based archives is a better and faster way to free scholarly literature than waiting for each discipline to embrace author self-publishing in its own proprietary way. However, this is by no means clear and the same OAI framework that supports interoperability between institution-based archives also supports interoperability between discipline-based archives. We expect that, whatever the final outcome, there will be increasing numbers of both institution- and discipline-based archives in the near term. We think that the degree of interoperability between these archives will strongly influence their success.

9. References

Arms, William Y. (2000). Automated Digital Libraries How Effectively Can Computers Be Used for the Skilled Tasks of Professional Librarianship? D-lib Magazine 6. available at http://www.dlib.org/dlib/july00/arms/07arms.html.

Harnad, Stevan (1995). The Postgutenberg Galaxy: how to get there from here. available at http://www.cogsci.soton.ac.uk/~harnad/THES/thes.html.

Kling, Rob and Geoffrey McKim (2000). Not Just a Matter of Time: Field Differences and the Shaping of Electronic Media in Scholarly Communcication. Journal of the American Society for Information Science 51(14), 1306-1320.

Van de Sompel, Herbert, Thomas Krichel, Micheal L. Nel-son, et al. (2000). The UPS Prototype project: explor-ing the obstacles in creating a cross e-print archive end-user service). Old Dominion Computer Science Tech Report, available at http://openlib.org/home/krichel/upsproto.ps.

Varmus, Harold (1999). E-BIOMED: A Proposal for Electronic Publications in the Biomedical Sciences. available at http://www.nih.gov/about/director/ebiomed/ebi.htm.

Electronic Publishing '01 –
2001 in the Digital Publishing Odyssey
A. Hübler et al. (Eds.)
IOS Press, 2001

Distributed Parallel Multi-Channel Publishing System

Wei Li, *Framkom*, Rebecca Dahlin, *Framkom*

Abstract

With more and more electronic media appearing and popularly accepted, the publishing industry is facing a greater challenge than anytime else before. The only solution to cope with these problems is to extend the traditional publishing to cover both print publishing and electronic publishing business. This paper intends to propose an integrated system solution to assist this transition. *Distributed Parallel Multi-channel Parallel Publishing*, as one of the outcomes of *DIP* (Digital Information Processing) project, sponsored by *SITI* (Swedish IT Institute) aims to propose a comprehensive solution to cover both paper-based and electronical media publishing, based on advanced distributed software system architecture and field-related up-to-date standards. In the DIP project, the new standard of news industry, *NewsML* is adopted as the authoring, storing and transforming format. *JDF* (Job Definition Format) is partly employed to monitor and assist the control of the entire paper-based publishing process. On the aspect of software system architecture, Java-based distributed network technology, Jini, acts as the infrastructure of the system.

0. Introduction and Motivation

Nowadays, with the rapid evolution of Internet and web technology, publishing industry is experiencing a revolution on all steps of its process. One publication has to be delivered parallelly in different transferring formats as well as display layouts, according to various accessing client devices, such as web browser*s*, PDA*s*, mobile phone*s* and PDF format for printers etc. This gives birth to multi-channel publishing.

Multi-channel publishing refers to a new publishing model, which leverages the advantages of XML and XSL technologies to separate the content and layout of a publication, allows information to be authored with standardized templates, so that the same information can be re-purposed and redistributed across those multiple delivery channels with or without the same "look and feel" as the original print document. This maximizes the document's value and makes it easier to update and reuse. Multi-channel publishing will change the present publishing model.

However, there are still some necessary studies to be carried out in order to achieve a highly automated multi-channel publishing system: how to describe and store the publication resource; how to deliver content and layouts according to different client devices; how to bridge the gap between the traditional printing publishing and electronic media publishing process, as well as the consideration on the scalability issue and some other attentions on the software system architecture.

This paper intends to provide an integrated system solution to cover both paper-based and electronical media publishing, based on the study of DIP (Digital Information Processing) project, sponsored by SITI (Swedish IT Institute). In the following of the paper, section 2 gives a analysis of the current problems existing in the publishing industry. Section 3 briefly introduces some concepts and terminology, including popular web content description standards XML specification and advanced middleware technologies. Section 4 elaborates in depth on the essence of these new technologies and points out the relevent issues and approaches in a pragmatic way. Then section 5 lays out the concepts and technologies under the specific scenario of multi-channel publishing, where a comprehensive solution is illustrated together with some up to date publishing industry standards. And the last section concludes the whole work and present some future perspectives on it.

1. Problems in Publishing Industry

The history of the printing industry officially starts back in 1439 when Johann Gutenberg first experimented in using lead figures to print books. But some people argue that the art of printing is much older in that Chinese people have used screen-printing technology for more than 1500 years. Either way the printing industry is old and have distinguished heritage. However when entering the internet and web epoch, the status of this old-lined industry looks no longer steady enough:

The traditional paper-based newspaper product is losing ground on the benefit of digital products. The editions are constantly decreasing and so is the biggest income for the newspaper producers – advertisement fees. In the near future news publishers have to find a way to charge the readers for information and companies advertising on any output medium.

Publishing materials include text, pictures, videos and audio data. These materials are highly required for reuse and sharing. However, due to various reasons, such as centralized storage, copyrights, ownership of the publishing materials, it is quite difficult to share and reuse the materials. Thus, it causes a big waste of these valuable resources.

Other problems that the newspaper producers struggle with are of a more organizational nature. Today every publishing medium means extra work. One has to rewrite or adjust the material to be suitable for the specific output medium. Most times the technical knowledge of the reporter is too limited to fulfill this and it is also hard for newspaper company to afford the cost for every transformation. It is most desirable that this adjustment be automated as much as possible.

All these problems force the publishing industry modernize its way of work, and the burgeoning computer technologies provide the possibility to update the old-fashioned work model.

2. Concepts and Terminology

2.1 XML and related Specifications

2.1.1 XML

Extensible Markup Language (XML) is a meta-markup language that provides a format for describing structured data. XML describes a class of data objects called XML documents and partially describes the behavior of computer programs which process them [1]. XML documents are designed to be easy for computer processing, as well as be defined human-legible and reasonably clear. This facilitates more precise declarations of content and more meaningful search results across multiple platforms. In addition, XML is enabling a new generation of web-based data viewing and manipulation applications.

2.1.2 DTD and XML Schema

XML provides mechanism to define and check the structure of XML document, with which constraints on the storage layout and logical structure could be imposed on XML document. By far, there are two standards DTD (Document Type Definition) and XML Schema for this purpose [2]:

DTD is used to define the legal building blocks of a XML document. It defines the document structure with a list of legal elements. It uses document-orient syntax and can be declared inline in XML document, or as an external reference. XML schema is a set of constraints for describing the structure of domain information. It describes an internal and inter-document structure for the whole class of documents. The Schema provides a set of validation rules for the organization of XML documents.

XML can use DTD or XML Schema to validate XML documents. Compared with DTD's deficits: more document-oriented and not easily extensible, XML Schema can be a advanced replacer. However, XML Schema specification is released recently, most of the XML documents at present are still using DTD for construct and validation.

2.1.3 XSLT (Extensible Stylesheet Language Transformation)

XSLT enables and empowers interoperability between XML documents and other web documents. It provides mechanism for converting a XML document to other web document, e.g. HTML document [3]. More commonly, it is used now to convert a XML document to its XHTML [4] counterpart for displaying the document in a standard web browser. Moreover, it can also be used to merge logic (script codes) part into a web page when converting a XML document to a XHTML document. This feature can be used to separate the logic description from the content of web pages.

2.2 Middleware and Mobile Agent

Middleware is connectivity software that consists of a set of enabling services that allow multiple processes running on one or more machines to interact across a network. Middleware is essential to migrating mainframe applications to Client/Server applications and ability of communication across heterogeneous platforms. During 1990s, it evolves to support interoperability in terms of object-orient component technology. There are 3 widely-publicized middleware models: Object Management Groups' *CORBA* [5]; Microsoft's *COM/DCOM* [6] and Sun's Java-specific *RMI* [7]. Now, more middleware platforms are written in Java, which support more than one model and can easily talk with different models to reuse the existing software legacy. Middleware technology makes distributed application easily constructed and gives more advanced features such as load balancing to the software architecture.

The increasing development of distributed systems requires more and more efficient technologies to ensure the access and the management of the network resources. In this context, mobile agent technology is considered an enhancement of distributed technologies as it provides powerful and efficient mechanisms to develop applications for distributed and heterogeneous systems.

Mobile agent technology has become popular primarily because of the efficient way it provides for the access and the manipulation of remote information. The mobile agent architecture considers that local interaction is more efficient than the remote one. The solution proposed by mobile agents is for software to migrate to remote hosts, where information is stored, so that the user's request can be executed locally. It means that agents can take decisions or fulfill previously designed operations in an autonomous way on the remote site, even if the home host becomes temporary unavailable. This feature, called mobile logic, gives flexibility to the design of distributed systems.

2.2.1 Message System and Publish/Subscribe mechanism

Messaging System, built from loosely coupled components communicating through messages, is used to build highly reliable, scalable, and flexible distributed applications. A messaging system allows separate, uncoupled applications to reliably communicate asynchronously.

A Publish/Subscribe messaging system is a typical model of Message System. It supports an event driven model where information consumers and producers participate in the transmission of messages. Producers "publish" events, while consumers "subscribe" to events of interest, and consume the events. Producers associate messages with a specific topic, and the messaging system routes messages to consumers based on the topics the consumers register interest in [8]. In Java application, message can be encapsulated as a Java object, which can wrap some possible behavior of the message data, and the delivery of the message is entitled the sense of mobile code. So far, Publish/Subscribe mechanism has been natively implemented in JMS and other middlewares.

2.2.2 Jini

Jini network technology provides a simple infrastructure for delivering services in a network and for creating spontaneous interaction between programs that use these services regardless of their hardware/software implementation [9]. Any kind of network made up of services (applications, databases, servers, devices, information systems, mobile appliances, storage, printers, etc.) and clients (requesters of services) of those services can be easily assembled, disassembled, and maintained on the network using Jini Technology. Services can be added or removed from the network, and new clients can find existing services - all without administration.

Jini builds on the concept of a *federation* of devices and software components. A federation is a temporary union of Jini clients and services that come together to get work done, *lookup* service is a full-fledged Jini service. It records information about the various services on the network. Services in Jini publish themselves by registering their proxies with one or more lookup services. A client uses the Lookup service to locate the services it needs, download the service's proxy object and start interaction with the service itself. In addition, Lookup service takes charge of bootstrapping Jini network.

3. Issues and Approaches

3.1 XML and Data Exchange

XML DTD specifies in advance the kinds of XML data elements expected and the structural relationships between them. Normally it is used to check XML document's validation, however it can be used to construct XML documents as well.

Based on a DTD, an application can easily grasp the document structure and create XML documents dynamically to communicate with another application. The receiver application that understands the same DTD can use a XML *parser* [10] (support DOM or SAX) program to fetch the desired information from the document for further operation. If the receiver application cannot understand the DTD of the sender application, there needs a transformation between these two applications: a XSLT can covert a XML document from one DTD to destination DTD. This processing can be deployed either in sender part or receiver part or an independent layer between them.

This is critically useful when data exchange takes place between different companies. So far, there are plenty of standards, which are used to model the similar facts in real world to store into computers, if all the data to be exchanged are XML-based, all the standards can be remained intact and the difficulty of interchange between them can be decreased greatly. The main work will be to define a XSLT transformation between different standards.

XML Schema can be a good substitute of DTD, since it uses the XML syntax then when reading the structure of document, a same XML parser can be use and a extra DTD parser is not necessary, furthermore, XML Schema give more exact type description than DTD.

3.2 XML Storage

The best way to store and retrieve XML format documents is to have a database that supports XML. However, different means can be applied to the storage regarding to the type of XML documents. XML documents fall into two broad categories: *data-centric* and *document-centric*.

Data-centric documents are those where XML is used as a data transport, e.g. sales orders and invoices. In these documents the order of sibling elements is often unimportant. They are constructed from known, regular sets of data and the content of each element, is subject to update independently. *Document-centric* documents are those characterized by irregular structure and mixed content and their physical structure is important. Examples include written text such as articles and advertisements. Normally, document-centric XML document contains static content that will only be updated by replacing the entire document.

To store and retrieve the data in data-centric documents, one needs a database that is tuned for data storage, such as a relational or object-oriented database. With relational database, the structure of the data in the document will be mapped as tables in the database. To document-centric documents, store and retrieve a single, intact XML document as a CLOB or BLOB is a good strategy, since it contains static content and is delivered from the database as a whole. However, the feature of index, query and efficient retrieve are necessary to be taken into consideration.

3.3 E-Media Multi-Channel Publishing

The reason entitling XML the universal data standard is that a XML document can be easily converted to a new one conforming to another XML document structure (DTD or Schema) after a XSLT transformation. This is significantly useful for data exchange between departments or companies supporting different data standards. When under the scenario that different client devices and programs (e.g. web browsers and wap phones) support different formats as HTML, WML etc, a corresponding XSLT transformation has to be applied to cater to client in its understandable format. For example, a conversion from HTML to WML to enable WAP phone users to read the content of web pages. This process, from the viewpoint of message itself, gives same content different presentations conforming to the different client devices and programs. This is the essential concept of multi-channel publishing.

In a more practical way, the raw content of information is constructed as a separate XML document. Every XSLT transformation for different presentations is defined in separate XSL layout stylesheet documents. When an HTTP request reaches, the web server determines the client type through an HTTP_USER_AGENT parameter in the request.

Then it retrieves the corresponding content document, chooses the matched XSL stylesheet and applies the stylesheet on content to produce and send the transformed document to client. The whole procedure can be fulfilled on the fly without the client noticing. Different clients receive the right content and layout to display on their accessing devices.

3.4 Remote/Local in Jini Services

In most means of implementation within object-based distributed computing architecture (CORBA or COM/DCOM), a server publishes its services as interface for access from clients. The interface will be compiled to generate *stub* and *skeleton* working for communication between client and service implementation respectively. In other words, any client requesting for service has to bind a stub with him through which to interact with server-side Skeleton on behalf of service itself.

Jini service replaces the *stub* with *service proxy*, which can be treated as mobile object traveling from service to client machine via lookup service. In addition, the proxy can be customized to carry logic from server, which is much more advantageous than Stub/Skeleton generated to only take charge of conforming network communication and calls to predefined formats. With this property Jini services can be designed in flexible ways which can be categorized roughly as types below:

- A proxy runs entirely locally on client side.
- A proxy as stub to communicate back to the logic on the service.
- A proxy that has logic on both the client and service.

With this flexibility, one can design and deploy logic freely between the client and server sides, or more widely, over the Jini network. The Jini service can be treated as a mobile-service register in the first type, every service visitor will receive integrated application logic to run locally in run-time. The second type looks like the CORBA model, however, it can help to make reuse of legacy system services an easy thing. For example, to incorporate a legacy service into Jini network, the proxy can be implemented as a wrapping of the original stub object to move to client and interact with service directly with any originally specified communication protocol. The third type gives freedom to application logic deployment to make the logic run efficiently on the machine benefiting from data retrieve or computing processing. No matter what type the service is implemented actually, the client program can be a same one and the server (service proxy and service implementation) can switch among the different types described above as needed later.

4. Integrated Application Solution

The integration of XML and Jini technology gives revolutionary change on software system architecture. In our DIP project, we apply the concepts and technologies we discussed above to achieve a distributed parallel multi-channel publishing system.

4.1 System Goals

As a completed printing and publishing solution conforming to the up-to-date field standards, our system intends to achieve support for traditional printing publishing and electronical multi-channel publishing. Other than trying to reach multi-channel access from various client devices, streamlined printing workflow and authoring and maintenance of publications will also be taken into consideration intensively. Generally speaking, our publishing system will have the following features:

- The sense of *parallel processing* permeates all over the system: The same materials can be published to printing machines and various web-based electronic means concurrently. The processing steps in the publishing procedure can be carried out parallelly. And on other aspect, all the system components necessary run simultaneously to collaborate with each other to fulfill the whole publishing, making the whole task visual and controllable.
- Publishing Information stored in resource database is sharable and reusable from other departments or outside the company, through the advanced subscribe/publishing mechanism.
- Web-based e-media publishing can serve for various clients, using various receiver devices (wap phone, web browser, PDF reader etc) to receive correct content and layout for display automatically.
- Automated information authoring, management and publishing which will ease the work of journalist and publishing department.
- Intelligent workflow tracing and assistant are targeted on printing publishing.
- Excellent scalability and high performance benefiting from advanced implementation of distributed system architecture.

4.2 Publishing Industry Specifications

NewsML

NewsML [11], proposed by IPTC (International Press Telecommunications Council), is a XML encoding for news. It is intended to be used for the creation, transfer, delivery and archiving of news. NewsML is media independent, and allows equally for description and representation of the evening TV news and a simple textual story. Not only specially be set out to meet the use of electronic news production, archiving and delivery, NewsML also include features for paper-based publishing and other specific production environments.

JDF (Job Definition Format)

JDF is an extensible XML-based interchange data format proposed by four companies prominent in printing industry, which aims to unify the pre-press, press, and post-press aspects of any printing job. JDF provides a mechanism to explicitly specify the controls needed by each process in printing process, which may be specific to the devices that execute the processes. JDF works together with a corresponding format Job Messaging Format, (JMF). JMF provides the means for production components of a JDF workflow to communicate with system controllers and administrative components. It relays information about the progress of JDF jobs and gives MIS (Management Information System) the active ability to query devices about the status of processes.

4.3 System Design

Based on the understanding of an entire publishing procedure, process can be divided generally into 2 steps: authoring and publishing. Comprehensive analyses are placed on these 2 processes to meet the demands with their different features.

4.3.1 Authoring

To accomplish good multi-channel publishing and to be able to adjust content as well as layout according to media and/or the readers expressed wishes, the news story created by the journalist needs to be extended with additional information – meta data. This meta data can be divided into two main categories; layout- and content related information.

Layout related meta data concerns information that is useful when processing information for publishing. It could be the size of a text, the format of a picture but also more administrative information such as the authors name and what company that owns the material.[12]

Content related meta data is additional information that describes what the story is about and how it is structured. We identified three levels of content related meta data that most be considered to be able to automatically adjust news content. All news stories handle one or more subjects, for example sports, domestics, political statements or celebrity gossip. The topics give a first clue on what the story is about. Then the news story is build up according to a template. A common structure could be headline, byline, abstract, sub headline, text, picture, text to the picture and the name of the person taking the picture. The third and most exciting level of meta data is the weight added to identify the importance of different parts of the story. The weight could be added to a hole story, to the different components it is build up by or to specific paragraphs of sentences in the text.

Based on these three levels of content related meta data personalized news products can be produced automatically and without the journalist having to write different stories for different purposes. However it is impossible to totally avoid additional work for the journalist since it is only he who is capable of adding the meta data. Nobody else could decide what is the most important parts in the material.

In the DIP project we have developed a news editor program that will support the journalist when writing the story and above all when adding the meta data necessary. The NewsEditor is written in Java and is based on NewsML. It allows the journalist to add both layout related meta data as well as all three levels of content related meta data.

The story is composed by journalist and reviewed by editor who decides (with a importance value attached on every story) whether or when to publish it. When the story is written and the meta data is added all information is stored within a document-centric resource data base as a NewsML document. Once stored information could be shared among organizations or distributed to the readers through publisher/subscriber technology. (see figure 1.)

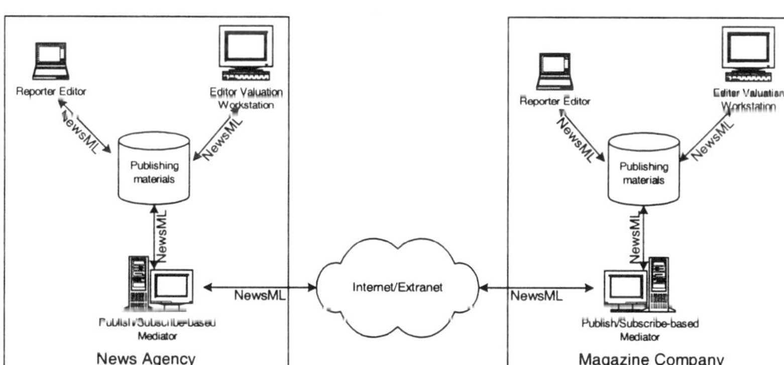

***Figure 1**. Publishing Materials Exchange*

4.3.2 Publishing Process

With publishing content ready, publishing materials are prepared to publish in different media terms. In this step, most work is focused on layout design and publishing workflow. However, due to the inherent difference between different publishing means, We divide this step into two procedures: Paper-based printing publishing and web-based e-media publishing, so that the appropriate architectures and technologies will be applied respectively to meet their diverse demands.

4.3.2.1 Printing Publishing

Paper-based printing publishing includes typically newspaper, magazine, pamphlet and brochure, which are more printer-related, and already have mature workflow. The workflow of paper-base printing publishing can be described generally as Create, Prepress, Press and Postpress steps. And furthermore each step can be resolved: Prepress as Trapping, Imposition, Color Correction; Press as Ripping, Plate-making, Printing; and Postpress as Cutting, Folding, Binding.

All these processes have been considered and fully described in JDF. To make the print job fulfilled, JDF specification designed Job Messaging Format (JMF), specifically defined to describe communication between the controller and the work centers or devices within the production system.

The four components required to create, modify, route, interpret and execute a JDF job are named as *agents*, *controllers*, *devices* and *machines* [13] in the specification, based on which we will implement our JDF-based workflow system:

The overseer of the relationships between all of the units in a workflow is *Management Information Systems*, a macrocosmic controller. It is responsible for dictating and monitoring the execution of all of the diverse aspects of the workflow. It must remain in contact with the actual production facilities. This can be accomplished typically using JMF messaging.

Referring to concepts and description in JDF specification, we design our printing publishing workflow system based on Jini infrastructure (see figure 2.), each device providing printing service is defined as an independent service in Jini network. When a print job begins, a federation of demanding services will be constructed dynamically following a predefined publishing processing sequence.

- A *Job Composer* defines the publishing job before the job begins to carried out, all the jobs will be saved in Workflow Database as JDF format. Job Composer can be treated as the implementation of the agent in JDF specification.
- A *Job Dispatcher* queries Workflow Database to acquire the Jobs to be fulfilled, and puts them into a Job queue. Every job in the queue will be loaded to execute one by one.
- Through Jini Lookup service, Job Dispatcher finds the required service available within Jini network, and receives corresponding service proxy to run locally interacting with remote service implementation.
- During the processing period, service implementation records status switches, and sends them back to store in Workflow Database, then Job Dispatcher can monitor the status of every process from Workflow Database. Here service implementation can be thought of Devices in JDF and service proxy Controller.
- Considering that not all the processes could be done by computers and some physical equipments have no interface for computer control automatically. Some services can be implemented as computer terminals with which operators who take charge of these processes will check the processing status and input feedback manually as the result information to be converted into JDF and JMF format to save in Workflow Database. In this case, remote service can be implemented as an information input window program.

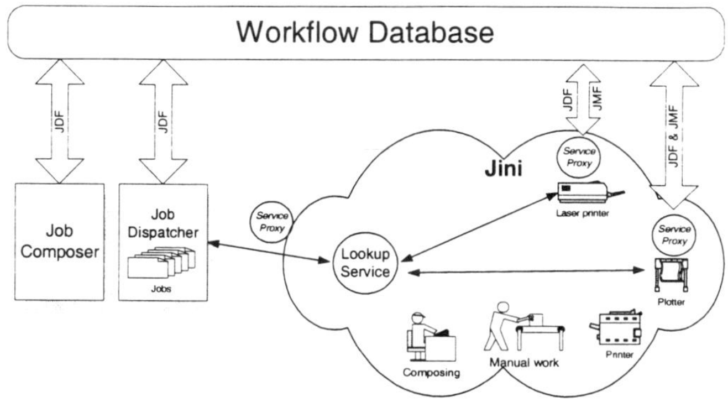

Figure 2. Paper-based Print Publishing

4.3.2.2 E-Media Publishing

Web-based Publishing is innately different from traditional printing publishing as it has many special features, such as no restricted size limits; rich media terms, video and audio. However on the background it requires bulks of labor work of maintenance and updating. We target to give a solution to make this exhausting work flexible and automated.

The three key processes of web publishing are Content design, Layout design and Logic design, which are in fact independent of each other, although most present solutions mix them together. We will treat them separately, since it is close to the fact that the technicians who work on a certain part of these three are hard and also not necessary to understand the technology knowledge of other two parts. Then they can just utilize their specialized skills focusing on problem solving in their domains.

In our integrated publishing solution, the materials are stored in the resource database. The database can output the NewsML format datastream, based on which, there are only two steps left, Layout design and Logic design. (see figure 3.)

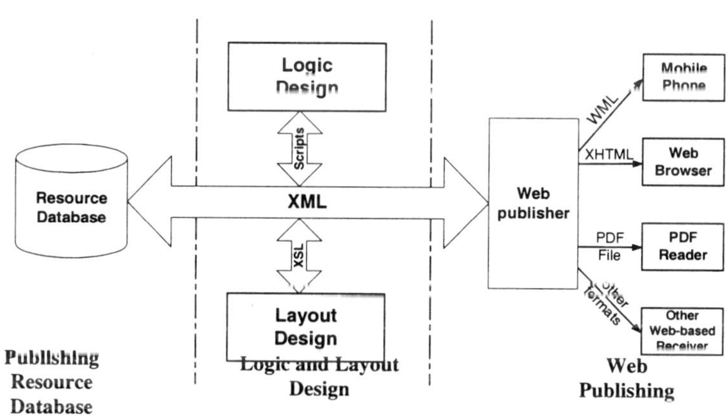

Figure 3. Web-based E-media Publishing

The *Publishing Material Database* is the legacy of printing publishing solution. As described in former parts, all the content is saved as NewsML format and easy to convert to other XML-based format standards.

Layout and Logic Design are separated to fulfill, and any third-party assistant tools e.g. XSL Editor and Script Builder can be used to aid design, there is no limit on these extra extensions.

Normally, to each different output medium, a layout stylesheet file will be designed and saved separately, e.g. a same news content will have a NewsWML.xsl for mobile phone display, a NewsXHTML.xsl for web browser, and some extra stylesheets for other accessing means. These stylesheets can be used as predefined templates for all the same structured NewsML documents and the same mechanism to applying logic template.

In Information Publishing part, the e-media multi-channel publishing technology is imployed as discussed in 4.3. Client's web request is passed on by web server to a servlet. The servlet checks the client device type, retrieves corresponding content, layout and logic templates from database and applies the XSLT transformation to produce different final document to deliver to client devices for presentation. The whole process can be fulfilled on the fly. To provide a better access performance when request amount is large, the static logic and content parts can be transformed in advance to store as semi-final version at a predefined time interval, then only one XSLT stylesheet is needed when accessing.

At present, the supporting access means includes wap phones, PDAs, web browsers, PDF reader, VoxML and more media are to be supported soon.

5. Conclusion and Perspective

XML is becoming the universal data standard, and Java is a platform independent network programming language. Jini infrastructure walks further more, extending the Java application "write once run everywhere" mode to "write once run from everywhere". A skillful combination of use of these two advanced technologies can empower great functionality and flexibility to software system architecture.

Distributed Parallel Multi-Channel Publishing is an integrated application of XML and Jini technology on publishing domain. Within this specific scenario, we fulfill a publication content management system consisting of authoring tool, XML encoding NewsML-based storage and multi-channel clients access, applying Java-based Jini infrastructure to trace and monitor printing workflow defined in JDF. On e-media publishing aspect, we fit in various devices for access of news publication. There are still some meaningful work to increase the value of the solution, such as to make the workflow more flexible and efficient means, a fine loading algorithm worth study, the alarm and status message should be able to send to operator's portable devices collaborating with each other in Jini network especially when manual manipulation is urgent. Also, many concepts and approaches adopted in our project can be adapted to other scenarios. For example this solution can be adopted in a ubiquitous computing environment, Jini supporting cooperation between all the portable devices, XML-based message transferring over Jini federation. Along this road, XML-based distributed software system architecture will be a prior choice for various software applications.

6. References

[1] W3C, Extensible Markup Language (XML) 1.0 (Second Edition) , 6 October 2000
http://www.w3.org/TR/2000/REC-xml-20001006
[2] W3C, XML Schema, 2001-03-16
http://www.w3.org/XML/Schema
[3] W3C, Extensible Stylesheet Language (XSL), 21 November 2000
http://www.w3.org/Style/XSL/
[4] W3C, XHTML™ 1.1 - Module-based XHTML, 6 April 2001
http://www.w3.org/TR/xhtml11/
[5] OMG, CORBA 2.4.2 specification, 2001-02-01
http://www.omg.org/cgi-bin/doc?formal/01-02-01
[6] Microsoft, Component Object Model (COM)
http://www.microsoft.com/com/
[7] Sun Microsystems, Remote Method Invocation (RMI)
http://www.javasoft.com/products/jdk/rmi/index.html
[8] Sun Microsystems, JAVA MESSAGE SERVICE API
http://www.javasoft.com/products/jms/index.html
[9] Sun Microsystems, Jini network technology
http://www.sun.com/jini/index.html
[10] Apache XML Project
http://xml.apache.org/
[11] IPTC, NewsML Specification, Oct, 2000
http://www.iptc.org/site/NewsML/index.html
[12] Framkom, DIP report, April 2001
[13] CIP4, JDF Specification Version 1.0, April 10, 2001
http://www.cip4.org/documents/jdf_specifications/index.html
[14] Gamma etc, Design Patterns, Elements of Reusable Object-Oriented Software, Addison-Wesley, 1997.
[15] Oracle 8i Application Developer's Guide - XML Release 3 (8.1.7) September 2000
[16] Richard Martin, Building E-Commerce with XML, Beijing Hope Electronic Press, Jan. 2001
[17] Sing Li, Professional Jini, Wrox Press, Aug. 2000
[18] IFRA, "IFRAtrack in practice", describing several publishing operations in which IFRAtrack helps staff meet ever-increasing demands for speed, correct quality, high service level, safe deliveries and cost efficiency. 1999.
[19] Suchitra Gupta, Jeffrey M. Hartkopf, Suresh Ramaswamy, "Event Notifier: A Pattern for Event Notification", in Java Report Magazine, July 1998.
[20] The Research Group on Ubiquitous Computing and Communication
http://www.dsv.su.se/research/k2lab/ucc/
[21] Nathan Finstein, "Notes on an Editorial Expert System (in Prolog) at TV Guide"
[22] Stig Nordqvist et al., "XML-based IFRAtrack: the glue for integration in business-wide media workflow management systems", in Proceedings of XML Europe 2000, Paris, France, June 2000.
[23] Brett McLaughlin, Java and XML 1st Edition, June 2000

Electronic Publishing '01 –
2001 in the Digital Publishing Odyssey
A. Hübler et al. (Eds.)
IOS Press, 2001

A framework for automatic combination of media contents by minimising information redundancy. Case: Integrated publishing in multimedia networks

Anneli Heimbürger [(*)], Paula Silvonen and Caj Södergård
VTT Information Technology
P.O. Box 1204
FIN - 02044 VTT
Finland
[(*)]*Email: anneli.heimburger@vtt.fi*

Abstract

Information redundancy becomes a crucial problem in the Web when contents from different resources are automatically combined to produce a new WWW–publication. Information retrieval, natural language processing and the latest WWW–activities offer a challenging framework to approach the information redundancy problem of automatically combined news articles. It seems reasonable, that minimising information redundancy should be performed by a hybrid technique that combines some elements of these approaches. The purpose of this exploratory study is to introduce a theoretical and practical framework for clarifying the information redundancy problem in the case of integrated publishing.

0. Introduction

For millions of Internet users, resource discovery from the World Wide Web would be a more fascinating and efficient experience if there were automatic or at least semiautomatic methods of detecting and filtering out information redundancy. The information redundancy problem becomes crucial in dynamic, distributed Web database applications in which heterogeneous information is automatically integrated from different data resources. One such application area is integrated publishing, where materials coming from several Web newspapers and TV news are automatically combined to form a new integrated Web–publication or a news service.

If the Web-based news service provides a user with a set of related documents that might overlap to a certain extent, the user is probably interested in the union of these news articles where similarities are eliminated. In this paper, news is defined as information about recent national and international events of general interest currently reported by news bureaux, newspapers, radio, television and Web news services. The focus of this exploratory study is on textual news items.

The exploratory study presented here is a part of the integrated multiple media publishing research and development work currently in progress in VTT Information Technology, one of eight research institutes that make up the Technical Research Centre of Finland (VTT) (Södergård et al. 1999). The case environment of the study is the Web-based integrated publication system for TV–programmes and newspaper articles called IMU (http://www.vtt.fi/imu2). IMU is being developed by VTT Information Technology together with Finnish universities and enterprises. The IMU system has been designed to work with mobile devices as well. Minimising the information redundancy of news articles is of special importance in mobile news services.

The IMU system has two channel types: common and personal channels (Figure 1). The channel is defined as a news composite. The common channel offers general news items and the personal channel can be personalised according to user's interests. From the point of view of an IMU user, one ideal solution would be to provide a user with a short summary concerning a certain news topic. The summary could be generated or extracted automatically from the IMU system, and it could also have a list of links to articles in different newspapers and TV news stories dealing with the topic concerned. We could define this kind of a summary as a meta-summary or a meta-ingress. However, in the current IMU-implementation the common and personal news channels overlap to some extent. The same or almost the same news story can appear several times with different or slightly different titles depending on how the newspapers have dealt with the topic and how sensational the news topic has been. The main reason for this is that the newspapers base their stories on common news items from national and international news bureaux.

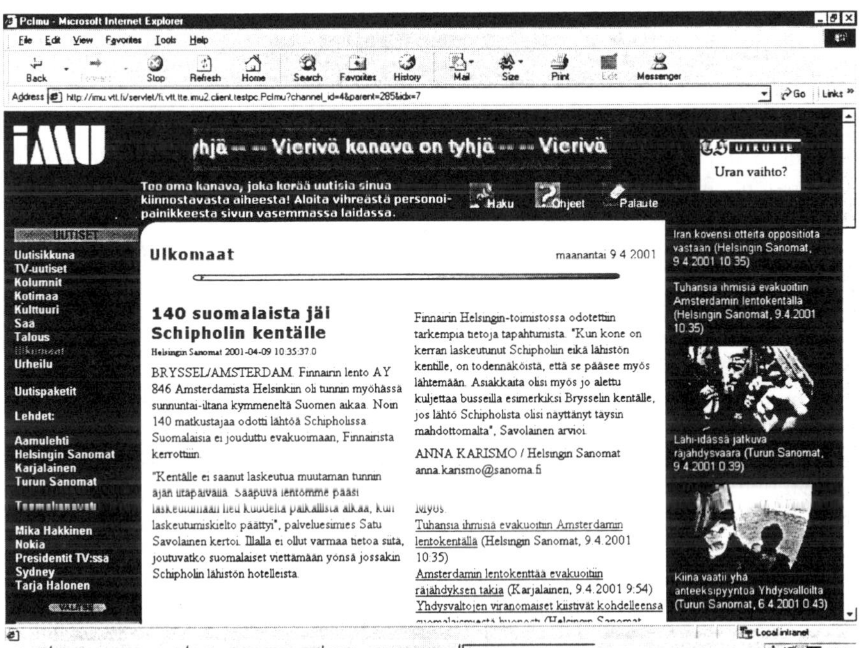

Figure 1. The IMU system has two channel types on the left: common and personal channels. The common channel offers general news items and the personal channel can be defined by the user according to his/her interests.

Minimising information redundancy can be divided into two phases: detecting redundancy and filtering out redundancy. A step-by-step approach to solve the problem seems a reasonable way to start. The process of determining whether one news article is similar to another one involves two main steps: (a) extracting appropriate information from the incoming news article and (b) comparing its features against those previously extracted from news articles in the database. What features to use and how they are compared are the two primary issues to be resolved. The more reliable the feature extraction is, the better the result. In terms of computational efficiency the feature-comparing –step must be very fast if the database is large and real-time performance is desired. After semantic similarity is somehow and on some level detected, the articles should be clustered around different topics, and meta-ingresses generated or extracted inside the topic clusters.

There are several scenarios when the elimination of information redundancy can be useful. For example, Web search engines often retrieve identical or nearly identical documents. A redundancy detection mechanism could be used as a filter for search results, excluding documents that overlap with documents above a certain threshold. Another application could be to highlight the differences between these documents. The goal of automatic information extraction and integration techniques is to construct combined descriptions of the information coming from multiple heterogeneous resources.

Classic and modern information retrieval, natural language processing, the latest WWW–activities, journalistic and communication research, and usability engineering provide a multidisciplinary approach to solving the problem of information redundancy in news articles. In this study we concentrate on the first three issues. It seems obvious that detecting and filtering out information redundancy should be performed by a hybrid technique that combines elements of these issues.

There are several research projects working on electronic news delivery systems (see Section 4). As far as we know our approach differs from others in two ways:

- In the IMU system the integration of news articles from several Web resources is automatic.
- The detection and filtering out of information redundancy focuses on the semantic metadata of news articles, which can be automatically extracted from the relational database of the IMU system.

The purpose of this exploratory study is:

- to introduce elements of the framework for clarifying and formalising the information redundancy problem in the case of integrated publishing,
- to describe experimental arrangements to test the detection and filtering out of information redundancy,
- to identify relevant problems for more precise investigation.

The remainder of this paper is organised as follows. A framework for approaching the information redundancy problem of news articles is introduced in Section 2. The working hypothesis for the experimental arrangements is described in Section 3. Related work is reviewed in Section 4. Future work is discussed in Section 5.

1. Elements for the theoretical framework

Information retrieval together with natural language processing offer some methods to approach the information redundancy problem. Recent developments in World Wide Web techniques, such as the Resource Description Framework (RDF), the Topic Maps –standard, ontologies and the concept of the Semantic Web as a whole are essential tools to be considered for automatic metadata extraction and semantic markup generation. All of these provide interesting possibilities for developing the Web news services of the future.

1.1 Information retrieval

The main objective of information retrieval research is to develop methods for retrieving all the documents which are relevant to a user query. "Find related/similar" and duplicate detection –types of algorithms are interesting from the viewpoint of our research problem.

Clustering methods with distance measures can be used to reduce information by grouping together similar items, and to generate simplified descriptions and summaries of documents. An optimal clustering method loses as little relevant information as possible discussed in documents. Combining different distance measures may provide a new approach to similarity detection. This is one issue for our future work.

1.2 Natural Language Processing

Natural language gives freedom for enormous variation in expression, from choosing between synonyms to using different styles, emphasis, different levels of abstraction, and metaphoric expressions. Authors have their own individual writing styles, which depend on their background, knowledge, profession and personal style of communication. One basic problem is that the same idea can be presented in several ways.

In a useful text analysis method, synonymous expressions should be encoded similarly. The goal of natural language processing is to use the semantic information of documents as well as statistical information to enhance the clustering of documents. In our research we use a string-matching algorithm with a thesaurus (see Section 4).

1.3 Semantic Web

The Semantic Web is an idea of World Wide Web inventor Tim Berners-Lee, Director of the World Wide Web Consortium (Berners-Lee 1999; W3C 2001). The word "semantic" in the context of the Semantic Web means "machine-processable". Berners-Lee explicitly rules out the sense of natural language semantics. The aim of the Semantic Web is to have data on the Web defined and linked in a way that it can be used by machines not just for display purposes, but for integration and reuse of information across various applications.

Markup languages define the markup rules, which add meaning to the structure and content of documents. The Standard Generalised Markup Language (SGML) is an international standard for defining markup languages, and it is designed to promote text interchange (ISO 8879 1986). The Extensible Markup Language (XML) is a subset of the SGML, and it is usable over the Internet. Like SGML, an XML document consists of marked up data using tags. XML documents can have a document type definition, but it is not necessary. The textual contents of IMU news articles are stored in the XMLNews-Story format that defines the structural components of a news article (XMLNews-Story Specifications 2001).

The Resource Description Framework (RDF) is another application of XML (W3C 2001). RDF is a general framework for describing any Internet resource. Such descriptions are often referred to as metadata or "data about data". An RDF description can include the authors of the resource, the date of creation or updating, key words, subject categories, and so forth. The RDF language is an important schema for the description of resources and their types. Recent developments in markup allow domain-specific information to be expressed as document metadata.

Above this, according to the Berners-Lee Semantic Web architecture, there is the ontology layer. An ontology is a set of concepts - such as things, events and relations - that are defined, for example, in domain-specific controlled language in order to create an agreed-upon vocabulary for exchanging information (Guarino 1995). To standardise semantic terms, many areas use specific ontologies, which are hierarchical taxonomies of terms describing certain knowledge topics (Crow and Shadbolt 1996; Miller 1995; Motta et al. 2000; Staab et al. 2000). In the IMU system the classification of news into basic topics can be seen as a very rough ontology.

The Topic Map –standard might provide an interesting possibility to define a machine-processable ontology for the IMU news service. Topic Maps are defined by the ISO/IEC 13250 standard (ISO/IEC 13250 2000). The base notation of Topic Maps is SGML. As XML is a subset of SGML, it can be also used as a base notation for Topic Maps. A topic map expresses its creator's view about what the topics are, and which parts of an information set are relevant to which topics.

Finally, we put these theories, models and methods in perspective and collect them into a unified framework. The introduced framework provides us with methods to approach the information redundancy problem and to construct the experimental environment for testing. It also gives us ideas for future work as well (Figure 2).

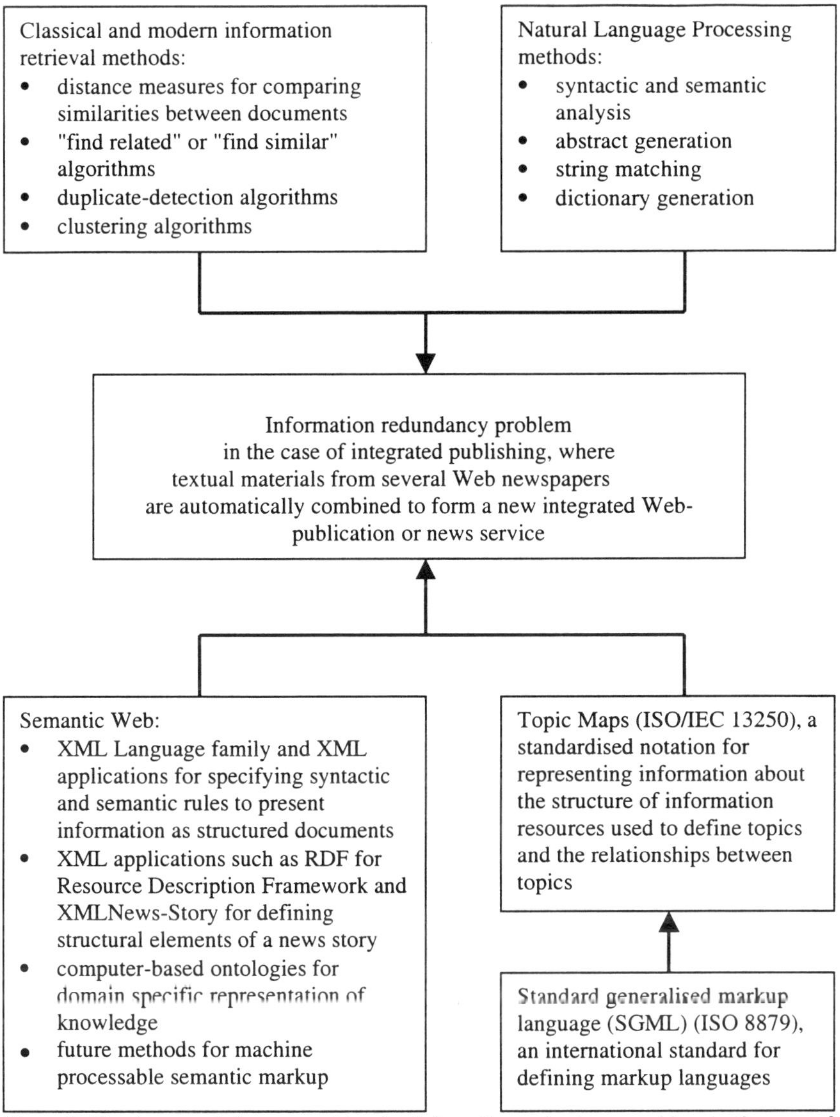

Figure 2. The framework for approaching the information redundancy problem in the case of integrated publishing.

2. Towards a practical framework

The case environment of our experimental research on minimising information redundancy will be based on the integrated publication system for TV–programmes and newspaper articles called IMU (http://www.vtt.fi/imu2). A continuously updated WWW-multimedia publication is created by combining the contents of databases from several newspaper houses and TV companies. The users read the news service from the Internet on their PC's with normal WWW-browsers, or from television sets connected to the Internet through set-top –boxes. The content can be accessed with WAP phones. The news can also be downloaded as synthesised speech into portable MP–players. This is a service of special interest for the visually impaired.

The heart of the IMU system is an active media server. Articles from four Finnish newspapers and TV news from one Finnish company are deposited in its database. The IMU system analyses the Web version of the newspaper, divides it up into structural elements, and separates off the necessary metadata. In the same way, the TV news is broken down into news items, using video analysis and closed caption texts. The contents are deposited in the database as objects, which are then combined to form a publication tailored to the reader's preferences.

At the moment the IMU consists of three types of information as follows, each type with related descriptive and/or semantic metadata.

- television news broadcasts: video and metadata. A video news article containing text, picture and metadata is generated for each news item within the news broadcast.
- news articles: text, pictures and metadata
- events and programme information: text, metadata like locations, start and end times.

The textual content of articles, images and video files are stored in the file system. The textual content of articles is stored in the XML-based XMLNews-Story format. The metadata of an article is stored in the relational database.

We divide a Web news article into separate components at different levels of precision. A textual news article N on the Web can be presented as follows:
Level 0: N = (n),
Level 1: **N** = (M, C),
Level 2: **N** = (**M**, C),
Level 3: **N** = (**M**, **C**),
Level 4: **N** = (**M**, A, **C**),
Level 5: **N** = (**M**, A, **C**, **L**), where

- n is the news article as a whole
- M is for metadata and C is for content
- **M** = (m_1, m_2), m_1 for descriptive metadata and m_2 for semantic metadata. Descriptive metadata describes, for example, by whom, how and when documents were created. Semantic metadata characterises the actual subject matter that can be found within the document's contents.
- **C** = (c_1, c_2, ... c_n) is for content where c_i, i = 1, 2, ... n are structural elements of the news story, for example, according to the XMLNews-Story DTD
- A is for an abstract.
- **L** = (l_1, l_2) is for links, where l_1 represents outgoing links and l_2 incoming links.

We could continue the analysis further by taking account of visual information (graphics, stills, animation and video) and audio information (speech, music, voice and other sounds) materials with related time dependence and with different types of links etc. However, this is not done in this work. The analysis will help us to identify different components and combinations of components on which the information redundancy detection and filtering can be focused, and to generate ideas for experimental arrangements.

Demonstrations of minimising information redundancy in the automatic combination of media contents will focus in the IMU case on textual information in the first place. In the Figure 3 our working hypothesis for experimental tests is presented. The semantic metadata elements such as titles, photo captions, article descriptors and ingresses are automatically extracted from incoming news articles, which are stored on the IMU active server and tagged according to the XMLNews-Story specification. Semantic similarity analysis will be carried out in the first phase between article titles, in the second phase between article photo captions, in the third phase between article descriptors, and finally, if necessary, between article ingresses. The predefined value of a similarity threshold function will define whether the process of the similarity analysis proceeds to the next phase.

The similarity calculations will be performed using the UNIFIER algorithm, which was developed at VTT Information Technology. Unifier is a Java-based software that analyses string similarity by applying the minimum edit-distance metric and dictionary lookup. The system can be utilised, for instance, in analysing the content similarity of text documents and in spelling error correction. The minimum edit-distance metric is expanded to whole words instead of only characters (Jurafsky and Martin 2000). In addition to minimum edit-distance calculation, a thesaurus is utilised in phrase similarity analysis. Thesaurus entries define synonyms that do not look alike and so cannot be matched with the edit-distance method.

The edit-distance or Levenshtein distance is defined in our approach using the following types of string difference:

- Substitution – one letter or word is replaced by a different one (*peoole* vs. *people*; on phrase level *Bond 007* vs. *Bond James*)
- Deletion – one letter or word is missing from the string (*peole* vs. *people*; *Bond* vs. *Bond James*)
- Insertion – one extra letter or word is inserted into the string (*peopple* vs. *people*; *Bond, James Bond* vs. *Bond James)*
- Transposition of two adjacent letters or words (*pepole* vs. *people*; *James Bond* vs. *Bond James*)

The system considers these string distance types and their combinations when it calculates similarity measures both for words and phrases.

After the similarity analysis, article elements with pointers to articles will be clustered around topics. If the news stream comes from the personal channels, then the topics are already defined by a user. In the case of the common news channel the topic clusters must be generated. The news topics can be the main categories of the IMU system or a more precise classification in which ontological methods and the Topic Maps –standard could be applied. Links to other articles inside the cluster should also be created.

Then we have to decide inside one topic cluster which news ingress we show for a user. The decision can be made according to the Euclidean distance in the cluster. There are also other approaches, such as a time stamp priority and a front-page story priority.

Finally, the user interfaces for multiple media devices should be designed. For mobile phones the textual interface is a natural choice. For PCs and other mobile devices such as communicators, there are more degrees of freedom to visualise news clusters and the similarity relations between news articles by graphical views.

3. Related work

There are several research projects working on electronic news delivery systems. To the best of our knowledge our approach differs from others in that we focus on the information redundancy problem and our approach is based on the semantic metadata of XMLNews-Story tagged news articles, which can be automatically extracted from the relational database of the IMU system. Most of the research on electronic news delivery systems concentrates on searching news (Hunter 2001; Maybury 2000; Mock and Vemuri 1997; Watters and Wang 1998, 2000).

Information retrieval research provides a set of concepts, models and methods that seem to be useful when approaching the information redundancy problem in our case. One very good starting point for information retrieval research is the home page of the Center for Intelligent Information Retrieval (CIIR) (http://ciir.cs.umass.edu/). There are a number of issues such as information extraction, interfaces and visualisation, topic detection and tracking being studied with the general aim of improving the effectiveness of access to and organisation of large text databases (Croft 2000). CIIR's topic detection and tracking (TDT) research project has investigated the state of the art in finding and following new events in a stream of broadcast news stories. The goal of the research is to organise television, radio and print news according to the event-based topics that they discuss.

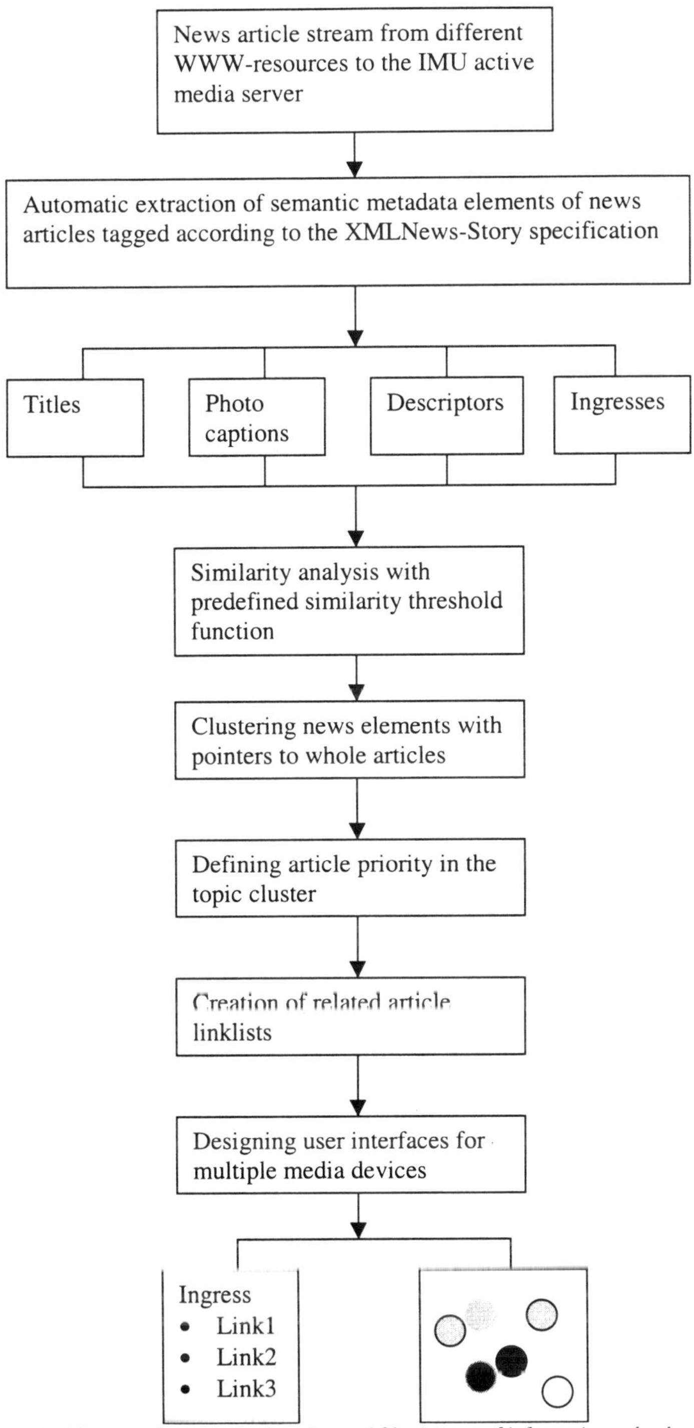

Figure 3. A practical framework to test the detection and filtering out of information redundancy.

Information extraction (IE) systems analyse unrestricted text in order to extract specific types of information. IE research has been reported by, among others, Appelt (1999), Cowie and Lehnert (1996), Endres-Niggemeyer (2000), Fuketa et al. (2000), Liu et al. (1999), Moens and Dumortier (2000), and Salton et al. (1997). Automatic text categorisation and summarisation has potential in many text-based applications including text routing and filtering (Lam et al. 1999; Moens and Dumortier 2000; Salton et al. 1997). From a natural language perspective, information extraction systems must operate at many levels, starting from word recognition and sentence analysis and ending up at comprehension of the full text document (Jurafsky and Martin 2000).

Much research has been done on similarity measures and clustering (Baeza-Yates and Ribeiro-Neto 1999; Kohonen 2001; Kok et al. 1999; Kowalski and Maybury 2000; Modha and Spangler 2000; Skarmeta et al. 2000; Zhang and Korfhage 1999). Carrick and Watters (1997) and Watters et al. (1998) have studied the automatic association of text and photo news items in their Electronic News Delivery -project. Bergamaschi et al. (2001) have studied semantic similarity and calculation of the semantic similarity degrees in the context of integrating data from heterogeneous database systems.

Many systems have been proposed to find similar or related documents in the World Wide Web (Dean and Henzinger 1999; Hui and Goh 1998; Netscape Communications Corporations 2001; Vu and Li 2000).

Intellectual property protection and work on duplicate detection has concentrated mostly on exploring extracted features of document image databases (Brin et al. 1995; Lopresti 2000) or CAD applications (Kahng et al. 1999). Monostori et al. (2000) have studied methods for detecting plagiarism in large text collections.

There are also interesting projects going on in the EU's Information Society Technologies (IST) –programme such as the Multimedia Indexing and Searching Environment (MUMIS). The project focuses on technology for indexing and retrieval of data from different media sources and in different languages (Hiddink 2001).

4. Discussion and future work

The exploratory study has concentrated on the methodological and technical issues related to minimising information redundancy. In this study the theoretical framework for minimising the information redundancy problem in the case of automatic combination of media contents in integrated publishing has been introduced. The hybrid framework contains elements from information retrieval research, natural language processing and the latest developments of the World Wide Web. The experimental arrangements in the IMU environment have been described as a practical framework of the study.

In this study the following problems were identified for further research:

- a better understanding of the possibilities of existing metadata in the IMU relational database,
- a more precise understanding and identification of different information redundancy categories in the common and personal channels of the IMU system,
- a systematic analysis of the effect of the similarity threshold function value to the results,
- a better understanding of the characteristics of news materials and the effects of their time dependence on the study of information redundancy,
- a more precise understanding of distance measures and their possible combinations that could have the potential to provide a new approach to similarity research,

- a more precise understanding of the role of ontologies, the Topic Map –standard and semantic markup methods in the conceptualisation and management of media contents,
- a systematic analysis of the information redundancy problem in mobile news services.

Furthermore, the increased availability of multi-lingual materials in all areas of the public and private sector is driving demand for systems that facilitate integration of the contents from multi-lingual Web resources. Developing methods for minimising news material redundancy in automatic combination of multi-lingual media contents in mobile news services challenges the future of the Semantic Web.

5. References

Appelt, D. E. 1999. Introduction to information extraction. AI Communications, Vol. 12, No. 3, pp. 161-172.

Baeza-Yates, R. and Ribeiro-Neto, B. 1999. Modern information retrieval. New York: ACM Press. 513 p. ISBN 0-201-39829-X.

Bergamaschi, S., Castano, S., Vincini, M. and Beneventano, D. 2001. Semantic integration of heterogeneous information sources. Data & Knowledge Engineering, Vol. 36, No. 3, pp. 215 - 249.

Berners-Lee, T. 1999. Weaving the Web. New York: HarperSanFrancisco. 226 p. ISBN 0-06-251586-1.

Brin, S., Davis, J. and García-Molina, H. 1995. Copy detection mechanisms for digital documents. In: Proceedings of the 1995 ACM SIGMOD International Conference on Management of Data, May 22 - 25, 1995, San Jose, CA, USA. Pp. 398 - 409.

Carrick, C. and Watters, C. 1997. Automatic association of news items. Information Processing and Management, Vol. 33, No.5, pp. 615 - 632.

Cowie, J. and Lehnert, W. 1996. Information extraction. Communications of the ACM, Vol. 39, No. 1, pp. 80 – 91.

Croft, W. B. 2000. Recent research from the Center for Intelligent Information Retrieval. Boston: Kluwer Academic Publishers. 306 p. ISBN 0-7923-7812-1.

Crow, L. and Shadbolt, N. 2001. Extracting focused knowledge from the semantic web. International Journal of Human-Computer Studies, Vol. 54, No. 1, pp. 155 - 184.

Dean, J. and Henzinger, M. R. 1999. Finding related pages in the World Wide Web. Computer Networks, Vol. 31, No. 11 - 16, pp. 1467 - 1479.

Endres-Niggemeyer, B. 2000. SimSum: an empirically founded simulation of summarizing. Information Processing and Management, Vol. 36, No. 4, pp. 659 - 682.

Fukcta, M., Lee, S., Tsuji, T., Okada, M. and Aoe, J-I. 2000. A document classification method by using field association words. Information Sciences, Vol. 126, No. 1-4, pp. 57 - 70.

Guarino, N. 1995. Formal ontology, conceptual analysis and knowledge representation. International Journal of Human and Computer Studies, Vol. 43, No. 5/6, pp. 625 - 640.

Hiddink, W. 2001. MUMIS Multimedia Indexing and Searching Environment. (referred 4.4.2001). Project description: <URL: http://www.ctit.utwente.nl/Docs/projects/international/mumis.html>.

Hui, S-C. and Goh, A. 1998. Information filtering of on-line news using dynamic abstract generation. Cybernetics and Systems, Vol. 29, No. 6, pp. 577 - 591.

Hunter, A. 2001. Get your news on the Web. Information World Review, January 2001, No. 165, pp. 20 - 21.

ISO 8879. 1986. Information Processing - Text and office systems - Standard generalised markup language (SGML). Geneva: ISO. 155 p.

ISO/IEC 13250. 2000. Information Technology - SGML Applications - Topic Maps. Geneva: ISO/IEC. 39 pp.

Jurafsky, D. and Martin, J. H. 2000. Speech and language processing: an introduction to natural language processing, computational linguistics, and speech recognition. Upper Saddle River: Prentice-Hall, Inc. 934 p.

Kahng, A. B., Kirovski, D., Mantik, S., Potkonjak, M. and Wong, J. L. 1999. Copy detection for intellectual property protection of VLSI designs. In: Proceedings of the 1999 International Conference on Computer-aided Design. Pp. 600 - 605.

Kohonen, T. 2001. Self-organizing maps. Third edition. Berlin: Springer (Springer series in Information Sciences 30). 501 p. ISBN 3-540-67921-9.

Kok, Y. H., Goh, A. and Holaday, D. A. 1999. Using cluster analysis to determine the media agenda. Aslib Proceedings, Vol. 51, No. 10, pp. 361 - 371.

Kowalski, G. J. & Maybury, M. T. 2000. Information storage and retrieval systems. Theory and implementation. Second edition. Boston: Kluwer Academic Publishers. 318 p. ISBN 0-7923-7924-1.

Lam, W., Ruiz, M. and Srinivasan, P. 1999. Automatic text categorization and its application to text retrieval. IEEE Transactions on Knowledge and Data Engineering, Vol. 11, No. 6, pp. 865 - 879.

Liu, J., Wu, Y. and Zhou, L. 1999. A hybrid method for abstracting newspaper articles. Journal of the American Society for Information Science, Vol. 50, No. 13, pp. 1234 - 1245.

Lopresti , D. P. 2000. String techniques for detecting duplicates in document databases. International Journal on Document Analysis and Recognition, Vol. 2, No. 4, pp 186 - 199.

Maybury, M. 2000. News on demand. Communications of the ACM, Vol. 43, No. 2, pp. 33 - 34.

Miller, G. A. 1995. WordNet: A lexical database in English. Communications of the ACM, Vol. 38, No. 11, pp. 39 - 41.

Mock, K. J. and Vemuri, V. R. 1997. Information filtering via hill climbing, wordnet, and index patterns. Information Processing & Management, Vol. 33, No. 5, pp. 633 - 644.

Modha, D. S. and Spangler, W. S. 2000. Clustering hypertext with applications to web searching. In: Proceedings of the 11th ACM on Hypertext and Hypermedia, May 30 - June 3, 2000, San Antonio, TX USA. Pp. 143 - 152.

Moens, M-F. and Dumortier, J. 2000. Text categorization: the assignment of subject descriptors to magazine articles. Information Processing & Management, Vol. 36, No. 6, pp. 841 - 861.

Monostori, K., Zaslavsky, A and Schmidt, H. 2000. Document overlap detection system for distributed digital libraries. In: Proceedings of the 5th ACM conference on ACM 2000 Digital Libraries, June 2 - 7, 2000, San Antonio, TX, USA. Pp. 226 - 227.

Motta, E., Buckingham Shum, S. and Domingue, J. 2000. Ontology-driven document enrichment: principles, tools and applications. International Journal of Human-Computer Studies, Vol. 52, No. 6, pp. 1071 - 1109.

Netscape Communications 2001. What's Related FAQ (referred 16.3.2001) <URL: http://home.netscape.com/escapes/related/faq.htm>.

Salton, G., Singhal, A., Mitra, M. and Buckley, C. 1997. Automatic text structuring and summarization. Information Processing & Management, Vol. 33, No. 2, pp. 193 - 207.

Staab, S., Angele, J., Decker, S., Erdmann, M., Hotho, A., Maedche, A., Schnurr, H.-P., Studer, R. and Sure, Y. 2000. Semantic community Web portals. In: Proceedings of the 9th International World Wide Web Conference, Amsterdam, The Netherlands, Elsevier Amsterdam. Pp. 473 - 491.

Södergård, C., Aaltonen, M., Hagman, S., Hiirsalmi, M., Järvinen, T., Kaasinen, E., Kinnunen, T., Kolari, J., Kunnas, J. and Tammela, A. 1999. Integrated multimedia publishing: combining TV and newspaper content on personal channels. Computer Networks, Vol. 31, No. 11-16, pp. 1111 - 1128.

Vu, Q. and Li, W-S. 2000. Exploring link topology for associating Web pages. Poster in the 9th International World Wide Web Conference, Amsterdam, May 15 - 19, 2000. 3 pp.

W3C The Technology & Society Domain: Semantic Web Activity (referred 12.3.2001) <URL:http://www.w3.org/2001/sw/>.

Watters, C. and Wang, H. 2000. Rating news documents for similarity. Journal of the American Society for Information Science, Vol. 51, No. 9, pp. 793 - 804.

Watters, C., Shepherd, M. A. and Burkowski, F. J. 1998. Electronic news delivery project. Journal of the American Society for Information Science, Vol. 49, No. 2, pp. 134 - 150.

XMLNews-Story Specifications (referred 9.4.2001) <URL: http://www.xmlnews.org/XMLNews/>.

Zhang, J. and Korfhage, R. 1999. Distance and angle similarity measure method. Journal of the American Society for Information Science, Vol. 50, No. 9, pp. 772 - 778.

An integrated multiple media news portal

Caj Södergård [*,1], Matti Aaltonen [2], Christer Bäckström [1], Ari Heinonen [4], Timo Järvinen [1]
Timo Kinnunen [1], Pauliina Koivunen [3], Sari Lehtola [2], Ville Ollikainen [1], Katja Rentto [2],
Mikko Seppälä [4], Antti Tammela [2]

[1] *VTT Information Technology, P.O. Box 1203, FIN-02044 VTT, Finland*
[2] *VTT Information Technology, P.O. Box 1206, FIN-33101 Tampere, Finland*
[3] *University of Jyväskylä, Information Technology Research Institute, P.O. Box 35, FIN-40351 Jyväskylä, Finland*
[4] *Journalism Research and Development Centre, FIN-33014 University of Tampere, Finland*

[*] *Corresponding author*

Abstract: The emerging multiple media portals accessed by a variety of terminals require semi- and fully automatic procedures for managing the material. The IMU (Integrated Publishing in Multimedia Network) trial system, developed in this work, automatizes parts of the news content acquirement and processing work of the portal web master. The IMU active proxy server extracts the metadata from news web sites and from the television news broadcasts through video analysis making an automatic classification and linking of related articles and TV clips possible. The deeply integrated material is partitioned into news composites called channels, which can be personalised by the user. The automatically computed event and media calendar allows for a new type of integration of news and up-coming events. The news content is refined by setting up filters for monitoring of the business environment. Through our interfaces for PC, TV, WAP and MP3 terminals, the user accesses the same news content at work, at home in the living room and on the move. To balance the automatic procedures with journalistic judgement, we created web tools for human editors to control and override the automatic operations and for creating new content. The community feature enables groups to share news and to discuss topics internally. The trial including closely 400 users with PC, TV and WAP terminals showed a stable interest in the service. The typical user retrieved a few fresh articles including a TV clip at prime time in the evening. The television set user retrieved two times more material than the PC user, but proportionally less news. The most popular channels for the TV-user were TV programme schedules and TV clips. The community channels attracted the TV set users. Personalization was used scarcely and searches even more seldom. The interviews showed that the system was well accepted, except for navigating in the TV-IMU application with the remote controller.
Keywords: Portals, Integrated publishing; Multiple media publishing; Personalization; Video analysis; Semiautomatic editing; Community building; Environmental scanning

0. Introduction

Portals, like Yahoo[1] and MSN[2], are common entry ports into the WWW. To gain in popularity, they are including more and more features like common and localised news,

---

[1] http://www.yahoo.com/
[2] http://www.msn.com/

search engines, chat, communities, calendars, personalization and e-commerce. Audio and video multimedia material are increasingly being added creating *multiple media portals* [1]. In this environment, content – even if primarily intended for a certain medium – is repurposed for a multiplicity of distribution channels and receiving terminals. A goal is, that the media consumer can get content versions independently of the terminal device at use at the moment, be it a PC, TV, WAP telephone or a PDA.

The management of these multiple media and personalisable portals poses a significant challenge. The editors and web masters must use a wide variety of semi- and fully automatic procedures. In a recent paper [2], we presented the IMU trial system[3] for integrating newspaper and television news on personal channels. In the extensive user studies of the IMU system, the value of this deep source integration was clearly recognised and a even broader integration with more – and fresh - information sources was wished for. Editorially prepared feature articles interested the readers significantly more than ordinary news and more editorial touch was in general hoped for. The television set was by many – especially the media house people – seen as the preferred terminal for this type of content.

In the second phase of the IMU work reported here, we have addressed these observations by including constantly updated news sources as well as an editorial system for human editors. A journalistic team was founded for doing the editorial work. The television set is included as a terminal on equal footage with the PC. Personalization is tried in a more professional application for scanning of the business environment. In addition, communities have been integrated creating a link between the large-scale news creation in major media houses and the small-sized content production and discussions in local communities.

Maintaining an event calendar is tedious job for the web master. In this trial, we have created an automatic procedure for setting up calendars.

1. Principles behind our work

1.1 Personalisation of news, event and media calendar and environmental scanning

As described in [2], IMU offers a set of channels. The channel is a stored database query that in [3] is called a semantic bookmark. One channel type are *common channels* to which the reader can subscribe (Top News, 'the weather' etc). The coverage of these channels cannot be changed by the user. In addition to these fixed channels, the user can tailor so-called *personal channels* according to his or her interests. The reader creates personal channels by selecting one or more news or event and media sections from the ones made available by the IMU content producers. The reader can, for example, make a sports channel by combining the sports sections from one TV station and one newspaper. The articles covered by the channel can be further personalised by using a query clause. A third type is the *environmental scanning channel.* Environmental scanning is defined as the acquisition of information external to an organisation, the knowledge of which would assist management in planning future courses of action [4]. Strategic planning is closely connected to environmental scanning (e.g. see [4], [5], [6]), since adaptation to environmental demands and the ability of staying ahead of environmental challenges are

---

[3] http://www.vtt.fi/imu/

vital to an organisation's success. The user can, for example, select a 'technology environment' channel and personalise it by different search terms.

Event and Media Calendar automatically fetches from the supplements of two web newspapers. The material consists of television and radio programme schedules, movie theatre information, theatre and movie reviews, and information on different events (music concerts, art exhibitions etc.). The television schedules are utilised via the TV interface to set the set-top-box to record television programmes.

1.2 Semiautomatic editing – the IMU editorial environment

Automatic selection sometimes results in an inadequate news offering. News items are placed in wrong departments, the main news are not always necessarily the most important ones, and links are incorrect. Therefore, we have developed an editing and information managing application for the IMU newsroom.

The IMU newsroom combines the benefits of automatic news generation and the professional expertise of journalists. The human editors administer the news flow, personalise thematic news channels and create news packages from the material fetched from our news sources (Fig. 1). The news packages offer a broader view on particular topics than the separate pieces of news that are scattered all over the IMU departments.

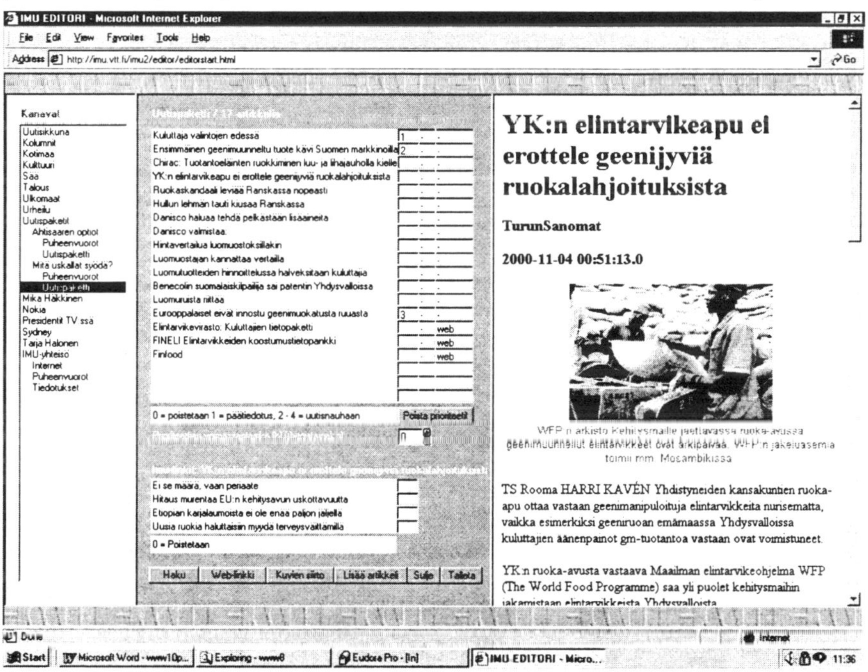

Figure 1. The IMU editor, where a news package about food is under preparation. The package consists of an editorial introduction and links to articles in the IMU database (middle).

News discussion forums are attached to the news packages. Thus, the audience can have their say regarding the daily news topics. The IMU editors take actively part in the discussion forums. The editors can always override the automatic choices and select the news for the main news slots (on the front page and news departments), delete repetitive news and delete incorrect links.

1.3 Communities

Communities link the large-scale news creation in major media houses and the small-sized content production in different communities. For the three communities in the trial we have set up communication spheres (channels) consisting of a bulletin area, a discussion forum and a personalised news channel. Some community members work as moderators producing material for their community channel. The IMU newsroom staff work in close co-operation with the moderators. The moderators use the same editing application as that in the IMU newsroom.

The community members access their own dedicated channels through the IMU front page seeing therefore the daily news feed. The communities are also able to create their own personalised news channels. These community news channels present a filtered selection of all the IMU content.

2. The functions and the user interface

The system functions and user interface were designed in a multistage process – starting from a brain storm with the project companies, proceeding through a requirement description, ending up in a user interface description that was implemented and put into the trial.

As described in above, the IMU system combines related articles, video clips and media events into channels. Video articles, mostly TV news, and text-based articles are treated and presented in a similar way. There are three main areas on the front page (Fig. 2) (from the left) 1) *Channel selection area* where the user can select and modify the available channels. The main groups are News, Personal Channels (personalised channels and community channels) and Event and Media Calendar. 2) *News area* where the most topical news item is opened in the upper window; in the lower window are the headlines of other news items. 3) *News banner* with top news headlines, mostly with pictures. In addition to these areas, there is a *scrolling channel* – a sort of news ticker – in the uppermost part of the front page. From the front page the user can proceed to the various news departments and other services of IMU.

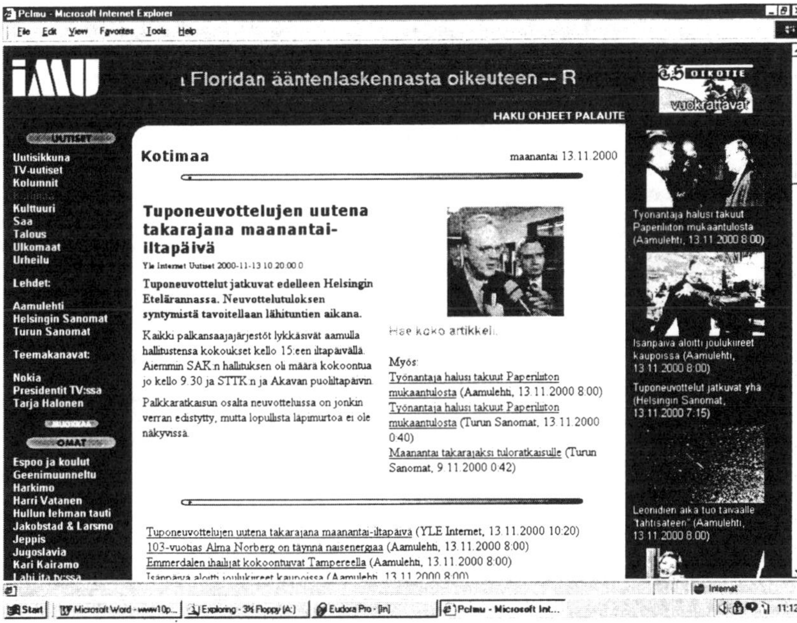

Figure 2. The IMU publication, where the channels (common and personal) are presented on the left. The channel "Kotimaa" is selected. The channel contains the domestic news headlines and TV news drawn from several newspapers and TV stations. A News banner with the top headlines is displayed on the right.

In the Event and Media Calendar the user can switch between four fixed channels: television and radio programme, movie theatre schedules, and events information (e.g. music, exhibition, and drama (Fig.3).

Figure 3. The Event and Media Catalogue gives the user TV and radio programs, movie theatre offerings, and other event information.

The PC and TV interfaces are very similar. The same information can be retrieved via the TV and the PC. Of course, the smaller resolution of the television screen affects the way in which the elements are shown. For example, the news stories cannot be scrolled as on the PC, and have therefore to be paginated. The remote control device has to be taken into account, when designing the TV interface (Fig. 4). Most of the commands should be given with the buttons on the remote control.

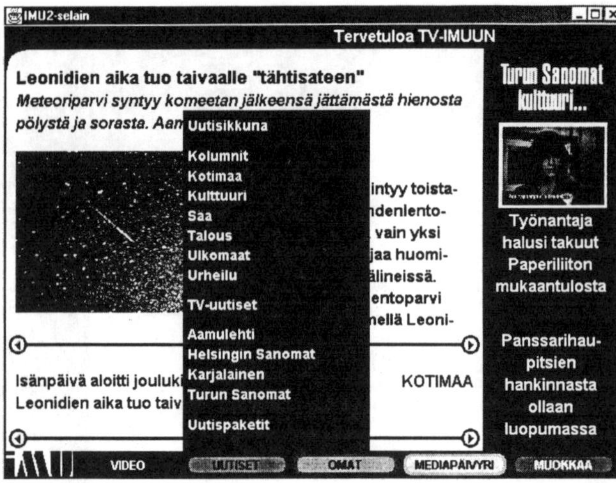

Figure 4. The TV-IMU is used with a TV remote controller. The menu Common channels is selected with the remote control red button. The channel "Kotimaa" is selected with the arrow keys. The browser is written in Java.

The WAP-IMU service provides personalised news for the users (Fig. 5). The metaphor behind the user interface is the channel. It is also possible to search the IMU news database with a WAP-IMU.

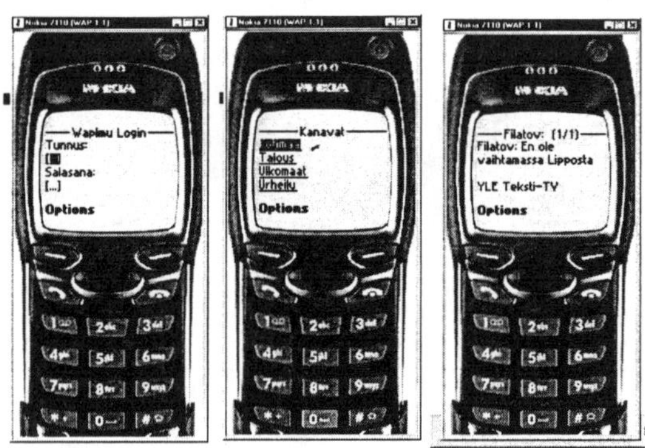

Figure 5. The WAP-IMU publication, where the user at first logs in, selects a channel (Kotimaa), a heading and finally gets a short article.

3. The system architecture

The three-tier software architecture implemented with Java is a natural, almost self-evident, choice for a modern web application. How to implement each tier is a more interesting question.

3.1 Client

In our case, where Java was chosen as the implementation language, Java applets and Java applications represent the fat client approach, and Java servlets represent the thin client solution.

3.1.1 PC

On the PC, we mainly developed a thin client. One servlet takes care of most user interaction tasks. All data needed for the user interface is kept in Java objects that remain active throughout the session. The model of the visible user interface is kept internally in a DOM (Domain Object Model)[4] tree structure. Normally each interaction from the user causes some parts of the DOM object to change, but as much as possible of the object is kept constant to reduce computing load. After each interaction the whole DOM tree is written out as an XML document.

The XML content is converted into HTML by the browser according to rules given in an XSLT style sheet attached to the XML file. The layout has been constructed using HTML tables in the style sheet. Separating the model handling from the graphical representation makes it much easier to generate HTML dynamically with servlets. Most of the user interface consists of HTML documents without frames. Only the scrolling channel is an applet. All selectable items cause a call to the interface servlet.

There is also a third alternative to the thin and fat client. Here, the user interface is implemented as a simple applet and the application logic is handled by a servlet that communicates with the user interface applet. This architecture has been used for the personalization wizard of the PC client. The communication between the personalization applets and the corresponding servlet is done using HTTP tunneling [7], where serialized Java objects are passed between the client and server using HTTP reducing firewall problems.

3.1.2 Other clients

The TV client uses a fat client architecture, where the browser is written as Java application. The WAP client is a scaled down version of the PC client. The biggest difference is that XSLT style sheets and applets cannot be used on the client side. WML documents must be generated by the server servlet directly.

The applet-servlet combination was used to implement the Editor depicted in Fig. 1. The Editor could have been implemented with servlets, but applets handled the complex user interactions better.

The Editor consists of several applets communicating with each other using a static class. One of the applets is active through the whole editing session. The other applets are invoked as needed.

---

[4] http://www.w3.org/DOM/

3.2 Server

3.2.1 Server platform

There are two NT server computers in the system: the media server and application server. The media server stores Microsoft ASF content to the file system and serves it by using Microsoft's streaming media server software. The server-side part of the IMU application runs completely in the application server. In addition to middle tier software, i.e. Microsoft's web server and JRun servlet engine, the database runs in the application server.

3.2.2 Middle tier

Despite the fact that the J2EE (Java 2 Enterprise Edition) technology[5] is quickly emerging as a platform for multitier enterprise applications, Java servlets were chosen as the middle tier technology. Java servlets have strong benefits in a research project.

3.2.3 Database

The database consists of persistent data storage and database API (Fig. 6).

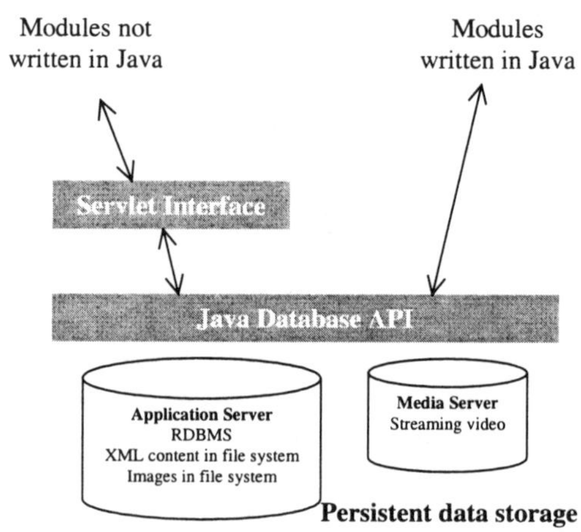

Figure 6. Database architecture.

The database uses XML only as the storage format of textual content of articles. Each article is stored in the file system as an XML file that conforms to the XMLNews-Story[6] DTD. Article, images and video clip, metadata, i.e. data needed for article selection and displaying article lists, is stored in the RDBMS. The database API, written in Java, retrieves data from the RDBMS and returns it to the client modules as Java objects that are instantiated from classes that represent IMU objects such as users, channels and articles. The Java objects contain URIs to images and videos. The textual content of the articles is passed as DOM objects.

---

[5] *http://java.sun.com/j2ee/*

[6] *http://www.xmlnews.org/*

3.3 Video segmentation

Television news broadcasts are segmented into stories. Even if the segmentation methods resemble those in the literature, see e.g. [8], we are applying them in a new way (Fig. 7). The appearance of the news anchor and various kinds of visual effects governs the setting of boundaries for a story (Fig. 8). A story is further segmented into separate scenes with associated stills determined from the first scene following the news anchor. The segmented news stories are labelled with news transcripts retrieved from closed caption texts.

Figure 7. The channel "TV news" is selected. The news transcript retrieved from closed captions is in the middle. The news topics found with video analysis are listed together with their representative stills at the right. Links to related newspaper articles are below.

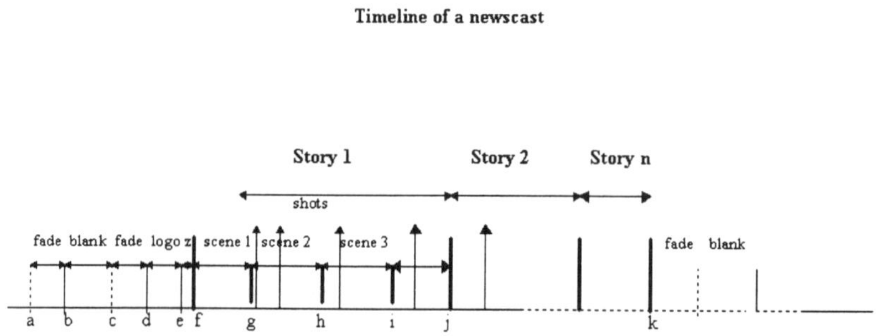

Fig 8. Time representation of typical video segmentation. The above timeline represents events within the video. Fade-out is represented by a-b, blanks by b-c, fade-in by c-d. During d-e the news show logo is displayed. During e-f the news anchor is zoomed in. The news program and the first story begin at transition f. The periods f-g, g-h, h-i and i-j signify scenes in the first story. At j starts a new story usually found by similarity search. Event k represents the beginning of a fade-out, this also represents the end of the news program.

3.4 TV Client

A PC-based Set Top Box (STB) was built to study, how an integrated media terminal – mixing computer and television - could be used as an integral part of everyday life in a living room. The STB has DVD playback, facilities to record and replay television programmes and an infrared remote controller, which complies with the NorDig specifications [9].

The televison schedules are used for interactive programming resembling the services available for digital recorders TiVo [10] and ReplayTv [11]. Television trailers, MPEG2 ML@MP compressed at up to 8 Mb/s, are. It is also possible to use STB as television tuner with an instant recording capability. STB has a Nicam [12] tuner to receive and record digitally transmitted stereo audio.

3.5 Environmental scanning

A telephone interview concerning strategies of business environment scanning was administered to randomly selected 150 Finnish SMEs employing more than 10 and less than 250 people in February 2000. The goal of the interview was to form topics of interest to the scanning wizard discussed above. Interviewees were asked how important it is to find information from different areas of the environment and how often they scanned the areas. Frequency of scanning is connected to the perceived importance of the issues scanned ([14], [15], [16]). The question format of frequency of scanning is derived from Hambrick's [13] study validated by Farh et al [17].

The environmental areas were named according to Daft et al [16] as competition, customer, technological, regulatory, economic and socio-cultural sectors. Natural environment was added as one sector (see e.g. [18]). New topics included were potential competitors [19], changes in customer's business area, suppliers [19], new developments, changes or circumstances in the business area, environmental activists [20], natural environment [18]. Different environmental sectors were used as channels in the IMU-publication, and separate topics as search keywords in the scanning wizard.

The interviews showed that scanning was considered to be most important in competition, customer and technology sectors. The scanning wizard was based upon this.

4. The trial system

News articles are fetched daily from four on-line newspaper web-sites: Aamulehti, Helsingin Sanomat, Karjalainen and Turun Sanomat (Fig.9). Television news is digitized from Finnish Broadcasting Company (YLE) broadcasts. Up-to-the-minute news articles as well as teletext news are acquired from the YLE website. Teletext news provide shorter text-only versions of YLE news articles and are therefore suitable for WAP phones. Event information covers culture offerings in the cities of Helsinki and Tampere.

The content is viewed over fast networks on PC and TV platforms. In addition, WAP phones and voice synthesis devices are available terminals.

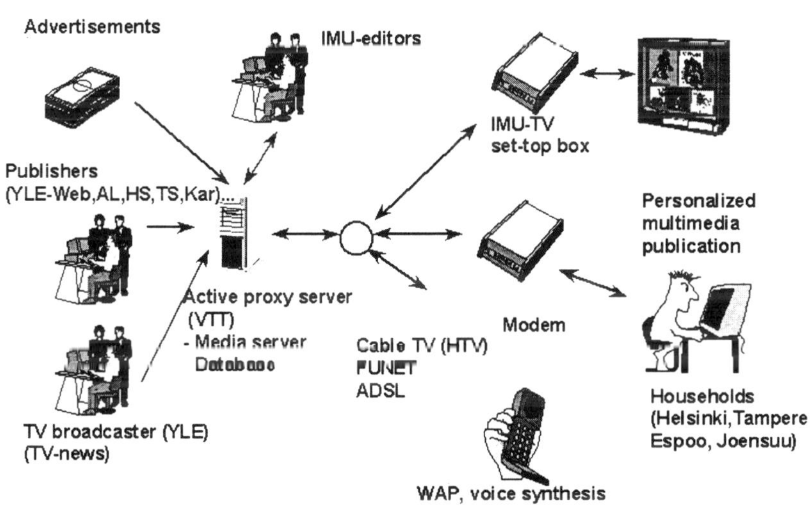

Figure 9. The trial set-up, where the active proxy server processes the content from the media houses. The IMU editors control the machine-made choices and produce own news packages. The publication is used on different terminals.

4.1 IMU2 Content Acquisition

The content acquisition not only fetches content from on-line publications, but it also extracts keywords and metadata from source content, generates news items from digitized TV news broadcasts and finally stores content and metadata into the database to allow a deep level of integration of different content items (Fig. 10).

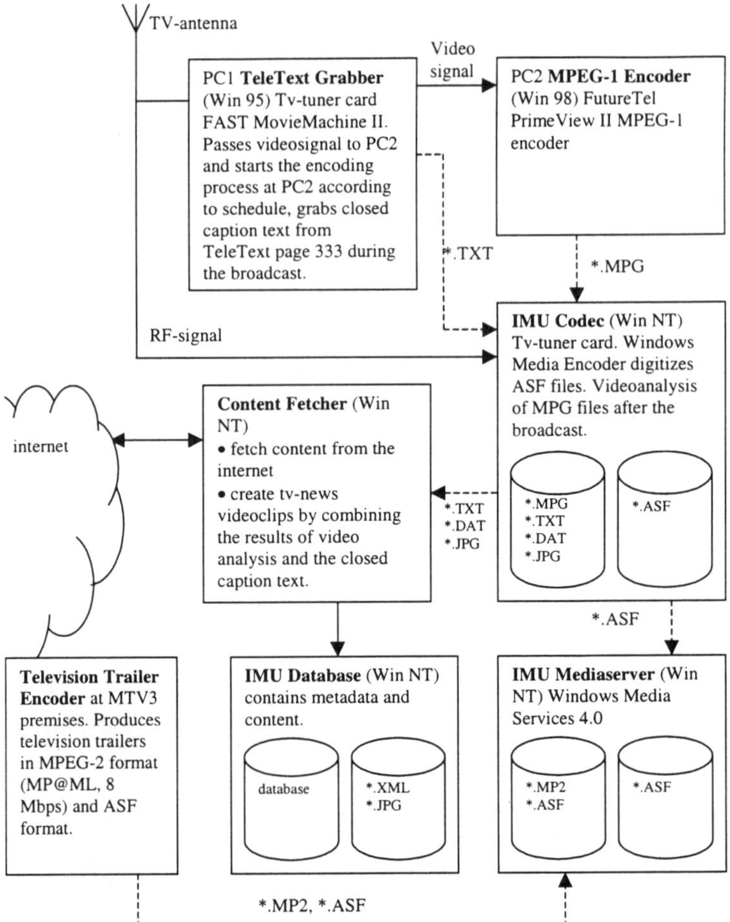

Figure 10. The IMU Content Acquisition

The fetched HTML-pages are parsed according to predefined rules coded into each different fetcher. Content data keeps the article ingress, bodytext, subtitles and caption, a JPEG- or GIF-file, which contains picture data and television news broadcast in Advanced Streaming Format[7]. Closed caption text with timestamps are grabbed from teletext page in real-time. This transcript of the speech in the broadcast is combined with video analysis to produce a video news article.

The fetchers are written in Java (JDK version 1.2.2)[8] and the HTML-parsing is done using Java Swing-classes. The Java Secure Socket Extension (JSSE 1.0.1)[9] and HTTPClient Java package written by Ronald Tschalär (HTTPClient Version

---

[7] http://www.microsoft.com/asf/
[8] http://www.javasoft.com/products/jdk/1.2/
[9] http://java.sun.com/products/jsse/

0.3-2)[10] is used. Other parts of the content acquisition system (Teletext Grabber, MPEG-1 Encoder and the Video Codec) have several "glue" applications written in C.

4.2 The TV-settopbox

4.2.1 Hardware and software

The user interface was made for 640x480 display. An infrared remote control reader was made and installed into STB case. On top of Windows operating system, there is a Java application for browsing the IMU pages (Fig. 11). Behind the browser window there is Visual C++ application, which takes care of remote controller control, video card controls, DVD and streaming video playback and programme trailer handling. The application receives commands from IMU server and the browser in a XML tagged file using a subset Louth VDCP commands [22].

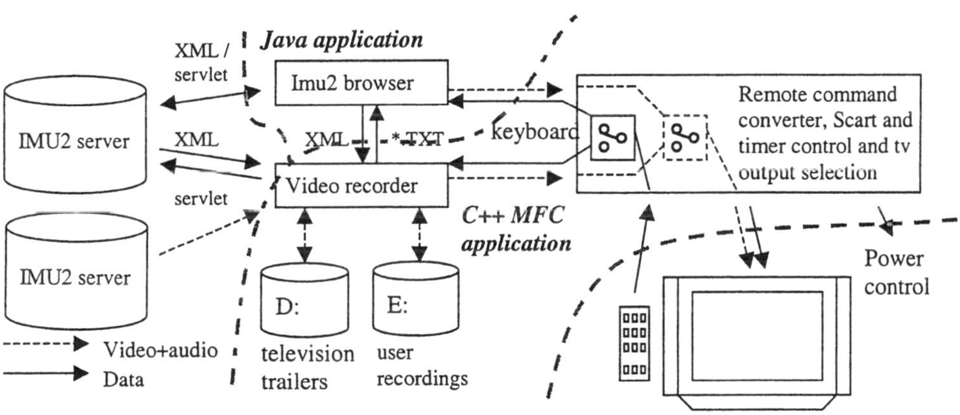

Figure 11. Block diagram of IMU Set Top Box application software

4.2.2 Using IMU Set Top Box

The STB has four different operating modes. In TV-IMU and IMU modes the browser is visible and at user's command. In TV-IMU there is also a small TV window on top of the browser showing the real time television programme. In the video mode the user can view his own recordings, television trailers, IMU news clips or DVD's. In television mode the STB serves as a television.

Commands, menus and links are adressed in a sequence by pushing the arrow buttons on the remote controller. The activation path starts at the advertisement in the upper right corner and goes through the news banner titles to the right to the opened article and the article list.

[10] http://www.innovation.ch/java/HTTPClient/

5. User trials

5.1 Description of users and the usability evaluation

The trial system was tested in households in the Helsinki, Tampere, and Joensuu area (Table 1). Of these 412 potential users, 360 has actively used the system.

Table 1 . The user groups in the trial.

User group (potential users)	Size
Cabel modem users	233
Students using the Helsinki University of Technology network	44
Students using the University of Tampere network	33
ADSL users	27
Iidesranta community	21
Merihaka community	12
WAP users	16
Environment watching users	10
Journalist trial	9
TV-IMU-users	12
Total (IMU community)	412

Most users represented single (n=147) or two (n=148) person households 278 of all respondents reported not to have children.The users are a very "computerised": over 98 percent have a computer in their household and 99 percent uses Internet daily or almost every day.

5.2 Usage patterns

During the research period (18.9.-3.12.2000) the PC users logged in IMU on average 11 times. The most active user logged in IMU 152 times. The sessions lasted on average 11 ½ minutes. During each session the PC users chose on average 3,2 articles. During the first week IMU was in most active use (Fig 12).

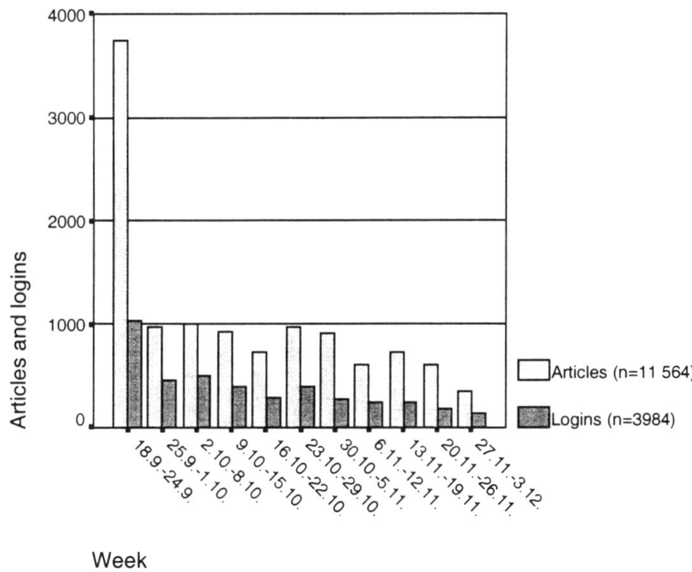

Figure 12. Amount of articles retrieved per week

The IMU *prime time* for both PC and STB users was, like in the previous trial [2], between late afternoon and late evening hours (3 p.m. - midnight), which resembles the habits of television viewing. Morning use was more common to the STB users than the PC users.

By far, the most popular channel in IMU is television news (Fig. 13) with around 22 percent of all channels chosen. In the interviews, 65 % of the users wished for more television content.

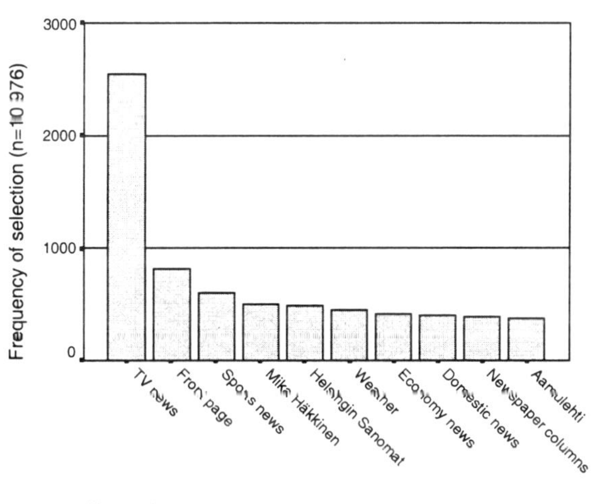

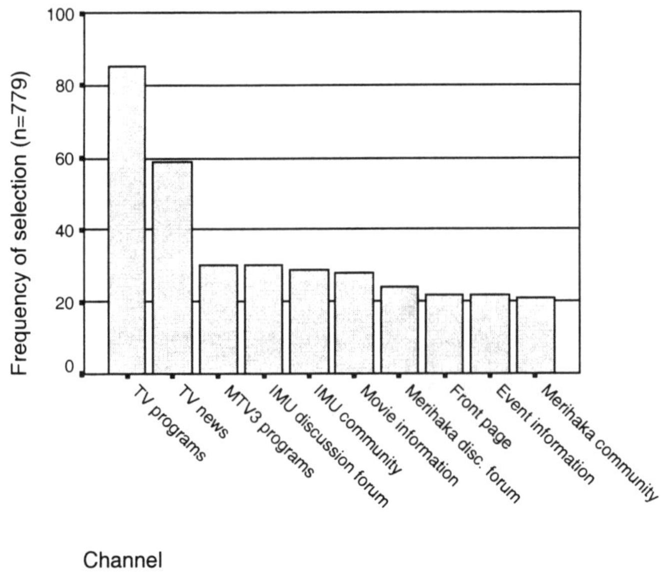

Figure 13. The top ten of IMU channels for PC (upper) and TV-users (lower)

The main difference between PC and TV user groups is that the TV users follow the news a lot. The TV users have been able to use the Media Calendar ; the most popular of all channels are channels showing television programme schedules. Most of the TV-IMU users are also members in two of the communities, which is seen in the popularity of the community channels. The proportion of community channels chosen by PC users is noticeably smaller.The average TV-IMU user selected roughly two times more articles than the PC user.

Fairly few used personalisation. 360 users personlized only 130 own channels. However, these channels were frequenly selected - on the average 8 times. Articles were searched for 0,56 times per user and a certain TV-broadcast was searched only exceptionally (0,09 times per user). The corporate users considered the environment scanning feature a good idea, but wanted more distinct categories and more news material in order to use the feature more frequently – now only one third had made personal channels and only 5 % an environmental channel.

6. Conclusions

The emerging multiple media portals with extensive features need semi- and fully automatic procedures for managing the material. Especially the content delivery to multiple terminals types like PC, TV and wireless devices requires plenty of automatic conversions and appropriate user interfaces. The IMU trial system developed in this work automatises parts of the news content acquirement and processing work of the web master. The IMU active proxy server extracts the metadata from the content of news web sites and from the television news broadcasts through video analysis. Through our interfaces for PC, TV WAP and MP3 terminals, the trial user could access the same news content at work, at home in the living room and on the move. Technically we use both thin and fat client architectures.

In spite of the merits of automatic procedures, journalistic skills and judgement cannot be overtaken by machines. Therefore, we have developed an applet based editor for journalists to control and override the automatically made operations. The journalistic team set up in the trial also created there own news packages.

The trial with PC and TV terminals showed a stable interest in the service. The typical user retrieved a few fresh articles at prime time in the evening. One fourth of the retrieved articles on PC was television news topics. The television set user selected two times more articles than the PC user, which supports our initial belief that the TV set is most suitable for this type of material. The most popular channels for the TV-user were TV programme schedules, TV clips coming in second. Fairly few used personalisation, but users were active. Searches were very scarce. News packages were used only marginally. The interviews showed that the system was well accepted, except for the navigating in the TV-IMU application with the remote controller.

The IMU media portal environment can be extended in various way. We are developing a system, where personalized news content through speech synthesis is converted into MP3 files that are downloaded on portable MP3 players. The main users of this system are visually impaired people.

7. Acknowledgements

We thank for the financial support and advice the National Technology Agency and 11 Finnish companies in the media and communication sector. In addition to the authors, Marjo Huusko, Mikko Kojo, Eija Ruotsalainen and Minna Suovirta have participated in the project.

8. References

R.G Picard., 2000. Changing Business Models of Online Content Services. The International Journal on Media Management, Vol. 2, pp. 60 – 68.

C. Södergård, M. Aaltonen, S. Hagman, M. Hiirsalmi, T.Järvinen, E.Kaasinen, T. Kinnunen, J. Kolari, J. Kunnas, A. Tammela, Integrated multimedia publishing; combining TV and newspaper content on personal channels. Proceedings of the 8th International World Wide Web Conference, Elsevier Science, Amsterdam, 1999, pp. 1111 – 1128.

S.Staab , J.Angele , S.Decker, M.Erdmann, A.Hotho, A.Maedche, H.-P.Schnurr, R.Studer , Y.Sure, Semantic Community Web Portals, Proceedings of the 9th International World Wide Web Conference, Elsevier Science, Amsterdam, 2000, pp. 473 – 491.

F. Aguilar, Scanning the Business Environment, Macmillan Co, New York, NY, 1967.

R. Beal, Competing Effectively: Environmental Scanning, Competitive Strategy, and Organizational Performance in Small Manufacturing Firms, Journal of Small Business Management, 2000, vol 38, no.1, pp. 27-57.

B. Boyd & E. Reuning-Elliot, A Measurement Model of Strategic Planning. Strategic Management Journal, 1998, vol 19, pp.181-192.

K. Moss, Java Servlets, McGraw-Hill, New York, 1998.

S. Boykin, A. Merlino, Machine Learning of Event Segmentation for News on Demand. Communicarions of the ACM, February 2000, Vol.43, No. 2, pp. 35 - 41

NorDig I Digital Integrated Receiver Decoder Specification for use in cable, satellite and terrestial networks. Available at http://www.nordig.org

TiVo Experience. Available at http://www.tivo.com

What is ReplayTV? Available at http://www.replaytv.com

Television Systems; NICAM 728: Specification for transmission of two-channel digital sound with terrestial television systems B, G, H, I and L. European Telecommunication Standard ETS 300 163 November 1994. European Telecommunications Standards Institute Sophia Antipolis Valbonne France. Available at http://www.etsi.org

D. Hambrick, Environmental Scanning and Organizational Strategy, Strategic Management Journal, 1982, vol 3, pp. 159-174.

B, Boyd, Perceived Uncertainty and Environmental Scanning: A Structural Model, Ph.D. Dissertation, University of Southern California, 1989.

C. Choo, Environmental Scanning: Acquisition and Use of Information by Chief Executive Officers in the Canadian Telecommunications Industry, Ph.D. dissertation, University of Toronto, 1993.

R. Daft, J. Sormunen & D. Parks, Chief Executive Scanning, Environmental Characteristicsm and Company Performance: an empirical study. Strategic Management Journal, 1988, vol 9. pp.123-139.

J. Farh., R. Hoffman. & H. Hegarty, Assessing Environmental Scanning at the Subunit Level: a Multitrait-multimethod Analysis. Decision sciences, 1984, vol. 15, no.2, pp.197-220.

P. Kotler, Marketing management; Analysis, Planning, Implementation and Control, Prentice Hall, New Jersey, 2000.

M. Porter, How competitive forces shape strategy. In H. Minzberg & J. Quinn (eds.), The strategy process. Concepts, Context, Cases, Prentice Hall, New Jersey, 1996, pp. 75-82.

R. Freeman, Strategic management: a stakeholder approach, Pitman, Marsfield, 1984

Louth Video Disk Communications Protocol. June 1999, http://www.louth.com

Electronic Publishing '01 –
2001 in the Digital Publishing Odyssey
A. Hübler et al. (Eds.)
IOS Press, 2001

Navigating a corpus of journal papers using Handles

Christopher Chapman & David F. Brailsford
Electronic Publishing Research Group
School of Computer Science and IT
University of Nottingham
NOTTINGHAM NG8 1BB
UK

ABSTRACT

For some years now the Internet and World Wide Web communities have envisaged moving to a 'next generation' of Web technologies by promoting a globally unique, and persistent, identifier for identifying and locating many forms of 'published objects'. These identifiers are called Universal Resource Names (URNs) and they hold out the prospect of being able to refer to an object by *what* it is (signified by its URN), rather than by *where* it is (the current URL technology). One early implementation of URN ideas is the Unicode-based Handle technology, developed at CNRI in Reston Virginia. The Digital Object Identifier (DOI) is a specific URN naming convention proposed just over 5 years ago and is now administered by the International DOI organisation, founded by a consortium of publishers and based in Washington DC. The DOI is being promoted for managing electronic content and for intellectual rights management of it, either using the published work itself, or, increasingly via *metadata* descriptors for the work in question.

This paper describes the use of the CNRI handle parser to navigate a corpus of papers for the *Electronic Publishing* journal. These papers are in PDF format and based on our server in Nottingham. For each paper in the corpus a metadata descriptor is prepared for every citation appearing in the *References* section. The important factor is that the underlying handle is resolved locally in the first instance. In some cases (e.g. cross-citations within the corpus itself and links to known resources elsewhere) the handle can be handed over to CNRI for further resolution.

This work shows the encouraging prospect of being able to use persistent URNs not only for intellectual property negotiations but also for search and discovery. In the test domain of this experiment every single resource, referred to within a given paper, can be resolved, at least to the level of metadata about the referred object. If the Web were to become more fully URN aware then a vast directed graph of linked resources could be accessed, via persistent names. Moreover, if these names delivered embedded metadata when resolved, the way would be open for a new generation of vastly more accurate and intelligent Web search engines.

0. INTRODUCTION

One of the most striking recent developments in electronic data interchange has been the specification of XML [1, 2] as an 'enabling metasyntax' and its subsequent enthusiastic adoption on the World Wide Web and elsewhere. XML is rapidly transforming every aspect of the way digital documents are internally structured and how they are externally accessed via hyperlinks.

Metadata (i.e. 'data about data') for 'publications'—in the widest sense—has been collected, somewhat haphazardly, by commercial and academic publishers for many years.

A secondary publishing industry has developed via companies such as ISI, Science Citation Indexes and BioMedNet based on creating and selling metadata for scientific papers (e.g. metadata items such as Title, Author, Date, Abstract, Keywords etc.). Given that metadata is usually well structured, human-readable and plain text in nature, it is natural to want to use XML to represent it.

The World Wide Web Consortium (W3C) answered calls for an XML metadata framework by creating the Resource Description Framework, usually known by its abbreviation of RDF. Using RDF, complex and structured metadata can be specified in XML syntax. RDF is capable of representing a directed graph of properties and relationships but the underlying XML syntax ensures that the basic ability to parse RDF is already present in the latest generation of XML-based software.

The next section examines how the linking of a URN to metadata about a digital object – as a staging point before a possible linking to the object itself – can confer great benefits in searching for, and acquiring, information on the Web.

1. PERSISTENT IDENTIFIERS AND METADATA

An area of Internet and Web development that has received much attention is that of URNs (Universal Resource Names) or 'persistent identifiers'. Like the familiar URL, a URN is a member of a wider set known as Universal Resource Identifiers (URIs) [3]. But while URLs refer to a file's physical location, URNs are intended to be independent of such details.

The URN paradigm is to call objects by a unique name. The name chosen need not be inherently meaningful, but there are obvious advantages if this is the case. The additional requirement is that URN identifiers shall be global and persistent – they will, essentially, never expire. URNs can also utilise existing naming schemes, such as ISBN, simplifying the transition of legacy systems to the new technology.

The subject of URNs is still surrounded by considerable, and often heated, debate. Much of this discussion centres on the scalability of URN implementations, given that the extra burden on the Domain Name Service (DNS), and ultimately on hardware such as routers, will be considerable if a future DNS has to query servers with a URN to find a 'nearby' instance of an object rather than following a step-by-step resolution of a URL to a specific server. Controversy rages also on what the permitted subset of characters should be that can be used by a URN. The handle implementation of a URN, used in this paper, allows the full Unicode character set to be used but it has been argued [4] that exotic characters chosen from tens of thousands of possibilities are not a good foundation for maintainable and persistent identifiers; the restricted 7-bit ASCII subset would, perhaps, be a much more stable basis. Ultimately these discussions will produce results that have far-reaching implications for future URN development but for the purposes of our investigations we wanted a persistent identifier system that was sufficiently well developed to use in a real application, but with sufficient flexibility that the principles of our research could be easily transferred to any future URN system.

The Handle system, developed at the Corporation for National Research Initiatives (CNRI) in Reston, Virginia, is one such system [5]. It is described as a global, distributed name resolution system. A handle is a persistent, global identifier, and looks something like:

```
hdl:1034/example-handle
```

Note that `hdl:` is the name of the protocol, not part of the handle itself. It is analogous to the `http:` part of a URL. The `1034` is the handle code that has been assigned to Nottingham, and is unique to our institution.

The remainder of the identifier is the name of the particular handle in our namespace. Since we are a handle naming authority (number 1034), we have full control over this namespace, and the handles we create within it. This means we can create our own naming scheme, or migrate from an existing scheme, for our part of 'handle space'.

In some ways, similarly to the DNS, the Handle system resolves the name of a handle (the address) to data. Unlike DNS, however, which resolves to a single IP address, a handle resolves to an arbitrary series of name/value pairs. These data can be considered the *contents* of the handle itself.

Any type of data can be stored within a handle, including metadata. The advantages are clear – using DNS, a single identifier (a URL) would be resolved to a single file somewhere on a server. Using handles, we can resolve a handle identifier to one or more files (or even multiple copies of the same file on different servers), to administrative information, and also to document metadata. Because the metadata is stored *as a part of the handle itself*, it can be accessed separately from the document. Indeed, a handle can be created for a document that does not exist in electronic form. The handle for such a document would probably not contain any URLs, since there is no electronic document to redirect to, but the metadata could still be present – and this has value in itself.

Thanks to the software and libraries developed at CNRI, the Handle system is sufficiently mature to use in applications. At Nottingham we run a handle server, written in Java by CNRI and freely downloadable from their website. This server deals with any queries from our locally administered handle space, by returning the data associated with a handle to the user who made the query. Our server is also part of the global Handle network, so if it receives a request to resolve a handle administered by some other naming authority, it can potentially hand off the request to an appropriate server somewhere else in the world.

At Nottingham we are creating handles for each document in our test corpus – the EP-odd archive (see section 3). We are also, as part of our test domain, creating handles for all documents referenced from within papers that are part of the corpus – papers from other publications, for example, that are referred to in the *References* sections of the papers we host. In most cases these handles will resolve to a metadata descriptor for the referenced item, but in the case of intra-corpus references i.e. a reference to another paper in the EP-odd archive, it is possible to resolve the handle further and to deliver the document itself.

In a future where most items on the Web possess a URN the preparation of such descriptors would not be necessary – the publisher of the item, be it an individual or a publishing company, would already be maintaining URNs for their resources and ensuring that, at the very minimum, they resolve to correct metadata. Clearly, this is an area that will need careful attention. Standard measures will need to be specified (probably using digital signatures and public key encryption) for validating URNs and their implicit metadata. Only in this way will it be possible to have multiple instances of a URN around the Web and to know that each one is a faithful replica of the original that is guaranteed to be maintained in perpetuity by the owner of the item being referred to. The DOI initiative [6] uses handles for its URNs and in addition to promoting the DOI for e-commerce and rights trading in digital documents is also emphasising to publishers their responsibilities in maintaining the persistence of the DOIs they issue and the integrity of the metadata associated with them.

1.1 Dublin Core metadata and RDF

The Dublin Core metadata schema [7], developed from a series of workshops beginning in Dublin, Ohio in 1995, is a set of 15 common metadata elements which, for the most part, can be applied to any object – and not just digital objects. The element set has proved to be useful in many applications – ranging from medicine and libraries (both traditional and digital) to museums. Dublin Core is probably the most widely used metadata schema today.

We chose it for our metadata research because of its simplicity and popularity, but our research is not particular to any one schema – to a large extent, the precise nature of the metadata we are dealing with is irrelevant to the project.

One of the W3C's principal contributions to the metadata field is RDF, which is now a W3C Recommendation for the representation and serialisation of structured metadata in XML format [8]. RDF provides a framework for the representation of any metadata from any schema, to very high levels of complexity and is a cornerstone of the W3C's Semantic Web activities [9].

The RDF model is that of a directed graph with 'objects' as the nodes. Objects in this context can be documents, chapters, organisations, authors or indeed anything that has properties or relations to other objects. The eventual aim is that every concept on the planet can be linked, through relations like these, into one huge, vastly interconnected, graph. It is debatable when, if ever, this will be achieved but RDF is intended to be the framework for this mammoth task.

RDF can, initially, be very daunting and as the complexity of relationships within a given schema increases so also does its readability decline very quickly. However, simple applications, such as the use of RDF to store Dublin Core metadata are far more manageable. We are using RDF for precisely this purpose and thus leaving much of the expressive power of RDF untapped — linking *all* of the resources within a document corpus, with RDF, would be the basis of a much larger project.

2. THE EP-odd ARCHIVE

The Electronic Publishing research group at Nottingham hosts a corpus of documents in PDF format, comprising almost 200 papers from the journal *Electronic Publishing — Origination, Dissemination and Design* (EP-odd). These papers were originally published by John Wiley & Sons Ltd. in the period 1988–1995, and the internally hyperlinked PDF files were the result of the CAJUN project undertaken at Nottingham in 1993 [10]. The PDF files are stored locally, and are also accessible on the Web through the EPRG's website [11].

The EP-odd archive, aside from its value as a public resource, is used within our research group as a test domain for new projects. In 1999, we set out to define descriptive document metadata for every paper in the corpus, allowing the collection to be more easily searched and browsed. Our starting point was a set of metadata for EP-odd that had already been compiled: Nelson Beebe's bibliographies website at the University of Utah [12] contains metadata for a large number of computing journals and publications, including metadata that has been compiled for eight years of EP-odd. This metadata is in BibTeX format and one of our first tasks was to map it to Dublin Core (DC) metadata.

A mapping between the BibTeX and DC schemas was generated by comparing the descriptions of each element in both schemas and matching them as closely as possible. A Perl script performed the conversion of the metadata from one schema to the other, taking the BibTeX as input and producing a set of DC RDF files, one per document, as output.

These RDF files were given the same filenames as the PDF files they each represented, but with an additional `.rdf` suffix.

The mapping of BibTeX to DC was not one-to-one. Some of the DC elements had to be filled with generic data (which was usually common across the whole corpus – the Publisher field did not vary, for example), but the mapping was close enough to produce meaningful DC metadata. The end result was a set of simple RDF XML files, each containing descriptive metadata fields for a single PDF file.

These RDF metadata descriptors then formed the basis of a Web search interface to the EP-odd archive. The system was written as a number of Perl/CGI scripts that accessed the RDF files directly. The result is a Web search engine that enables the EP-odd archive to be searched by fields such as title (`DC:Title`) and author (`DC:Creator`), and which displays the metadata (formatted for Web viewing) when the user clicks on a search result in the list. The metadata descriptor pages do, of course, contain a link to the PDF document itself. This system has proved to be a robust and fast interface to the EP-odd archive, and it is publicly accessible at `http://www.cs.nott.ac.uk/~clc/epodd.html`.

Having completed this proof of concept, our focus shifted to the references in the PDFs themselves. Could we hyperlink these so that if users click on a reference in the Acrobat document window, they see metadata for the referenced paper, with the option of getting the whole paper? Many of the references found in the EP-odd archive were to papers from other publications. For these, we often had no electronic copies of the papers, nor did we have any metadata, so we created this metadata manually. Research into metadata inference, for example, pulling out certain fields of metadata from the reference text itself, is continuing, and touches upon important questions such as 'how do we know with confidence that two apparently similar references, in different PDF documents, really do refer to the same target document?'

Our current work is centred on hyperlinking all cited reference within these PDFs by creating handles for every document referred to in the corpus, and assigning metadata to each one. We are developing Acrobat plugins to allow for resolution, in a variety of ways, for the embedded handle links in PDF files. We are also building on the work of the Open Journal Framework project (1995-1998) [13] to achieve the superimposition of hyperlinks into PDF documents where they do not already exist. The situation is complicated by the fact that some of the references already contain absolute links to other papers, which we need either to preserve in some fashion, or to remove entirely.

3. FUTURE PROSPECTS USING XAP

A recent development has opened up exciting new possibilities for metadata within PDF documents. We are referring to XAP, Adobe's metadata initiative, which was unveiled with the release of Acrobat 5.0 in April 2001.

XAP (eXtensible Authoring and Publishing) is a framework that allows document authors to add structured metadata directly into a PDF file. XAP was conceived for both the storage of application-specific and general descriptive metadata; its framework is almost a full implementation of the W3C's RDF specification and allows for the embedding of RDF metadata inside PDF documents.

A block of XAP metadata can be assigned to a whole document, and also to individual document components (images, font dictionaries, or any other PDF object). These metadata objects can be stored as uncompressed, unencrypted XML text streams within the file. This, in turn, greatly eases the burden of developing standalone tools to access XAP metadata inside a PDF, because, at least at the level of descriptive metadata for the whole document, it is not necessary to parse the PDF contents in detail – a simple text search for embedded RDF metadata in XML syntax will suffice.

Adding XAP metadata to every document in the EP-odd archive was a natural progression of our continuing work. Since we already have RDF metadata available for every document in the corpus, the task is to insert this data into the PDF files. To this end we are developing a small program which uses the Acrobat System Development Kit (SDK).

The newfound ability to store structured metadata inside a PDF in a standardised way is an exciting one, and will undoubtedly spawn a host of tools and applications that take advantage of it. At least one major search engine already includes normal PDF files in its indexes – it will be interesting to see how soon search engines look for XAP metadata in PDF files given that the process of extracting XAP metadata is much simpler than that of extracting page text from the PDF document.

But the new ability to store this metadata inside a PDF document raises an important issue. Storing document metadata within the document itself (as XAP does) is logical. The metadata *belongs* to the document, and should ideally be as close to it as possible. Users should be able to view the metadata easily, and if they are able to edit the document the metadata should be available in the editing process – in other words the metadata should be *internalised*, and should be a basic part of the document itself.

But we mentioned earlier the need to access metadata without forcing the user into retrieving the whole document file, since the full document may not be what the user wants. Barring complicated server-side solutions where the metadata (and only the metadata) is extracted from the PDF file, and delivered to the user every time it is requested, this means keeping an *external* copy of the metadata. Indeed, when we consider documents that we want to read the metadata for, but which are not available in an electronic form or have distribution restrictions, *externalised* metadata is the only way to make the metadata publicly available.

The issue of metadata duplication is one that raises considerable academic debate, with all sides advancing compelling arguments. How many different copies of metadata should exist for a single object? How are multiple copies to be kept synchronised, and what happens if that synchronisation breaks?

Working on the principle that convenience to the end user is the most important factor, we decided upon an approach of storing the Dublin Core metadata both internally, within the PDFs, *and* externally, as values in the associated handles. This decision raises difficult questions of consistency and synchronisation, and these questions will be a keynote of our future research.

4. CONCLUSIONS

Our system, as developed so far, shows on a small scale the immense possibilities for discovery of resources once one can 'link everything to everything', as originally envisaged in the Microcosm project [14] and now re-visited in the idea of the Semantic Web [9]. But, having found a resource, it may not be free to download, and one of the obvious applications for URNs and document metadata is precisely in the area of e-commerce. Indeed, the whole thrust of the DOI initiative is towards e-commerce and Rights management rather than search and discovery [6].

Another avenue for further study is opened up by the possibility of storing component XAP metadata inside a graphically rich format such as PDF. This opens up new possibilities for e-commerce: instead of licensing a whole document for reuse, a customer might be able to purchase the rights to play a movie clip or to reprint just a single image or table.

However, if metadata is to be used to carry out transactions in digital property, this raises the question of trust. How does the user know that the metadata is correct? What is to stop a competitor releasing false metadata records, linked to a URN of some sort, in order to damage an organisation's business or reputation? The need for robust digital signatures, scalable URN implementations and comprehensive 'anti-spoofing' measures are just a few of the many technical issues to be resolved before the next generation of Web technologies can become commonplace.

5. REFERENCES

[1] Tim Bray, "Beyond HTML: XML and Automated Web Processing", *View Source* online magazine (September 1997).
http://developer.netscape.com/viewsource/bray_xml.html
[2] Jon Bosak and Tim Bray, "XML and the Second-Generation Web", *Scientific American* **280**, 5, pp. 89–93. (May 1999)
[3] T. Berners-Lee, "Universal Resource Identifiers in WWW: A unifying syntax for the expression of names and addresses of objects on the network as used in the World Wide Web", *World Wide Web Journal* 1, 2 (1996), pp 3–19. See also
http://www.faqs.org/rfcs/rfc1630.html (June 1994).
[4] J. Kunze, "The ARK Persistent Identifier Scheme", Internet Draft
http://www.ckm.ucsf.edu/people/jak/home/ark-01.txt (March 2001)
[5] Sam X. Sun and Larry Lannom, "Handle System Overview",
http://www.handle.net/overview-current.html (August 2000).
[6] "DOI System Overview", http://dx.doi.org/10.1000/203 (2001)
[7] For the latest version of the Dublin Core Schema see
http://www.dublincore.org/documents/dces/ (1999)
[8] Ora Lassila, "Introduction to RDF Metadata",
http://www.w3.org/TR/NOTE-rdf-simple-intro (1997)
See also http://www.w3.org/RDF/FAQ (March 2001) and
http://www.w3.org/TR/REC-rdf-syntax (February 1999)
[9] Tim Berners-Lee, James Hendler and Ora Lassila, "The Semantic Web", *Scientific American* **284**, 5 pp. 34–43 (May 2001). See also
http://www.scientificamerican.com/2001/0501issue/0501berners-lee.html
[10] Philip N. Smith, David F. Brailsford, David R. Evans, Leon Harrison, Steve G. Probets and Peter E. Sutton, "Journal Publishing with Acrobat: the CAJUN project",
Electronic Publishing—Origination, Dissemination and Design **6** (4), 481–493
(December 1993)
[11] See http://cajun.cs.nott.ac.uk/compsci/epo/papers/epoddtoc.html
for the original EP-odd archive and http://www.cs.nott.ac.uk/~clc/epodd.html
for the DC search engine.
[12] Nelson Beebe's bibliographic archives can be found at:
http://www.math.utah.edu/~beebe/bibliographies.html
with a direct link to the EP-odd metadata at:
http://www.math.utah.edu/pub/tex/bib/epodd.html
[13] David F. Brailsford, Steve G. Probets, Les Carr and Wendy Hall, 'Dynamic Link Inclusion in Online PDF Journals', *Proceedings 7th International Conference on Electronic Publishing (EP98)* pp.550–562. (Springer Verlag 1998)
[14] S. Hitchcock, F. Quek, L. Carr, W. Hall, A. Witbrock and I. Tarr, 'Linking Everything to Everything: Journal Publishing Myth or Reality?' *ICCC/IFIP conference on Electronic Publishing 97: New Models and Opportunities*. (1997)

Electronic Publishing '01 –
2001 in the Digital Publishing Odyssey
A. Hübler et al. (Eds.)
IOS Press, 2001

CABRef: Cross-Referencing into an Abstracts Database

Ann Apps and Ross MacIntyre
MIMAS, University of Manchester,
Oxford Road, Manchester, M13 9PL, UK
Email: ann.apps@man.ac.uk, ross.macintyre@man.ac.uk

Abstract: This paper describes a prototype system, CABRef, which provides seamless linking from a citation in the bibliography of an electronic journal article to a detailed abstract of the cited work, within a particular research domain. Publishers of journal articles will query CABRef to determine the URL links to embed in their article bibliographies which enable end-user cross-reference navigation. The abstracts within CABRef, and their discovery metadata, are encoded in XML and processed with XML-aware software. The CABRef XML abstracts database is updated using data exported from the CABI abstracts production database on a regular basis when abstracts are 'published', involving a simple extra step in the CABI abstracts production process.
Keywords: abstract, cross-reference, linking, Dublin Core, XML

0. Introduction

CABI *Publishing* [1] create and publish a comprehensive, bibliographic database, including high-quality abstracts, which covers the world-wide published research literature in all aspects of applied life science, including agriculture, forestry, veterinary science and human health and disease. Electronic access to these CABI abstracts and associated material is normally available on a subscription basis or pay-per-view via online hosts.

During recent years, CABI *Publishing* has funded MIMAS [2] at the University of Manchester to perform a programme of electronic publishing research and development. The programme's principal themes were SGML/XML production and linking technologies, with the emphasis on practical implementation rather than theory. The CABRef prototype system, described in this paper, was developed during this collaboration and allows free access to a single abstract for an end-user. Typically this will be via a link from a reference in a journal article, the system being enabled by Web links, incorporating appropriate CABRef identifiers, embedded into the Web display of that article by its publisher. The initial version of CABRef provides access to abstracts of journal articles, which constitute 85% of the records in the CABI abstracts database, but it is possible that later versions of CABRef would include other genres such as conference papers or books.

1. Overview

Research into journal article cross-referencing [3] indicates that there are three major components for constructing systems to support reference linking. Firstly, persistent, unique identifiers are needed for the target resources. Secondly, a 'look up' mechanism will be employed to discover the identifier of a resource from a citation. And thirdly, a mechanism is required to deliver a particular, identified item to an end-user. The CABRef identifier is a unique identifier for each CABI abstract. The CABRef system consists of two parts: CABRef *Look Up* is provided for publishers to determine the CABRef identifiers of references in their journal articles using basic citation information; CABRef *Abstract Display* provides a Web display of the CABI abstract of a cited work.

A cross-referencing paradigm could be seen as 'discover – locate – request – deliver'. In CABRef, 'discover' is performed by a publisher ascertaining a CABRef identifier for a citation using CABRef Look Up. CABRef abstracts are currently available in only one database, so 'locate' simply involves the embedding of the CABRef URL, along with the discovered identifier, into a journal article reference. The end-user 'requests' the abstract when activating this link, causing 'delivery' of the abstract by CABRef Abstract Display.

2. CABRef Look Up

CABRef Look Up returns the CABRef identifiers for a list of citations supplied in a prescribed text string format, via a Web page. Look up is performed on an XML [4] *Match File*, which is created and updated from information exported from the CABI abstracts database.

2.1 CABRef Query

In general, publishers will request CABRef identifiers for a list of citations via a batch interface. In the initial prototype this is a Web page interface into, and from, which a publisher can 'cut-and-paste' a list of citation queries and replies. It is hoped to provide an email batch citation query service in the future, and a demonstration version of this has been produced.

Each citation query is a list of fields, separated by '|' and terminated by '|#'. The list of citation queries is returned to the publisher with their CABRef identifiers, and possibly comments, appended. For a journal article this query string is:

J|*JournalTitle*|*Year*|*Volume*|*Page*|*Author*|*PublisherRef*|**#**

where: *JournalTitle* is the full journal title; *Year* is the publication year; *Volume* is the journal volume number; *Page* is the start page of the article; *Author* is the first author in plain text as 'FamilyName Initials', and is optional; and *PublisherRef* is the publisher's own reference identifier for this citation. The returned query is:

J|*JournalTitle*|*Year*|*Volume*|*Page*|*Author*|*PublisherRef*|*CabRefId*|*CabRefComment*|**#**

where: *CabRefId* is the CABRef identifier of the citation or 'NotFound'; and *CabRefComment* is a possible diagnostic comment, for example 'UnmatchedAuthor' when the remainder of the citation query indicates a valid bibliographic reference except for the first author's name.

For the CABRef prototype, journal title abbreviations, for which there is no single standard, are not supported. Supplying the ISSN instead of the journal title is also not available, because ISSNs do not generally appear in journal article bibliographies. A wildcard or truncation character is not provided in CABRef queries, it not being the intention to provide a general search interface into CABI abstracts.

Example citation queries sent to CABRef may be:

```
CITATIONS
J|Telopea|1999|8|297|Mabberley DJ|MR020|#
J|Journal of Bacteriology|1999|181|3193|Wilck A|MR021|#
J|Journal of Great Lakes Research|1998|24|343|Dawson VK|MR022|#
J|Hayvancilik Arastirma Dergisi|1998|8|52|Kurtoglu F|MR023|#
J|Gartenbauwissenschaft|1999|64|97|Krug H|MR024|#
J|Gene|1998|225|67|Zeiss CJ|MR025|#
J|Journal of Park and Recreation Administration|1999|17|65|Norris PA|MR026|#
```

CABRef would return the following, where CABRef identifiers are in the penultimate field of each citation query reply:

```
CABRef CITATIONS
J|Telopea|1999|8|297|Mabberley DJ|MR020|19990310140||#
J|Journal of Bacteriology|1999|181|3193|Wilck A|MR021|19991109241|UnmatchedAuthor|#
J|Journal of Great Lakes Research|1998|24|343|Dawson VK|MR022|19990505783||#
J|Hayvancilik Arastirma Dergisi|1998|8|52|Kurtoglu F|MR023|19991412031||#
J|Gartenbauwissenschaft|1999|64|97|Krug H|MR024|19990310186||#
J|Gene|1998|225|67|Zeiss CJ|MR025|19990107152||#
J|Journal of Park and Recreation Administration|1999|17|65|Norris PA|MR026|19991809359||#
```

In order to assist publishers in resolving individual citations, a single citation query Web form is provided. Details of a citation can be entered into the appropriate fields of this form, and CABRef will return the identifier for the citation. Information about the format of a citation query may be obtained by sending 'Help' to the CABRef batch interface.

The CABRef citation query interface is based on the PubMed [5] 'Citation Matcher' model, which provides an email and a web batch interface for determining identifiers. CrossRef [6] uses a similar format for Digital Object Identifier (DOI) look up queries [7]. When designing the CABRef query format, this model was enhanced to include: a leading field indicating the genre of the abstracted resource ('J' for a journal article), thus allowing for later extension to other document types; a field for a returned diagnostic comment in addition to the identifier; and a terminating character ('|#') to obviate problems caused by newline characters, which are sometimes inadvertently introduced by intermediate software.

Possible alternative designs of CABRef queries could have utilised the 'object metadata zone' of the emerging OpenURL [8] standard, or defined an XML interchange format. An example, hypothetical CABRef citation query reply encoded as a partial OpenURL [9] might be (without the line breaks):

```
sid=CABI:CABRef&genre=article
&title=Gene&date=1998&volume=225&spage=67&aulast=Zeiss&auinit=CJ
&pid=<pubref>abc1234</pubref>
&<cabrefid>19990107152</cabrefid>&<comment></comment>
```

Encoding the same citation query reply in XML could be:

```
<cabrefQuery>
<genre>journal article</genre>
<journalTitle>Gene</journalTitle>
<year>1998</year>
<journalVolume>225<journalVolume>
<startPage>67</startPage>
<firstAuthor><snm>Zeiss</snm><inits>CJ</inits></firstAuthor>
<pubref>abc1234</pubref>
<cabrefid>19990107152</cabrefid><comment></comment>
</cabrefQuery>
```

For the prototype version of CABRef it was decided to use the more concise '|' separated text string for citation queries. As the designers of the CrossRef query interface [10] found: "one unresolved issue in implementing an all-XML query interface is the lack of an industry-standard XML query language", although this situation may be remedied when the definition of XML Query [11] is complete.

2.2 The CABRef Match File

CABRef Look Up determines CABRef identifiers by matching citations submitted through the interface described above against XML records in the CABRef *Match File*. The Match File is a single XML file which holds a record for each abstract in the CABRef system, generated from data extracted from the CABI abstracts database. The fields within each record are only those required for citation matching against the citation query requests, rather than the full data record for an abstract. An example XML record in the Match File for an abstract is:

```
<cabcit>
<Identifier>19990107152</Identifier>
<Type>journal article</Type>
<JnlTitle>Gene</JnlTitle>
<JnlVolume>225</JnlVolume>
<JnlPage>67</JnlPage>
<Creator><snm>Zeiss</snm><inits>CJ</inits></Creator>
        <!— Publication Year -->
<Date Qualifier="Created" Scheme="W3CDTF">1998</Date>
        <!— CABRef load date -->
<Date Qualifier="Available" Scheme="W3CDTF">2001-04-01</Date>
</cabcit>
```

Because the purpose of the Match File is for 'look up' text matching, the contents of its contained XML elements are all plain text and do not contain any XML character entities or typesetting elements. Only journal article records are included in the Match File, although the source data extracted from the CABI abstracts database will contain information about other types of work such as books and conference papers.

Look Up is performed by an OmniMark [12] program which extracts the elements of the citation queries from the input string, and then searches for the citations in the Match File. The Match File is processed as an XML file by parsing it against its Document Type Definition (DTD).

The initial prototype version of CABRef will hold data from 1997 onwards. It is hoped that CABRef will include earlier data in the future. The Match File will be updated at regular intervals, possibly weekly, with newly published CABI abstracts. It is possible that for future versions of CABRef this simple Match File will be replaced by a database. Although the Look Up data is essentially of simple structure, mapping to a single table in a relational database, holding it in a database may improve the performance of CABRef Look Up.

3. CABRef Abstract Display

It is expected that a publisher of a journal article will ascertain the CABRef identifiers corresponding to the references in the bibliography section of the article using CABRef Look Up described above. The publisher will then embed a CABRef display URL, appended by the appropriate CABRef identifier, alongside a reference in the HTML of the Web version of the article, to provide a link for an end-user to follow. The process used by a publisher for finding CABRef identifiers and embedding links from the references would be similar to that already used for including links to PubMed. When an end user follows one of these CABRef links the corresponding CABI abstract is displayed

3.1 CABRef Abstract XML Files

The CABI abstracts available within CABRef are held as XML files, which are created and updated at the same time as the Match File, using data extracted from the CABI abstracts database. Display of an XML abstract is by an ‘on-the-fly’ conversion to HTML using an OmniMark program.

An example CABRef abstract in XML is:


```
<crab>
<dc:title>TIMP-1 expression is increased in X-linked progressive retinal atrophy despite its
exclusion as a candidate gene.</dc:title>
<dc:creator><cr:snm>Zeiss</cr:snm><cr:inits>C. J.</cr:inits></dc:creator>
<dc:creator><cr:snm>Acland</cr:snm><cr:inits>G. M.</cr:inits></dc:creator>
<dc:creator><cr:snm>Aguirre</cr:snm><cr:inits>G. D.</cr:inits></dc:creator>
<dc:creator><cr:snm>Kunal</cr:snm><cr:inits>R.</cr:inits></dc:creator>
<dc:creator><cr:aff>James A. Baker Institute for Animal Health, College of Veterinary Medicine,
Cornell University, Ithaca, NY 14853-6401, USA.</cr:aff></dc:creator>
<dc:subject Scheme=“CABRef”>UU600</dc:subject>
<dc:subject Scheme=“CABRef”>LL070</dc:subject>
<dc:description>X-linked progressive retinal atrophy (XLPRA) of dogs is an animal model
for...</dc:description>
        <!— Publication Year -->
<dc:date Qualifier=“Created” Scheme=“W3CDTF”>1998</dc:date>
        <!— CABRef load date -->
<dc:date Qualifier=“Available” Scheme=“W3CDTF”>2001-04-01</dc:date>
<dc:type Scheme=“CABRef”>Journal article</dc:type>
<dc:identifier Scheme=“CABRef”>19990107152</dc:identifier>
<dc:identifier Scheme=“CRCite”>
        <cr:JnlTitle>Gene</cr:JnlTitle>
        <cr:JnlVolume>225</cr:JnlVolume>
        <cr:JnlIssue>1/2</cr:JnlIssue>
        <cr:JnlPages><cr:ppf>67</cr:ppf><cr:ppl>75</cr:ppl></cr:JnlPages>
</dc:identifier>
<dc:language>En</dc:language>
<dc:relation Qualifier=“IsPartOf” Scheme=“ISSN”>0378-1119</dc:relation>
</crab>
```

The fields of the abstract are described within the XML files using Qualified Dublin Core [13] elements (in a *dc* namespace) where applicable, with extensions within a CABRef (*cr*) namespace. The *dc:subject* fields contain CABI subject categories, which are not used or displayed by CABRef at present, but may have future uses when adding functionality such as 'more like this'. The *dc:language* field gives the language of the corresponding article, according to a CABI coding scheme but translated into the language's name for display, rather than the language of the abstract which is generally in English. Other fields in the XML record for a CABRef abstract which are not displayed are: *dc:type* which is always 'Journal article' in the CABRef prototype; and the 'Available' *dc:date* which is the date when the abstract was added to CABRef and for internal use only. Within the XML DTD, a further *Scheme* 'DOI' is allowed for *dc:identifier*, which would allow for the future addition of a Digital Object Identifier (DOI) of the abstracted article. CABI abstracts contain more data fields than are captured in a CABRef abstract, such as species and geographic descriptors, but it was decided to restrict the fields displayed through the free CABRef interface.

3.2 Display of an Abstract

The above example XML abstract would be displayed to the end user as:

CABRef Abstract 19990107152

TIMP-1 expression is increased in X-linked progressive retinal atrophy despite its exclusion as a candidate gene.

Author(s): C. J. Zeiss, G. M. Acland, G. D. Aguirre, R. Kunal
James A. Baker Institute for Animal Health, College of Veterinary Medicine, Cornell University, Ithaca, NY 14853-6401, USA.

Journal: Gene
ISSN: 0378-1119
Volume 225 Issue 1/2, 1998, pp 67-75

Abstract:

X-linked progressive retinal atrophy (XLPRA) of dogs is an animal model for ....

Language: English

3.3 Dublin Core for Journal Article Metadata

Using Dublin Core elements to capture the abstract is not strictly necessary because these XML elements are used only within the CABRef system. The main purpose of Dublin Core metadata is for simple resource discovery and for interoperability. However it seems reasonable to use a standard encoding scheme and to follow best practice rather than inventing a specific CABRef one. If, in the future, there is a requirement to make CABRef interoperable with some other system the task of transforming the metadata elements to standard ones will be simplified.

Using Dublin Core to capture journal article metadata does present some problems, particularly in capturing author details and citation information, hence the addition of application specific elements within a CABRef namespace. In addition, some elements have application-specific *CABRef* schemes which are not strictly Qualified Dublin Core.

Dublin Core does not currently allow for a means of capturing the separate elements of an author's name. Thus CABRef includes sub-elements of *dc:creator* to capture the family name (*cr:snm*), the initials (*cr:inits*) and any suffix (*cr:extra*), or a corporate author (*cr:corpau*). It also includes a further sub-element, used in a separate instance of *dc:creator,* to hold the affiliation (*cr:aff*). CABI abstracts contain only one affiliation which means it is not necessary to link affiliations to authors within this application.

Within the Dublin Core community discussion is on-going to define a recommended way of capturing the citation information for a journal article, i.e. its containing journal, volume, and issue and its page range within that journal volume. A Dublin Core Citation Working Group recommended a best practice encoding scheme using either a structured string or XML sub-elements (a 'structured value') within the *dc:identifier* element. This recognises the fact that this set of citation information *identifies* the journal article. Although this 'dc:citation' encoding has not been endorsed by the Dublin Core Metadata Initiative it has been used in practice for capturing this information about journal articles [14]. The citation information encoding within CABRef largely follows this recommendation, albeit with slightly different sub-element labels within the CABRef (*CRCite*) namespace. The journal's ISSN is captured within a *dc:relation* element using an *isPartOf* qualifier. This reflects the fact that the ISSN is information about the containing journal rather than the article itself. In fact, all the citation information is about the containing journal volume and issue, except for the page range which is pertinent to the article itself. Some may argue that this information should not appear in the metadata record for the article itself, but should be pointed to from the article's metadata. However this approach does not seem viable within CABRef where all the information about an article's abstract is held in one record, with little knowledge of, or ability to access, information about the journal apart from its ISSN. The end-user will expect to see all the information from the abstract including its citation details within one web page.

4. CABRef System Architecture

An outline of the CABRef system architecture is shown in Figure 1.

Source abstract data records are exported from the CABI abstracts production database, for published abstracts, on a regular basis, in a tagged text format. These are converted into two sets of XML [4] records, one for the Match File and one for the CABRef abstracts database, which is a set of XML files. This translation is by an OmniMark program which verifies the resulting XML records by parsing them against the relevant DTDs. CABRef abstract XML files are organised within a file directory structure according to their CABRef identifiers.

When a publisher sends in batch citation queries, ascertained from references within journal articles, these are processed and returned by the Look Up program, another OmniMark program which searches the Match File to find the citation CABRef identifiers.

The publisher would use the returned CABRef identifiers to add Web links to journal article bibliographies. When an end-user clicks on one of these links, the Abstract Display program, also OmniMark, is called via the Web's Common Gateway Interface (CGI). This program processes the requested abstract's XML file by parsing it against its DTD and generating appropriate HTML which is returned to the end-user's Web browser.

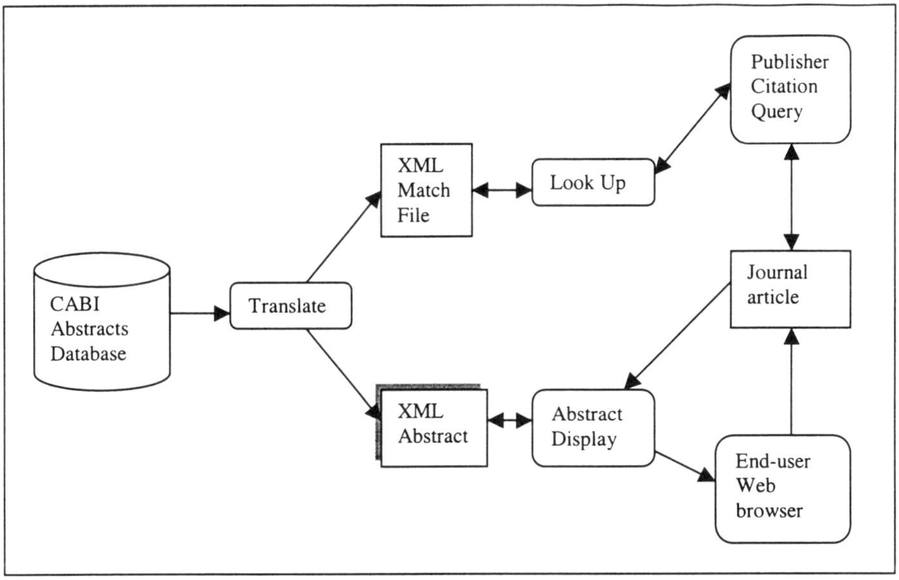

Figure 1. CABRef system architecture.

OmniMark [12] is an SGML/XML-aware 4th generation programming language which includes powerful pattern analysis and manipulation facilities. OmniMark was chosen as a software platform because, being XML-aware, it seemed appropriate for developing an XML application. The language includes Web CGI utilities which simplify the coding of the Web interface, is portable, and is available for most generally used platforms. At the beginning of the project OmniMark version 5.5 was freely available and was used for SGML-based journals production work within CABI, both of these influencing the choice.

CABRef is hosted on a Windows NT machine with an IIS Web server, but the code was initially developed on a Unix Solaris machine running an Apache web server. Porting the code required little intervention other than configuring the IIS web server to run OmniMark.

5. Future Development

CABRef is currently a prototype system and so has not been released for general use. It is hoped that several publishers within the applied life science domain will be encouraged to look up and include CABRef identifiers and links within the references of their electronic journal articles. It is intended that such links will be included within the primary full text journals published by CABI. Only when some of these links are in place can CABRef be developed and become generally used. But it will be essential that the CABRef abstract display URL remains persistent once it has been embedded into published articles.

The CABRef look up searching mechanism currently requires exact matching on the journal title, the volume number and the start page number. This primitive search algorithm has been built as a 'proof of concept'. A production version of CABRef will probably need the introduction of a database, rather than the simple XML Match File, to improve searching performance, although, because this is a batch operation, 'instant' response is not a requirement. It is also likely that some fuzzy matching algorithm will be necessary to improve the 'hit' success rate.

At present, CABRef provides links to abstracts of journal articles only, but it could be extended in the future to include other genres such as books and conference papers. CABRef could also be enhanced to provide associated information and 'more-like-this' abstracts to CABI subscribers, but free access is likely to be always to a single abstract.

Future development possibilities could be envisaged of linking on from the abstract to its corresponding full text, via initiatives such as CrossRef [6], SFX Context Sensitive Reference Linking [15], or other resolution services. For older works possibilities could be envisaged of linking to library OPACs or Inter Library Loan document delivery services. The CABRef Abstract XML DTD already allows for inclusion of the article's DOI and CrossRef provide a mechanism for ascertaining DOIs. Resolution services such as SFX which attempt to find the 'appropriate copy' of an article for an end-user make use of OpenURLs [16,8] to transport the article's metadata. The CABRef XML abstract contains all the metadata elements, based on Dublin Core, which would be needed in such an OpenURL [9], thus making its on-the-fly generation easily possible. Adding future functionality becomes viable because the CABRef instances of CABI abstracts are held as XML files which can be processed using XML software.

CABRef will provide free 'taster' access to high quality abstracts for researchers within the applied life science domain, adding value to the bibliographic references in a journal article. Thus CABRef is a step on the way to providing academic researchers with seamless, 'joined-up' cross-referencing within their subject domain.

6. Acknowledgements

The CABRef prototype was developed as part of a research project within MIMAS at the University of Manchester funded by CABI Publishing. The authors would like to thank Andrea Powell, Product Development Director, and members of the CABRef team, in particular Carol Steel, Fiona Maclean and Christopher Plummer, at CABI Publishing, for their contribution within the project.

7. Note about Authors

Ann Apps has been actively involved in the Dublin Core Citation Working Group and is a member of the recently formed NISO OpenURL committee. Ross MacIntyre is the MIMAS senior project manager for digital library and electronic publishing research and development.

8. References

1. CABI *Publishing*, the publishing division of CAB International. http://www.cabi.org
2. Electronic Publishing at MIMAS, a UK Higher and Further Education data centre. http://epub.mimas.ac.uk
3. Caplan, Priscilla and Arms, William Y. (1999) Reference Linking for Journal Articles. *D-Lib Magazine* **5**(7/8) (July/August 1999). doi://10.1045/july99-caplan
4. XML (eXtensible Markup Language). http://www.w3.org/XML
5. National Center for Biotechnology Information, National Library of Medicine, PubMed. http://www.ncbi.nlm.nih.gov/PubMed
6. CrossRef. http://www.crossref.org
7. CrossRef Query Specification. http://www.crossref.org/docs/CrossRef_query_spec.pdf
8. OpenURL Syntax Description. http://www.sfxit.com/OpenURL/openurl.html

9. Powell, Andy and Apps, Ann. (2001) Encoding OpenURLs in Dublin Core metadata. *Ariadne* **27** (March 2001). http://www.ariadne.ac.uk/issue27/metadata
10. Atkins, Helen; Lyons, Catherine; Ratner, Howard; Risher, Carol; Shillum Chris; Sidman, David and Stevens, Andrew. (2000) Reference Linking with DOIs. *D-Lib Magazine* **6**(2) (February 2000). doi://10.1045/february2000-risher
11. XML Query. http://www.w3.org/XML/Query
12. OmniMark Technologies Corporation. http://www.omnimark.com
13. Dublin Core Metadata. http://www.dublincore.org
14. Apps, Ann and MacIntyre, Ross. (2000) Dublin Core Metadata for Electronic Journals. *Proceedings of the 4th European Conference on Research and Advanced Technology for Digital Libraries (ECDL2000)*, Lisbon, Portugal, 18-20 September 2000. *Lecture Notes in Computer Science* (Springer-Verlag) **1923** pp 93-102.
15. SFX, Context Sensitive Reference Linking (Ex Libris). http://www.sfxit.com
16. Van de Sompel, Herbert and Beit-Arie, Oren. (2001) Open Linking in the Scholarly Information Environment Using the OpenURL Framework. *D-Lib Magazine* **7**(3) (March 2001). doi://10.1045/march2001-vandesompel

Electronic Publishing '01 –
2001 in the Digital Publishing Odyssey
A. Hübler et al. (Eds.)
IOS Press, 2001

The Role of the First Macedonian Internet portal "Macedonia Search" in Enhancing of the Development of Digital Communication and the Associated Problems

Zoran Gligorov[i]

Macedonia Search
http://www.org.mk,
http://www.macedonia.eu.org
gligorov@osi.net.mk

Abstract: One of the often-overlooked aspects of today's modern electronic information spread is that not all people speak English. Since the software applications are mainly made for areas where they sell best, smaller and poorer nations with a local language and alphabet are often ignored and forgotten by the software industry. The situation today is that the people who do not speak English and would like to use their own language are somewhat deprived and as a result - sometimes quite reluctant to start using electronic communication.

This paper concerns itself with the sources, consequences and means to solve this problem. The issue is discussed in regard to real-life example of situations with the use of the Macedonian language and a comparative analysis of the solutions applied. The examples concentrate on Internet publishing using the Macedonian language and its effects and popularity among the Macedonian-speaking individuals.

The paper provides an analysis of the current situation from which conclusions applicable to other cultures can be extracted.

"Welcome to our first global village. It is Macedonian because it is ours, and we are proud of it. It is global because it connects all of us, it brings us together to unity much more powerful than each of us. No matter what we are, or how much we have achieved in our lives, we are here together. To show our cultural heritage. To show what we know and what we have inherited from the past generations. However, we are here to learn too, to go forward and to leave much more for the generations to come. Still, we have to fill the gap left by the five hundred years slavery, humiliation and tyranny.

In this small village you will find a bit of everything and a lot of warmth. It is well categorized and, although the communism ended, it is self-governed. Don't abuse it. Look at the richness it has.

Don't leave quickly from our village. We are a hospitable nation. Have a chat with us or with those who have the same interests in the discussion groups. Even if you don't have much time, have a peek - they may brighten your day.

Even if you have a business to do, there is something for you. Send faxes, paging and SMS messages, or call the World. Yes, we want to see you happy whatever you do.

For our own good."

- Welcome words of Macedonia Search, www.org.mk

0. Introduction

About a year and a half ago, on 1 January 2000, the first Macedonian "Yahoo" was born. It was called, and still is called "**Macedonia Search**", a then small Internet portal developed in the very similar fashion as Yahoo – two student programmers and a vision. That was a vision for a better, brighter future. There was no commercial company, no registered non-profit organization, just two students: Zdravko Stafilov and Zoran Gligorov in a virtual company called "The Imperial Network".

Macedonia saw its first Internet portal more than half a decade after the World saw Yahoo. Why is Macedonia so late? Some may argue that this is due to the general latency of things in Macedonia. There are strong facts holding this theory. However, we don't believe that this is the main reason of the half-decade latency. That is why this paper is written; and that is why **Macedonia Search** believes the future is bright.

*"We, the team of **Macedonia Search**, believe that the Internet is the best chance for Macedonia. Chance for the common Macedonian citizen to overcome the barriers present in this region for so long. Maybe the biggest gain of Internet is the proven great influence in building an individual, democratic consciousness. Totalitarian forces, censorship and racial hate cannot stay for long. That is why we believe that exactly the Internet, if it becomes an everyday tool for every Macedonian citizen, will incredibly help solving the current, quite serious problems in the country. In the same time, Internet is a tremendous chance for our economy. Still, chances come and go and it is up to us to grab them and prosper, or leave behind crying and mourning."*

1. What are the main concerns of an electronic publisher?

1. Input of the information, so it can be processed (using keyboard, speech-recognition software or any other method).
2. The compatibility of the product – can their published material be accessible and will it look the same on every computer and on every platform?
3. Providing the right content to right visitors.
4. Payment methods – can the user easily purchase the information required?

The basic conditions of the situation are that the Macedonian language is not English and uses an alphabet different than English. This is not uncommon, there are between three and four thousand languages spoken in the world today. It has been said that living in the world and speaking only one language is somewhat equivalent to living in an enormous mansion and staying in only one room. Thus, the problems and solutions apply to other non-English languages, too.

1.2 Background information

Macedonian language uses its own version of the Cyrillic alphabet, which has few characters different from the other Cyrillic alphabets (Russian, Serbian, Bulgarian). It is spoken by 2 million people, mainly in Macedonia, the neighbouring countries, Australia, Canada and the USA.

English is taken as a referral point because the standards for computer use, the software applications and the hardware itself are mainly designed by persons who use English Latin alphabet and speak English as a first language. This may have changed a little in the last years, having software engineering in India, Asia and Eastern Europe. However, the biggest share of the electronic publishing market today is the Western world and America, and one of the reasons for it is that the electronic publishing products have no difficulty to reach its *target audience in its own language*.

Language is one of the foundations of the culture because it is a tool that people use for thinking, and the success of the electronic publishing in non-English countries/cultures depends on the obvious, but often overlooked fact that it has to be done in the local language.

Although the English language is the lingua franca of computer technology and more and more people learn it as a second language, an electronic publisher in a non-English country cannot afford to set as a target only those persons who know it – there are simply not enough of them. This situation is evident in most developing countries and the countries of Central and Eastern Europe, including the Republic of Macedonia. In order to purchase a product, especially an intellectually related one, the user must be comfortable about using it with ease. This can only be accomplished if the local language is used.

This set of circumstances puts the speakers of Macedonian in a difficult position to make full use of the new technology. The majority of the problems appear to be in the user-computer communication. That is, when the information is entered using a keyboard that is not designed for that alphabet and when the viewing software cannot show the appropriate characters.

The problem has been partially solved by the makers of the operating systems initially designed to communicate in English. Some of them evolved and became more international, by supporting other languages. Unfortunately, all vendors invented their character sets for encoding the non-English alphabets, so today there are quite a few "standards" for encoding the Cyrillic alphabet. Only one has gone through the normal process of standardization, which is ISO 8859-5. However, the most common computers in Macedonia are Intel based PCs with Microsoft Windows operating systems. Microsoft seems to like its own Cyrillic encoding standard more, so Windows-1251 is the most used and best-supported standard for encoding the Cyrillic alphabet.

Macedonia Search conducted series of compatibility tests to find the perfect standard for encoding of the Cyrillic alphabet. The tests were performed on Windows, Linux and other operating systems and were discussed in the Macedonian discussion boards. No perfect standard was found, but three standards were found to be acceptable: Windows 1251, ISO 8859-5 and Unicode. All popular browsers had no problems presenting pages in those standards. However, serious problems appeared while trying to enter information using some of the standards. Those using Internet Explorer could write in Windows 1251, but sometimes some of the characters encoded with ISO were damaged. Netscape Navigator and Netscape Messenger showed similar results.

Macedonia Search prefers Windows-1251 for encoding Cyrillic text on the Internet.

2. Providing content in Macedonian

Choosing the standard is only the first step toward localised electronic publishing. The standard is only a tool to store and retrieve content. But who is going to provide the content? Furthermore, can we provide the right content to satisfy the interests of our visitors?

Macedonia Search started with its own search engine. All Macedonian Internet sites were indexed automatically, using a web spider. Care was taken to support all encoding standards, but results were shown using Windows-1251 standard only. The search engine was used to search only sites based in Macedonia, sites in Macedonian and sites for and about Macedonians. Those who wanted to perform wider searching were passed to the well-known search engines like Google, Alta Vista, Infoseek, Yahoo, etc.

The need for having a web portal with categorized links to all local sites was obvious. Categorizing the web sites is a completely different experience than programming a web spider or a search engine. It has to be done by hand, and in the case of **Macedonia Search**, with very limited human resources (i.e. two student programmers), so it took a while. Fortunately, doing something that has already been invented is an easier task and lessons can be learned without running into the same trouble as Yahoo or other similar services.

As a growing Internet portal, **Macedonia Search** started providing common services like web search, categories, free e-mail, weather forecast and discussion groups. It was increasingly popular, too. However, there was very little interaction with the visitors – they came, they saw what they were looking for and they went on. There were a few reasons for this: Too little right content for visitors' interests and general lack of interest to communicate with others on local basis.

How can a visitor be attracted to spend more time on a (localised) web site? How can a visitor be attracted to contribute to a web site? Web statistics show that 86 per cent of the visitors of **Macedonia Search** are located in Macedonia. The rest come mainly from the United States and Australia. This is not a common type of visitors. Some fields of interest are fairly easy to foresee. For example, a person living in Macedonia would not be that interested to see the weather forecast in New York, or London, but would be interested to see the local weather forecast. The same is true with the cultural or entertainment events. By providing informational resources such as the local cinema schedule, news, local weather forecast, games and entertainment, the popularity of **Macedonia Search** was up to over 2000 visitors per day.

2.1 Background information

Macedonia, a country of 2 million citizens, has between 20000 and 30000 Internet user accounts. Up to 4 000 of them are users who spend more than an hour per day on Internet. These are unofficial estimates.

3. Right tools in the right hands

As stated above, the majority of the problems appear to be in the user-computer communication. The standards for computer use, the software applications and the hardware itself are mainly designed by persons who use English Latin alphabet and speak English as first language. We, in **Macedonia Search**, believe that providing the right tools in the right language and with the right design will set up an incredible boost of the electronic publishing in the developing countries. Statistics show that Macedonia, although a developing country, has a fairly good production of engineers every year. Unfortunately, many of them leave the country in search for better jobs. Well, lets see if two engineers can do the job.

The web offers an incredible power to outstrip distances. There are many Macedonian engineers, writers, designers etc. around the world. Just like in any other developing country, many of the best people usually emigrate to Western Europe and the USA. However, we believe we can make them do something good for their own motherland.

Macedonia Search has developed a system for document storage, classification and retrieval. It is called "Knowledge Base", a place on the World Wide Web where all kinds of documents in Macedonian are stored. The interface is simple and straightforward, so anyone who speaks Macedonian can search, as well as add documents in many categories. Categories vary from science and technology to medicine, arts and entertainment. To add on quality, some of the top university professors stored their papers and books here. By providing good service free of charge **Macedonia Search** earned thousands regular users every day. A "user" is not just a visitor, but also a human who receives the information, and also thinks and transmits information to other fellow humans. It is a great pleasure to see the discussion groups very active and irc (Internet Relay Chat) chat rooms full.

Statistical analyses show that our most frequent users are high school and university students. We are very pleased to have an audience so curious and so full of energy. That is the reason why many of our services are aimed toward the interests of the secondary school and high school students. Further statistics are shown below:

Table 1: General stats for the period 11 May 2000 - 21 February 2001.

GENERAL STATISTICS	PERIOD 11 MAY 2000 – 21 FEBRUARY 2001
Total number of visits	7896331
Total visitors	294724
Total data transferred	19.92 gigabytes
Average hits per user	26.79
Average users per day	2518
Average hits per day	27513,35
Average data transferred per day	95 megabytes
Total unique IP addresses	46350

Table 2: Geographical location.

GEOGRAPHICAL LOCATION	PERCENTAGE
Macedonia (.mk)	86.14%
USA, commercial domains (.com)	3.00%
Australia	2.10%
USA, network domains (.net)	1.48%
Holland (.nl)	0.98%
Russia (.ru)	0.88%
USA, educational domains (.edu)	0.70%
USA, non-profit domains (.org)	0.57%
United Kingdom (.uk)	0.49%

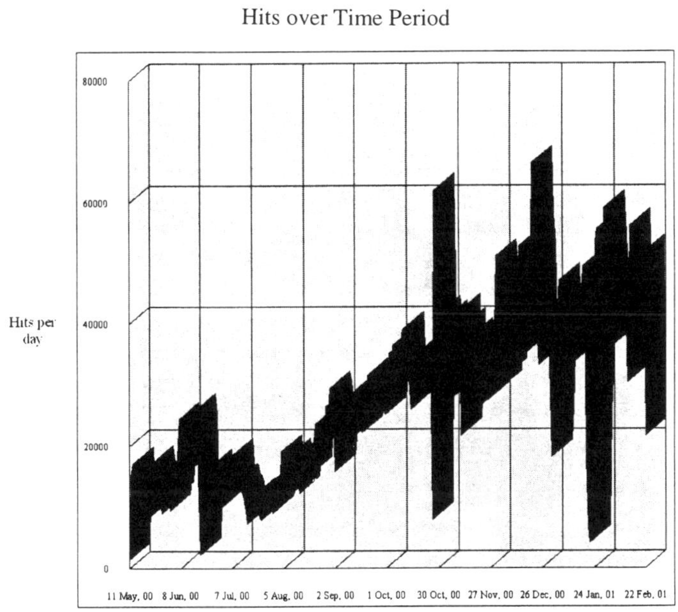

Fig. 1: Visitors per day between 11 May 2000 and 22 February 2001.

4. Payment methods – can the user easily purchase the information required?

What is the point of publishing a commercial product electronically, if there is no effective and friendly mechanism for collecting the payments? The USA and some of the Western Europe saw a great boom of e-commerce due to the well-organized systems for collecting credit-card payments. Even in the most developed countries there are flaws and changes to be done. Maybe the most important step forward was the electronic signature law, a law that promises a lot, but not just yet.

Although an electronic signature law has recently been passed in Macedonia too, a whole infrastructure has yet to be built. Macedonia is a country with a few bank scandals in the previous years, and many of the citizens prefer to keep the money "under a pillow" and not in banks. Credit cards are quite new to the population. However, most families with employed members have cheque accounts. The Macedonian Post also offers a pay on door services when the customer pays for the product when it is delivered. So there are means of selling goods and "atoms" as Nicholas Negroponte refers all objects that are actually delivered to your door.

Paying for electrons, i.e. information delivered by wire is not straightforward in Macedonia. The local banks do not offer means of collecting payments electronically, however a foreign service can be hired to handle the transactions. This will change, hopefully. A recent conference on e-commerce showed a great interest for providing the legal and technical tools for starting e-commerce in Macedonia.

5. Conclusion

The example of **Macedonia Search** shows that there is great potential for electronic publishing in the smaller developing countries, as well as an undiscovered potential customer base in countries with ethnic communities from these countries. This potential can be used if we access the nation's necessity for preserving its cultural identity.

6. Acknowledgements

The author would like to thank the following persons/institutions for their generous contributions for this project: The British Council in Macedonia, The Open Society Foundation in Macedonia, Electro Technical Faculty – Skopje and the collaborators Teodora Ajanovska, Zorica Lazarova, Nevena Shamoska, Filip Stojanovski, Simo Avramovski.

---

[i] Zoran Gligorov and Zdravko Stafilov are owners of the Macedonian non-profit internet portal "Macedonia Search". They can be reached at gligorov@macedonia.eu.org and stafilov@macedonia.eu.org

Electronic Publishing '01 –
2001 in the Digital Publishing Odyssey
A. Hübler et al. (Eds.)
IOS Press, 2001

Training in Electronic Publishing for Cultural Heritage Specialists: The Bulgarian Experience

Kalina Spasova Sotirova
Institute of Mathematics and Computer Science
bl. 8, Acad. G. Bonchev St., 1113 Sofia, Bulgaria
e-mail: kalina@math.bas.bg

Abstract: The issue at the heart of this article is an analysis of the actual condition of the publishing sector in Bulgaria and some predictions about the expected directions for its' future development in electronic environment. As the fourth great technique of writing, electronic text becomes unique medium for limitless exchange of human knowledge not only in the old continent, but in the world-wide scale.

Background

The e-publishing in Bulgaria is not widely spread and most publishers believe that the basic reason for this is financial. In spite of this many publishers show an interest in publishing in the new multimedia, recognising it as a priority type of publishing or intend to produce e-products in the future. What are the facts ? Most Bulgarian publishers (84%) produce only printed materials, 11% - both printed and electronic, and 1% - only electronic products. The book sector in Bulgaria survives with incredible difficulties in spite of increasing amount of private publishers (1,800 in 1998). The first Bulgarian e-publications were on display at the Sofia Book Fair in 1998, but the most of them were produced with foreign participation. Since then private companies showed growing interest in investing in this field and the tendency for future development is positive .

Education in Traditional and Electronic Publishing

A paradox in the local attitudes towards training appears in the difference between the clearly expressed need in training (53%) and the inclination to pay for it. Most Bulgarian publishers (61%) are not able to participate in training programmes offered by EU and do not invest in training activities in general. Higher interest in investment in training is observed in publishers already engaged with a new media (66%). The need in enriched access to training resources from abroad is expressed by 59% of the publishers. This makes Bulgaria a suitable country for running training programmes of EU. For 13% of the Bulgarian publishers e-publishing is an absolute priority and for 59% this sector does not offer advantages. The current situation in Bulgaria shows that local training is not flexible enough to meet the needs of a book sector in transition. The National Book Center (NBC) implements the governmental policy in the publishing area. A working state policy in the publishing sector requires active co-operation with non-governmental associations, e.g. Association of Bulgarian Publishers, Association of Bulgarian Writers, and Union of Translators.

Electronic Publishing for Cultural Heritage Specialists

The situation is even more complicated in the specialized field of e-publishing for cultural heritage. In the typical case cultural institutions do not have the staff, able to produce complete electronic publications. An indicative example of co-operation is the one between our team from the Telecommunications Dept. at the Institute of Mathematics and Computer Science and the National Library. This is a unique case of collaboration between institutions with different profiles on national and international level. Other such useful initiatives, supported by working governmental publishing policy will help for preserving the rich cultural heritage of Bulgaria.

0. Background

0.1 Bulgarian Book Sector in Transition

Since 1989 in Bulgaria there were numerous changes in the social and culture life, which reflected the publishing sphere. The transition made government unable to sustain the tradition of widespread access to books, centralized distribution and subsidized low pricing. In the collapsed infrastructure the abolition of the state monopoly opened up the market and print runs decreased by 50%. However, the privatization boosted the development in this area and the number of private publishers reached 1,800 in 1998. Most Bulgarian publishers (84%) produce only printed materials, 11% – both printed and electronic, and 1% – electronic products only (lower than the average value for the region). Nowadays the book sector survives with incredible difficulties, being vulnerable to the slightest movements in costs.

This article outlines the basic problems in the sphere of training for traditional and electronic publishers in Bulgaria. Main needs in the new technological context for publishing are related with the challenge of continuing professional development and acquiring competitive skills. To illustrate the most critical issues in e-books sphere in Bulgaria were used conclusions and statistics from the latest surveys: *Kingham 1998*[1], *LEONARDO project 2000*[2] *, a local study of the National Library*[3] *and a joint survey of the National Book Center and Gallup International.*[4]

0.2 Electronic Publishing Development

For e-books World Wide Web could be estimated as an entirely new method of publishing (print-on-demand), marketing and distributing. Until the end of 2001 the PCs, which will be connected to the World Wide Web will be 268 million, and in addition by 2003 500 million of human population will be Internet consumer. Concerning CEE region the electronic publishing makes its first big steps. The advantage for Bulgaria is the strong information technology potential. The first Bulgarian e-publications were on display at the Sofia Book Fair in 1998, but most of them were produced with foreign participation. Since then private companies showed increasing interest in investing in this field. The electronic publishing in Bulgaria (Internet and CD-ROM) is restricted by the educational market and the main consumers are libraries, universities and Ministries. 27% from the electronic books are for the business market, and 33% - for the educational market. This fact explains other interesting circumstance – the language for 73% of Bulgarian electronic products is Bulgarian, which would be an obstacle for presenting of the Bulgarian publishers in the world market. According to statistics data from LEONARDO 20% of publishers of electronic products had started more than three years ago. In collaboration with XEROX Bulgaria the new technology *print-on-demand* already works effectively in local environment. In Bulgarian cyberspace appeared over fifteen well-structured Bulgarian web portals for electronic book trade, following the model of AMAZON.COM. They offer widespread scale of Bulgarian and foreign titles,[5] but the searching is still slow. Low clients' activity remains the main restriction for the e-commerce in Bulgaria in general, not only for online book trade. The brake is the way of payment – a Bulgarian does not trust in electronic money. Other threat for the future of electronic publishing in general is increasing risk for intellectual property rights and business security, piracy, computer viruses, hackers etc. According Forrester Research by 2004 losses in electronic publishing would reach $1.5 bn. There are already several working tools for copyright protection and security of e-texts (*digital watermarking, 'wrapping', XEROX Content Guard*) but they are not popular in Bulgaria. The key word used by Bulgarian publishers concerning multimedia publishing industry is 'caution' and the main problem for successful development of electronic publishing is funding, lack of qualified staff, business partners and piracy. 66% of Bulgarian publishers admit that their staff need to improve existing, and to develop new, skills as a requirement for electronic publishing, and the way they prefer for this include training initiatives.

1. Education in Traditional and Electronic Publishing

1.1 State policy

The National Book Center (NBC) implements the governmental policy in the publishing area. It is a non-profit organization at the Ministry of Culture promoting the development of national writing, setting up the traditional *Sofia Book Fairs* and initiating legislation in the sector. Its' last activities are related with the *Book Support Programme.* NBC is also interested in developing electronic publishing. As a connection link between the government and private publishers NBC works in collaboration with ABPTOE (Association of Bookseller and Publisher Training Organizations). The aim is raising professional standards in the publishing field in local environment. A working state policy in the publishing sector requires active co-operation with non-governmental associations as well, e.g. Association of Bulgarian Publishers, Association of Bulgarian Writers, Union of Translators, EBCC (Euro Bulgarian Culture Centre).

1.2 Training Needs

Most of Bulgarian publishers (61%)[6] are not able to participate in training programmes offered by EU and do not invest in training activities in general. This situation is typical for the whole region. The need in enriched access to training resources from abroad is expressed by 59% of the Bulgarian publishers, which is considerably higher than in other countries from CEE. This makes Bulgaria a suitable country for running training programmes of EU. The recent low level of participation in any kind of training initiatives is explained by a lack of *specialized staff* (60%) and *technical problems* (33%). A significantly high number of publishers (43%) expect that a possibility for changing of training resources should arise in a years time. Higher interest in investment in training is observed in publishers engaged with a new media (66%). A paradox in the local attitudes towards training appears in the difference between the clearly expressed *need in training* (53%) and the *inclination to pay for it.* Most publishers give their preference to other areas of investment, e.g. new products (80%).

1.3 Training in Electronic Publishing

For 13% of the Bulgarian publishers e-publishing is an absolute priority and for 59% this sector does not offer advantages. When analyze the data from LEONARDO project have to be marked the fact that it is not concentrate on e-publishers, but covers whole sector. Therefore the results are representative for the publishing sector as a whole. The e-publishing is not widely spread and most publishers (*90% against the average for the region 79%)* believe that the basic reason for this is not lack of tradition, but financing. The current situation in Bulgaria shows that local training is not flexible enough to meet the needs of a book sector in transition. The participation in foreign training programmes is still unsatisfactory.

1.4 Current University Degree Programmes. Open and Distance learning - the alternative of the future

There are twenty-three universities in Bulgaria, but unfortunately students interested on publishing education, esp. electronic publishing have a little choice, although a number of universities (Sofia University, New Bulgarian University, American University in Bulgaria etc) offer degree programmes in Multimedia Computer Science etc. The Book Publishing Department at the Sofia University offers the one-of-a-kind professional education in the area. There is no formal training for bookselling and book distribution.

Regional Phare Distance Education Study Centre (RDESC) in University of Sofia provides distance education and training programmes in publishing and not only within and outside the region through its' local network It has branches, organized as local centers, in the New Bulgarian University, Medical University and Technical University. Associate centers towards RDESC are Bulgarian National Television and Bulgarian National Radio, which are involved in dissemination of the information about the different activities of the centre. RDESC develops a portfolio of distance education programmes targeted not only at students but at specialized training-the-trainers.

2. Electronic Publishing for Cultural Heritage Specialists

The situation is even more complicated in the specialized field of e-publishing for cultural heritage. The need to produce materials of specialized content and the difficulty to persuade institutions storing cultural heritage to give access to their holdings are amongst the key characteristics of this area. In the typical case cultural institutions do not have the staff, able to produce complete electronic publications. The professional e-publications will be a fact only through co-operation with experienced IT specialists. An indicative example of such co-operation is the one between our team from the Telecommunications Dept. at the Institute of Mathematics and Computer Science and the Manuscript Dept. of the National Library. One of our endeavors is to create an electronic catalogue of the departments' holdings within the frameworks of an EU-funded project MASTER[7], whose closing conference will be this summer in Sofia. Another current project aims to produce the first electronic edition of a mediæval Bulgarian manuscript, The Enina Apostle, dated XI century in co-operation with Dr. K. Kiernan from Kentucky State University, USA. This is a unique case of collaboration between institutions with different profiles on national and international level. Such joint activities could also be considered as an example of unconventional interdisciplinary training illustrating how the introduction of e-publishing changes the roles in the publishing sector in general. There is a big need of training in such interdisciplinary fields. Our team organized successfully two international summer schools in this area[8] .

3. Conclusions

In the digital age, the only source of sustainable and inimitable advantage lies on the power of ideas. Enabled by networks, intellectual capital comes to fore and new economic principles begin to govern the publishing sphere. Electronic texts will revolutionise human thrust for knowledge. Electronic texts are becoming a medium influencing new creativity where mass culture, mass media and mass literature will eventually produce a multimedia society. According to EU research between 8 and 18% of the book market should be

functioning on electronic grounds in the beginning of the new Millenium with higher values (between 20 and 30%) for the scientific, technical and medical literature.
Where will be the place of the Bulgarian publishing industry compared to this general picture? If we take into account the data on the current development of the local electronic publishing sector and the trends presented above, we cannot be optimists. At the same time if we analyze the situation we could see a good base for establishing a tradition in electronic publications.

The initiative INFOPROFESSION 2000, organised by Artefact Ltd and Martinus Nijhoff Bulgaria last October, put the main base for future active collaboration between infoprofessionals (publishers, computer specialists, non-governmental and educational institutions and individuals, related with publishing area and esp. e-publishing.) The need for adequate presentation of real condition and trade possibilities of Bulgarian publishing sector had motivated creation of web portals, which structure was discussed at the conference. Annually conferences, new contacts will help for sharing the various experiences of Bulgarian infoprofessionals and will coordinate their efforts aimed at creating professional e-publications in local environment. Creators of Bulgarian publishing industry are supported by an old tradition of active readership and high level of literacy of the Bulgarians. They are open to take the advantage of the future and this is a good base.

A closed system has no future in the information society in the beginning of New Millenium and we have to work together for opening it. A working state publishing policy in Bulgaria, on which the government is working recently, international collaboration of non-governmental institutions and future consolidation of Europe in addition, will help to preserve the rich cultural heritage of one of the oldest countries in Europe.

4. References

[1] BULGARIA: A Book Sector in Difficulty. A report by David Kingham for the joint activity 'Governments love Books (electronic books too)' of the Council of Europe, UNESCO and Börsenverein des Deutschen Buchhandels, Strasbourg, 1998
[http://www.osi.hu/cpd/govermentslovebooks/bulgaria01.html]

[2] The *LEONARDO DA VINCI* project of EC *"Needs of Publishing Training in Europe in the Information Society"* (III 2 A) is the first specialised research for publishing activities in the CEE region and the fullest one available till now. It is made among all publishers, not only electronically specialised ones and it is not a representative for software houses occupied mainly with electronic publishing. The second part of the project includes quantitative and qualitative research of publishing realities in ten candidates for associated membership in EU (Bulgaria, Latvia, Lithuania, Poland, Slovakia, Hungary, Czech Republic, Slovenia, Romania and Estonia) [http://www.sca.bg/publications/frames/htm , in Bulgarian]

[3] *Book production in Bulgaria 1985–1995*, Bibliometrical analysis of the National Library. In: Informational Support of the Book Sector, Plovdiv 1996

[4] *Data on the Bulgarian Book Publishing,* research of BBSS Gallup International made on request of the National Book Center at the Ministry of Culture, in Bulgarian, Sofia, 1998

[5] The Bulgarian Book (http://www.bgbook.dir.bg) is the first Bulgarian web site, which proposed online orders and delivery for Bulgaria. It has weekly title renewal and 10% discount. Other pioneer in the area is ARTEFACT Ltd., the biggest private subscription company and the first one offering online subscriptions. The first Bulgarian Internet bookstore (http://www.bgstore.com) is specialised on computer and IT area. Nowadays the richest choice (over 11,000 titles) offers virtual bookstore HELIKON (http://www.helikon.bg). Other sites showing the level of Bulgarian electronic book trade are:
http://www.pazar.bg,
http://www.easyshop.bg,
http://webgate.bg/global/tema/1.htm,

http://www.books.bg,
http://www.bgob.net,
http://www.slaveikov.com ,
http://edel.bulgarvoice.com,
http://stalker.dir.bg/book/bookshop.htm,
http://www.bora.exco.net

[6] The data in this section are based on the research *"Needs of Publishing Training in Europe in the Information Society*", see note 2.

[7] Manuscript Access through Standards for Electronic Records [http://www.cta.dmu.ac.uk/projects/master/]

[8] http://www.math.bas.bg/~dpm
http://www.math.bas.bg/~aitbs

Electronic Publishing '01 –
2001 in the Digital Publishing Odyssey
A. Hübler et al. (Eds.)
IOS Press, 2001

High quality electronic publishing in universities using XML - the DiDi principle

Peter Schirmbacher, Susanne Dobratz, Matthias Schulz

Humboldt-University Berlin, Computing Centre
Unter den Linden 6
10099, Berlin, Germany
http://dochost.rz.hu-berlin.de
(dobratz | schirmbacher | matthias.schulz.1 @rz.hu-berlin.de)

The number of electronic documents, which are to be handled, archived and made accessible to the public by university libraries in cooperation with other institutions, is highly increasing. Using an SGML/XML-based publishing concept enables universities not only to unlock their information and research resources but also to set up new services, like a document management or a printing on demand with higher quality as by using conventional publishing concepts. There are three main arguments for using an SGML/XML-based publishing strategy not only for theses and dissertations at Humboldt-University Berlin but also for university publications like conference proceedings, public readings, technical reports and other material, that is subsumed under the term "Grey Literature": 1. Archiving, 2. Retrieval and 3. Reusability of structured documents. This paper will describe the policy and technology that stands behind the local electronic publishing concept.

1 Enabling technologies

"SGML and XML are markup languages for presenting information as structured documents. They are often called "enabling technologies". To cite Oxford English Dictionary: *Enable, v. To Supply with the requisite means or opportunities to an end or for an object.* Markup Languages do not, by themselves give off-the-shelf answer to questions related to electronic publishing... They provide an opportunity. An opportunity to take a look at the information from a more abstract level. Not as pages or lines, but as packets with a label. When information is "tagged", it means you have classified its distinct logical elements. It is like turning your information into a miniature library, searchable, retrievable, useable.[1]

When talking about an SGML/XML-based publishing concept, there is always the question for the costs of material, tools and workload and its relation to the result. One can barely see that the technology behind a book or a document server is based upon those markup languages. And as long as we cannot provide new and better services, that motivate users to use those digital libraries, those questions have to been answer. Thinking in terms of "Digital Libraries" those new service demands include an availability of services 24 hours a day at 7 days a week independently from the location of the user, giving free access from the desktop to an unlimited repository and a sustainable digital

[1] Tuija Sonkkila in her invitation to the RAJU2001 Seminar, 23.4.2001 Otaniemi, Espoo, Finland. (http://kirjasto.oulo.fi/raju2001/)

archive. More than ever do the typical responsibilities of a library become important: the acquisition, exploitation and the offer of access to information resources. Building systems that provide a better user-oriented retrieval and a higher quality of access to digital literature at low costs becomes therefore essential, if libraries want to survive in an information society.

2 Arguments for an SGML/XML-based publishing concept

2.1 Archiving

Archiving electronic texts and documents is a highly discussed topic during the last years. Here two major aspects have to be taken into consideration: first, the question for the hardware, which is used for saving documents and second, the questions for an appropriate document format. Answering the question for the document format, which should be used for archiving, the following points seem to be essential to be considered:

- to guarantee a long term preservation for 10 years and more
- the availability of the document format on different hardware platforms
- the possibility to convert into several document formats without loss of information or data and therefore the possibility to choose a presentation format
- standardization of the archive format by an independent international consortium
- the possibility of inclusion of multimedia objects in their native format

2.2 Retrieval and Knowledge Management

Searching within collections of digital publications is often performed by a full text search engine in combination with a search within bibliographic metadata, such as title, author, and keywords according to a classification schema and abstracts. Using semantic and semi-semantic parts of digital documents offers new perspectives for a more detailed retrieval, which leads to search results, containing higher value of information. Arguments for SGML/XML are e.g. the possibilities:

- of using document structure and semantic tags for retrieval and new services like a printing on demand
- for detailed search facilities
- for automated cataloging
- for information extraction (e.g. citation index) and the use knowledge management functionality
- of deriving highly structured information, which is more valuable than information provided in standard text documents, e.g. in PDF

The call back of a search for a specific term in a full text database includes a lot of hits, which are not really relevant for the user. Searching, e.g. in headings of captions for this word decreases the number of hits and led to information, which is more important to the user, because it is scientific practice to use scientific terms or keywords in caption headings, in order to explain them in the following section.

The local decision for using an SGML/XML based publishing strategy was done by using experiences made in the German Medoc-Project as well as own evaluations[2]. The

[2] see Ohst, Daniel: Dateiformate für das elektronische Publizieren, Studienarbeit am Institut für Informatik, Humboldt-Universität zu Berlin, Berlin, 1998, http://dochost.rz.hu-

experiences and tools were also taken for evaluation and distribution within the German Dissertation Online project, which was funded by the Deutsche Forschungsgemeinschaft from April 1998 until October 2000.[3]

3 Electronic publishing

There are different views on electronic publishing:

View of Authors: Authors want to create and edit electronic publications in their native text-processing environments. For them publishing means disseminating their research results. So they first of all focus on the content rather than on the writing behaviour itself. To publish their documents very fast and worldwide is often the main argument to choose an Internet publication. But often questions as how to ensure intellectual property rights or copyrights often withhold them from choosing this method of publication.

View of Users: Users want to access digital publication, regardless of time and location. The possibilities of retrieving only the wanted rather than all available information for a certain topic seems to be rather essential for them. Another interest of this group is the possibility to prove the identity, integrity and authenticity of documents on servers. Did the author indicated on the front page really write this paper? Can the publishing date secured in a way, that ensures the originality of the information, that can be linked to inventions or patents that have to be secured? Is it possible to prove whether the author or anybody else has altered this document after publication?

View of Libraries: The main duty of libraries is the acquisition, exploitation, and long term archiving of printed materials. These duties now apply to digital documents as well. Libraries are also in charge of ensuring authenticity and validity of electronic publications.

View of Computing Centres: Computing centres usually approach this problems from a perspective where terms like physical availability of servers, bandwidth of computer-networks, quality of retrieval tools, long term archiving hardware, search machines, and storage capacity play a major role.

View of Publishers Publisher consider electronic publishing first of all as an technological process, that has to be handled in co-operation with several partners, such as authors, lectors and service providers.

Launching an electronic publishing project at a university can therefore only be a joint effort of the different institutions that are involved in a publication process:

Research Institutions as the producers of publications

Libraries as the publishing house, being responsible for dissemination

Computing centres as the institutions that holds most of the knowledge of the technology

Media centres as the institutions that provide knowledge for non textual enhancements.

Such a concept was taken when launching the "Digitale Dissertations" project at Humboldt-University.

---

berlin.de/docserv/buecher/ohst-daniel/HTML/ or Schirmbacher, Peter: Dateiformate ein zentraler Punkt des elektronischen Publizierens, Vortrag auf dem "Expertenworkshop". Neue Organisationsformen elektronischer Veröffentlichungen: Angebote wissenschaftlicher Bibliotheken, Dortmund, 23.-24.11.1998, http://eldorado.uni-dortmund.de:8080/bib/98/workshop/schirmbacher

[3] see results at http://www.dissonline.de

4 The Digital Dissertations project at Humboldt-University

The project "Digitale Dissertationen" at Humboldt-University in Berlin was sponsored for 3 years (Sept. 1997 - Dec. 2000) by a German government programme for multimedia applications for universities (Hochschulsonderprogramm III). Organised by the University Computing Centre and the University Library, it aimed to build up a digital library of theses and dissertations, access to which is available via the Internet. The project has a number of objectives upon which effort was concentrated. These include:

Addressing security and archiving issues - by the use of digital signatures, electronic time stamping services, and the appropriate use of SGML/XML standards.

Implementing a high quality retrieval system

Ensuring that support is available for authors who are producing their work in electronic format - by providing courses and guidelines as well as special services for scanning and preparing audio, graphical and video information

developing a workflow model for the submission and handling of digital publications within the university - giving considerations to cataloguing, storage and organisation of theses, and the work involved for the staff of the Library and the Computing Centre

This project was extended with the participation within the German "Dissertationen Online" project undertaken by the Initiative of Information and Communication of the German Learned Societies. This project was funded by the German Research Foundation (DFG: Deutsche Forschungsgemeinschaft) for 2 years. The final conference took place at Berlin in October 2000. It worked at a more integrative level and aimed towards a German wide initiative to bring scholarly publications online which are usually lost in libraries, such as dissertations, diploma and master theses. Through the joint work of 6 academic disciplines (mathematics, physics, chemistry, educational sciences, computer science and libraries as the State and University Library Lower Saxony (SUB Göttingen) and the German National Library (DDB: Die Deutsche Bibliothek)) which took place at several locations (Duisburg, Oldenburg, Erlangen, Berlin, Göttingen, Frankfurt) was highly successful in Germany and elsewhere. So a tight co-operation with the Networked Digital Library of Theses and Dissertations (NDLTD[4]), set up by Edward Fox from the Virginia Polytechnic Institute and State University, USA, was established.

5 Developing a electronic publishing concept for Humboldt-University Berlin

By now the project has moved out of the project status into a "normal" workflow between those two institutions. The developments are likely to guide the university to establish an electronic publishing house, but as those decisions have not been made yet, the organisational and technical concept is considered as the most important part. By May 2001, Humboldt-University has tested and established three major publishing lines, that are cover different fields of "grey literature":

Electronic dissertations and professorial dissertations,

Proceedings of the EUNIS2001 conference

Public readings of the university.

For those three different applications different publishing strategies were developed and used.

---

[4] http://www.ndltd.org

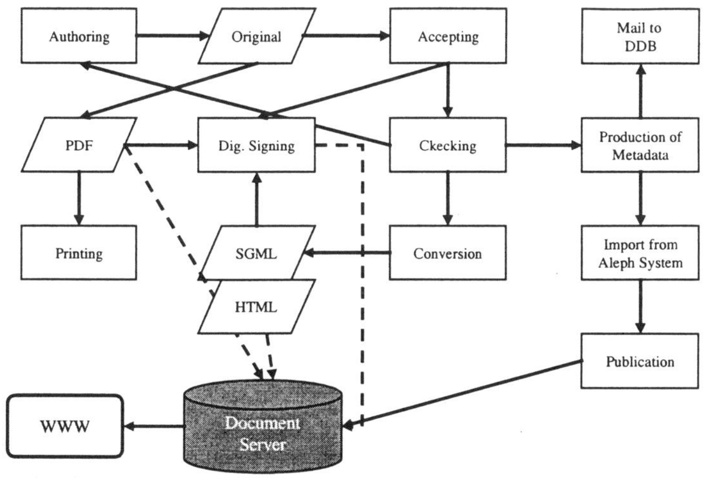

Figure 1: The whole publication workflow that is supported by a self-programmed workflow system

A very sophisticated task was to establish a common workgroup of staff from both participating institutions: library and computing centre and to develop a workflow. The workflow is supported by a workflow system that is easy to use for all parties and allows a detailed control of subtasks and contains a messaging and alerting system for the participating persons. Throughout long discussions and by reorganising of parts of old workflow within both institutions it took nearly 3 years to reach a result, that works independently from the actual project group. The underlying systems is based on a Sybase database, and maintained in the computing centre. The major workflow components are WWW-interfaces programmed using PHP4. So platform independence and an IP-based security strategy was reached by using the HTTP-protocol as basis.

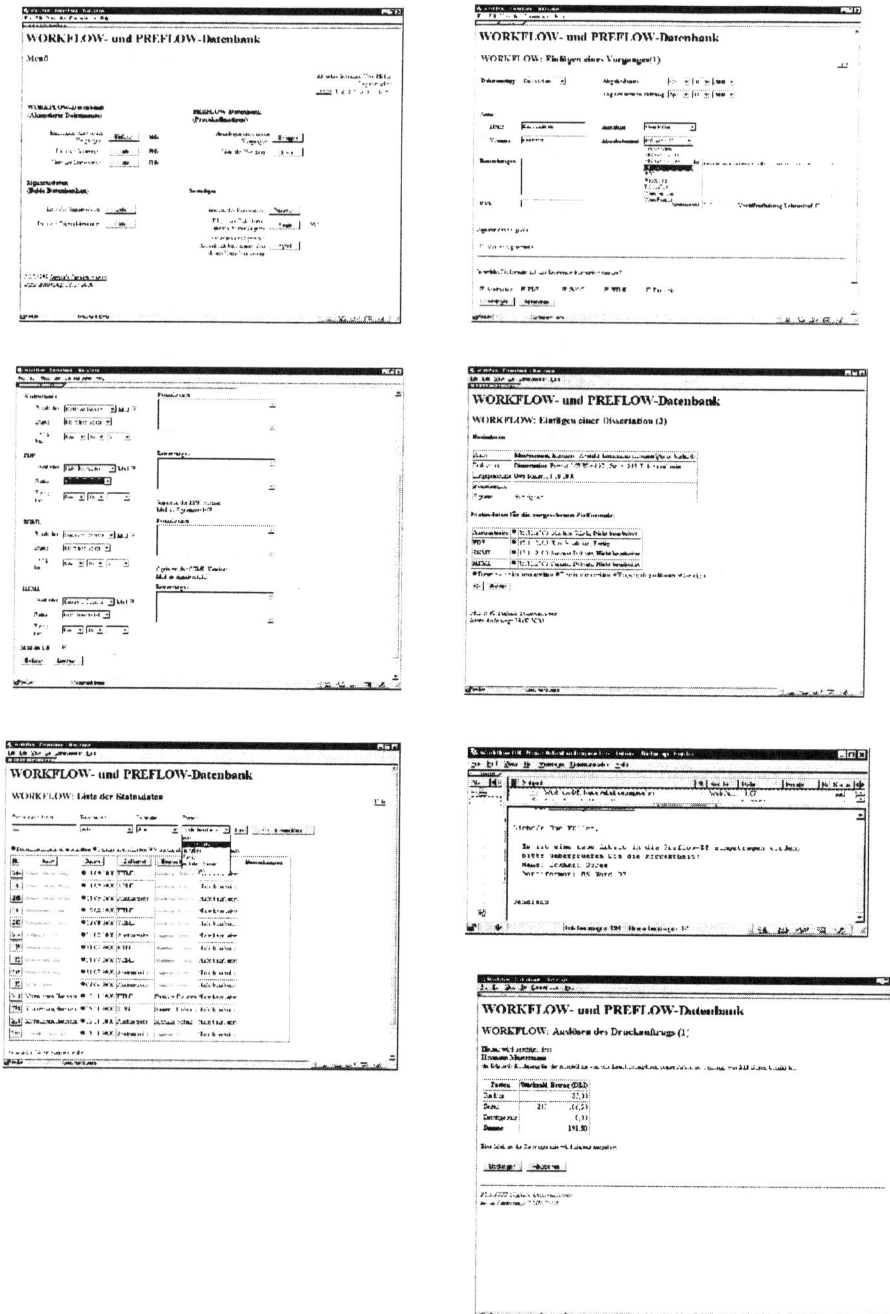

Figure 2: Screenshots of the workflow database user interface

5.1 Electronic dissertations

Why dissertations? In Germany dissertations have to be published by law. A doctoral candidate has to submit his dissertation using one or the other method to provide his or her dissertations to the university library in order to gain the doctor's degree. Usually the doctoral candidate fulfilled this requirement by providing 40 up to 120 paper copies (depending on the department) to the library or to provide a certain amount of microfilm copies to the library or to publish the whole dissertation in an publishing house or as an special issue in an well known journal in his field. All those conventional methods usually put a heavy financial burden upon mostly young scientists. So in 1997 the "Kultusministerkonferenz" (Conference of the Federal Ministries of Culture) decided to advise universities to allow a digital publication as additional method to fulfil the publication duty. Like every university in Germany, this advice had to be put into local law by the university itself. Humboldt-University did so by establishing the legal basis in March 1998, with an addition to all "Promotionsordnungen".

5.1.1 Document Conversion Workflow

The aim to collect a critical mass of documents and to develop a conversion strategy to SGML/XML was soon reached. By April 1998 the basic conversion concept was in place and documents could be converted from Microsoft Word into SGML instances. This technology has been improved throughout the entire project time, so that by now, a nearly automated conversion could be performed, which takes about half an hour for an average dissertation of about 200 pages, including several tables and figures.

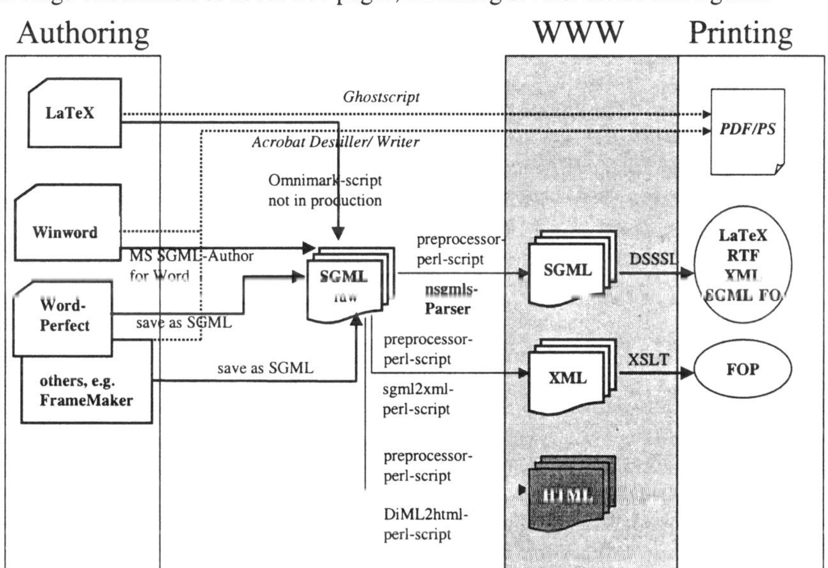

Figure 3: Schematic view onto the conversion process (FOP: Formatting Object to PDF engine; SGML-FOT: SGML: Formatting Object Tree; RTF: Rich Text Format)

The usage of Markup Languages like SGML/XML is not an easy task. First, a DTD (document type definition) giving the structured demands for the documents was designed. Instead of starting from the spread, the project used developments from the Virginia

Polytechnic Institute and State University[5] (Virgia Tech). This ETD.dtd was adopted to meet the German demands and renamed into DiML.dtd (Dissertation Markup Language). The technology of Virginia Tech using a tool "Microsoft Author for Word" was improved for certain details as table model, bibliography model, etc. and put into practice.

The first idea within the project was to provide an SGML/ XML -based editor to the authors in order to get "tagged" documents. A survey that was conducted in early 1998 appeared with a result that was not surprising. Potential authors wouldn't accept a higher effort, e.g. to learn the usage of a new text formatting system or XML-based writing systems in order to publish electronically. So supporting authors within their native word processing system in order to obtain pre-forms of achievable originals became a major task for the project. Especially as 75% of the authors used Microsoft Word, the focus turned towards this user group. A high quality authors support, resulting in the offer of a choice of 2 4-hour Word courses, which teach the usage of style sheets and Word features was established. Whereas project staff conducted the first courses they became a stable offer of the computing centre and are now held by staff of the computing centre.

Table 1: Usage of word processing systems at Humboldt-University

Word 6-9	166	75%
LaTeX	47	21%
Corel Wordperfect 7-8	5	2,3%
FrameMaker	3	1,4%
QuarkXpress, PageMaker	0	
Total of submitted dissertations (Jan. 1998 - July 2000)	221	100%

5.1.2 Metadata workflow

The German "Dissertationen Online" (DissOnline.de) project developed a Dublin Core metadata set for electronic theses and dissertations[6] that has been agreed by all German libraries. With this basic technology, a metadata database, covering several functions has been built upon a Sybase system using Java as programming language. It serves the following tasks:

Create catalogue entries for the digital documents and establish an interface to the Libraries Online Public Access Catalogue

Providing access to the digital documents through a highly configurable and reusable WWW-interface, that supports navigation within the archive and search using the Dublin Core fields.

Reporting new documents nearly automatically to the German National Library (Die Deutsche Bibliothek (DDB)), that has the duty to collect all German language literature.

The metadata workflow is an essential part of the whole publication process and is a major part of the workflow supported by the workflow database. Only if the librarian has finished cataloguing the publication, she or he can give the entry free for public access. This online publication than becomes visible for WWW-users and is part of the list of available publications shown in the screenshot below.

[5] http://www.etd.vt.edu

[6] see actual information at http://deposit.ddb.de/metadiss.htm

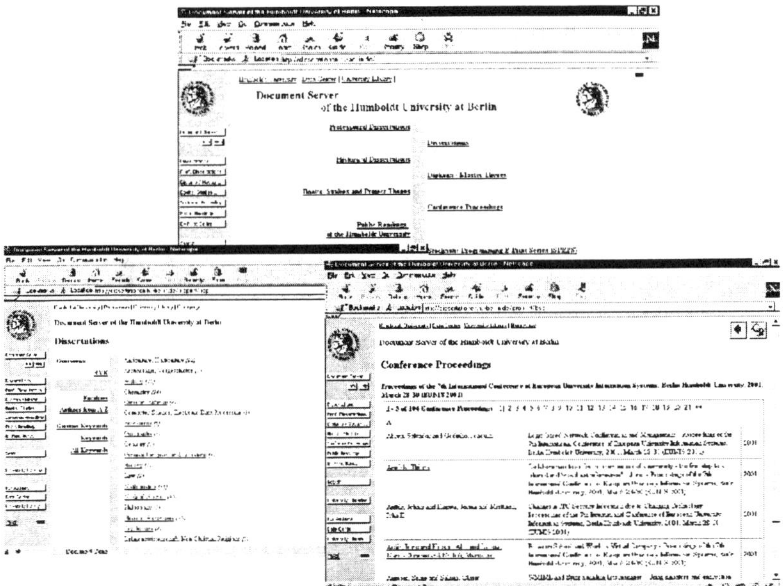

Figure 4: List of available publications, e.g. Dissertations that is automatically produced by the metadata database at the university library

5.2 EUNIS 2001 proceedings

According to the developed workflow, the concept was proved while applying it to another type of documents. The difficulties that arose with the EUNIS 2001 articles for the conference proceedings were the following ones:

The Word style sheet was designed using German version of Word. This was not acceptable at Word systems in other languages, e.g. Russian, Bulgarian, etc. Problems with character sets are in focus as well as the different naming of standard paragraph and character styles.

The Dissertation word template was much too comprehensive for the document type article.

The Word Macros written in WordBasic partially failed to work for several reasons: character sets, naming of styles (the macros were build based on German style names). This was esp. difficult to handle for the bibliography database, that the authors were obliged to use.

The authors had severe problems in using the Word template. Mostly the reason for that was that in contrary to the authors of dissertations who usually undergo a detailed introduction to that topic, those authors were not at all used in structured publishing. So most of the received articles had to be structured by the local publishing group.

Many problems were caused by the inclusion of graphics within the documents. As detailed instructions were given on how to save images, photographs and graphics, most of the authors failed to do so. Painting diagrams in Word was one of the major mistakes that were made.

The conversion technology applied to the conference proceedings was basically the one used for the dissertations (Microsoft SGML Author for Word 97). For the conference proceedings, the digital preliminary printing stage was set in an SGML based styling system 3B2[7]. So the whole proceedings were printed directly from the SGML source code. In order to accomplish a cross media publishing using the same document sources, the SGML documents were proceeded using a perl-script, so that they became XML documents. Those XML documents were not, as it is the technology for the electronic dissertations, by another perl-script converted to static HTML documents, that could be viewed on the web. They are on-the -fly generated using the Apache[8]/Cocoon[9] XSLT-Server technology.

5.3 Public Readings of Humboldt-University

As Microsoft is not developing their conversion tool further on[10], although it guarantees a high quality of conversion, another additional conversion technology had to be found. Therefor a comprehensive test of FrameMaker + XML 6.0 as conversion tool was conducted. It was tested with public lessons of Humboldt-University, which are basically the entrance readings of professors or readings at special occasions. This document type distinguishes itself from the other through the fact, that there is just one author, who is responsible for the publications. That person works in the research department of the university and usually receives the documents without any formatting as Word files. The previous publishing strategy used QuarXPress with bare formatting and structuring in order to produce a layout for a printed brochure. In order to reuse the document for a high quality internet publication, the decision was made to use FrameMaker as new layout tool because it supports this task in a very professional manner and additionally it is able to deliver also structured versions of the documents. So a complete XML environment has been set up, consisting of:

a new Document Type Definition: OVL.dtd

an FrameMaker+XML SGML application

an EDD (Element Definition Document) for applying structure to a FrameMaker document

a conversion table to map those FrameMaker elements to XML elements according to the new OVL.dtd

a layout style that can be applied to the FrameMaker EDD elements (and for production of the printed / PDF version)

an XSLT an a CSS style sheet for applying a layout to the exported XML document for usage on the WWW (a server side XSM/XSLT processing using Cocoon has been installed)

As a usage of this originally intended conversion technology for the electronic dissertations, this comprehensive test resulted in the realisation, that for a heterogeneous author environment this technology is much too complicated to be used. As the usage of FrameMaker for writing demands much more skills in order to produce pre-structured documents, this technology cannot be recommended for the electronic dissertations.

6 Printing-on-Demand Service with Apache/Cocoon

Digital Libraries which using their document servers as long term electronic archives will not make printed information dispensable. On the contrary for users of these

[7] http://www.3b2.com

[8] http://www.apacheorg

[9] http://xml.apache.org/cocoon/index.html

[10] The latest version of Word it is available for is Word97. As Word 2000 has the same internal document format (doc) those documents can be converted using Word97.

information systems the desire for printed documents is increasing. In most cases this desire often focuses not on the whole document as such, but on particular parts of it like chapters, citations and so on. For that reason our printing on demand project aims on the development of a technology which allows the users to print the wanted part of a certain document only.

For the printing on demand component with XML the usage of Apache/Cocoon was chosen. This software uses an XSLT-engine to produce an HTML or PDF-Version on the fly. "The Cocoon Project is an Open Source volunteer project under the auspices of the Apache Software Foundation (ASF), and, in harmony with the Apache web server itself, it is released under a very open license. Even if the most common use of Cocoon is the automatic creation of HTML through the processing of statically or dynamically generated XML files, Cocoon is also able to perform more sophisticated formatting, such as XSL:FO rendering to PDF files, client-dependent transformations such as WML formatting for WAP-enabled devices, or direct XML serving to XML and XSL aware clients. "[11]

As Cocoon does not consist of a printing on demand component (especially a selection feature) a small workaround using different XSLT-style sheets had to be done. The users view, containing an HTML-view onto the actual document includes check boxes, which the user can use to select parts of a specific document. This view is produced by the XSLT-Broker style sheet which calls a default style sheet, that produces HTML (XSLT-Style sheet with option document.xml?format=html) if the user selects certain parts of the document by clicking in the checkboxes. Then by clicking on the "OK" button a perl script (PHP-Choice) is called. This script selects the desired chapters and sections of the document by using XPath-expressions (http://dochost.rz.hu-berlin.de/proprint/bsp/slides.xml?CHAPTER=3 and http://dochost.rz.hu-berlin.de/proprint/bsp/slides.xml?CHAPTER=4) and cuts those parts out of the document and holds them in the main memory. This procedure is carried out by the XSLT-Broker-style sheet that is now been called with the XML-option (document.xml?format=xml). These parts are added to one single XML-document (all in the main memory!) and processed by the XSLT Broker-style sheet either with the print option or the HTML option (document.xml?format=pdf or document.xml?format=html)

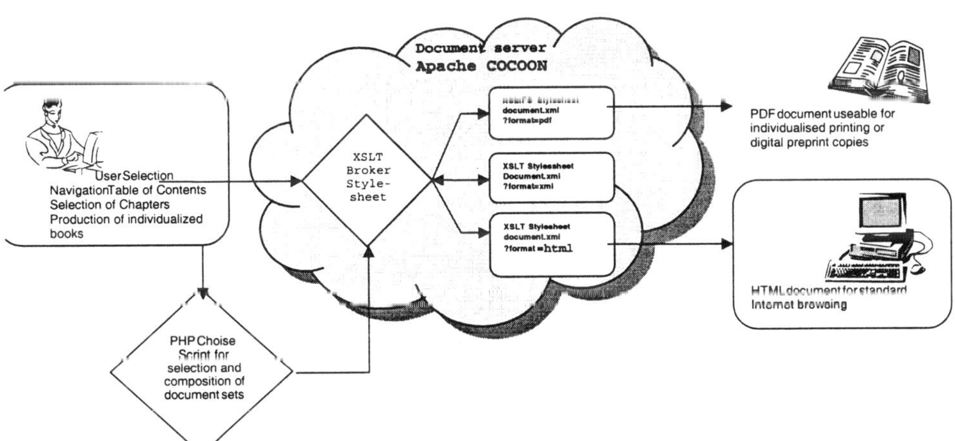

Figure 5: Usage of Apache/Cocoon for Printing on Demand

[11] http://xml.apache.org/cocoon/index.html

7 Further Developments

Looking at the local developments made within the past 3 years, it is now inevitable to establish a broader publishing policy that covers ideally all university publications. Such a policy should also include concepts regarding:

a reviewing system

a payment policy and component

a broad distribution and marketing policy

The education of students in the field of scientific (electronic) publishing from the beginning of their study.

All those ideas can only become reality of not only the service institutions, but also the university management are working together on that issue.

Further developments regarding the technical question of conversion will lead to more support for authors and therefor the investigation into alternative word processing systems, the customisation of XML editing solutions and developments made for a server side automated usage of conversion tools will proceed.

*Electronic Publishing '01 –
2001 in the Digital Publishing Odyssey
A. Hübler et al. (Eds.)
IOS Press, 2001*

Dealing with large documents in the Digital Library : a case study of ETD documents

F. Role & S Chaudiron & M Ihadjadene

Francois.Role@wanadoo.fr
stephane.chaudiron@u-paris10.fr
ihadjade@u-paris10.fr
Département Information-Communication (llphi)
Université de Paris10
200 avenue de la république, 92001 Nanterre Cedex, France
Tel: (33) - 01 40 97 73 54
Fax: (33) - 01 40 97 59 81

Abstract :
This paper presents the first results of the CodeX project ; this project aims at conceiving and developing a software platform for visualizing electronic documents according different contexts of use. We introduce and define the term "multiple view" which is the core of our approach and we present the technical choices we made to develop this user oriented approach. We conclude by drawing some perspectives based particularly on the generation of multiple and dynamic views and the integration of language engineering tools. The Codex Project demonstrates that the XML format can successfully be used to provide electronic access to theses. While the project focusses on a prototype implementation using CODEX data, the approach will be general enough that it can be adopted by any group for implementing a digital library. Discussion of research results and ideas for future work appear in conclusion

Keywords: CodeX, multiple view, electronic documents, XML, language engineering, ETD, metadata, browsing.

0. Introduction

The widespread use of the Web and the increasing occurrence of the thesis as an electronic document raise opportunities for the wider dissemination of a thesis electronically. The true benefit of a ETD (Electronic Thesis and Dissertation) digital library, however, comes not from the replication and enhancement of traditional library functions, but rather in the ability to make possible tasks that would not be possible outside the electronic environment, such as the hypertextual linking of related texts, full text searching of holdings, and the integration of filtering information tools, data visualization with the texts in the digital library.

Many doctoral dissertations and masters theses are valuable and interesting sources of knowledge, but too often rarely read. The relatively restricted access to print theses is the predominant reason for their underutilisation. (Fox,1997) (PHANOURIOU, 1999). The largest university-based collection of ETDs is maintained by the NDLTD (Networked Digital Library of Theses and Dissertations), a consortium of research universities (see http://www.ndltd.org). The largest for-profit collection is stored by UMI, University

Microfilms International, a division of Bell and Howell (see http://www.umi.com). A few additional for-profit organizations are creating digital libraries of ETDs, including http://www.dissertations.com.

In France, there are some efforts to publish ETDs online. For example, the ANRT (atelier national de reproduction des thèses) , projects Callimaque[1] and CITHER[2]. Such systems use TIFF image or PDF. Most ETDs are traditional dissertations written in Microsoft Word and then transferred into Adobe's PDF. (see for example http://www.ndltd.org) . We will first describe why we chose to base our representation on XML as opposed to PDF or Postcript formats which are more commonly used when dealing with big documents. PDF has many advantages including:

- PDF files can easily be created from most word processors, including WordPerfect or Word;
- is readily accessible, cross platform, using the free and freely available high quality Acrobat Reader viewer;
- offers high levels of document security;
- in addition to viewing a publication, full text searches can be performed on PDF files. Full text searching allows a user to locate specific words or sentences in a document, making research and citation faster and easier.

ETD documents in PDF format are derived from text originally produced for other purposes (e.g., print publication , archiving), and little work is invested in adapting them for use in an electronic environment. As it has been pointed out by several studies comparing the reading of paper versus on-line documents in the psychological and ergonomics (Dillon,1991), (Dillon,1992), (Hass,1992) (O'Hara,1997) (VAN DIJK, 1980) , documents are not easily readable on a monitor. As a matter of fact, reading in the on-line condition is slow, laborious, and detracted from real conditions of reading.

As SAVAGE (1999) explains: "Studies [cited above] have made it clear that readers are reluctant to spend an inordinate amount of time reading a document on a computer monitor. Hence, after accessing a monographic document, the next task in using that information would be to download it to a hard drive and then to print it out."

In contrast to this approach, a limited number of academic institutions are attempting to publish ETDs in SGML/XML, including Cybertheses[3] (France) and the Helsinki University of Technology (Germany). The emergence of XML format raises new opportunities for dealing with ETDs in a more dynamic way where users can access and "visualise" only the relevant parts of documents using the system of multiple views.

In this paper, we describe the CodeX (Consultation et Organisation de Documents Électroniques à parisX) project which aims at studying and evaluating technologies for implementing an XML-based digital library of dissertations. We first introduce and define the term "multiple views" which is the core of our approach and we then present the technical choices we made to develop this user oriented approach. We finally conclude by drawing some perspectives based particularly on the generation of multiple and dynamic views and the integration of language engineering tools.

1. The "System of multiple views"

One needs to understand the "system of multiple views" as a knowledge-based tool which allows a user to access a document or a set of documents from different relevant

[1] available at : http://callimaque.grenet.fr

[2] available at : http://csdoc.insa-lyon.fr/these

[3] available at : http://www.cyberthese.org

perspectives according to its informational needs. In this respect, the "system" may be considered as a filtering and a visualisation tool.

By analogy, one may define the system of views as a consultation mode which allows the user to visualise differents sides of the same document or of the subset of the database. As an heritage of the relational databases world in order to design data extraction from tables, the term of "view" has then been used to design extraction of information shells from the logic structuration of the document.

In the present CodeX project, the goal is more ambitious as it plans to build the system of views, not only from the logical structuration of the document but also using content analysis of it. In this approach, we first need to distinguish between *static views* and *dynamic views*, and secondly, between *structure-based views* and *content-based views.*

Static views are so-called because they are pre-defined by the developers of the system interface and users cannot modify them. Among the views defined in the first phase of the project (Chaudiron, 2000), there are the following:

- visualisation of the content table;
- visualisation of the introduction, conclusion and content table;
- visualisation of the abstract made by the author;
- visualisation of the abstract made by the author and the bibliography.

Dynamic views allow the users to define their own views on the database. In this way, they can extract parts of documents in respect with the relevant level of granularity they need: it may be, for example, a subset of the document composed by the introduction, section 1 and the conclusion. Another dynamic view of the document, which is presently in test, is to give the users the possibility to explore the content of the document with linguistic tools such as automatic abstracting systems or automatic terms extraction systems.

The second distinction allows the distinguishing of the views based on the use of the logical structure of the document, which may be static or dynamic, and the views which are based on the analysis of the content of the document. The first type uses the XML structuration of the documents which directly determine the nature, the size and the number of the "granularity" of the document. The second type is based on the additional information given by the authors in the document text such as index, glossaries, different kinds of annotation, etc. These views are not part of the document itself but are derived from it and may be considered as *representations* of the content of the document (FRASER et al., 1999). Many interesting questions arise from this approach which are discussed in (ROLF and alii, 2001). Content-based views may also be the results of a linguistic processing achieved by a natural language processing system such as automatic summarization or semantic-based filtering.

2. Description of Codex

CodeX uses an XML-based format. XML is considered as an emerging standard for creating markup-languages. In the context of ETDs, it gives at least two interesting features:

- Advanced searching capability – An XML based archive of ETDs would allow users the capability of performing complex queries against the collection that would not be available to an archive of documents in PDF. The ability to search against all bibliographic entries would be one example.
- Dynamically created views – XML favours the separation of structure and presentation. By providing presentational information with the use of style-sheets, XML implementers can create multiple views for an XML document without changing the document itself. It gives users an appropriate view of structured data. Data delivered to the desktop can be presented in multiple ways. A local data set can be dynamically

presented in the view that is right for the user, based on factors such as user preference and configuration. XML document content can be dynamically generated from a database and user input.

Users specify the text they wish to browse; CodeX locates the XML file and associated metadata, determines which portion of the file contains the desired text section, applies appropriate styling rules, and presents the text in HTML form.

Currently, the CodeX system consist of three modules:

- a converter
- a metadata creation tool
- a visualization module

2.1 Converting to XML from Microsoft Word

The converter is a batch tool used to transform our collection of word documents (students thesis) into well-formed XML documents. In the first step of the process, we currently use a shareware filter application Majix (see http://www.tetrasix.com) that converts the RTF document to an XML. The primary weakness in this process is that the effectiveness of the conversion is largely dependent on the appropriate and consistent application of MS word styles throughout the source document. The list of potential Word styles can be as long as is necessary, but RTF to XML will return an error if it encounters a style that is not registered in the system. Currently more 30 ETD have been converted to XML documents.

While XML is seen as an ideal end product, the sticking point is still the perceived difficulty of XML and/or the lack of powerful, easy editors that make authoring dissertations in XML as easy as writing them in Microsoft Word.

2.2 Metadata creation tool

The metadata creation tool is a simple electronic form which is used to generate an TEI-based XML header associated with the documents. In addition to existing TEI fields and to take into account the specificities of theses and dissertations, we added some other fields such as: department, teacher, university name, diploma.

Such metadata can be included inside an ETD, making it a self-describing document, especially when XML is used. It is straightforward to encode CODEX based metadata in XML in a header portion of an XML ETD.

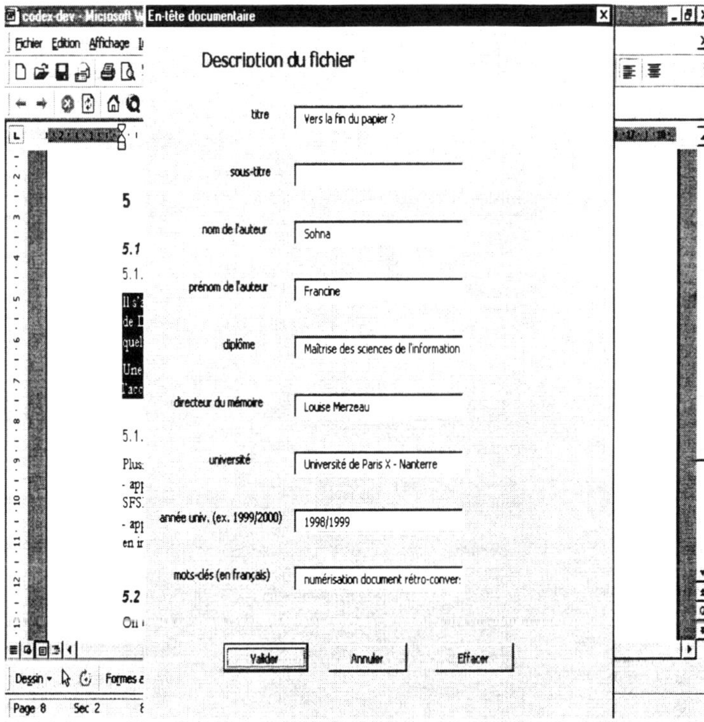

Figure 1: metadata creation tool

2.3 A visualization module

The visualization module is the core of the system. It uses the concept of "multiple views" to display documents generated by the two other modules in a wide variety of visual forms according to the informational needs of the users. When a user requests a document, our display system locates the XML file and its associated metadata, determine which portion of the file contains the desired text section, applies appropriate styling rules, and presents the text to the end user in HTML. As shown in figure 2, the visualisation module relies an XSLT style-sheet to execute on a Java-enabled web server (Apache).

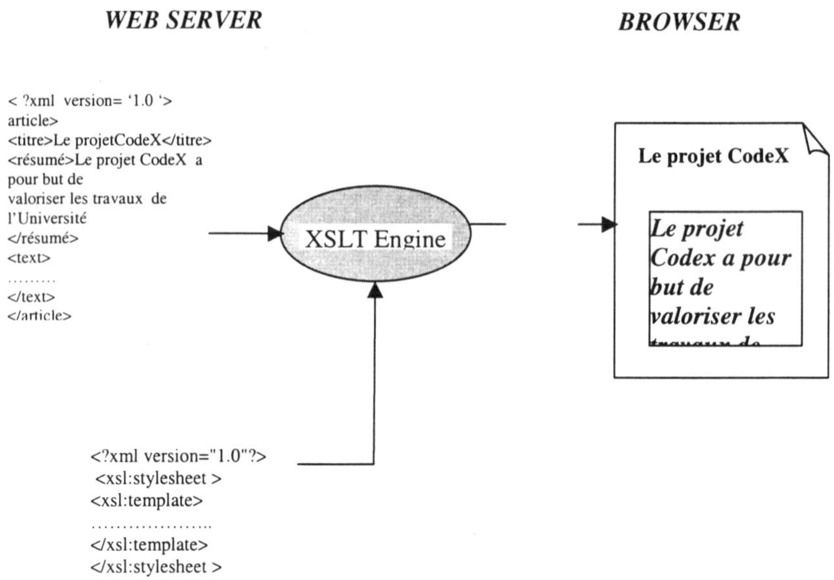

Figure 2: Using XSLT templates to generate specific views

3. Conclusion and Perspectives

In this paper, we have described an XML digital library. The Codex project demonstrates that the XML format can successfully be used to provide electronic access to theses and dissertations. XML provides a standard way for information providers to add custom markup to information-rich documents, in order to publish complex documents in a dynamic way. Codex tools were developed to extract structural and descriptive metadata from these documents and deliver document fragments on demand.

3.1 Index browsing

As most of electronic thesis present an index (generated automatically by software like Word), one current perspective of our work is to create a set of links from the index to the words in the ETD document. Such index will be represented in XML. In this approach, the design of the automatic hypertext generation is based on the content-based analysis of the ETDs. Content browsing applications provide information seekers with access to texts. Structured lists of index terms gives a preview of the content of an ETD.

3.2 Evaluation

We will perform tests to evaluate how useful such "dynamic views" are to users. Our hypotheses are that reading and browsing ETD documents this way will improve the user's satisfaction and save the reader's time. We will follow a user-centred approach (Borgman, 1996) (PERRIAULT, 1989).

4. References

(BALPE, 1999) Balpe J.-P. et al. (eds), Hypertextes, hypermédias et internet - Actes du colloque H2PTM'99, Paris, Hermes, 1999.
(BRINES, 1998) Brines-Moya Natalia & Hartill Julie, "Criteria for User-oriented Evaluation of Monolingual Text Corpora Interfaces", in First International Conference on Language Resources & Evaluation, Granada, ELRA, 1998, p. 893-898.
(BORGMAN, 1996) Borgman, C.L.; Bates, M.J.et al. Social Aspects Of Digital Libraries. Final Report to the National Science Foundation; Computer, Information Science, and Engineering Directorate; Division of Information, Robotics, and Intelligent Systems; Information Technology and Organizations Program. URL: (http://dlis.gseis.ucla.edu/DL/>).
(CHAUDIRON and al., 2000) CHAUDIRON Stéphane, ROLE François, IHADJADENE Majid, "CodeX : un système pour la définition de vues multiples guidées par les usages" in Actes du Colloque International sur le Document Électronique (CIDE'2000). 4-6 juillet 2000, Lyon, France ; p. 71-81.
(DILLON, 1991), Dillon A. "Reader's models of texte structures : The case of academic articles", in International journal of man-machine studies, n° 35, pp. 913-925.
(Dillon, 1992) Dillon, A. (1992). Reading from paper versus screens: A critical review of the empirical literature. *Ergonomics, Vol. 35(10),* 1297-1326..
(FOX, 1997) Fox, Edward A, John L. Eaton et al., "Networked Digital Library of Theses and Dissertations: An International Effort Unlocking University Resources", in D-Lib Magazine (September 1997). Available at: http://www.dlib.org/dlib/september97/theses/09fox.html.
(FRASER et al., 1999), Fraser B., Roberts J., Pianosi G., and al., "Dynamic views of SGML tagged documents", in Proceedings of the Seventeenth Annual International Conference on Computer Documentation, p. 93-98, 1999.
(Hass, 1992) Haas, C. " Writing Technology: Studies on the materiality of literacy". Mahwah, N.J.: Lawrence Erlbaum Associates.
(O'Hara,1997) K O'Hara " A comparison of reading paper and on-line documents" CHI'97 proceedings. Conference on human factors in computing. Atlanta.
(PHANOURIOU, 1999) Phanouriou Constantinos, Edward Fox et al., "A Digital Library for Authors: Recent Progress of the Networked Digital Library of Theses and Dissertations", in Proceedings of ACM Digital Libraries '99, Berkeley, CA, Aug. 11-14, 1999.
(PERRIAULT, 1989) Perriault, Jacques, La logique de l'usage : essai sur la machine à communiquer, Paris, Flammarion, p. 253.
(SAVAGE, 1999) Savage, William, "Reflections on a Sustainable Model for the Digital Publication of Theses and Dissertations", in Proceedings of UNESCO Workshop on the Electronic Dissemination of Theses and Dissertations, Paris 27-28 September, 1999 (available at: http://www/unesco.org/etd).
(VAN DIJK, 1980) VAN DIJK T A. "Macrostructures -An interdisciplinary study of global structures in discourse, interaction and cognition". Hillsdale, N. J., Erlbaum, 1980.
World Wide Web Consortium, Extensible Markup Language (XML) 1.0 (Second Edition), W3C Recommendation. http://www.w3.org/TR/REC-xml.
World Wide Web Consortium, XSL Transformations (XSLT) Version 1.0, W3C Recommendation. http://www.w3.org/TR/xslt.
(ROLE and alii, 2001), ROLE François, IHADJADENE Majid, CHAUDIRON Stéphane "Exploitation de l'indexation auteur pour le filtrage de documents structurés complexes" - 3ème Colloque du Chapitre français de l'ISKO- 5 et 6 juillet 2001, Université de Paris X/Nanterre.

*Electronic Publishing '01 –
2001 in the Digital Publishing Odyssey
A. Hübler et al. (Eds.)
IOS Press, 2001*

Negotiation of copyright in e-commerce of multimedia publishing material

Jaime Delgado[1], Isabel Gallego[2]

[1] *Universitat Pompeu Fabra (UPF), Departament de Tecnologia,
Pg. Circumval.lació 8, E-08003 Barcelona, Spain
jaime.delgado@tecn.upf.es*

[2] *Universitat Politècnica de Catalunya, Departament d'Arquitectura de Computadors,
Campus Nord, Mòdul D6
Jordi Girona 1-3, E-08034 Barcelona, Spain
isabel@ac.upc.es*

Abstract. Intellectual Property Rights (IPR) management in e-publishing is becoming a key issue for its full deployment. There is a real and urgent need to solve the problems associated with multimedia content copyright control that the spreading of the Internet and the WWW has created. Although many technical solutions to the problems already exist, there is still a lack of an efficient and agreed business model for e-commerce of e-publishing. Apart from introducing copyright information in the content to sell, there are other new specific needs related to IPR management in e-publishing. One of them is the possibility of negotiating the copyright conditions when buying multimedia material. This material could be directly bought by end-users, or, more interesting, by other publishers. An example of this situation could be the negotiation between an intellectual rights holder and a prospective publisher. In the paper, we present a specific approach to this IPR need, which is based on the use of metadata for representing IPR features, and on the specification of a protocol for negotiation of copyright at the purchase moment. Furthermore, the paper introduces the issues associated to IPR negotiation in a multi-broker environment.

0. Introduction

The paper is about the issue of Intellectual Property Rights (IPR), its representation, its negotiation and its use in e-business in the area of e-publishing. We concentrate on selling and distributing multimedia publishing material (mainly video information) using an intermediary or broker.

Apart from introducing copyright information in the content to sell, and from encrypting the content when considered necessary, there are other new specific needs related to IPR management in e-publishing. One of them, also related to the business models to follow, is the possibility of negotiating the copyright conditions when buying multimedia material. An example of this situation could be the negotiation between an intellectual rights holder and a prospective publisher.

In the paper, we present a specific approach to this IPR need. Our approach is based, first, on the use of metadata for representing IPR features, and, second, on the specification of a protocol for negotiation of copyright at the purchase moment.

It should be also noted that we assume that the multimedia material to be managed has some watermarking that helps to identify it. We do not worry about how this is generated, verified and extracted, and we also assume that is strong enough to be kept during manipulation, as it is normally the case. So our focus is on the two previous points.

Although our model is based, as introduced in section 3, on the existence of a broker to which users make requests, and that negotiates IPR conditions on behalf of a content provider, the final part of the paper introduces the issues associated to the extension of our single-broker model to a multi-broker one.

1. Intellectual Property Rights (IPR)

Intellectual Property Rights (IPR) are legal instruments that provide a limited monopolistic right to the owner of things such as patents, trademarks or copyrighted works. They provide an incentive for the creation of and investment in new works (music, films, print media, software, performances, broadcasts, etc.) and their exploitation, thereby contributing to improved competitiveness, employment and innovation.

This description is based on the Berne Convention [1] and the WIPO Copyright Treaty [2]. It is, as the sources state, broaden enough to ensure international applicability. There are local initiatives to implement these recommendations, as the EC Directive on Copyright [3] or the US Digital Millennium Copyright Act [4].

In the context of copyrighted works, IPR includes author's rights, which will be referred to later, sui generis rights (applicable for databases) and neighbouring rights (especially concerning artist-interpreters).

1.1 Author's rights (copyright)

All these rights are automatically given to originators of works (creators) by the simple fact of their authorship. They include:

- **Moral rights**
  Independent of the author's economic rights, and even after their transfer, the author has the following rights:
  - Dissemination Right: Exclusive right to disclose the work.
  - Paternity Right: Exclusive right to claim authorship of the work.
  - Respect Right: Exclusive right to object to any modification to the work prejudicial to his reputation.
  - Withdrawal Right: Exclusive right to withdraw the work.
- **Exploitation rights** (economic rights)
  Oriented to guarantee financial profit to originators of works. They include:
  - Reproduction Right: Exclusive right to authorise the reproduction, direct and indirect, permanent or temporary, in any manner or form.
  - Communication to the Public Right: Exclusive right for the authorization of any communication to the public of their works. These includes that members of the public may access them from a place and at a time individually chosen by them. Examples are: public performance, broadcasting, interactive on-demand transmission, etc.
  - Distribution Right: Exclusive right to authorize the making available to the public of the original or copies of the work by sale or other transfer of ownership. Relevant only to tangible objects.

2. Business Models

The Intellectual Property Rights (IPR) management in e-publishing is becoming a key issue for the full deployment of publishing in electronic commerce. The issue includes both copyright protection and the so-called Electronic Copyright Management Systems (ECMS).

Although in text-based creations things are not going so fast, the work in this area is strongly increasing when the published material has any multimedia-based content. This is because there is a real and urgent need to solve the problems of multimedia content copyright control that the spreading of the Internet and the WWW has created. There are different European projects related to IPR management like IMPRIMATUR [5], INDECS [6], COPEARMS [7], FILIGRANE [8], etc. that are good starting points.

Although many technical solutions to the problems already exist, there is still a lack of an efficient and agreed business model for e-commerce of e-publishing. Several solutions are being deployed, mainly in the area of music distribution, such as Soundwrap [9], DMDsecure [10], or DX3 [11], but none of them has succeeded as a model to follow.

Concerning selling of publishing material (books or e-books) on the Web, there are some initiatives that have IPR again as a key issue.

E-books are mainly sold from e-publishers and bookseller sites (a special case is selling directly by the author, like Stephen King's experience [12]). Some downloadable e-books are sold with specific viewing software, others use rather standard software. Sometimes, the term e-book refers only to those that are stored and read in specific hardware, not in standard computers.

With respect to copyright protection, publishers need to ensure that once an e-book has been purchased, it is not possible to be copied again. One simple schema is to encrypt each e-book so it can only be decrypted by the reader for which it was purchased.

There are different initiatives to digital rights management in e-books, such as EBX [13] and OEBF [14], and some XML based ones, such as XrML [15].

2.1 A model for IPR information representation

In order to deal with IPR, we have first to select a model in which to base IPR representation and negotiation. We have selected the IMPRIMATUR Business Model [5], which identifies a series of entities that may take different roles, such as Creator, Provider, Rights Holder, Distributor, IPR Data Base, or Watermarking & Fingerprint marking.

We are applying this model to an environment that consists on the use of a Broker (with the role of Distributor) in charge of being an intermediary between providers of multimedia publishing material (content providers) and the customers interested in buying that material and the corresponding rights for use and/or commercial exploitation. From a functional point of view, these copyrighted multimedia material providers may also assume the roles of Creator and Rights Holders in the same entity.

Furthermore, the broker stores and keeps up to date (with the help of content providers) the information about the multimedia material for sale in the system (from all content providers associated to the broker), and about the terms and conditions in which commercial electronic transactions are done, with the help of the IPR Database. Figure 1 illustrates this broker-based IPR model.

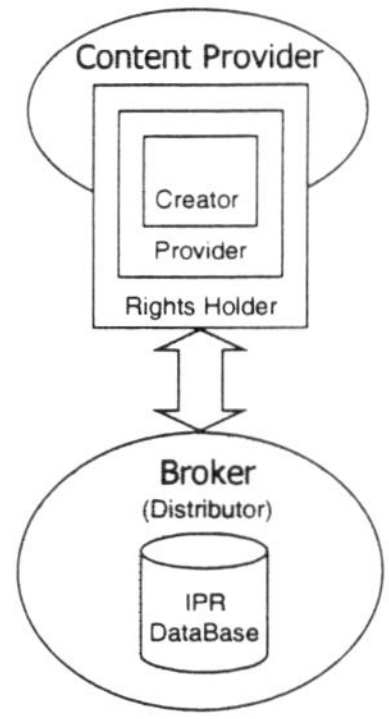

Figure 1. Broker based IPR Model

3. Use of metadata for IPR information representation

For managing IPR information, we need to represent it in some way. We have chosen a solution based on the use of metadata. A lot of work is going on in the area of metadata, from the widely used Dublin Core [16] to the MPEG7 standard [17] for audiovisual material. Our work is based on the alignment efforts we started in the context of an European CEN/ISSS Workshop [18], and on the work going on in the INDECS project [6], that focuses on metadata for IPR. We are currently implementing this solution in different projects, from brokerage of audiovisual material (in the HYPERMEDIA Project [19]), to broadband multimedia applications (the MARS Project [20]).

Basically, we use two kinds of metadata: general and IPR. General metadata, on the one hand, includes title, author(s), kind of publishing material, size, and other management attributes; and technical information, such as resolution, colour or shape. On the other hand, IPR metadata includes mark/no-mark, kind of mark, information associated to the mark (for further verification), rights owner, kind of rights, rights status and limits, etc.

This model just introduced has been implemented with RDF [21], extending the fundamental modelling concepts provided by the "RDF model and syntax" [22] and the "RDF schema" [23]. The schema utilisation policy of this framework allows the creation of a very flexible representation, not tied to any concrete initiative of metadata creation.

As said before, our system is based on a broker agent that is trusted by the content providers and the buyers (normally business users). It includes a database with references to the publishing material to sell. Since our implementation is focussing on video material, the multimedia metadata (information about the content to sell) stored in the broker can be divided in two types according to its use. First, there are video descriptive attributes (descriptive metadata) used to facilitate that the user locates the audio-visual material he's interested in. The second type encloses the part of the model concerned with intellectual property rights representation (IPR metadata). This information is structured following a metadata model that we have developed based on existing ones.

To start developing from a solid basis, the model has been constructed over INDECS basic model. This provides the general concepts that allow non-traumatic extensibility and a great adaptability to concrete and changing environments.

The descriptive metadata subset includes all those audio-visual material properties that permit the easy and rapid localisation of the audio-visual material needed. These properties can be packaged inside RDF schemes. A more detailed description of our metadata approach is given in [24].

4. IPR negotiation

Based on the IPR attributes set, when a buyer requests, to the broker, a purchase of audiovisual material subject to copyright, the broker extracts IPR information from its database (Clauses Templates) and presents an initial offer to the buyer (Contract by default). This information allows the buyer to take a decision on how to buy IPR, i.e., to know what are the copyright rules associated to the asset, to decide if he wants to re-sell it, etc. To facilitate this process, a negotiation mechanism is being developed based on a simple negotiation protocol. XML is used as interface to the IPR information in the broker's database. Since all metadata attributes are specified using XML, the implementation could be easily ported from one system to another. If the negotiation process finishes with agreement, it is complemented by the production of an electronic contract, which is signed by buyer, rights owner and broker (as TTP), and stored in the broker agent.

The negotiation protocol, that it is part of the "Agreement" phase in an e-commerce model [25], has three sub-phases:

- Initial offer (Contract by default),
- Co-operative contract production (kernel sub-phase) and
- Payment

The initial offer (Contract by default) is selected, between a set of clauses templates stored in the database of the broker agent.

In the Contract production sub-phase, the most complex and important one, there are few alternatives over which to work. First, the selling entity initiates the protocol with an initial proposal of digital rights conditions, normally taken from a pre-defined subset (Clauses Templates). After that, the buying entity has three alternatives:

1) Accepting the offer,
2) Making a counter-proposal and
3) Rejecting the proposal.

After the initial proposal, the negotiating entities elaborate the contract, using the negotiation protocol, from the sequence of proposals and counter-proposals until a final agreement is reached, forming then the final electronic contract.

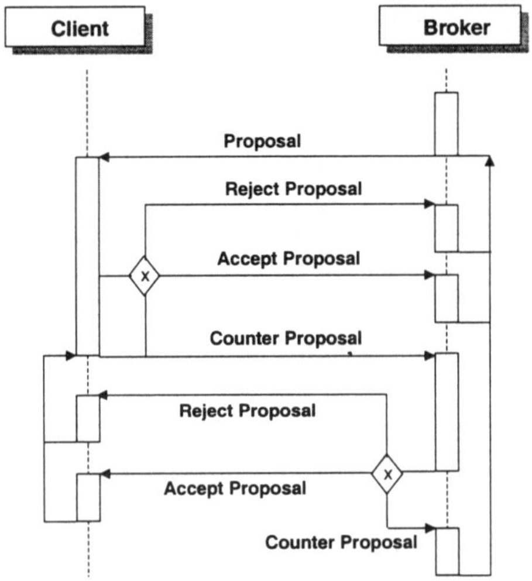

Figure 2. Kernel sub-phase of the IPR Negotiation Protocol

The graphic representation of the kernel sub-phase of this IPR negotiation protocol is given in Figure 2. More technical details are given in [26].

Accepting the offer is to accept a proposed clause of a contract (to add this entity to the list of entities who agree with this clause), making a counter-proposal is to add a new clause to the contract and rejecting the proposal is to remove the clause from the contract.

This "game" of proposals and counter-proposals could be extended under some rules (Negotiation Protocol). The negotiation is done through the broker, who has the unique legal copy of the contract. When the contract negotiation is finished, the broker generates the legal copy of the contract (Signed contract) and sends a copy of the contract to the entities involved.

Finally, although the rights negotiation protocol concludes when a proposal is eventually accepted or rejected, the IPR-related protocols continue in the context of the e-commerce "Post-Agreement" phase [25], that includes one step called "Post-negotiation", where the contract is executed and the fulfilment of the agreements in the contract is verified, following some workflow rules. It is in this "Post-negotiation" phase where the agent technology, which we are using for the implementation of the negotiation protocol, plays an important role (see [24]).

4.1 IPR contracts

Initially, the creator (writer, composer, actor, software programmer, etc.) of a work is holder of all the rights over it. Authors may not have the economic power to exploit their creations in an effective way. In such cases some or all exploitation rights can be transferred to publishers/producers specialized on this task.

This can be formalised in **author's contracts**. By them, publisher/producer becomes the exploitation rights holder of the work (Rights Holder). As a counterpart, the originator will receive royalties for the benefits derived from the exploitation of the work or/and initial fix revenue.

Publishers/producers do not usually have direct contact with end-users. They commercialise works to distributors (bookshops, libraries, Internet site providers, broadcasting companies, etc.), entities specialized in acquiring part of the rights of copyrighted works that allow them to satisfy final users demand of these works. Distributors may also encapsulate works with some services that facilitate this consumption, the added value they provide to the creations. Formalization of these agreements is made through **distribution contracts**, that may transfer some constrained exploitation rights or be mere licenses allowing the required actions to complete the commercialisation to end-users.

Finally, through distributors, copyrighted works arrive to their consumers. End-users acquire the right to access and use them by **purchase contracts**. These use rights may operate within the framework established in the distribution contract with the publisher/producer. The income distributor receives derived from these purchases will be also distributed, in a cascade manner accordingly to the royalties established in the different contracts so far, to publishers/producers and originators implied in the elaboration of the final product acquired by the consumer.

To ensure that fair economic returns arrive to authors and publishers/producers they can become members of collecting societies. These control the exercise of representation and reproduction rights of some types of intellectual works to enforce proper remuneration to their members.

4.2 An electronic IPR contract

Independently from the kind of contract agreed by means of the negotiation protocol already described, once an agreement is reached, there is a need to produce a contract to formalise the agreement. In the following paragraphs, we describe how to specify an electronic contract for this formalisation.

As already introduced, by IPR negotiation we mean the process in which, at purchase time, the buyer of some multimedia content and the rights owner (or his representative) negotiate the conditions (concerning rights) in which that material is sold. This process, run through a protocol with some interchange of information, is equivalent to creating an electronic contract. It could also be seen as a joint editing of a structured document (the contract), following pre-specified alternative rules.

The electronic contract, that should be electronically signed, has two parts:

- Mandatory part: It contains the minimum information necessary to formalise an electronic contract.
- Optional part: It contains optional information related to any kind of contract.

The mandatory part includes the following information:

- Type: To identify the kind of contract
- ContractSerialNumber: Contract unique identifier
- SignatureInformation: Information related to the signature of the contract
- NegotiationList: List of entities who participate in the negotiation of the contract
- Broker: Identification of the broker who has the TTP role
- Validity: Validity range of the contract

The optional part is a sequence of contract clauses. Every contract clause includes the following information:

- IdentifierContractClause: Clause unique identification
- Material: Multimedia material affected by this clause
- Right: Kind of right affected by this clause (right transfer, etc.)
- AgreeList: List of entities who agree with this clause
- Obligations&FallsList: List of obligations and associated punish actions
- PaymentInformation: Payment information involved with this clause
- ClauseDescription: Text description of the clause

5. A Multi-Broker Model

The second step of our work consists on the extension of the single-broker model to a multi-broker environment. In this case, it is necessary to add a protocol between brokers (broker-broker) able to allow a broker to sell publishing material that is managed by a different broker. Remember that our broker model is based on the fact that content providers give metadata information to brokers (while keeping the multimedia content in the provider's database) allowing them to sell their material to broker's customers.

Thus, apart from handling the broker-broker communication for selling purposes, this new broker-broker protocol also needs to be able to handle all copyright related issues, when IPR is associated to the multimedia material. ***Figure 3*** represents this new model.

Basically, what we have to do is to add extra functionality to the system with an operation able to update IPR information included in the broker's database. With this, it is possible for one broker to sell material managed by another broker. Then, the IPR information should normally be stored and updated in the responsible broker, not in the broker that is selling the content. Hence the need for this new functionality.

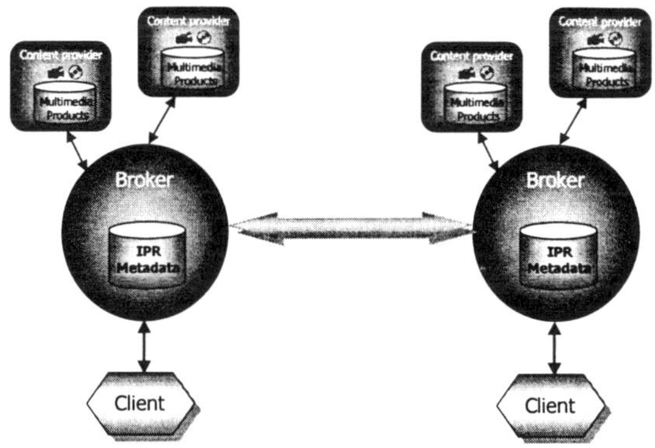

Figure 3. Multi-Broker Model

We are implementing this new feature with agents technology [27]. In this way, we can keep the information always in the system responsible for the publishing content and we can be sure that the information is always updated.

While the negotiation and contract preparation steps belong to the agreement phase in an e-commerce environment [25], this IPR information updating through a broker-broker protocol clearly belongs to a post-agreement phase [25].

In the multi-broker model we have two kinds of contracts: client-broker and broker-broker. The negotiation between brokers takes place when a broker is not able to provide publishing material requested by one of its customers, and has to look for the content in other places (we do not enter in the issue of how to find this external information, but the mechanism could be as simple as having the broker acting as a customer of another broker). In this case, the original client's broker has to negotiate with the content-owner's broker and produce a broker-broker contract to be able to sell the material to its customer, then producing a second contract, in this case a client-broker one. Figure 4 illustrates this combined negotiation and contract production.

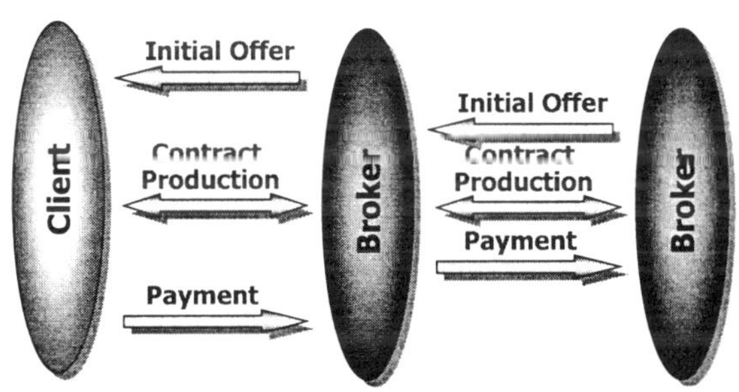

Figure 4. IPR Negotiation in a Multi-Broker Model

6. Conclusions

A business model for e-commerce of e-publishing where IPR is handled is still missing. Apart from introducing copyright information in the content to sell, there are other specific needs related to IPR management in e-publishing. One of them is the possibility of negotiating the copyright conditions when buying multimedia material.

In the paper, after introducing general issues about copyright and current business models, we have presented a specific approach for the representation and negotiation of

IPR. The representation is based on the use of metadata, by defining a structured set of attributes and an interface based on XML and RDF. This has been implemented in the MARS project, an application for e-commerce of audiovisual publishing material.

Concerning the negotiation of IPR, it is based on the specification of a protocol for the negotiation of copyright at the purchase moment. This is being implemented using agent technology. An electronic contract is also specified to formalise the agreements reached during negotiation.

Finally, the paper introduces the issues associated to IPR negotiation in a multi-broker environment. A new model with several brokers is introduced, and the needed operations, such as the update of copyright information, are identified.

7. References

1. Berne Convention for the Protection of Literary and Artistic Works, http://www.wipo.int/treaties/ip/berne/index.htm
2. WIPO Copyright Treaty, 1996. http://www.wipo.int/treaties/ip/wipo-copyright/index.html
1. EC Directive on Copyright, http://europa.eu.int/comm/internal_market/en/intprop/intprop/docs/index.htm
2. US Digital Millennium Copyright Act, 1998. http://www.loc.gov/copyright/legislation/hr2281.pdf
5. IMPRIMATUR Project, http://www.imprimatur.net
6. INDECS Project, http://www.indecs.org
7. COPEARMS, Project, http://www.ispo.cec-be/istka2/c4/actionline43.htm
8. FILIGRANE Project, http://www.filigrane.org
9. Soundwrap (Virtual Shrink-wrap for Music Distribution), http://www.soundwrap.com
10. DMDsecure (Digital Media Distribution), http://www.dmdsecure.com
11. DX3 (Digital Distribution Domain), http://www.dx3.net
12. Stephen King's personal web site, http://www.stephenking.com
13. EBX (Electronic Book eXchange), http://www.ebxwg.org
14. OEBF (Open eBook Forum), http://www.openebook.org
15. XrML (eXtensible rights Markup Language), http://www.xrml.org
16. DUBLIN CORE Home Page, http://purl.oclc.org/metadata/dublin_core
17. MPEG-7, http://www.cselt.it/mpeg
18. Metadata for Multimedia Information Workshop, CEN Information Society Standardisation System, http://www.cenorm.be/isss/Workshop/delivered-WS/MMI/Default.htm
19. HYPERMEDIA Project, http://www.corporacionmultimedia.es/hypermedia
20. MARS (Multimedia Advanced brokerage and Redistribution Surveillance) Project, http://www.upf.es/esup/dmag
21. RDF (Resource Description Framework), http://www.w3.org/RDF
22. RDFMS (RDF Model and Syntax Specification), http://www.w3.org/TR/REC-rdf-syntax
23. RDFS (RDF Schema Specification), http://www.w3.org/TR/rdf-schema
24. GALLEGO I., DELGADO J. and GARCÍA, R. "Use of Mobile Agents for IPR Management and Negotiation", 2nd International Workshop Mobile Agents for Telecommunication Applications (MATA 2000), 18-20 September 2000, Paris (France). Springer, ISBN 3-540-41069-4.
25. GALLEGO I., DELGADO J. and ACEBRÓN J.J. "Distributed Models for Brokerage on Electronic Commerce", International IFIP Working Conference Trends in Electronic Commerce (TREC'98), 3-5 June 1998, Hamburg (Germany). Springer, ISBN 3-540-64564-0.
26. DELGADO J, GALLEGO I. "Distributed Negotiation of Digital Rights", International Conference on Media Futures 2001, 8-9 May 2001, Florence (Italy) (To be published).
27. FIPA (Foundation for Intelligent Physical Agents), http://www.fipa.org

Electronic Publishing '01 –
2001 in the Digital Publishing Odyssey
A. Hübler et al. (Eds.)
IOS Press, 2001

Metadata interoperability for e-commerce of multimedia publishing material

Enric Peig, Jaime Delgado

Universitat Pompeu Fabra (UPF), Departament de Tecnologia
Pg. Circumval·lació 8, E-08003 Barcelona, Spain
{enric.peig, jaime.delgado}@tecn.upf.es

Abstract. Using metadata for referencing multimedia material is becoming more and more usual. This allows better ways of discovering and locating this material published on the Internet.

Several initiatives for establishing standards for metadata models are being carried out at the moment, but everyone focuses on their own requirements when defining metadata attributes, their possible values and the relation between them. From the point of view of someone who wants to seek and buy information (multimedia content in general) in different environments, this is a real problem, because he has to face different metadata sets, and so, must have different tools in order to deal with them.

In this paper, we present a model for the interoperability of different metadata communities, where neither the publishers nor the customers have to be aware that they all may be working with different metadata models. We are mapping the semantics of different metadata models with the objective of not loosing information when the user and the content provider use different metadata schemas. A "metadata agent" is used to carry out the interoperability information.

1 Metadata for multimedia initiatives

There are currently several international initiatives for the development of metadata schemes. Some of them are of general purpose and others have a very specific focus, many of them around multimedia information.

For our work, we are initially considering three of these initiatives, which are widely used and have a different focus. Since we want to develop metadata interoperability, there are good reasons to select these three metadata schemes. Although they have been initiated in very different environments, these initiatives have the objective of being as general as possible. However, interoperability is currently not possible. These initiatives are known as Dublin Core [1], MPEG-7 [2] and IEEE LOM [3].

1.1 Dublin Core

Dublin Core is a standard that represents a metadata element set intended to facilitate the discovery of electronic resources. Although it was born in the bibliographic domain, it has turned out to be a de facto standard for metadata on the web.

The metadata element set is formed by these 15 elements: Title, Creator, Subject, Description, Publisher, Contributor, Date, Type, Format, Identifier, Source, Language,

Relation, Coverage and Rights. The simplicity and conciseness of the set is one of the keys that explain its success.

Besides the metadata element set, a list of qualifiers is formally recommended, intended to sharpen the semantics of the 15 original elements, and thus, to adjust to specific domains and local implementations.

1.2 MPEG-7

The Moving Picture Experts Group (MPEG) is a working group of ISO/IEC in charge of the development of standards for coded representation. Among many others, it is now working on the MPEG-7 standard, formally named "Multimedia Content Description Interface", whose aim is to create a standard for describing multimedia data, and to offer tools to create and manage their descriptors. Its natural scope is the description of audiovisual information, be it analogue or digital, and be it broadcasted in real time from some source or recorded in media such as film, magnetic tape, CD, etc.

The MPEG-7 tools will allow users to create descriptors of content that may include information describing the creation and production processes of the content, information related to the usage of the content, information of the storage features of the content, structural information on spatial or temporal components of the content, conceptual information of the reality captured by the content, etc.

A description generated using MPEG-7 description tools will be associated with the content itself, to allow fast and efficient searching for, and filtering of material that is of interest to the user. MPEG-7 data may be physically located with the associated audiovisual (AV) material, in the same data stream, or in the same storage system, but the descriptions could also live somewhere else on the globe. When the content and its descriptions are not co-located, mechanisms that link AV material and their MPEG-7 descriptions are needed; these links will have to work in both directions.

The main tools used to implement MPEG-7 descriptions are the Description Definition Language (DDL), Description Schemes (DSs), and Descriptors (Ds). Descriptors bind a feature to a set of values. Description Schemes are models of the multimedia objects and of the universes that they represent; e.g. the data model of the description. They specify the types of the descriptors that can be used in a given description, and the relationships between these descriptors or between other Description Schemes.

1.3 IEEE LOM

The IEEE, through its Learning Technology Standards Committee, is working in a standard that aims to facilitate search, evaluation, acquisition, and use of learning objects, for instance by learners or instructors. Currently, this standard, called Learning Objects Metadata (LOM), is in the status of working draft.

The standard specifies a conceptual data scheme, formed by data elements that describe a learning object. Also, a Base Scheme is specified, which for each data element defines a name, an explanation, the size, the order, the value space, the data type and an illustrative example.

The data elements can be grouped into categories. The Base Scheme consists of nine categories: General, Lifecycle, Meta-metadata, Technical, Educational, Rights, Relation, Annotation and Classification.

2 The problem of metadata interoperability

The proliferation of different metadata schemes for published resources' description, like those just described, are making accessing this information difficult, since it is not always possible to view data in the same way from different applications. This situation requires applications to know all the schemes that may be found in different information providers guides to content. Furthermore, it is also usual to find storage systems containing objects referred to using different metadata schemes at the same time. There is yet another extra problem: we have to be aware of new metadata schemes that might appear, this will require applications to also adapt to these new schemes.

For these reasons, there is a need to develop interoperability systems between metadata domains, with the purpose of simplifying the discovery and access to this information, and to allow a high level of automation to this access.

2.1 A first approach to metadata interoperability

Several approaches to interoperability have been tried during the last years, but none of them has yet achieved a relevant result. An example of this, mainly at European level, is the work done by the CEN/ISSS (European Standardisation Committee / Information Society Standardisation System), where a Workshop was formed to deal with these issues, mainly focussing on metadata for multimedia information.

The results from the Workshop, entitled MMI (Metadata for Multimedia Information), were a few CWA (CEN Workshop Agreement) specifying a model for metadata and business requirements [4].

The MMI Model proposes a conceptual model for metadata for multimedia information in terms of classes of metadata, the roles of the different actors involved and the actions performed by each role. At the conceptual level, the same concepts and life cycle model can be applied both to information resources and to metadata.

The nine metadata classes recommended are:

- General: Basic reference to the resource and features independent of its use.
- Life Cycle: Information related to the different phases of the resource.
- Meta-metadata: Characteristics of the description rather than the resource.
- Technical: Technical features of the resource.
- Use dependent: Features that need to be interpreted according to the use of the resource.
- Rights Management: Information related to the control of transactions.
- Relation: Characteristics of the resource in relationship to other resources.
- Annotation: Comments on the use of the resource.
- Security: Metadata concerning security mechanisms.

Three roles are identified in the metadata model: Creator, Service Provider and User.

The actions performed by the Creator (of an information resource or of metadata) include: Author, Create, Capture, Prepare, Edit, Store. The actions performed by the Service Provider (of an information resource or of metadata) include: Maintain, Store, Backup, Integrate, Preserve, Archive, Discard, Validate, Quality Assure, Deliver, Provide Security Functions, Accounting, Advertise and Sell. The actions performed by the User (of an information resource or of metadata) include: Specify information required, Discovery, Selection, Establish right to use, Establish means to access/use, Access/retrieve the information, Verify, Transform and Use.

The MMI requirements do not attempt to produce a complete set of requirements for all uses of metadata, since this would be an endless task. On the contrary, the document is providing a metadata taxonomy and methodology to help identifying requirements for different sectors and applications.

The general requirements given in the requirements taxonomy are classified in:

- Information that metadata should provide.
- Facilities that should be provided in association with metadata.

The document can be used for different purposes in different ways. First, to have an overview about what are the general requirements for metadata; second, to check if some specific metadata requirements fit with the taxonomy; and, third (the most important use), to derive, from the described taxonomy, new specific requirements for new applications.

Finally, it should be noted that the MMI requirements is a "living" document that may be updated *1)* when new metadata requirements are developed for new applications; *2)* new applications discover their need for metadata; and *3)* if some new requirements are identified for the taxonomy.

As a conclusion, we could say that this work has been a good starting point and has identified the complexity of the problem, also showing that trying to cover all existing metadata schemes or trying to converge is not a feasible task. We should add that this Workshop has been disbanded once the CWAs were published, and has moved to a new Workshop, still running, focussing on Dublin Core.

3 A model for metadata interoperability

The model we are proposing, with a totally different approach to the CEN/ISSS one, is oriented to the search of metadata referenced multimedia material. Hence, how metadata are created or the relationship between attributes is of less importance compared with the issue of the meaning of every metadata element and the set of possible values. Therefore, our model is based, first, on a vocabulary that is common to the different metadata schemes and, second, on the semantic mapping with all of them. These are the key differences to other models.

This common vocabulary starts from the analysis of the most known metadata schemes, such as IEEE LOM, Dublin Core or MPEG-7. From here, the system has to be able to incorporate new elements and the corresponding mapping in case of finding other metadata schemes in which there were elements not already considered in the common vocabulary. To make this inclusion, it is clear that, as a first step, human intervention is needed, since tools to deduce the semantics of these elements are not currently available.

Table 1 illustrates the kernel of the common vocabulary and its mapping to the mentioned metadata schemes.

This mechanism of semantic mapping from a general vocabulary to the different metadata schemes is easily scalable, since we do not need to maintain crossed mapping among all existing schemes. It is clear, as also stated in [5], that the idea of supporting a matrix for crossed mappings between all possible schemes is not a scalable one.

What we propose then in our interoperability model is to only consider the mapping between different schemes and our common vocabulary. Then, for every new scheme that we want to add to our system, we only need to fill a column in the previous table, where the attributes with a semantic relationship with our vocabulary would appear.

Taking into account that the objective of the model we are presenting is the search of content in heterogeneous sources, our approach is that it is not necessary to keep an exhaustive and complete mapping of all the attributes of the metadata schemes. Hence, we can forget about those attributes that only appear in only one scheme but not in the others. In this way, our vocabulary would be a kind of intersection of all available systems we could find.

Table 1: Common vocabulary and its mapping

	Dublin Core	IEEE LOM	MPEG7
Identifier	Identifier	General.CatalogEntry	MediaInformation.MediaIdentification. Identifier
Title	Title	General.Title	CreationMetaInformation.Creation. Title.TitleText
Description	Description	General.Description	CreationMetaInformation.Creation. CreationDescription
Format	Format	Technical.Format	MediaInformation.MediaProfile. MediaFormat.FileFormat
Author	Creator	LifeCycle.Contribute.Entity	CreationMetaInformation.Creation. Creator
Creation_Date	Date	LifeCycle.Contribute.Date	CreationMetaInformation.Creation. CreationDate
Language	Language	General.Language	CreationMetaInformation.Classification. Language.LanguageCode
Rights	Rights	Rights	UsageMetaInformation.Rights.RightsID

Our model is also based on not imposing on information providers our proposed metadata scheme (our common vocabulary), but to use an agent that will be in charge of searching in the different information providers, at the request of the users of the system.

This *metadata agent* is the only element that knows about this common vocabulary and the mappings. In this way, the content providers and users searching for information are able to continue working with their own metadata schemes with the help of the agent.

Figure 1 shows how the different elements of our scenario are related.

We can see that the different elements (or actors) interchange two kinds of information. On one side, the user provides some keywords to the agent, so it can make the search in the provider system. As an example, we assume that users make queries such as "search for films from Director X" or "search for a painting from Artist Y between year Z1 and year Z2". Then, the agent has to map this information to the metadata schemes corresponding to the content providers where it will look for, in order to be able to deal with them, since we assume that they only understand queries following their metadata scheme.

On the other hand, we have the answers given by the content providers, which, in many cases, have the form of a metadata record following their own scheme. The task of the agent is then to provide the user with this information, that could follow their original scheme, the common vocabulary or the scheme requested by the user, if different.

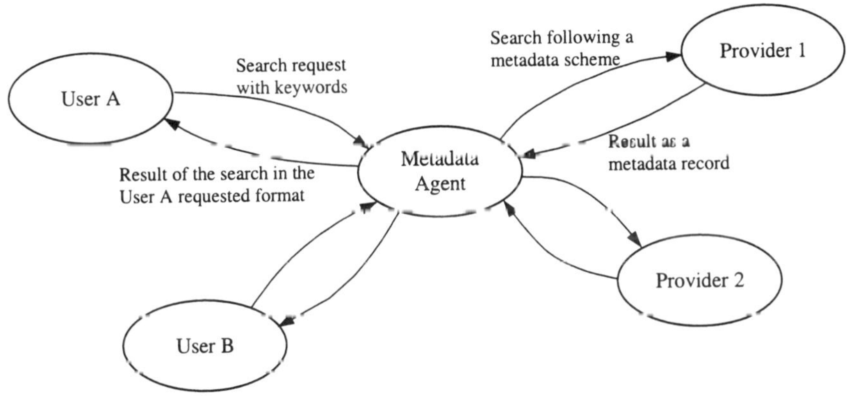

Figure 1: Relationship between elements

With this approach, users are able to make queries to different content providers without the need of knowing their metadata scheme, both at the moment of producing the query and when receiving the answer with the requested information.

4 Application to an e-publishing environment

The interoperability model we have specified, and its implementation with an agent[6], could be applied to very different environments. Apart from a typical application of information discovery and search, e-commerce and e-publishing are very promising areas.

Concerning general e-commerce, metadata is used in some applications for identifying content to be sold. The problem is that customers need to know the metadata scheme used by the multimedia content provider, or providers have to use too simple schemes in order to be accessed in an easier way. With the metadata agent, it is possible to identify content without the need of knowing about the metadata scheme used by content providers, which could be as complex as needed. Of course, this also helps providers in being accessed by more customers through the interoperability agent.

The previous approach could be also applied to an e-publishing environment, similar to the e-commerce one just mentioned. In this new case, the multimedia content to be sold is now multimedia publishing material, to be sold or not.

We have developed an application where users look for multimedia content to buy to be used for further publishing [7]. Both users and providers interact through a broker agent who will include, apart from the common e-commerce facilities and the handling of IPR [8], a metadata agent facility for metadata interoperability handling.

5 Conclusions

We have dealt with the problem derived from the fact that using metadata for referencing multimedia material is becoming more and more usual.

Although this allows for better ways of discovering and locating publishing material, this also leads to new problems. Because the current different initiatives for establishing standards for metadata models focus on their own requirements, a problem of interoperability is arising.

We are developing a model to solve this problem. We have considered the mentioned initiatives, such as Dublin Core, MPEG7, or IEEE LOM, and their different metadata schemes.

Our main objective is that neither the publishers nor the customers have to be aware that they all may be working with different metadata models. We are mapping the semantics of different metadata models with the objective of not loosing information when the user and the content provider use different metadata schemes.

Our model is based, first, on a generic metadata framework, which defines the common semantics between the most used metadata sets, and, second, on a "metadata agent" that will do the mapping between the different metadata models found and this generic model that we propose.

This agent, to be developed, will be integrated in applications that we have already developed in the area of e-commerce of multimedia publishing material.

6 References

[1] Dublin Core Metadata Initiative, http://dublincore.org

[2] "Overview of the MPEG-7 Standard", ISO/IEC JTC1/SC29/WG11 N4031, http://www.cselt.it/mpeg/standards/mpeg-7/mpeg-7.htm, March 2001.

[3] IEEE Learning Technology Standards Committee's Learning Object Meta-data Working Group, Approved LOM Working Draft 5 (WD5), http://ltsc.ieee.org/wg12

[4] Metadata for Multimedia Information Workshop, CEN Information Society Standardisation System, http://www.cenorm.be/isss/Workshop/delivered-WS/MMI/Default.htm

[5] J. Hunter, "MetaNet – A Metadata Term Thesaurus to Enable Semantic Interoperability Between Metadata Domains", Journal of Digital Information, volume 1 issue 8, http://jodi.ecs.soton.ac.uk/Articles/v01/i08/Hunter, February 2001.

[6] FIPA (Foundation for Intelligent Physical Agents), http://www.fipa.org

[7] MARS (Multimedia Advanced brokerage and Redistribution Surveillance) Project, http://www.upf.es/esup/dmag

[8] DELGADO J, GALLEGO I. "Negotiation of copyright in e-commerce of multimedia publishing material", 5th ICCC/IFIP International Conference on Electronic Publishing - ELPUB2001, July 2001, Canterbury (UK) (Published in this volume).

Electronic Publishing '01 –
2001 in the Digital Publishing Odyssey
A. Hübler et al. (Eds.)
IOS Press, 2001

Sponsoring Institutions

ICCC – International Council for Computer Communication

ICCC is an international council of approximately 100 governors, each a senior respected contributor to computer communication and related fields. Governors come from industry, academia and governments in over 30 countries. ICCC's strength lies in the multinational and multidisciplinary character of its governors.

ICCC is an Affiliate Member of the International Federation for Information Processing (IFIP) and the Internet Society.

ICCC Vision

ICCC, strives for a world in which global and regional policies give every community access to communication technologies and applications that will enhance life.

ICCC Mission

ICCC's mission is to shape the future of global communications by advocating those policies, applications, and research that will positively influence the social, cultural and economic impacts of computer communication. ICCC represents all regions of the world, covering the many disciplines, interests and fields of endeavor related to computer communication.

ICCC's strategic plan is discussed in a Business Plan document published in 1999, which includes specific actions to take in order to accomplish its mission.

Governance

The primary elements of ICCC's governance structure are the Council of Governors and its Executive Committee. Conferences committee, adhoc committees, strategic planning groups, and a regional office in Mumbai, India, currently support these bodies.

Council of Governors

ICCC governors are elected to terms of six years by Governors-in-office. Candidates are drawn from all disciplines, interests and fields of endeavor related to computer communication, e.g., scientists, technologists, equipment and system developers, service providers, users, economists, lawyers, and government officials. Council deliberations often are enriched by widely differing views on both technical and non-technical issues.

Governors, who are chosen on the basis of their willingness and ability to further the aims of ICCC, meet annually as a body, at which time new governors are elected. By statute the Council of Governors is limited to 125 members.

Groups

ICCC has created five strategic planning and oversight groups to formulate and carry out its initiatives. All groups contribute to the organization's three year strategic plan, which is reviewed and updated. The five groups are:

- Program Group
- Conferences Group
- Publications Group
- Marketing Group
- Internal Use of Technology Group.

The Program Group establishes the programmatic focuses for the organization as a whole, as it deems appropriate, and initiates projects. Within this overall focus, the remaining groups identify opportunities pertaining to their respective areas, develop initiatives and execute them.

The Groups also formulate policy recommendations for Executive Committee approval. Once approved, the groups enact and enforce policies in their respective areas. Group Leaders are assisted by their peers.

Conference Program and Organizing Committees

Large conferences are jointly managed by a Program Committee and a local Organizing Committee. Typically, a governor, assigned by the Executive Committee, leads the Program Committee and a person local to the conference site heads the Organizing Committee. A formal proposal is required for a flagship (biennial) conference. Topical and regional conferences are approved more informally due to their generally smaller size and lower risks.

IFIP - International Federation for Information Processing

The International Federation for Information Processing (IFIP) is a non-governmental, nonprofit umbrella organization of national societies working in the field of information processing. It was established in 1960 under the auspices of UNESCO as a result of the first World Computer Congress held in Paris in 1959. IFIP's creation was well timed. In the 1960s a veritable explosion in the growth of the computer industry and in the application of its products began. Since the inception of IFIP, information technology (IT) has become a potent instrument affecting people in many ways. It is a powerful tool in science and engineering, in commerce and industry, in education and administration and in entertainment. IFIP's principal aims are to

- foster international cooperation,
- stimulate research and development
- encourage education and
- disseminate information.

IFIP's mission

IFIP's mission is to be the leading, truly international, apolitical organization that encourages and assists in the development, exploitation and application of IT for the benefit of all people.

Principal elements

- To stimulate, encourage and participate in research, development and application of IT and to foster inter-national co-operation in these activities.
- To provide a meeting place where national IT societies can discuss and plan courses of action on issues in our field that are of international significance.
- To promote international co-operation directly and through national IT societies in a free environment between individuals, national and international govern-mental bodies and kindred scientific and professional organizations.
- To pay special attention to the needs of developing countries and to assist them in appropriate ways to secure the optimum benefit from the application of IT.
- To promote professionalism, incorporating high standards of ethics and conduct, among all IT practitioners.
- To provide a forum for assessing the social consequences of IT applications; to campaign for the safe and beneficial development and use of IT and the protection of people from abuse through its improper application.
- To foster and facilitate co-operation between academics, the IT industry and governmental bodies and to seek to represent the interest of users.
- To provide a vehicle for work on the international aspects of IT development and application, including the necessary preparation for the generation of inter-national standards.
- To contribute to the formulation of the programs for education and training needed by IT practitioners, users and the public at large.

Technical Activities

At the heart of IFIP lie its twelve Technical Committees (TCs) with their Working Groups (WGs) and Special Interest Groups, which count on the active participation of some two thousand people world-wide (for details please see „IFIP – Technical Committees (TC) & Working Groups (WG)"). Each of these Technical Committees works mainly on events and publications and manages its Working Groups. These groups work in a variety of ways to share experience and to develop their specialized knowledge. This includes open conferences, smaller working conferences, seminars, tutorials, circulated papers and, increasingly, electronic conferencing and e-mail. Further information about the IFIP TCs and WGs is available on the IFIP home-page (www.ifip.or.at).

Publications

Many IFIP events result in publications, there being some 30 to 40 new IFIP books annually, which are distributed worldwide. These books form a comprehensive library of developments in information processing as well as the current state of the art. A list is available on the IFIP homepage (www.ifip.or.at/public.html).

IFIP Newsletter

A vital element of IFIP's communication with its Members and with all who participate in our work is the IFIP Newsletter. This is published quarterly in both print and electronic form (www.ifip.or.at/newsletters/newsl.html).

Congresses and Major Conferences

IFIP's flagship event is its World Computer Congress, currently held biennially. The 15 th Congress was jointly held in Vienna, Austria, and in Budapest, Hungary. The 16 th IFIP Congress was held in Beijing, China. The 17 th Congress will be held in Montreal, Canada in 2002.

The nature of these Congresses has changed substantially over the years. Recent IFIP Congresses have consisted of a number of independent conferences, each dealing with a major specialized subject. These run in parallel so that some of the more general keynote addresses can be attended by all participants who can also share in social and other activities. In addition IFIP holds major international conferences organized by our Technical Committees.

IFIP – A Truly International Organization

IFIP has 45 societies and academies of sciences as Full Members, 4 as Corresponding Members, 1 as an Associate Member and 11 as Affiliate Members, representing countries from all regions of the world.

Relationships

IFIP maintains friendly connections with specialized agencies of the UN system and non-governmental organizations. First among these is UNESCO, which has commissioned, among other activities, several projects on computer education and which supports the participation in Congresses of people from developing countries. IFIP is also a Scientific Associate of
the International Council of Scientific Unions ICSU. IFIP collaborates with the following four international federations:

- IFAC (International Federation of Automatic Con-trol), a near neighbour of ours in Laxenburg, Austria,
- IMACS (International Association for Mathematics and Computers in Simulation),
- IFORS (International Federation of Operational Research Societies) and
- IMEKO (International Measurement Confederation).

How to get involved?

If you are interested in the work of IFIP, please access the IFIP Internet homepage (www.ifip.or.at), where you can find links to your Member Society and to the Working Groups of IFIP. You may also contact the IFIP Secretariat directly.

Author Index